Stand tall and be proud.

## RYOJI HIRANO

I'm so happy to be able to do what I love with a title I adore. I will treasure this forever! I hope readers who love *Demon Slayer* as much as I do will enjoy this book. Thank you to Gotouge Sensei and congratulations on completing the series!

P.S. The movie was deeply moving!

**Ryoji Hirano** is from Toyama Prefecture. He has been an avid reader of *Weekly Shonen Jump* from a young age. His one-shot "BOZE" inspired the *BOZEBEATS* manga. VIZ Media released the initial chapters of the series simultaneously with its Japanese debut.

# DEMON SLAYER: KIMETSU NO YAIBA— STORIES OF WATER AND FLAME

*Shonen Jump Edition*

*Story and Art by*
**RYOJI HIRANO**
*Original Concept by*
**KOYOHARU GOTOUGE**



**TRANSLATION** John Werry
**TOUCH-UP ART & LETTERING** John Hunt
**DESIGN** Jimmy Presler
**EDITOR** Jennifer Sherman



Printed in the U.S.A.

Published by VIZ Media, LLC
P.O. Box 77010
San Francisco, CA 94107

10 9 8 7 6 5 4 3 2 1
First printing, January 2022

ratings.viz.com
RATED T TEEN

**PARENTAL ADVISORY**
DEMON SLAYER: KIMETSU NO YAIBA–STORIES OF WATER AND FLAME is rated T for Teen and is recommended for ages 13 and up. This volume contains fantasy violence.

VIZ MEDIA
viz.com

SHONEN JUMP

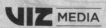

### STORIES of
### WATER and FLAME

*Story and Art by*
**RYOJI HIRANO**

*Original Concept by*
**KOYOHARU GOTOUGI**

# CHARACTERS

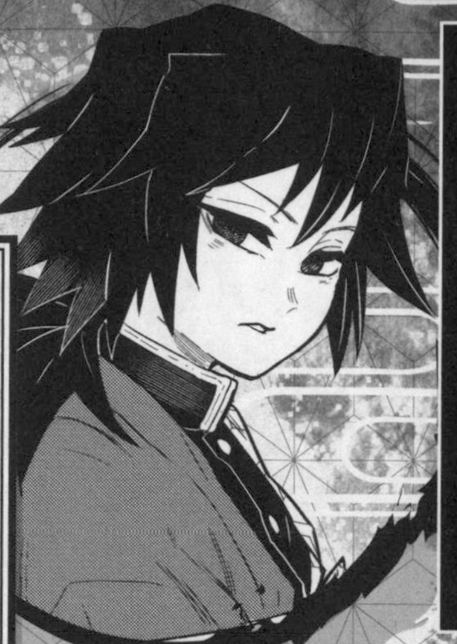

## GIYU TOMIOKA

Water Hashira in the Demon Slayer Corps. He's always calm and taciturn, which often causes misunderstandings. When he met Tanjiro, Tomioka invited him to join the Demon Slayer Corps.

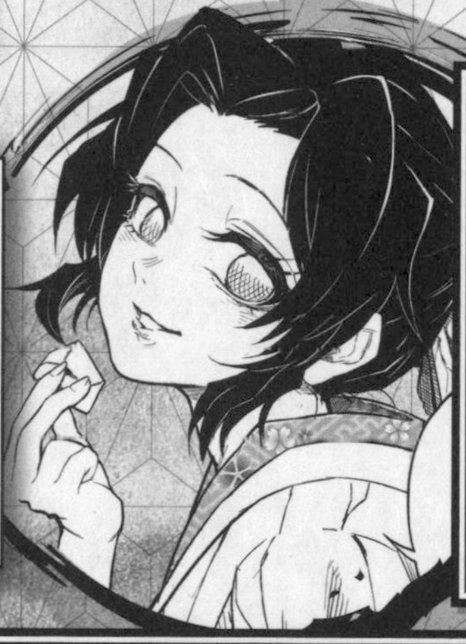

## SHINOBU KOCHO

Insect Hashira in the Demon Slayer Corps. She is familiar with pharmacology, and has created a poison that kills demons. She is pursuing the demon who killed her elder sister.

## DEMON SLAYER CORPS

This organization has existed since ancient times and is devoted to hunting demons. There are a few hundred members, but the government has not officially recognized it.

## DEMON

Staple food: humans. They have incredible physical abilities, and their wounds heal quickly. Some can change form and use superhuman skills. They only die when exposed to sunlight or decapitated with a special sword.

KYOJURO RENGOKU

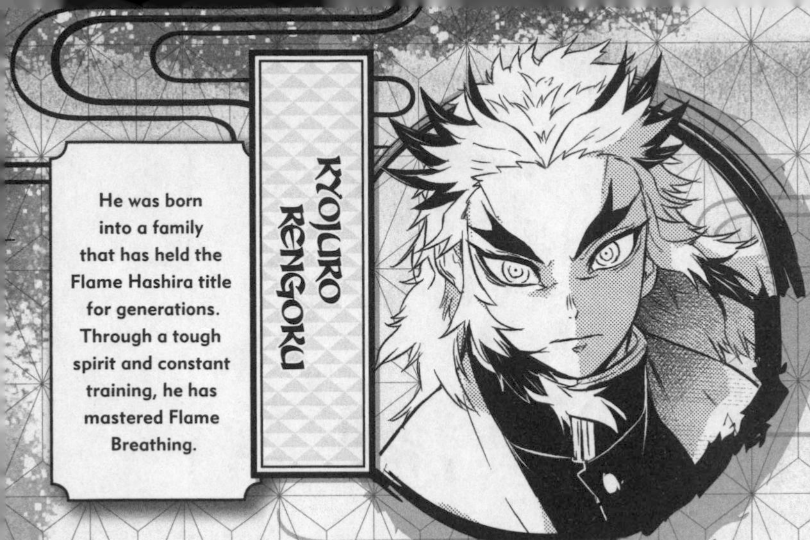

He was born into a family that has held the Flame Hashira title for generations. Through a tough spirit and constant training, he has mastered Flame Breathing.

MITSURI KANROJI

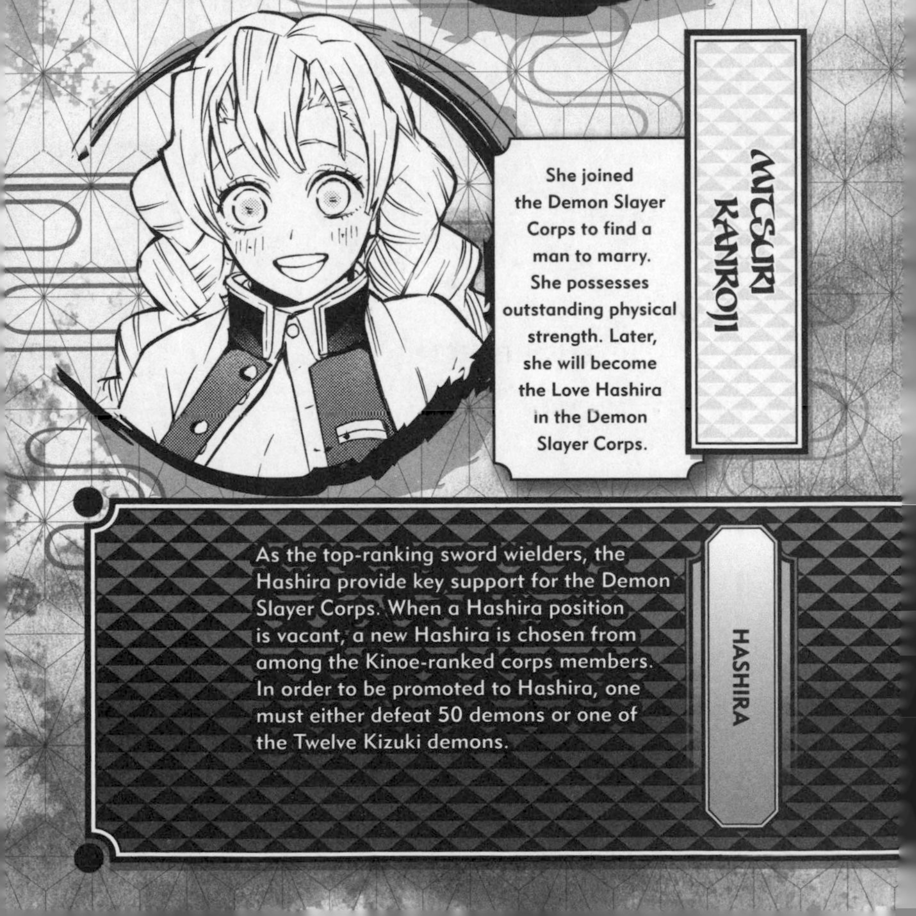

She joined the Demon Slayer Corps to find a man to marry. She possesses outstanding physical strength. Later, she will become the Love Hashira in the Demon Slayer Corps.

HASHIRA

As the top-ranking sword wielders, the Hashira provide key support for the Demon Slayer Corps. When a Hashira position is vacant, a new Hashira is chosen from among the Kinoe-ranked corps members. In order to be promoted to Hashira, one must either defeat 50 demons or one of the Twelve Kizuki demons.

# DEMON SLAYER
KIMETSU NO YAIBA
Stories of WATER and FLAME

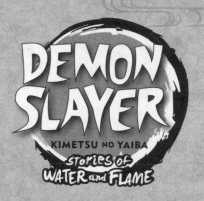

## CONTENTS

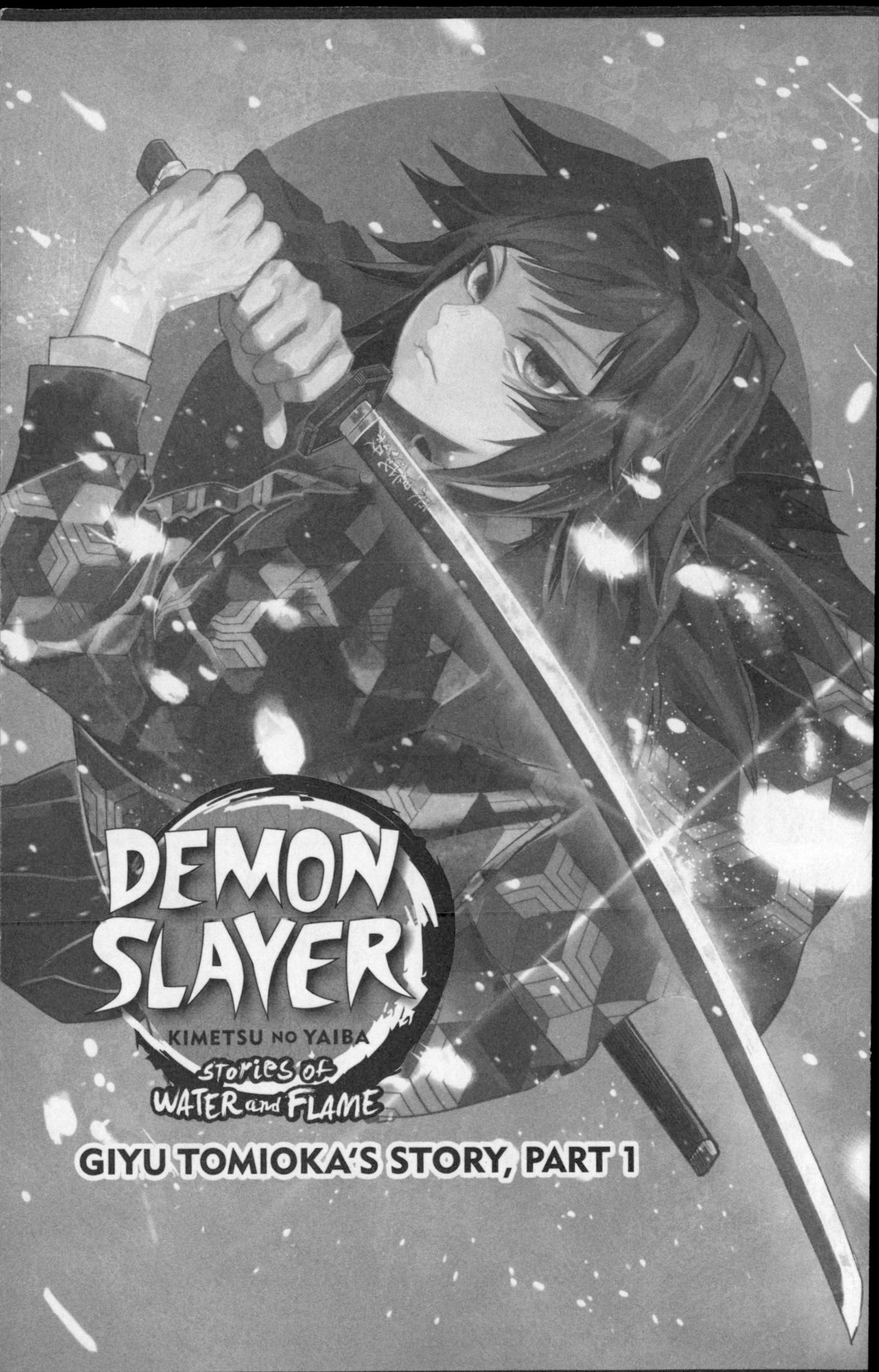
DEMON SLAYER
KIMETSU NO YAIBA
stories of WATER and FLAME
GIYU TOMIOKA'S STORY, PART 1

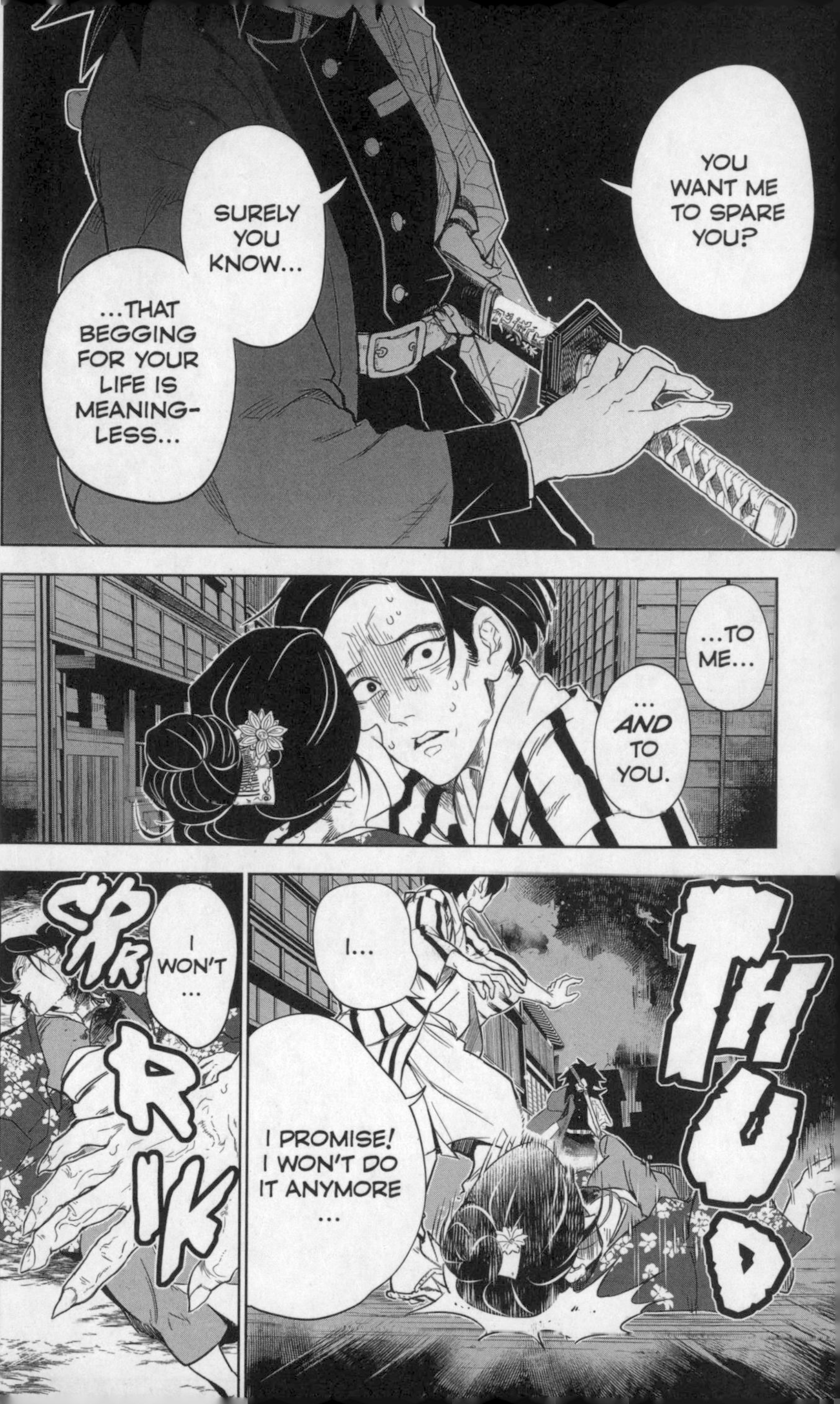
YOU WANT ME TO SPARE YOU?
SURELY YOU KNOW...
...THAT BEGGING FOR YOUR LIFE IS MEANING-LESS...
...TO ME...
... AND TO YOU.
THUD
I...
I PROMISE! I WON'T DO IT ANYMORE ...
I WON'T ...
SKRRIK

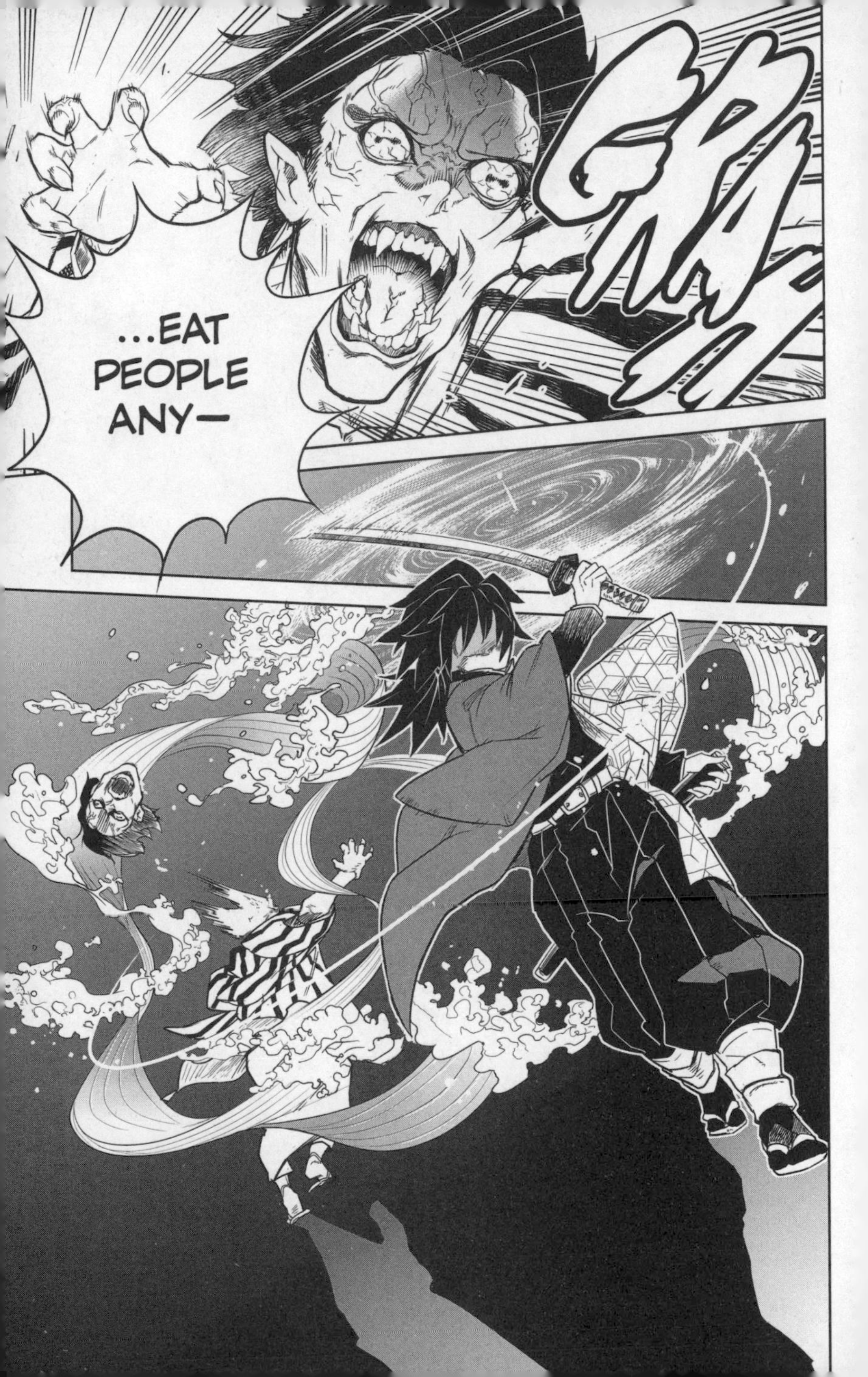
...EAT PEOPLE ANY—

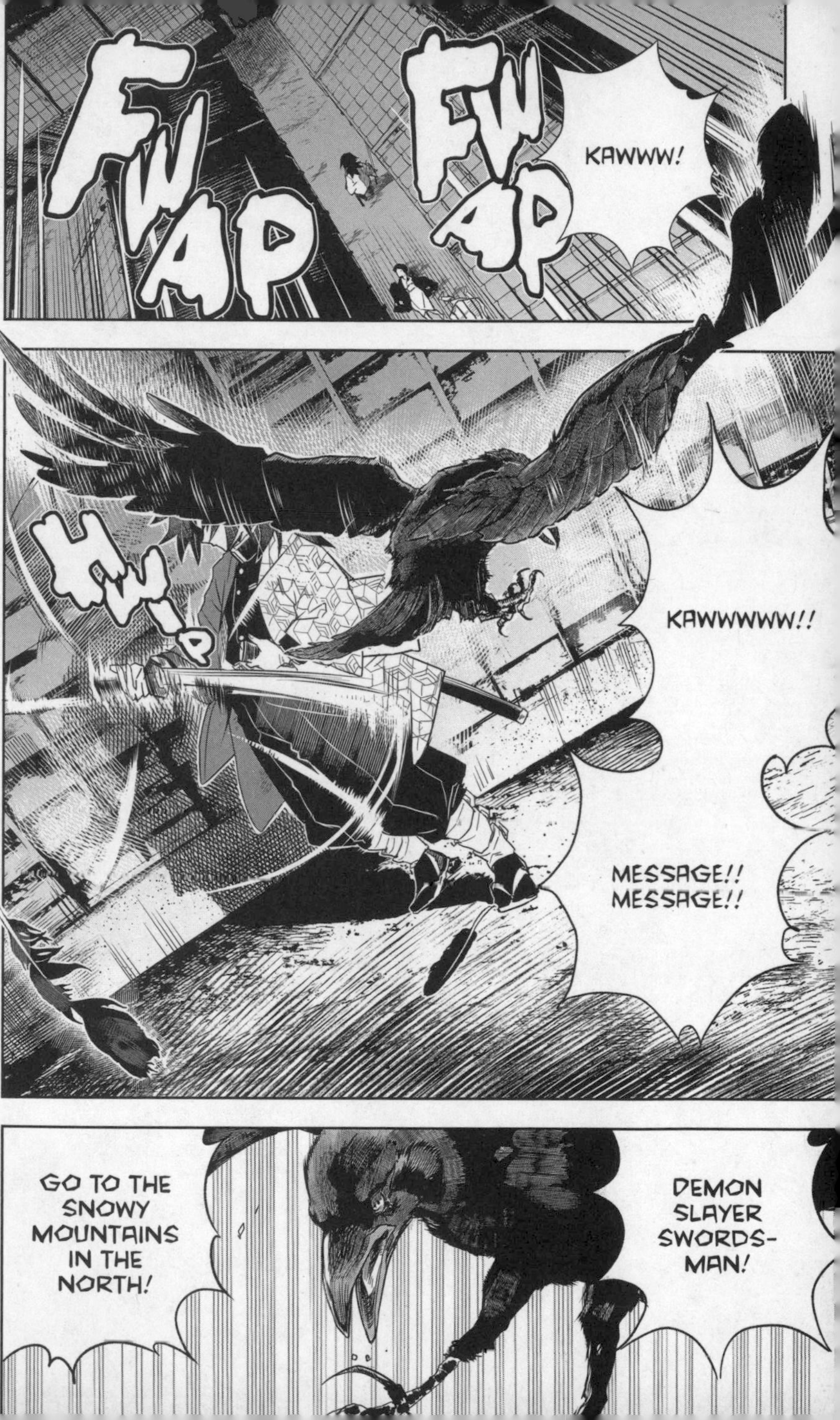
KAWWW!
FWAP
FWAP
KAWWWWW!!
MESSAGE!! MESSAGE!!
HWIP
DEMON SLAYER SWORDS-MAN!
GO TO THE SNOWY MOUNTAINS IN THE NORTH!

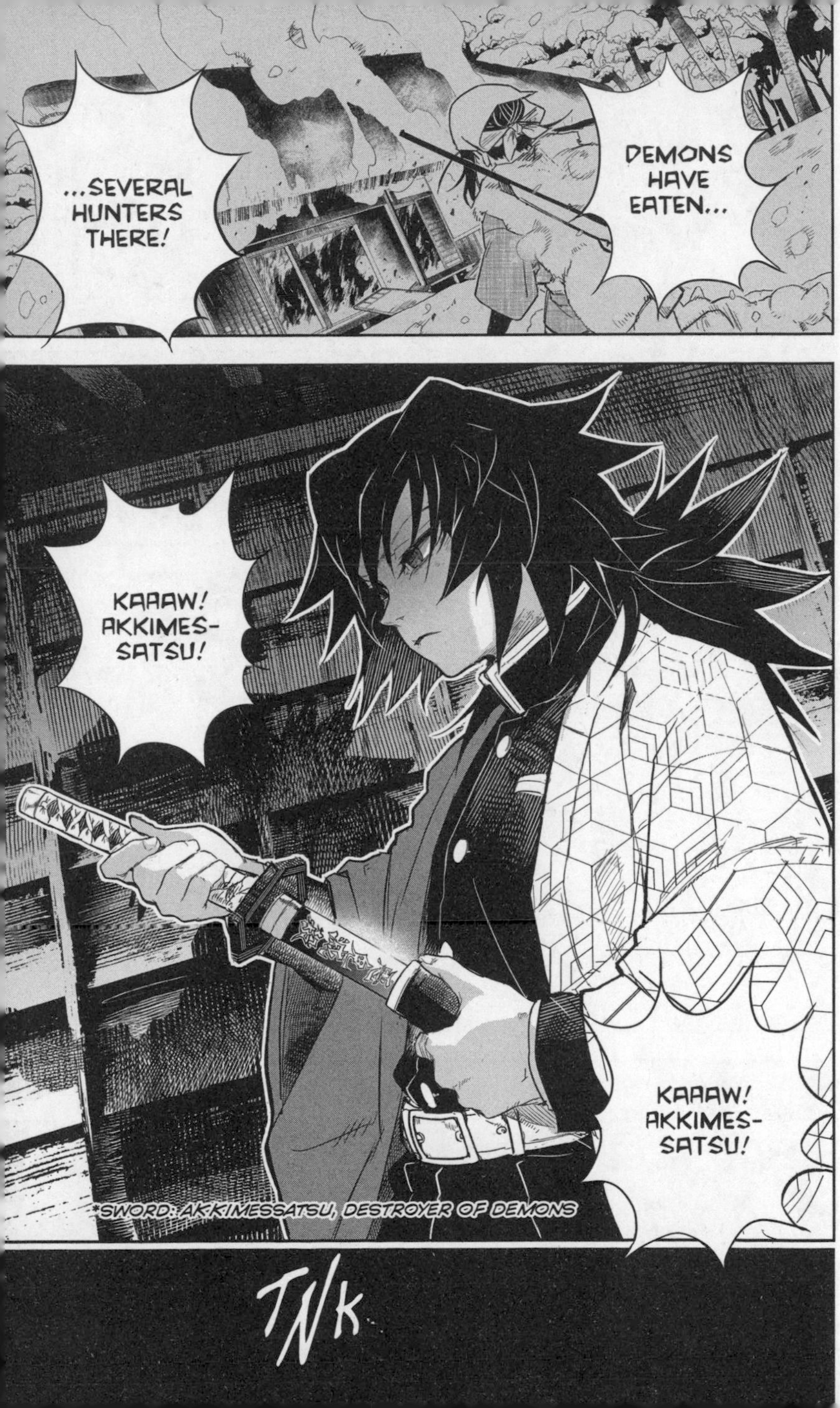
DEMONS HAVE EATEN...
...SEVERAL HUNTERS THERE!
KAAAW! AKKIMES-SATSU!
KAAAW! AKKIMES-SATSU!
*SWORD: AKKIMESSATSU, DESTROYER OF DEMONS
TNK

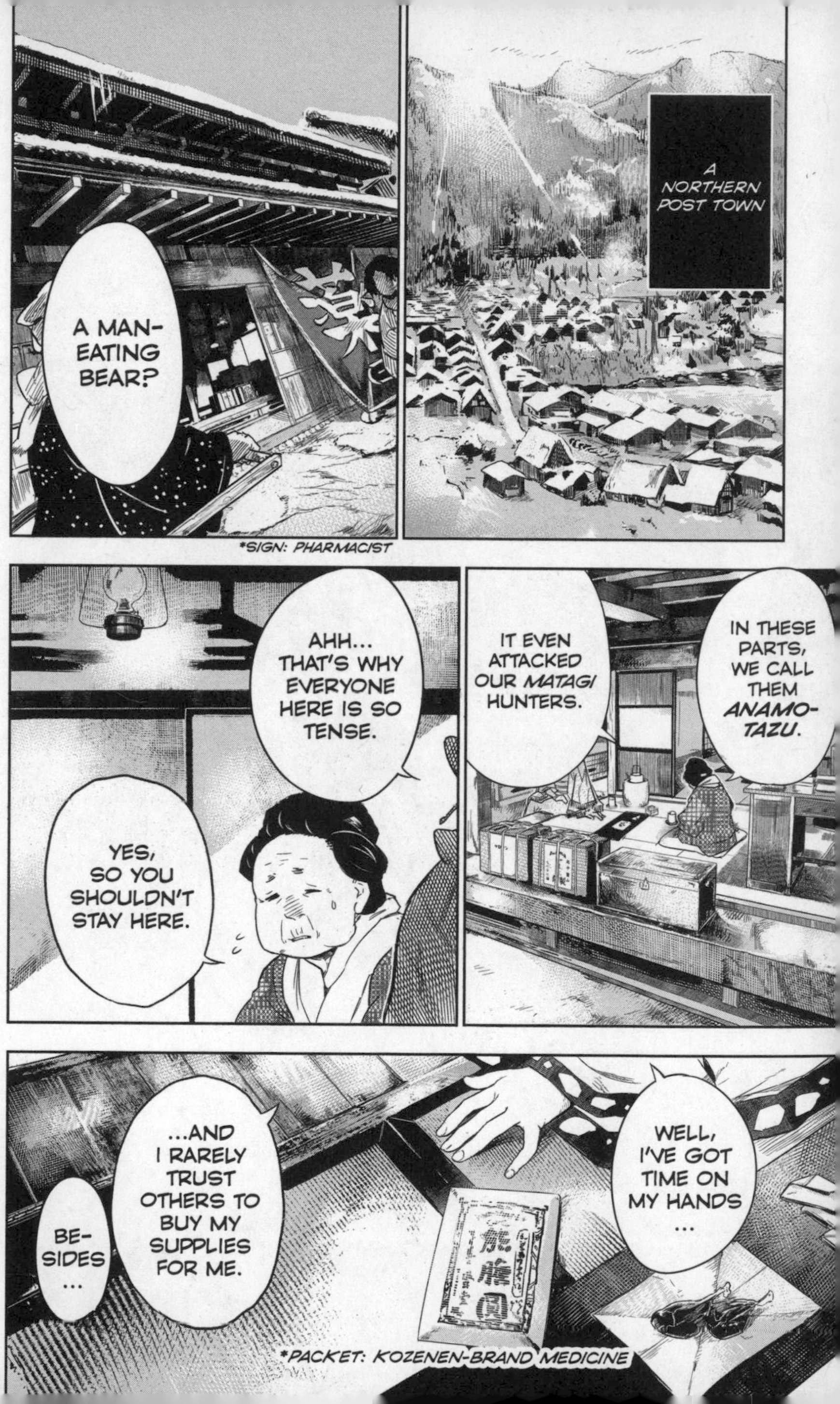
A NORTHERN POST TOWN
A MAN-EATING BEAR?
*SIGN: PHARMACIST
IN THESE PARTS, WE CALL THEM *ANAMOTAZU*.
IT EVEN ATTACKED OUR *MATAGI* HUNTERS.
AHH... THAT'S WHY EVERYONE HERE IS SO TENSE.
YES, SO YOU SHOULDN'T STAY HERE.
WELL, I'VE GOT TIME ON MY HANDS ...
...AND I RARELY TRUST OTHERS TO BUY MY SUPPLIES FOR ME.
BE-SIDES ...
*PACKET: KOZENEN-BRAND MEDICINE

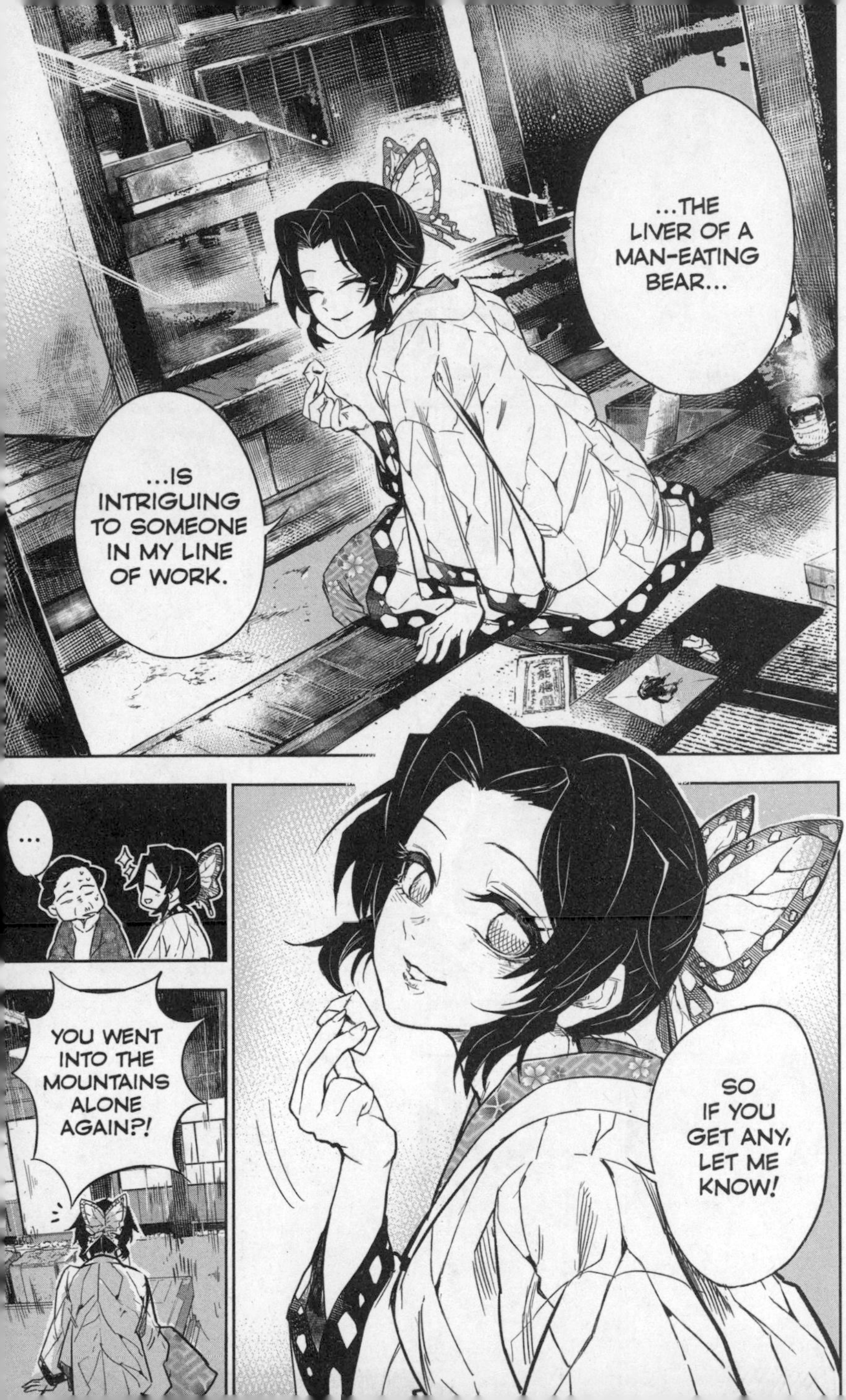
...THE LIVER OF A MAN-EATING BEAR...
...IS INTRIGUING TO SOMEONE IN MY LINE OF WORK.
SO IF YOU GET ANY, LET ME KNOW!
...
YOU WENT INTO THE MOUNTAINS ALONE AGAIN?!

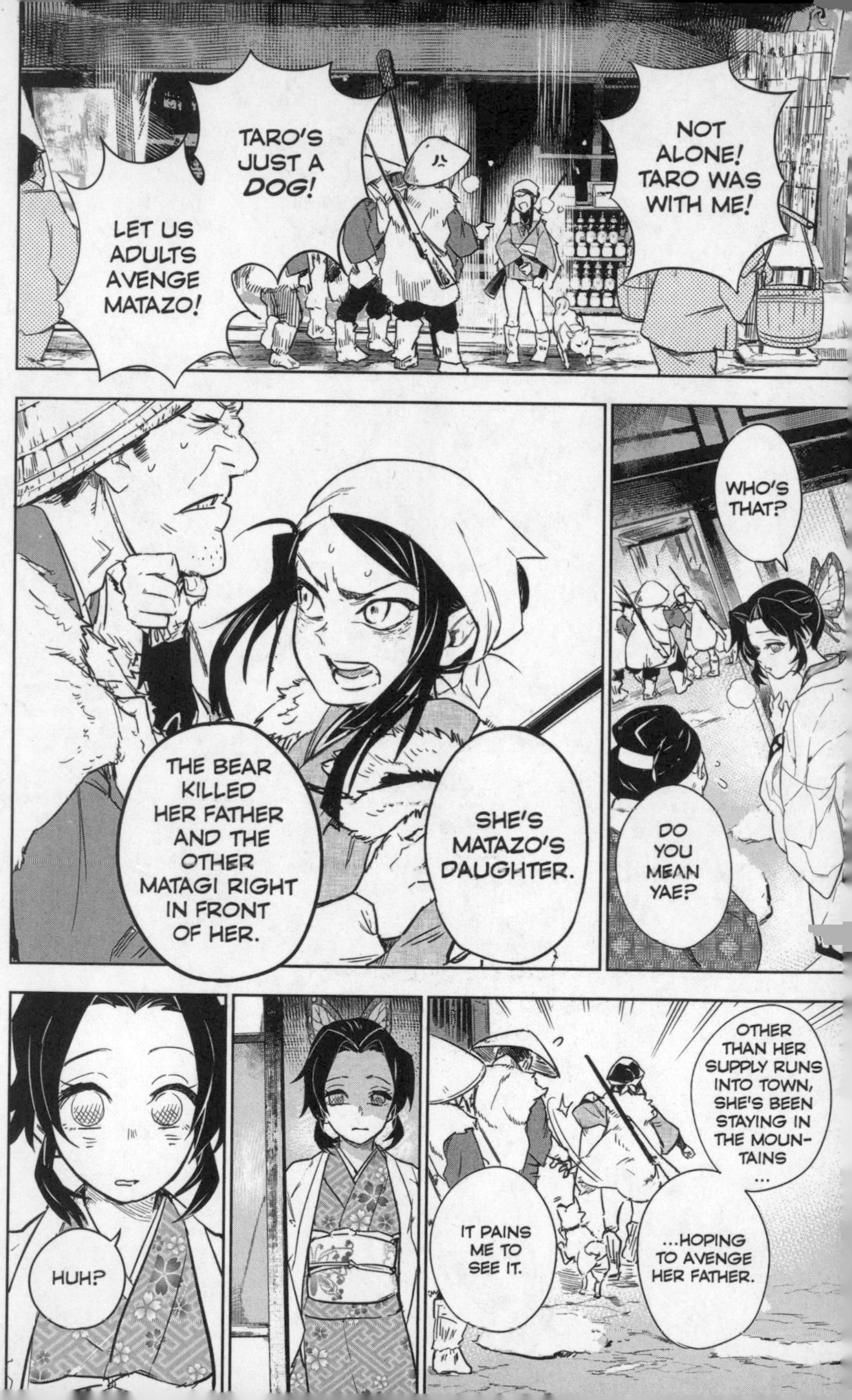
NOT ALONE! TARO WAS WITH ME!
TARO'S JUST A *DOG*!
LET US ADULTS AVENGE MATAZO!
WHO'S THAT?
DO YOU MEAN YAE?
SHE'S MATAZO'S DAUGHTER.
THE BEAR KILLED HER FATHER AND THE OTHER MATAGI RIGHT IN FRONT OF HER.
OTHER THAN HER SUPPLY RUNS INTO TOWN, SHE'S BEEN STAYING IN THE MOUN-TAINS...
...HOPING TO AVENGE HER FATHER.
IT PAINS ME TO SEE IT.
HUH?

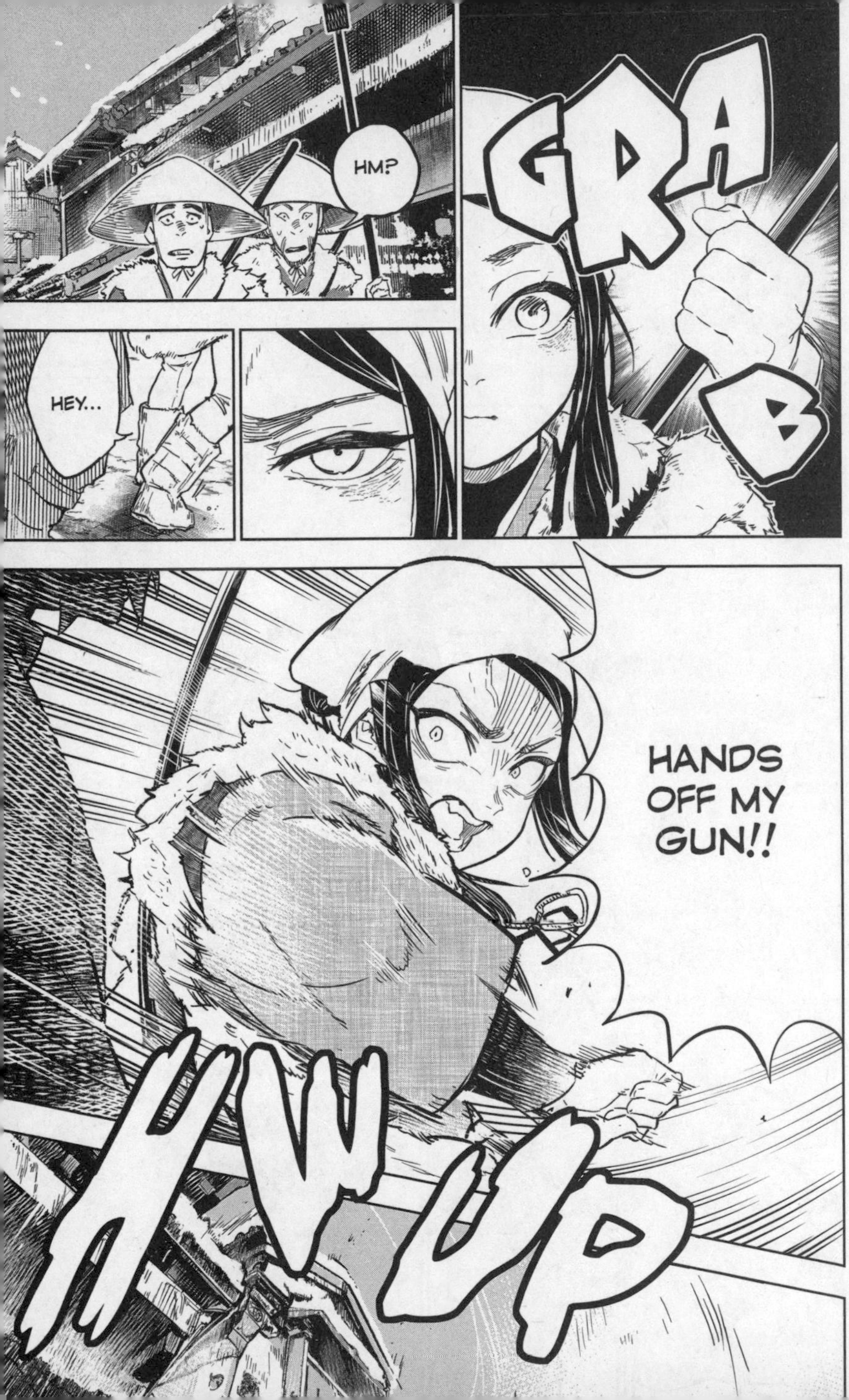
GRAB
HM?
HEY...
HANDS OFF MY GUN!!
HWUP

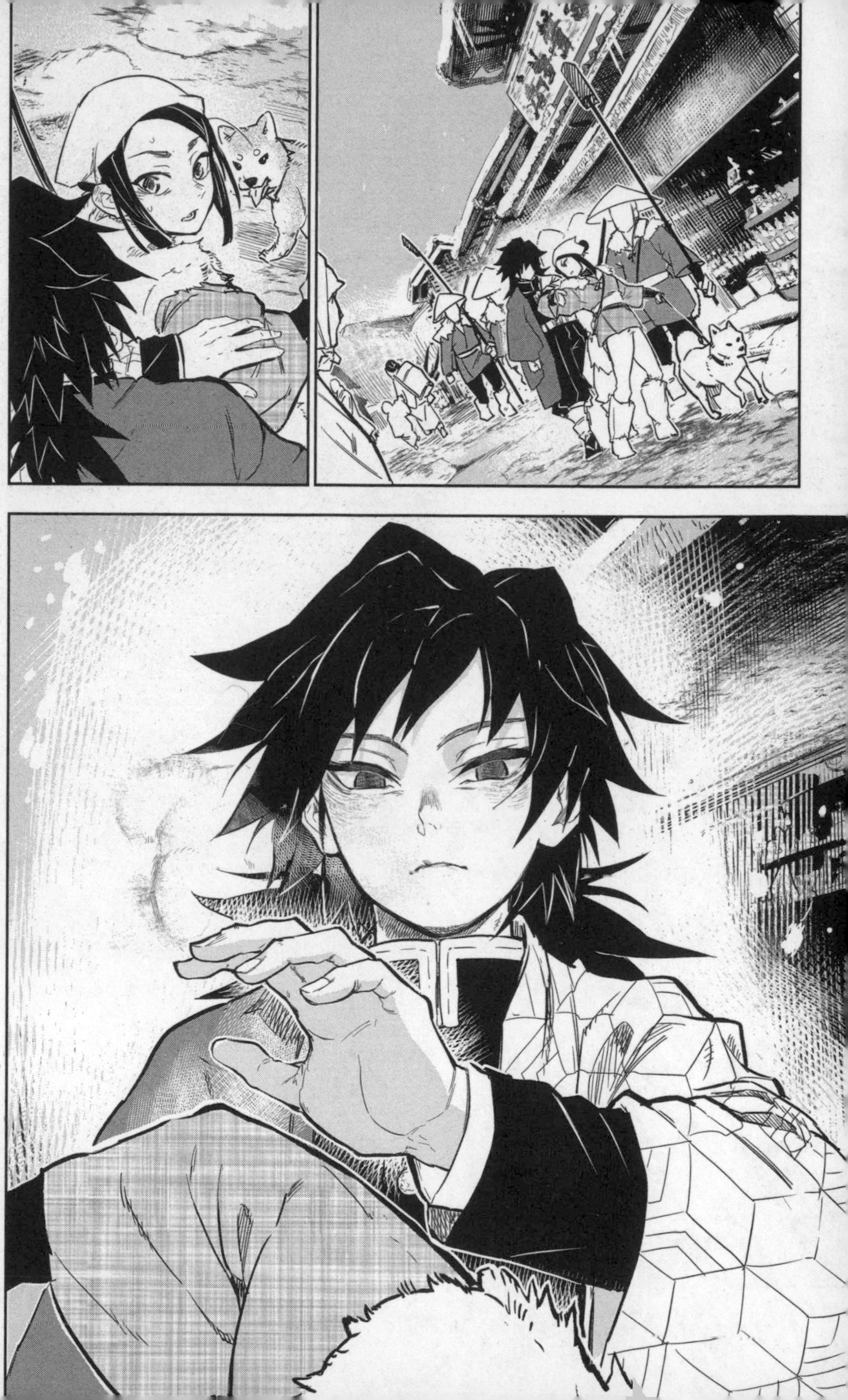

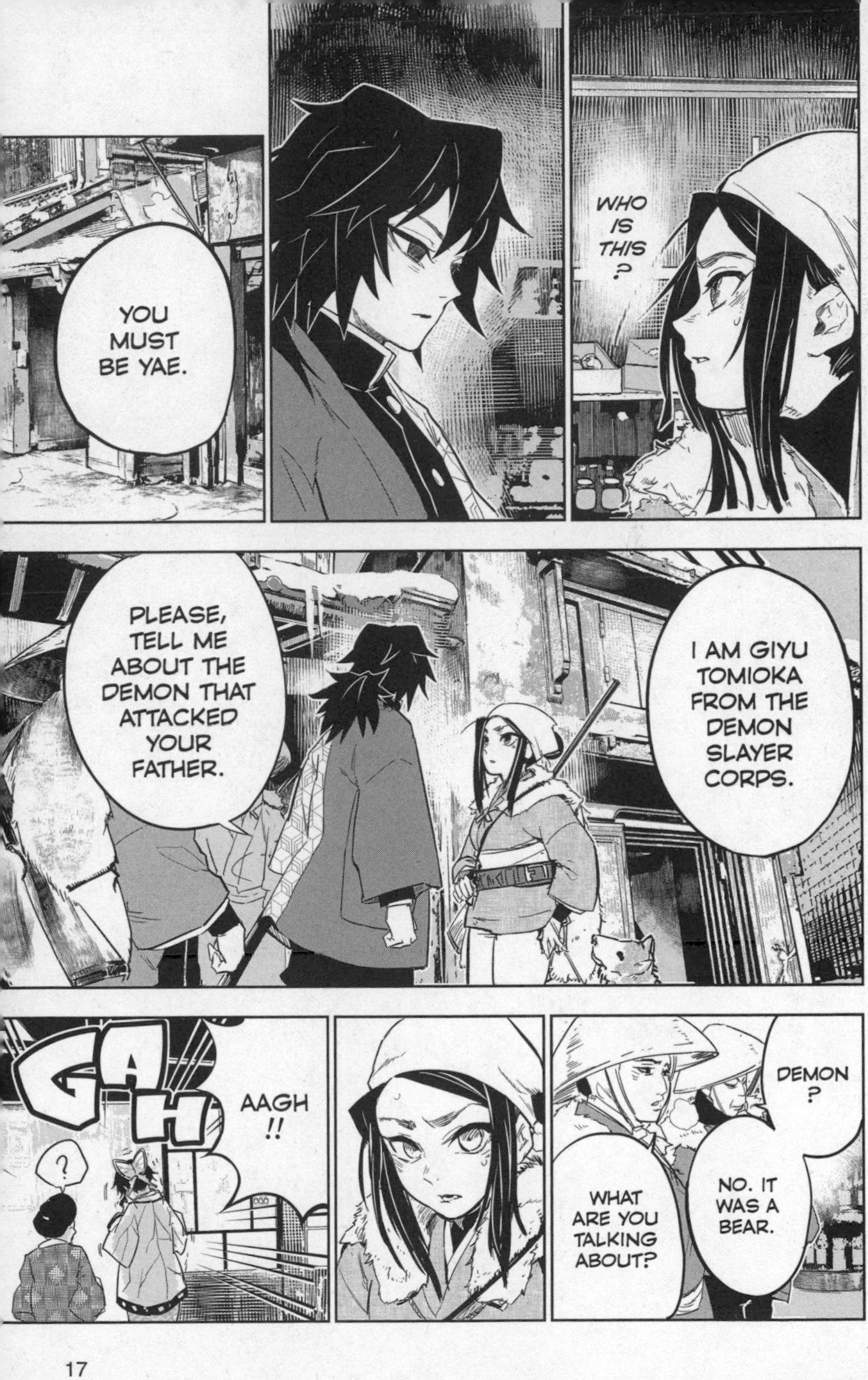
WHO IS THIS?
YOU MUST BE YAE.
I AM GIYU TOMIOKA FROM THE DEMON SLAYER CORPS.
PLEASE, TELL ME ABOUT THE DEMON THAT ATTACKED YOUR FATHER.
DEMON?
NO. IT WAS A BEAR.
WHAT ARE YOU TALKING ABOUT?
GAH
AAGH!!
?

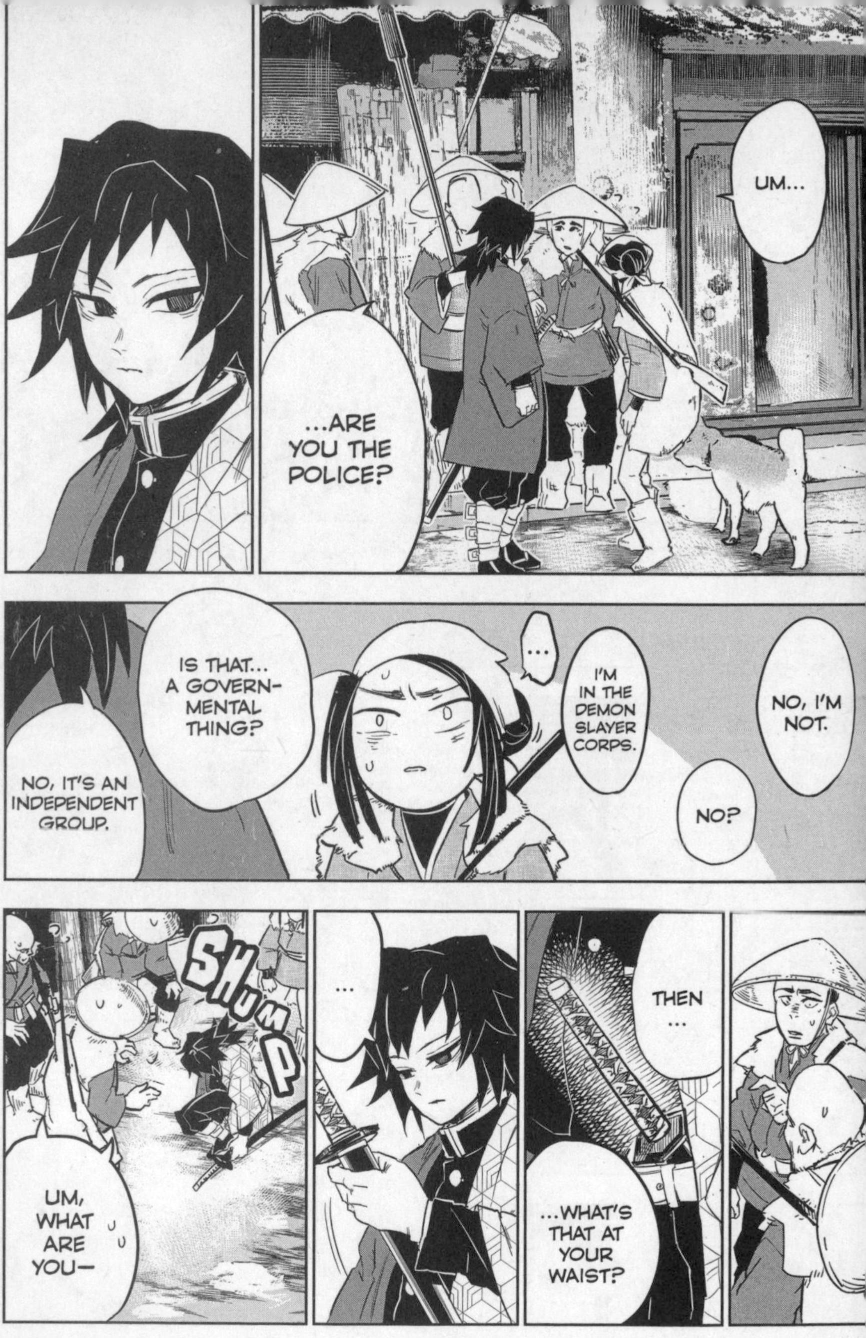
UM...
...ARE YOU THE POLICE?
NO, I'M NOT.
NO?
I'M IN THE DEMON SLAYER CORPS.
...
IS THAT... A GOVERN-MENTAL THING?
NO, IT'S AN INDEPENDENT GROUP.
THEN ...
...WHAT'S THAT AT YOUR WAIST?
...
SHUMP
UM, WHAT ARE YOU—

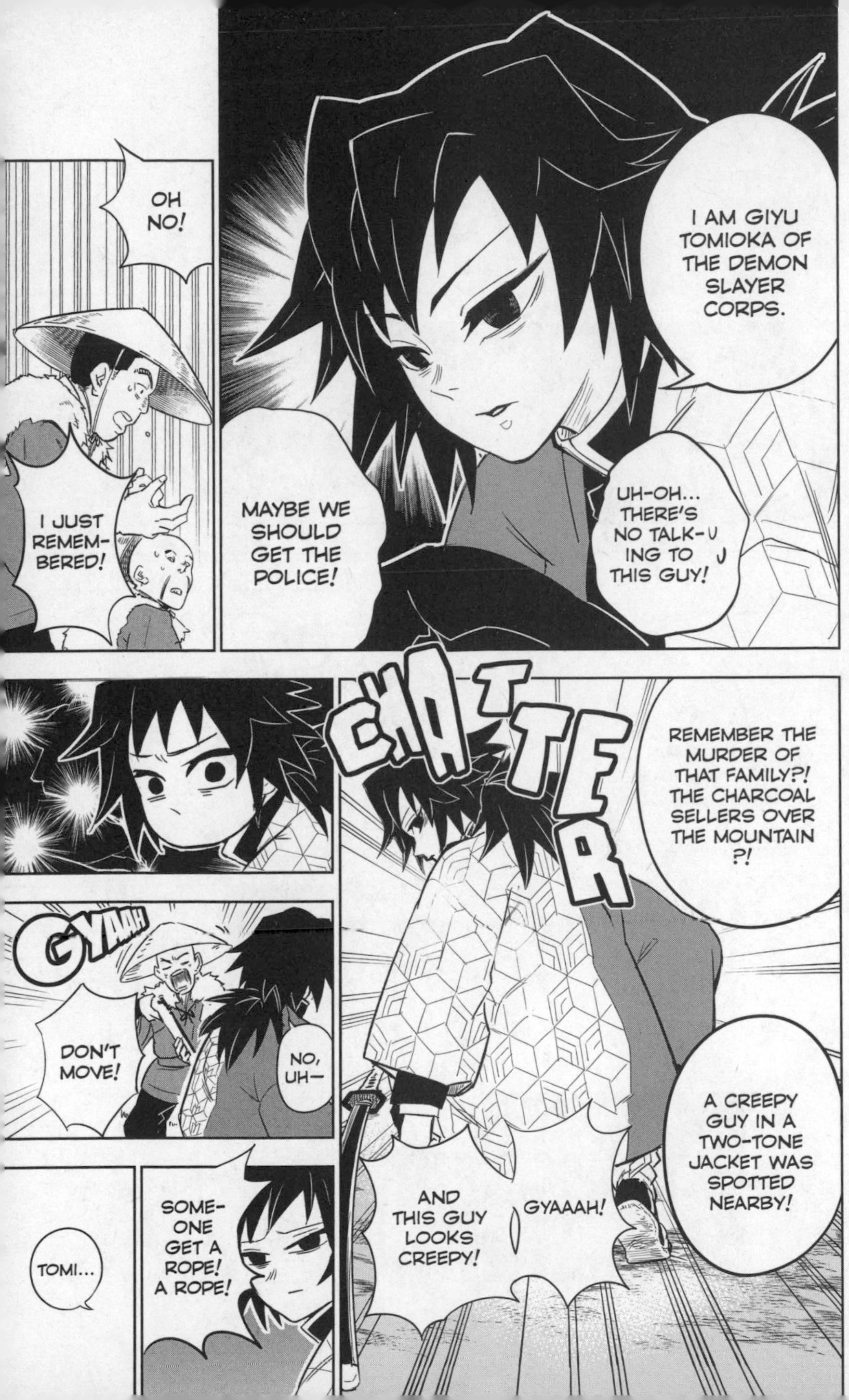
I AM GIYU TOMIOKA OF THE DEMON SLAYER CORPS.
UH-OH... THERE'S NO TALKING TO THIS GUY!
MAYBE WE SHOULD GET THE POLICE!
OH NO!
I JUST REMEMBERED!
REMEMBER THE MURDER OF THAT FAMILY?! THE CHARCOAL SELLERS OVER THE MOUNTAIN?!
CHATTER
A CREEPY GUY IN A TWO-TONE JACKET WAS SPOTTED NEARBY!
GYAAAH!
AND THIS GUY LOOKS CREEPY!
GYAAAH
NO, UH—
DON'T MOVE!
SOME-ONE GET A ROPE! A ROPE!
TOMI...

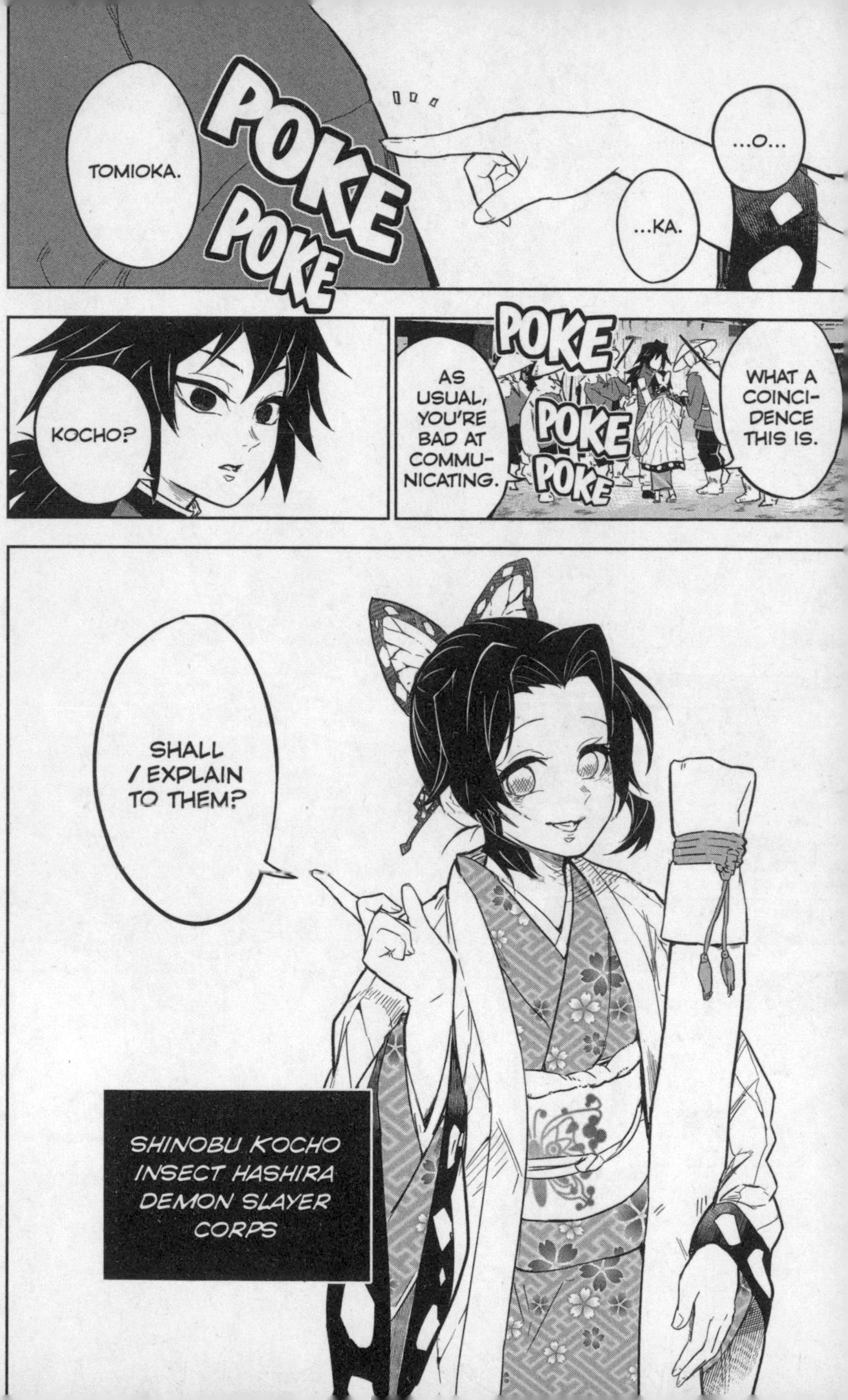
...O...
...KA.
POKE POKE
TOMIOKA.
WHAT A COINCI-DENCE THIS IS.
POKE POKE POKE
AS USUAL, YOU'RE BAD AT COMMU-NICATING.
KOCHO?
SHALL I EXPLAIN TO THEM?
SHINOBU KOCHO INSECT HASHIRA DEMON SLAYER CORPS

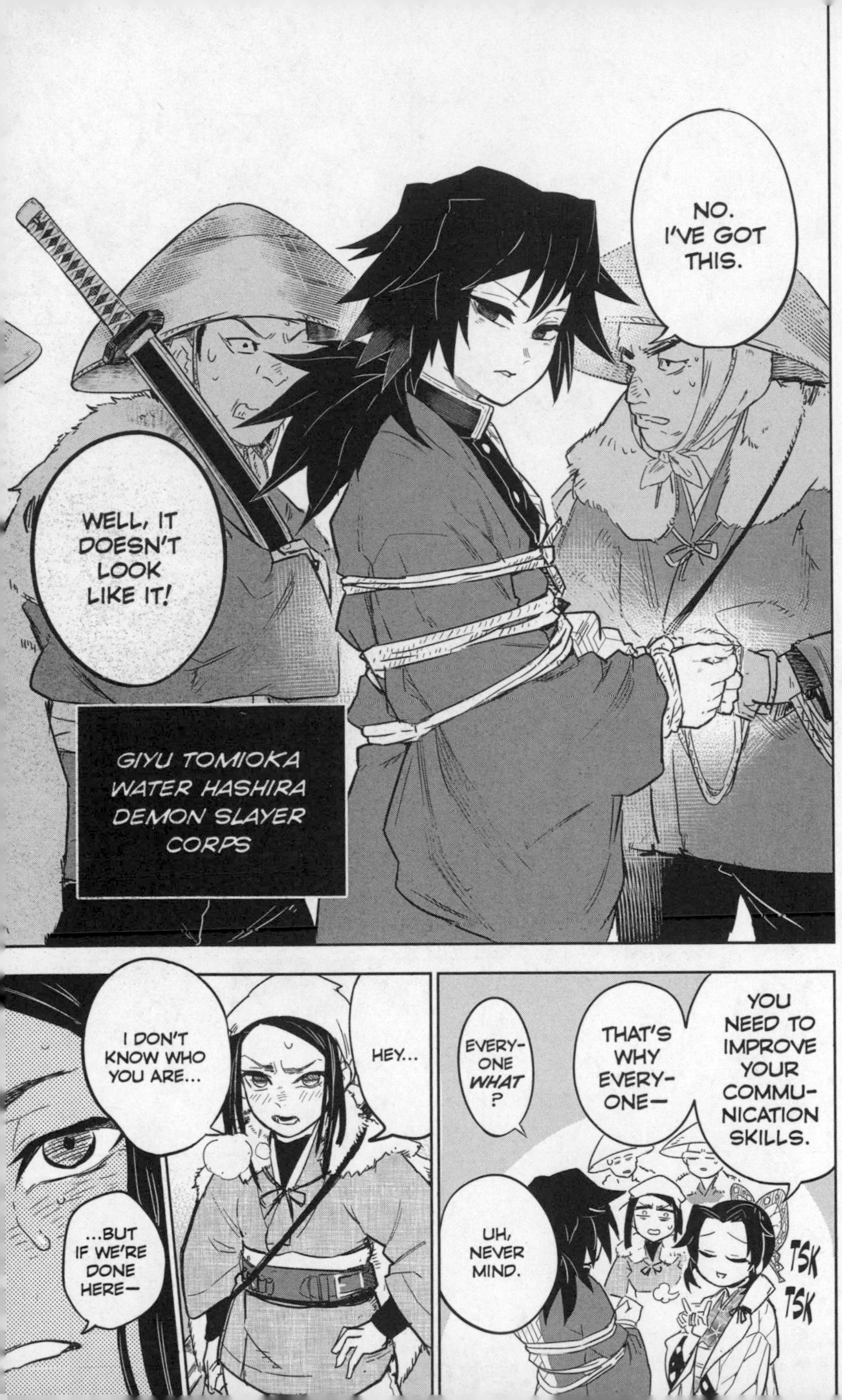
NO. I'VE GOT THIS.
WELL, IT DOESN'T LOOK LIKE IT!
GIYU TOMIOKA WATER HASHIRA DEMON SLAYER CORPS
YOU NEED TO IMPROVE YOUR COMMUNICATION SKILLS.
THAT'S WHY EVERYONE—
EVERYONE *WHAT*?
UH, NEVER MIND.
TSK TSK
HEY...
I DON'T KNOW WHO YOU ARE...
...BUT IF WE'RE DONE HERE—

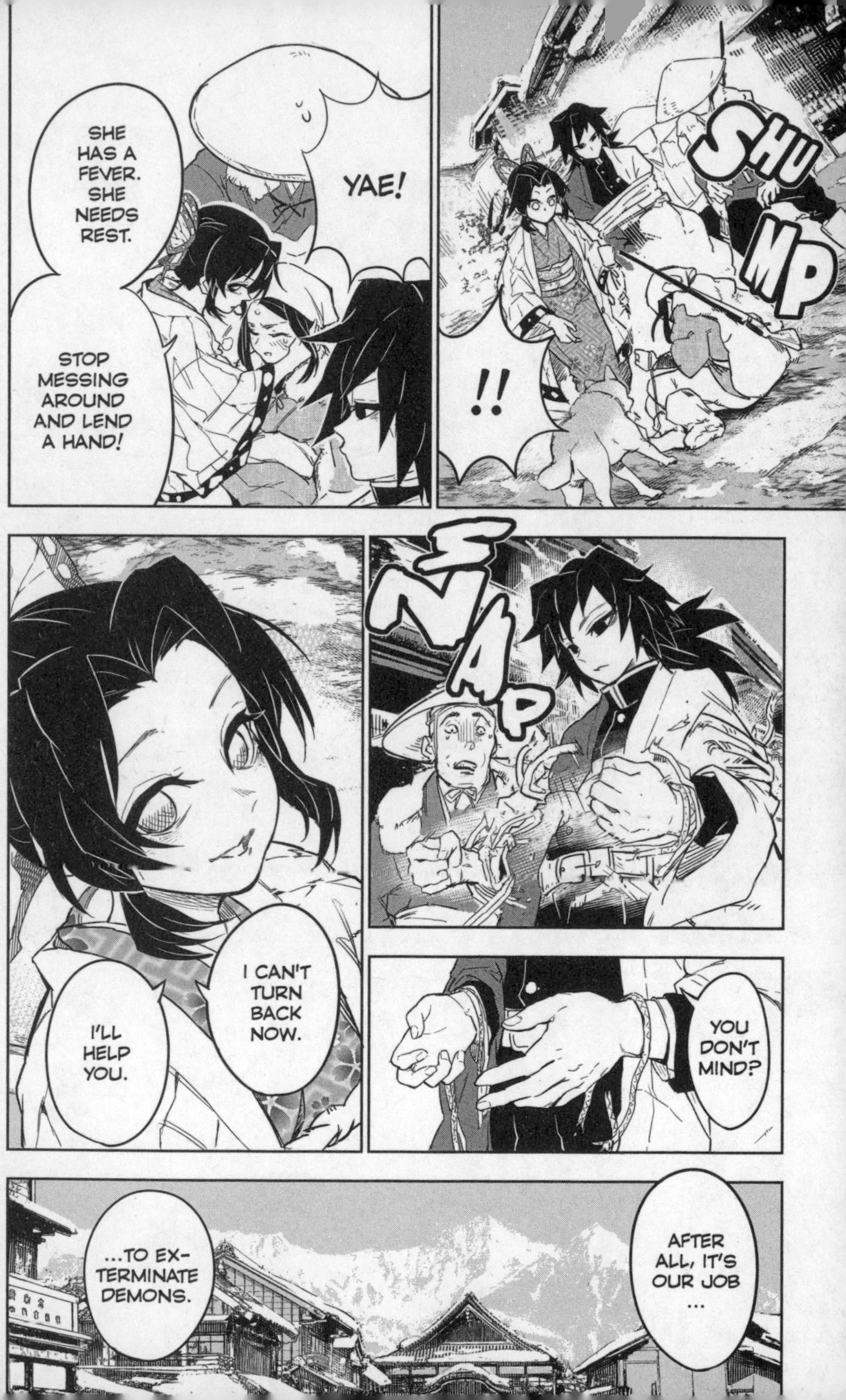
SHUMP
!!
YAE!
SHE HAS A FEVER. SHE NEEDS REST.
STOP MESSING AROUND AND LEND A HAND!
SNAP
YOU DON'T MIND?
I CAN'T TURN BACK NOW.
I'LL HELP YOU.
AFTER ALL, IT'S OUR JOB ...
...TO EXTERMINATE DEMONS.

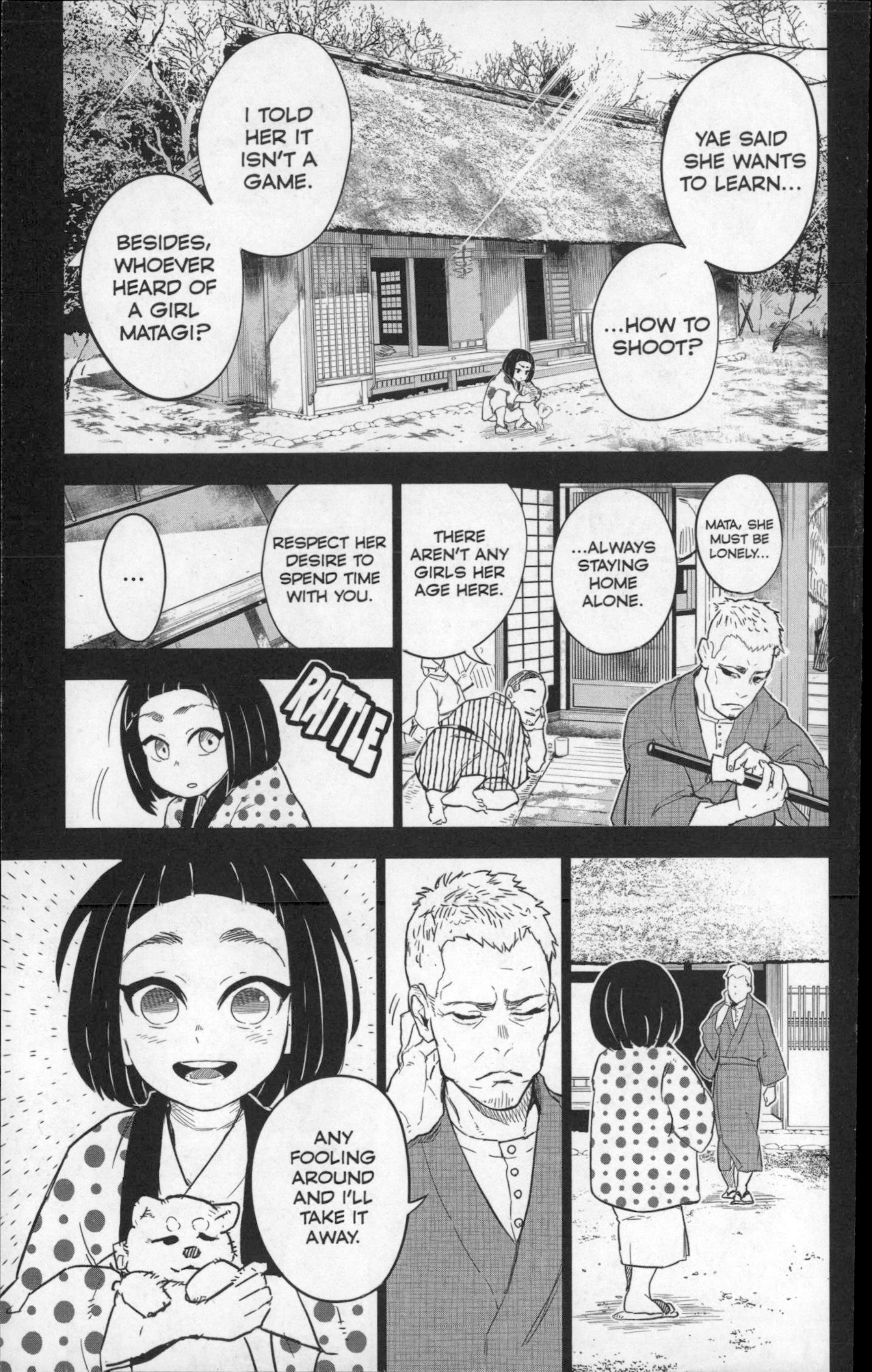
YAE SAID SHE WANTS TO LEARN...
...HOW TO SHOOT?
I TOLD HER IT ISN'T A GAME.
BESIDES, WHOEVER HEARD OF A GIRL MATAGI?
MATA, SHE MUST BE LONELY...
...ALWAYS STAYING HOME ALONE.
THERE AREN'T ANY GIRLS HER AGE HERE.
RESPECT HER DESIRE TO SPEND TIME WITH YOU.
...
RATTLE
ANY FOOLING AROUND AND I'LL TAKE IT AWAY.

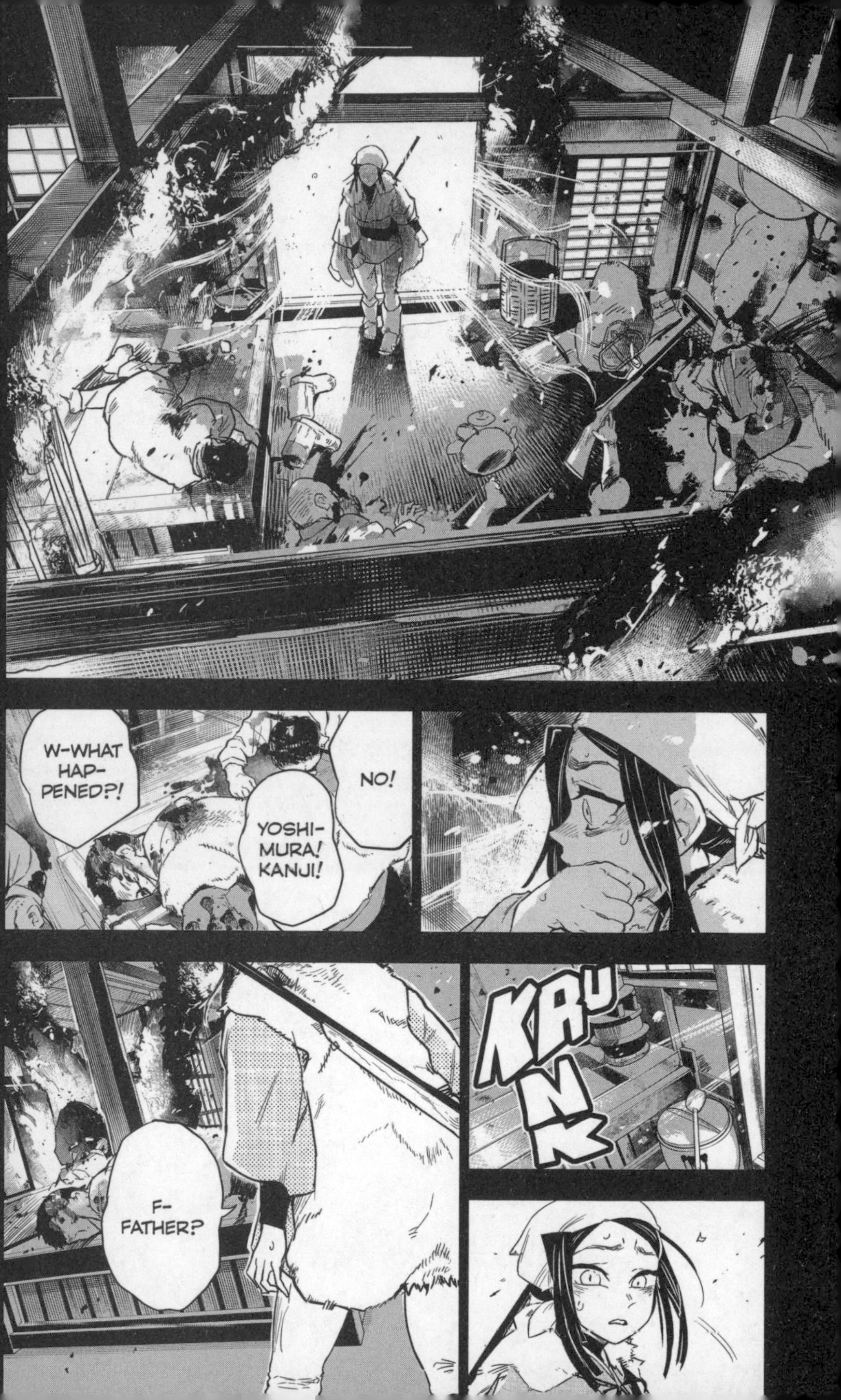
NO!
W-WHAT HAP-PENED?!
YOSHI-MURA! KANJI!
KRUNK
F-FATHER?

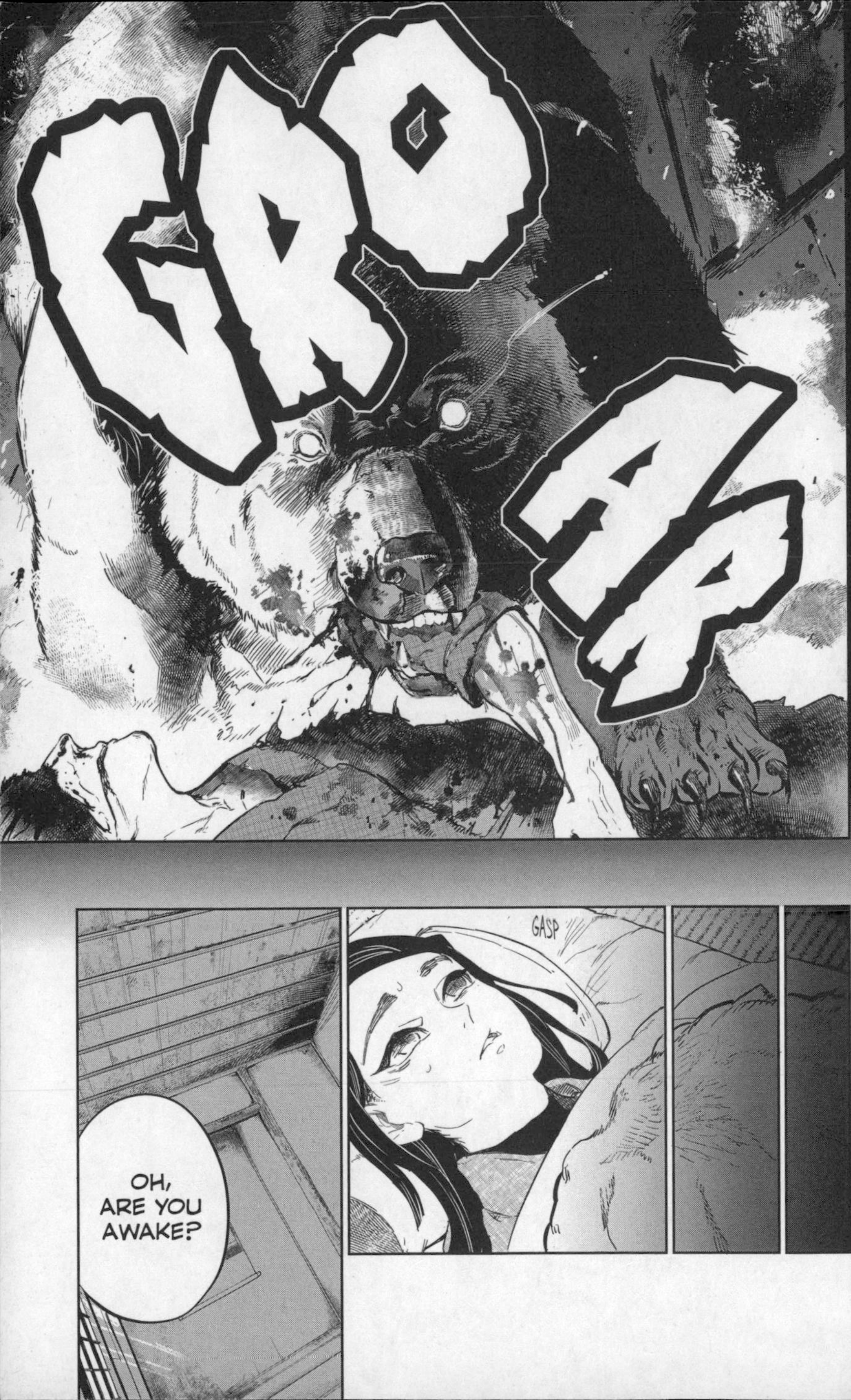
GRAOAR
GASP
OH, ARE YOU AWAKE?

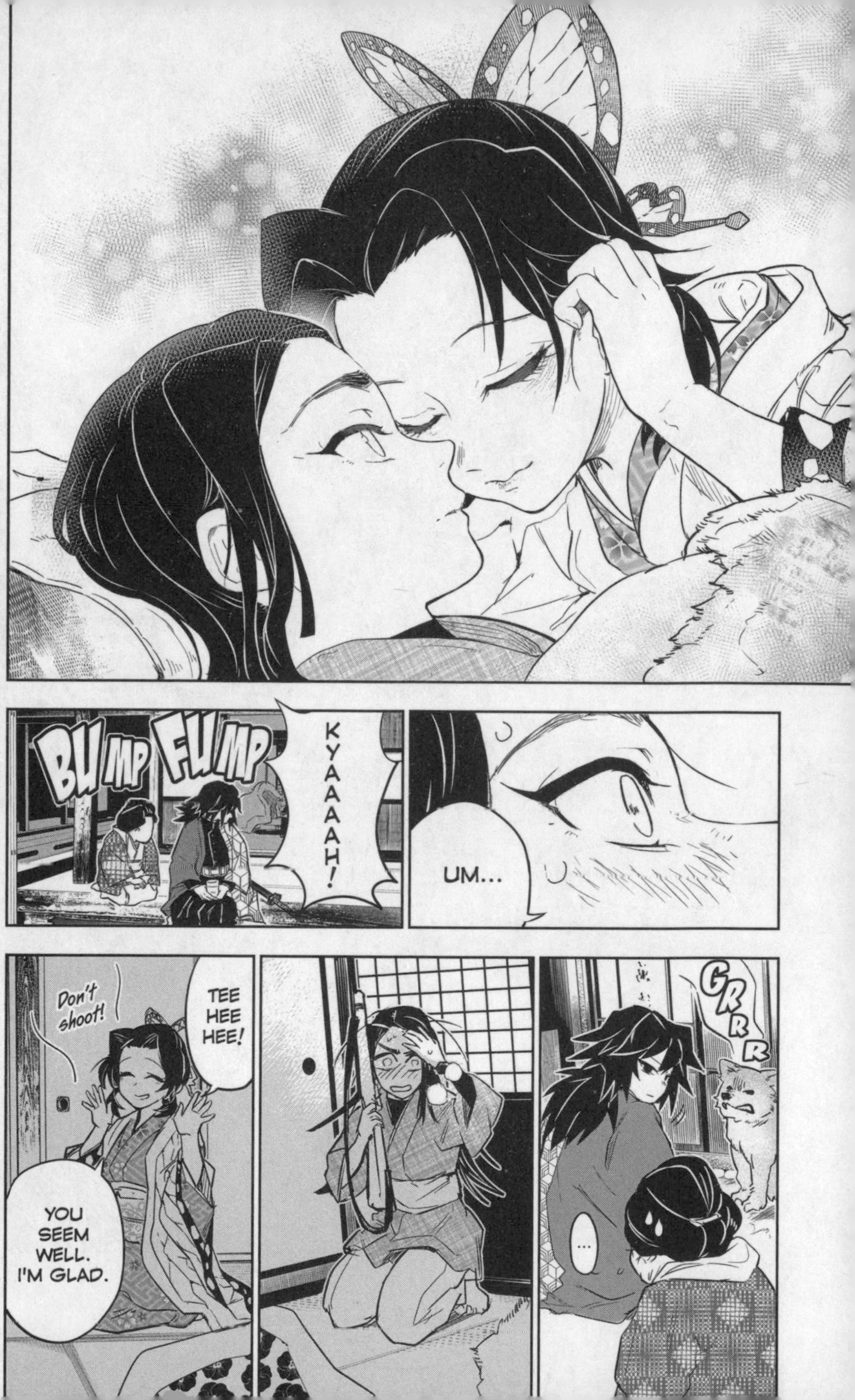
UM...
KYAAAAH!
BUMP FUMP
GRRR
...
TEE HEE HEE!
Don't shoot!
YOU SEEM WELL. I'M GLAD.

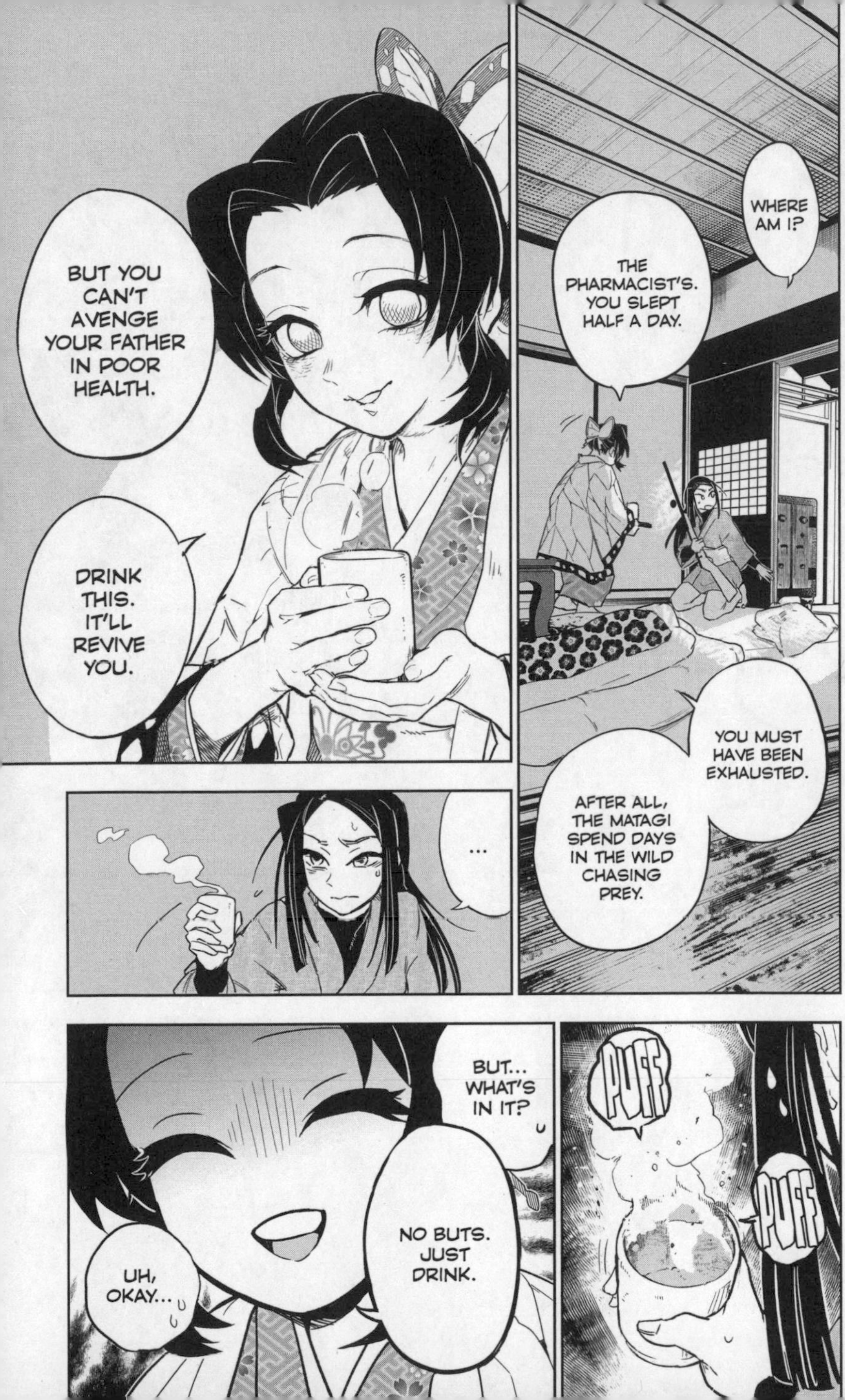
WHERE AM I?
THE PHARMACIST'S. YOU SLEPT HALF A DAY.
YOU MUST HAVE BEEN EXHAUSTED.
AFTER ALL, THE MATAGI SPEND DAYS IN THE WILD CHASING PREY.
BUT YOU CAN'T AVENGE YOUR FATHER IN POOR HEALTH.
DRINK THIS. IT'LL REVIVE YOU.
...
PUFF
PUFF
BUT... WHAT'S IN IT?
NO BUTS. JUST DRINK.
UH, OKAY...

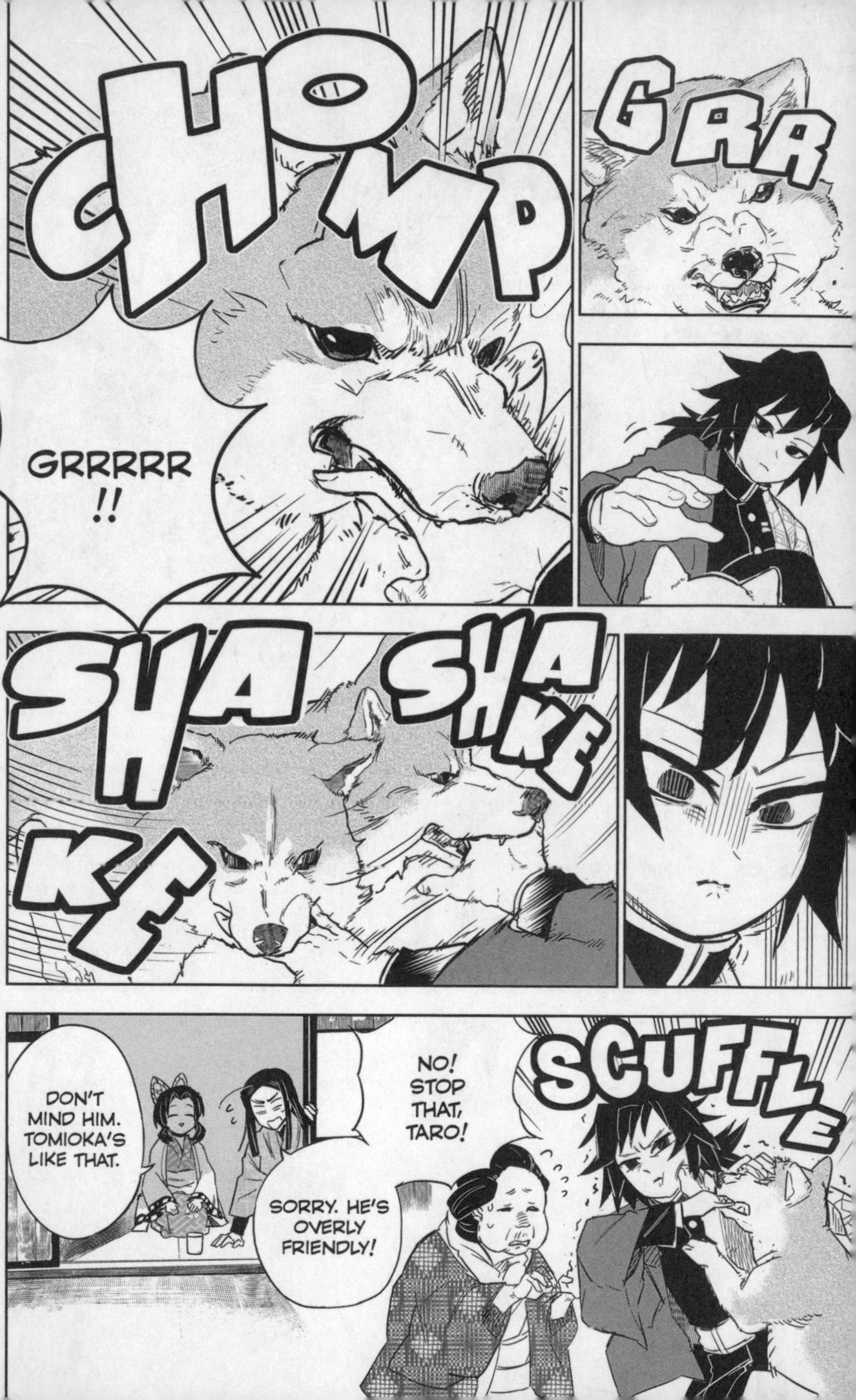
GRR
CHOMP
GRRRRR!!
SHAKE
SHAKE
SCUFFLE
NO! STOP THAT, TARO!
SORRY. HE'S OVERLY FRIENDLY!
DON'T MIND HIM. TOMIOKA'S LIKE THAT.

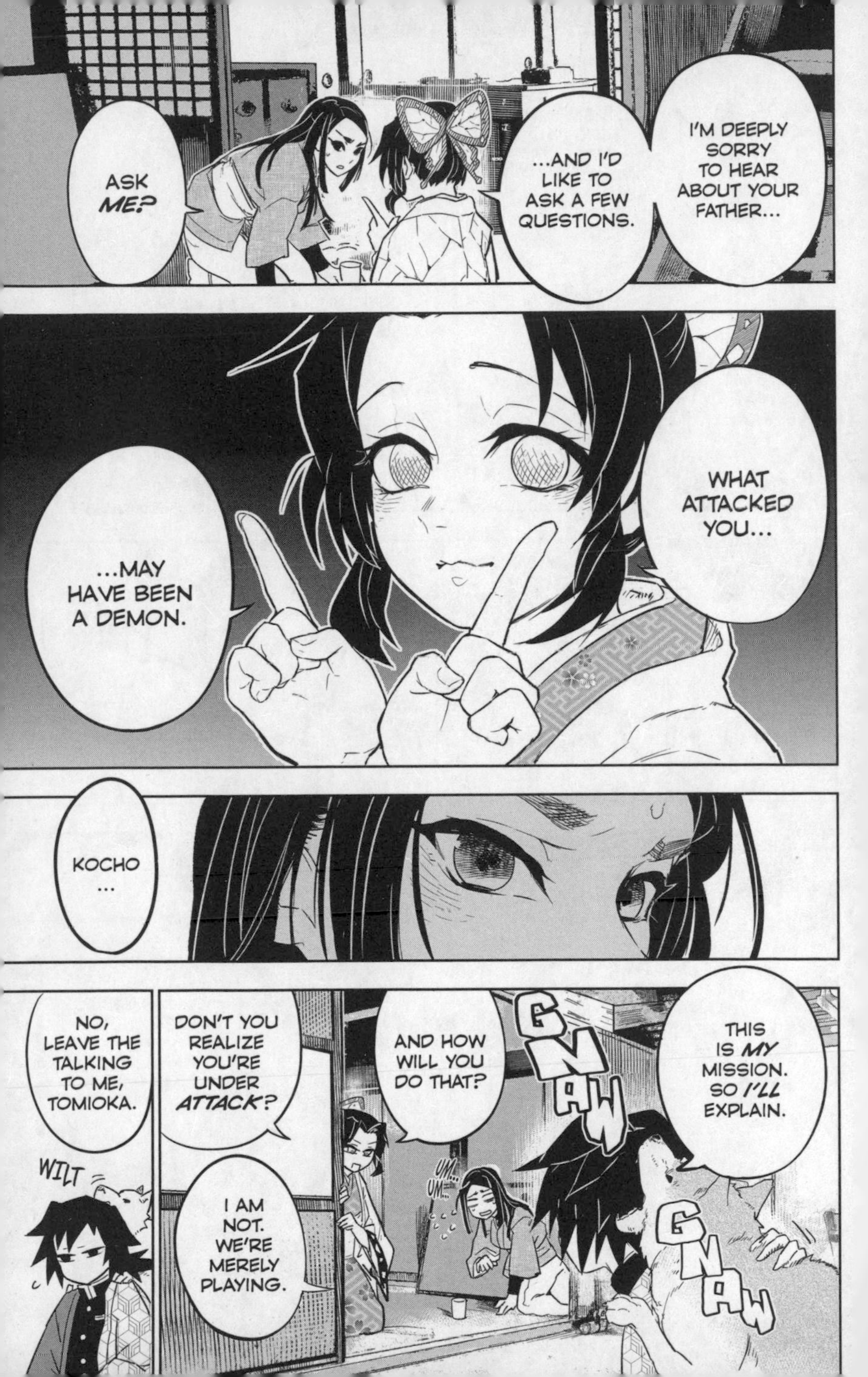
I'M DEEPLY SORRY TO HEAR ABOUT YOUR FATHER...
...AND I'D LIKE TO ASK A FEW QUESTIONS.
ASK *ME?*
WHAT ATTACKED YOU...
...MAY HAVE BEEN A DEMON.
KOCHO ...
THIS IS *MY* MISSION. SO *I'LL* EXPLAIN.
GNAW
GNAW
AND HOW WILL YOU DO THAT?
UM... UM...
DON'T YOU REALIZE YOU'RE UNDER *ATTACK*?
I AM NOT. WE'RE MERELY PLAYING.
NO, LEAVE THE TALKING TO ME, TOMIOKA.
WILT

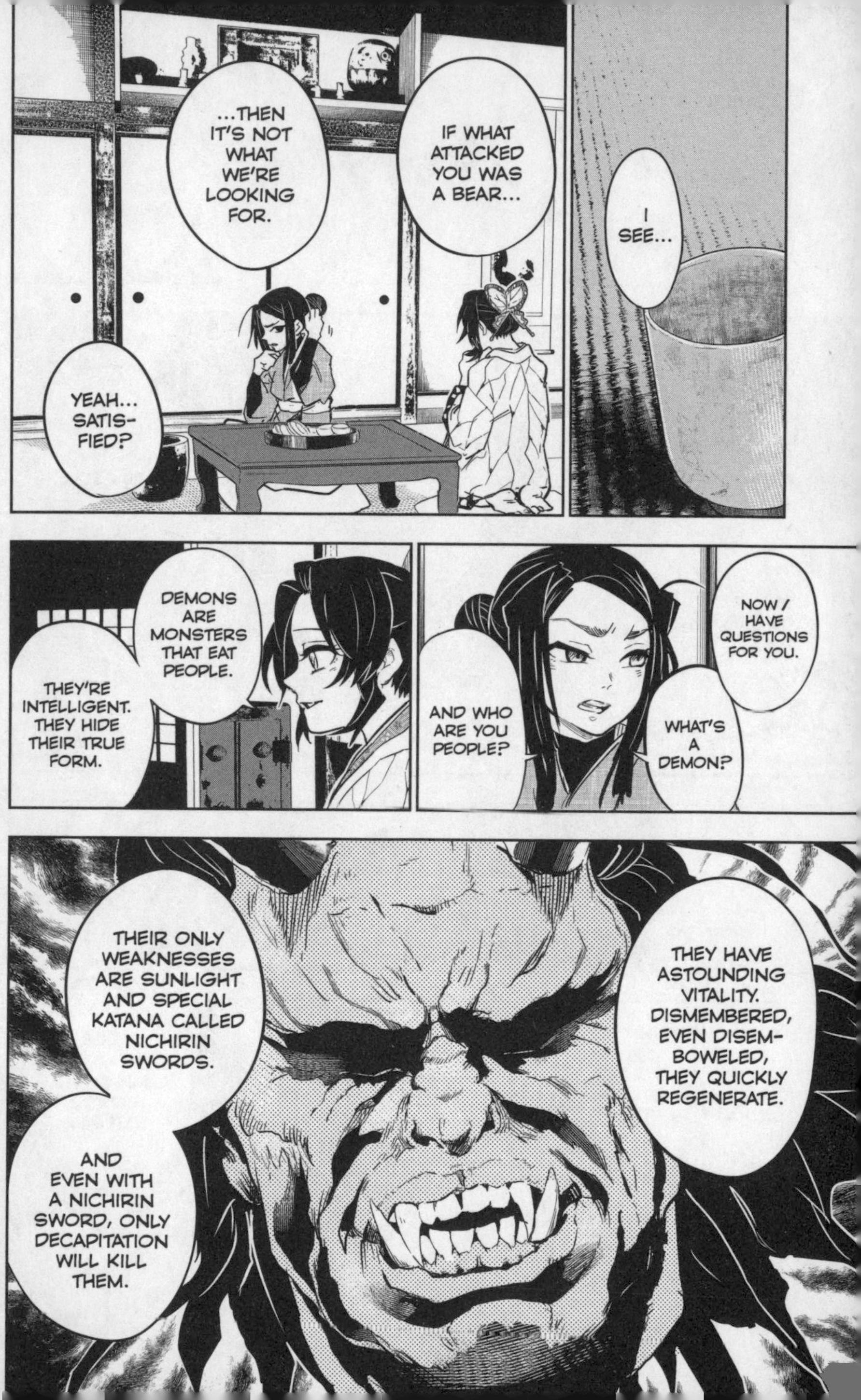
I SEE...
IF WHAT ATTACKED YOU WAS A BEAR...
...THEN IT'S NOT WHAT WE'RE LOOKING FOR.
YEAH... SATISFIED?
NOW I HAVE QUESTIONS FOR YOU.
WHAT'S A DEMON?
AND WHO ARE YOU PEOPLE?
DEMONS ARE MONSTERS THAT EAT PEOPLE.
THEY'RE INTELLIGENT. THEY HIDE THEIR TRUE FORM.
THEY HAVE ASTOUNDING VITALITY. DISMEMBERED, EVEN DISEMBOWELED, THEY QUICKLY REGENERATE.
THEIR ONLY WEAKNESSES ARE SUNLIGHT AND SPECIAL KATANA CALLED NICHIRIN SWORDS.
AND EVEN WITH A NICHIRIN SWORD, ONLY DECAPITATION WILL KILL THEM.

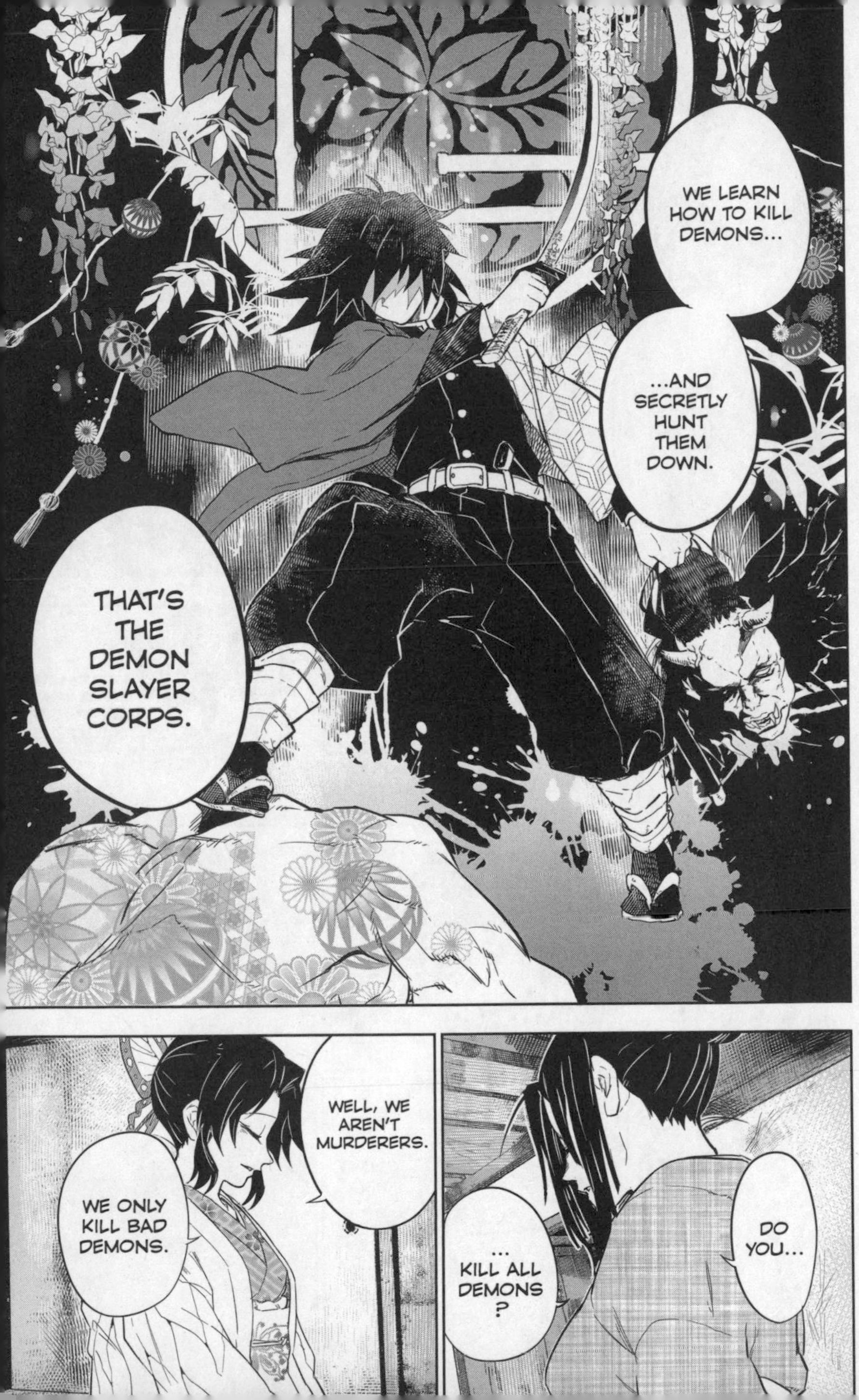
WE LEARN HOW TO KILL DEMONS...
...AND SECRETLY HUNT THEM DOWN.
THAT'S THE DEMON SLAYER CORPS.
DO YOU...
... KILL ALL DEMONS ?
WELL, WE AREN'T MURDERERS.
WE ONLY KILL BAD DEMONS.

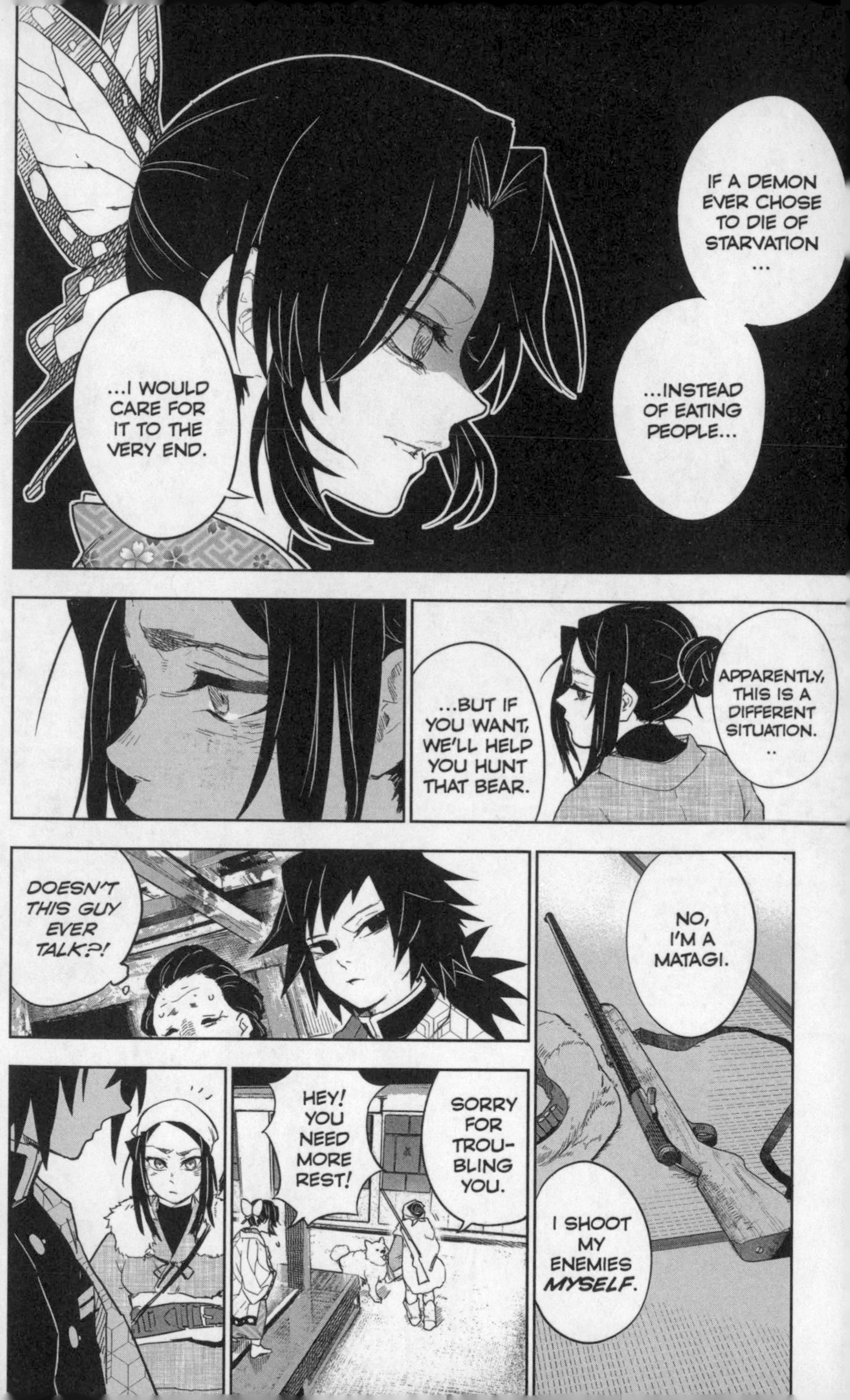
IF A DEMON EVER CHOSE TO DIE OF STARVATION ...
...INSTEAD OF EATING PEOPLE...
...I WOULD CARE FOR IT TO THE VERY END.
APPARENTLY, THIS IS A DIFFERENT SITUATION. ..
...BUT IF YOU WANT, WE'LL HELP YOU HUNT THAT BEAR.
NO, I'M A MATAGI.
I SHOOT MY ENEMIES *MYSELF*.
*DOESN'T THIS GUY EVER TALK?!*
SORRY FOR TROU-BLING YOU.
HEY! YOU NEED MORE REST!

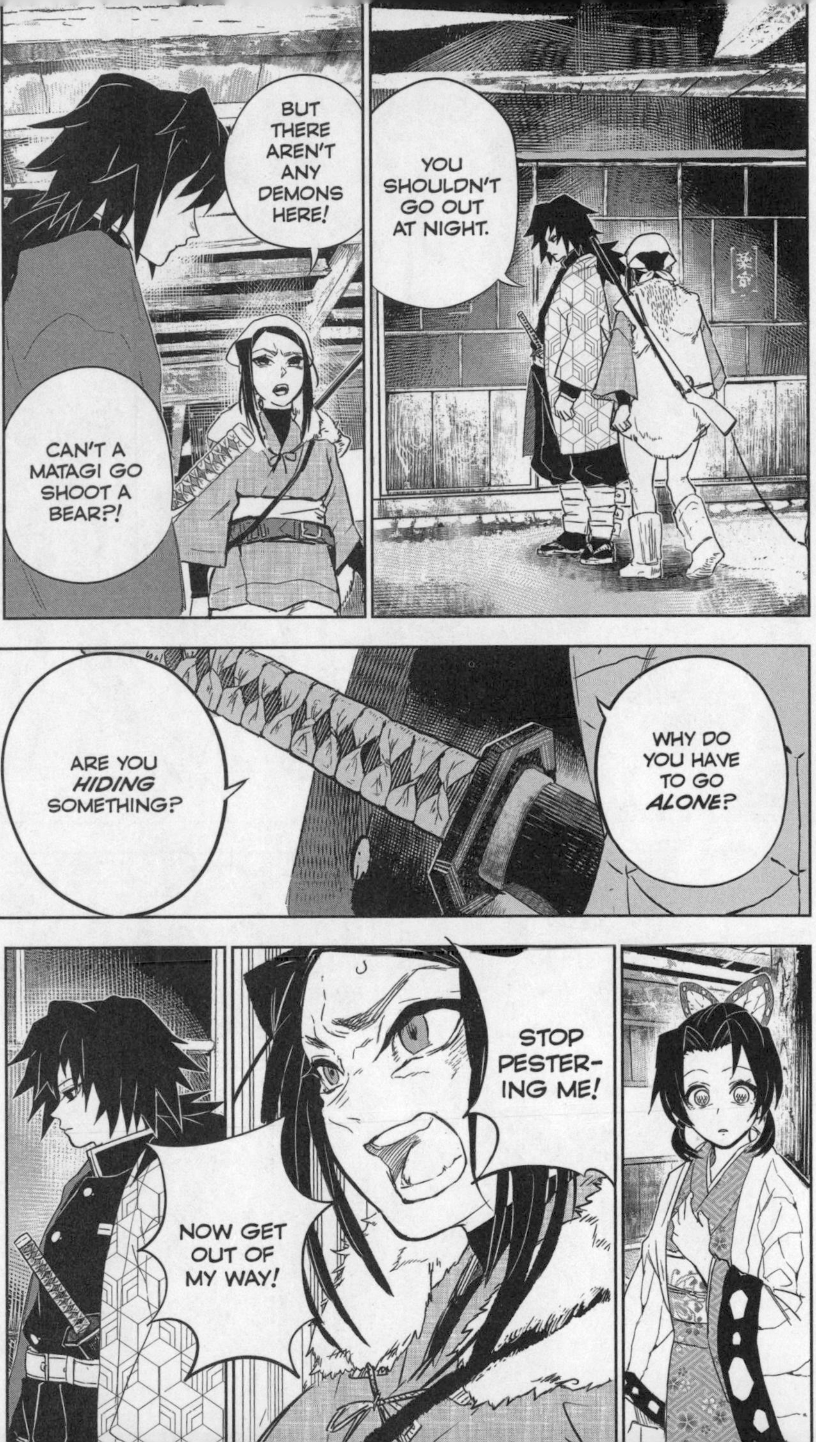
YOU SHOULDN'T GO OUT AT NIGHT.
BUT THERE AREN'T ANY DEMONS HERE!
CAN'T A MATAGI GO SHOOT A BEAR?!
WHY DO YOU HAVE TO GO *ALONE*?
ARE YOU *HIDING* SOMETHING?
STOP PESTER-ING ME!
NOW GET OUT OF MY WAY!

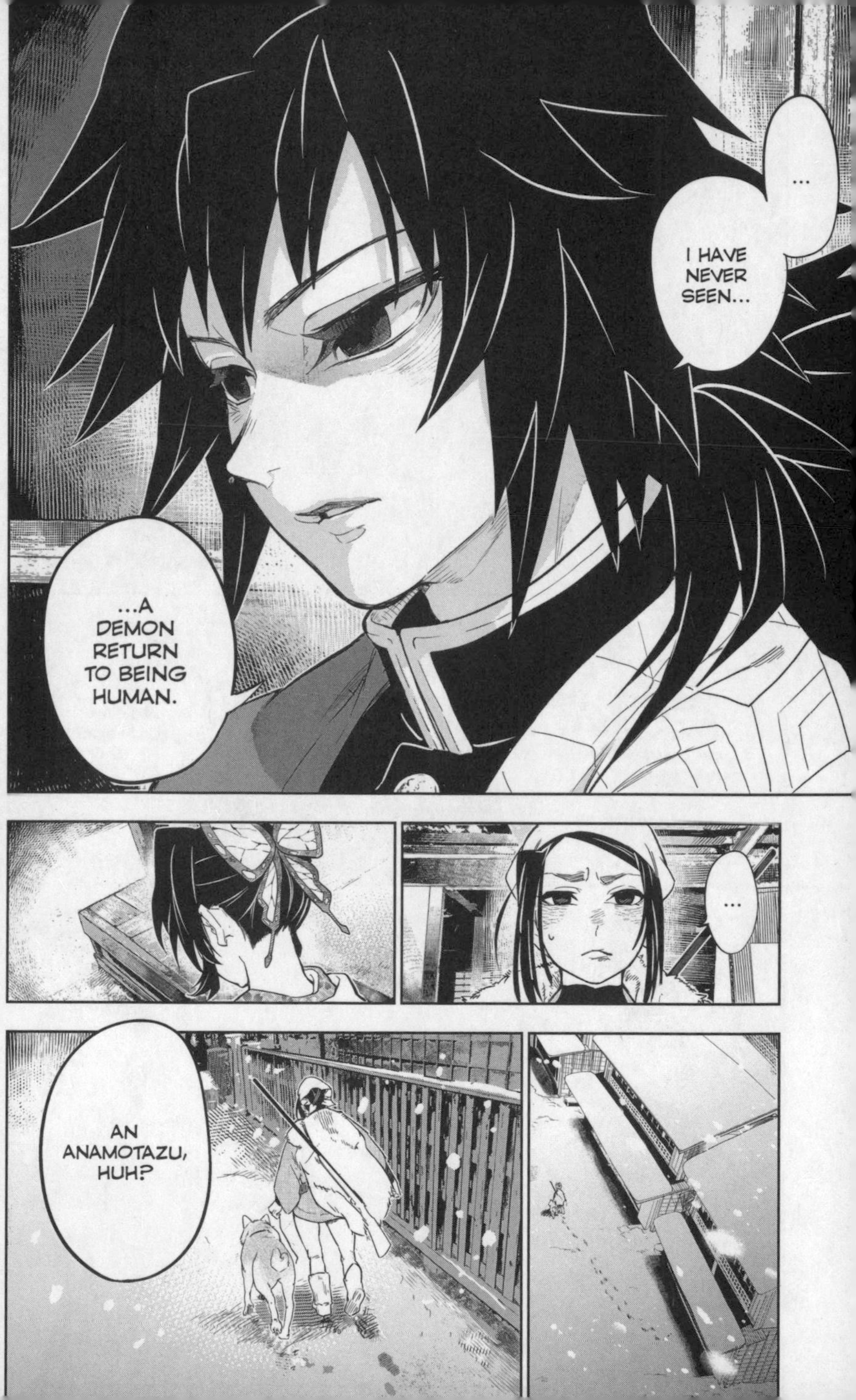
...
I HAVE NEVER SEEN...
...A DEMON RETURN TO BEING HUMAN.
...
AN ANAMOTAZU, HUH?

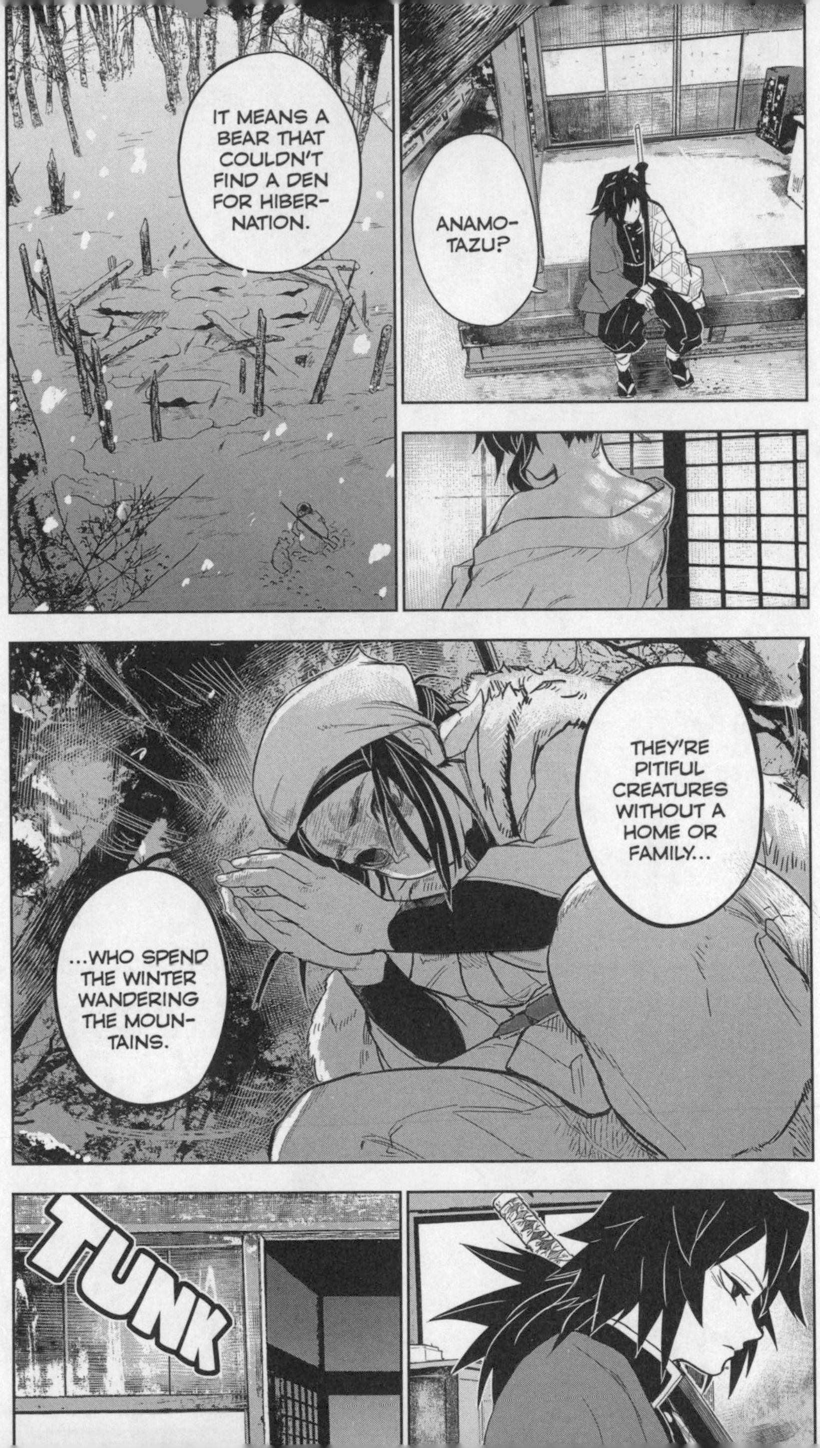
ANAMO-TAZU?
IT MEANS A BEAR THAT COULDN'T FIND A DEN FOR HIBER-NATION.
THEY'RE PITIFUL CREATURES WITHOUT A HOME OR FAMILY...
...WHO SPEND THE WINTER WANDERING THE MOUN-TAINS.
TUNK

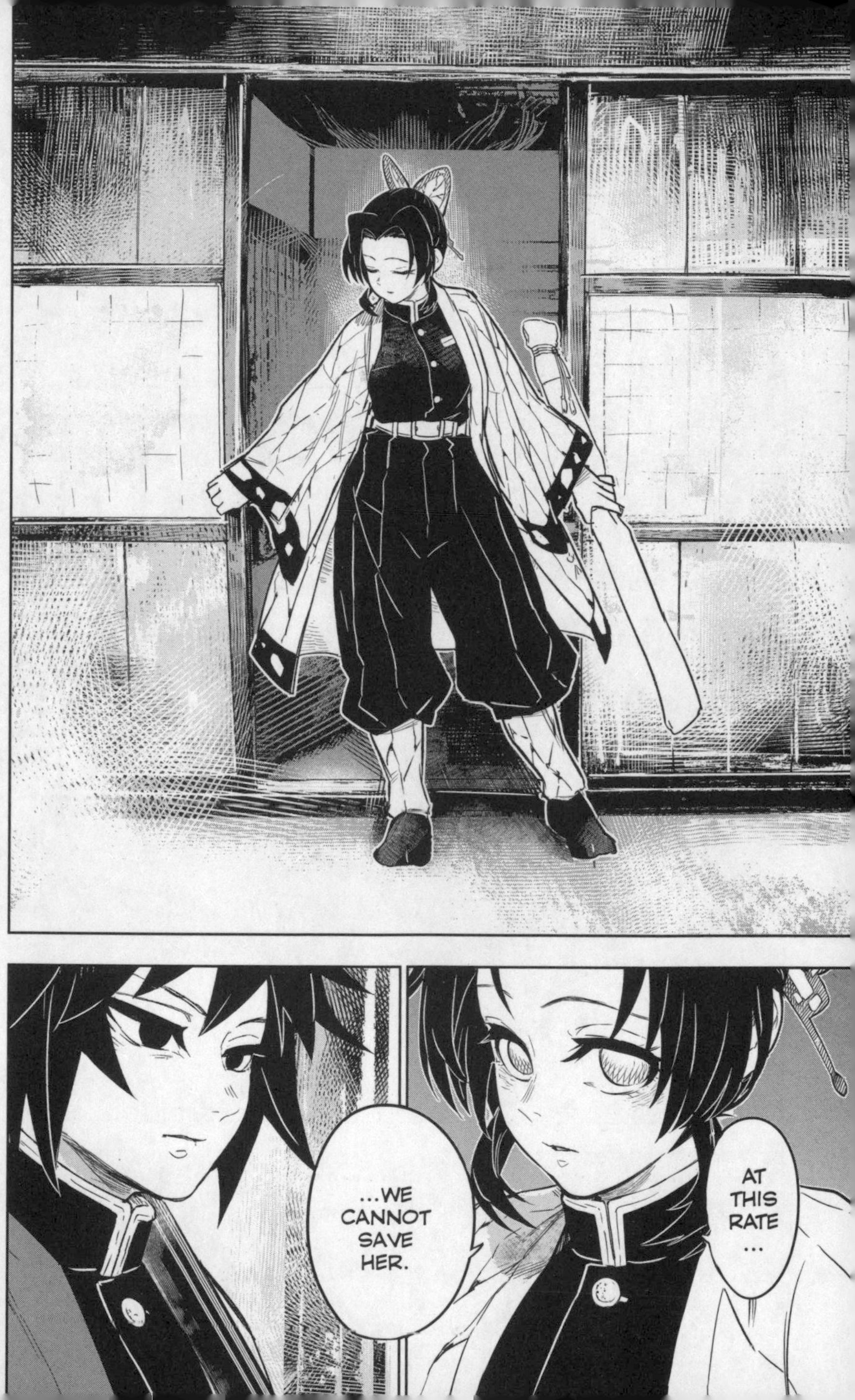
AT THIS RATE ...
...WE CANNOT SAVE HER.

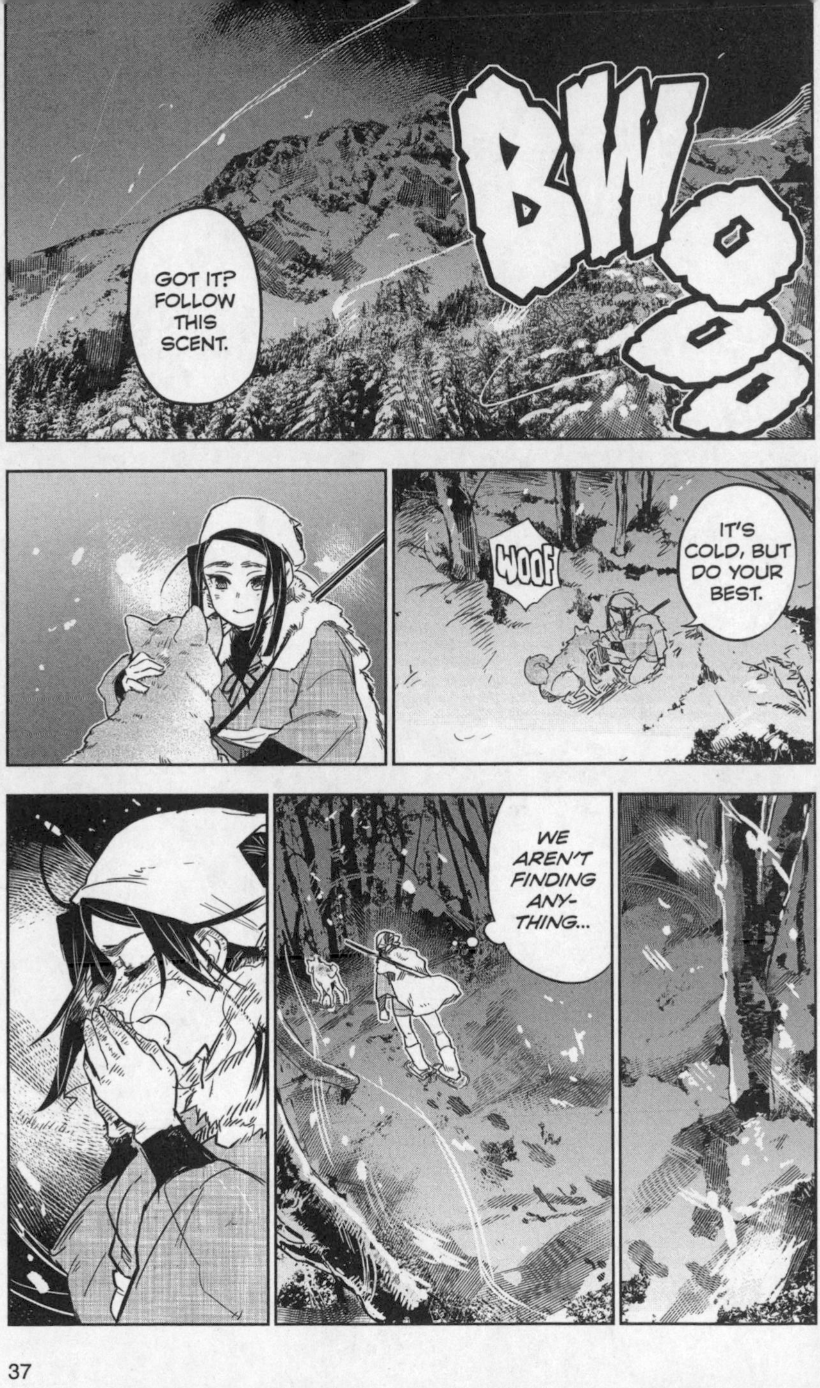
BWOOO
GOT IT? FOLLOW THIS SCENT.
IT'S COLD, BUT DO YOUR BEST.
WOOF
WE AREN'T FINDING ANY-THING...

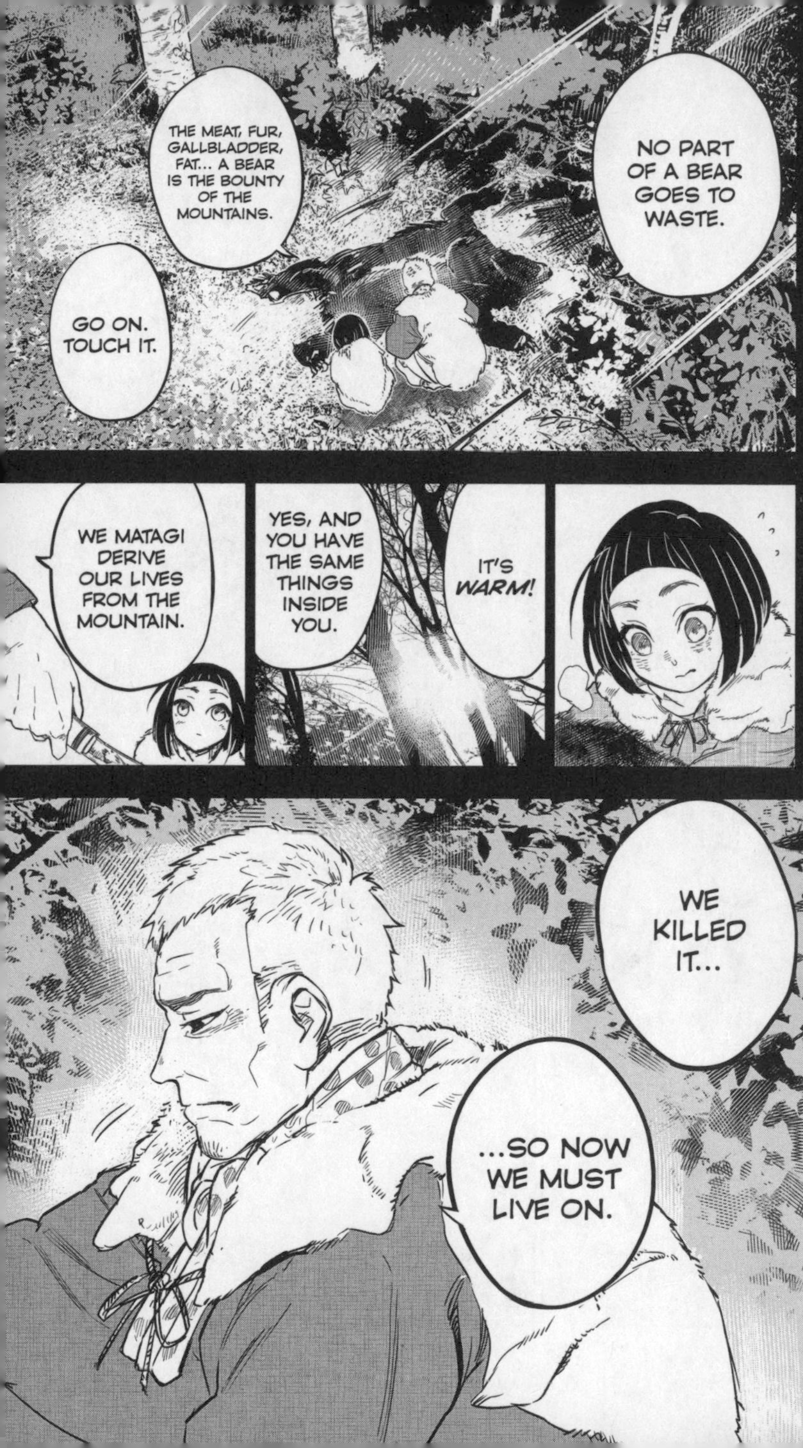

NO PART OF A BEAR GOES TO WASTE.
THE MEAT, FUR, GALLBLADDER, FAT... A BEAR IS THE BOUNTY OF THE MOUNTAINS.
GO ON. TOUCH IT.
IT'S *WARM!*
YES, AND YOU HAVE THE SAME THINGS INSIDE YOU.
WE MATAGI DERIVE OUR LIVES FROM THE MOUNTAIN.
WE KILLED IT...
...SO NOW WE MUST LIVE ON.

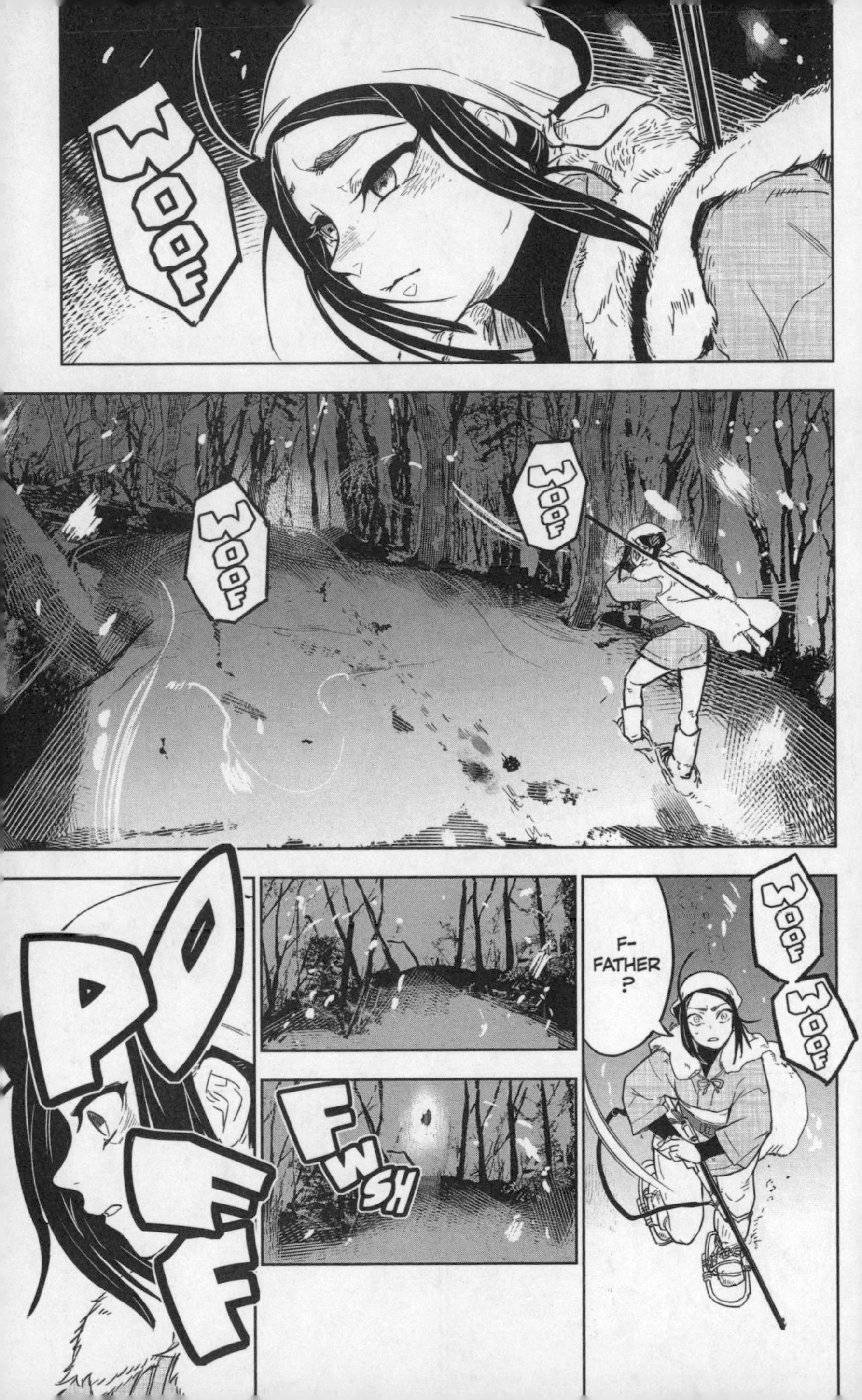
WOOF
WOOF
WOOF
WOOF
WOOF
F-FATHER?
FWSH
POOF

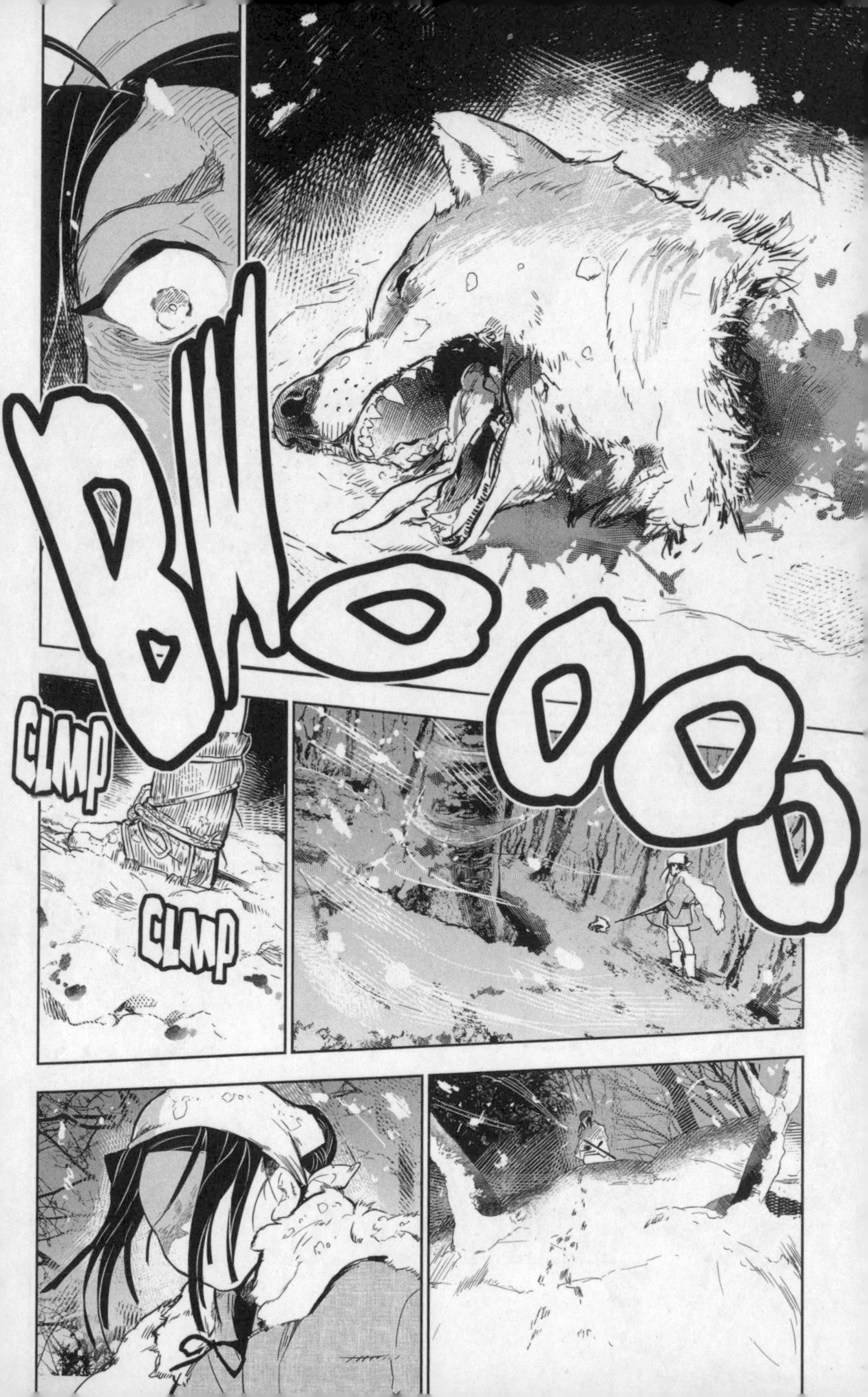
BWOOOO
CLMP
CLMP

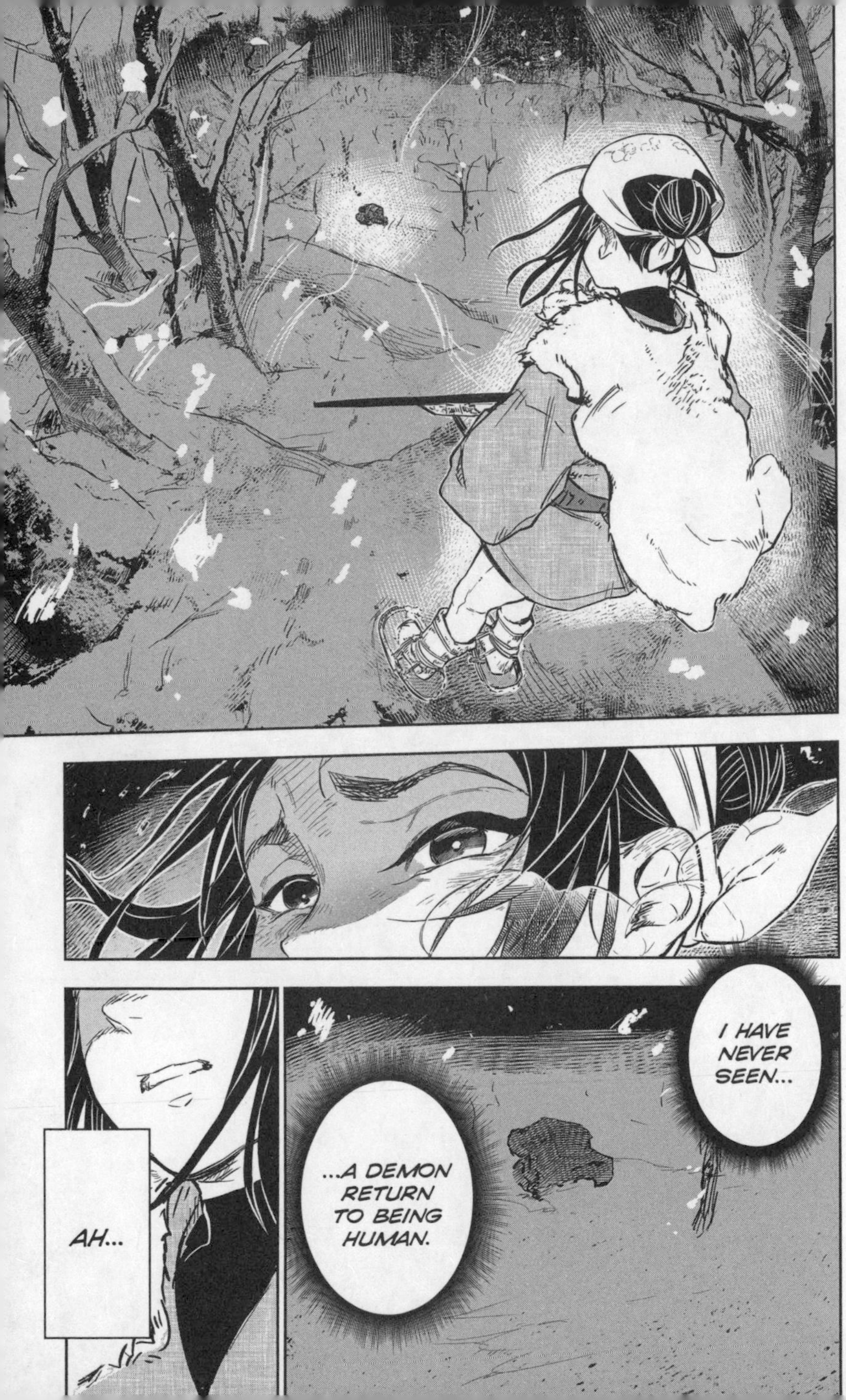
I HAVE NEVER SEEN...
...A DEMON RETURN TO BEING HUMAN.
AH...

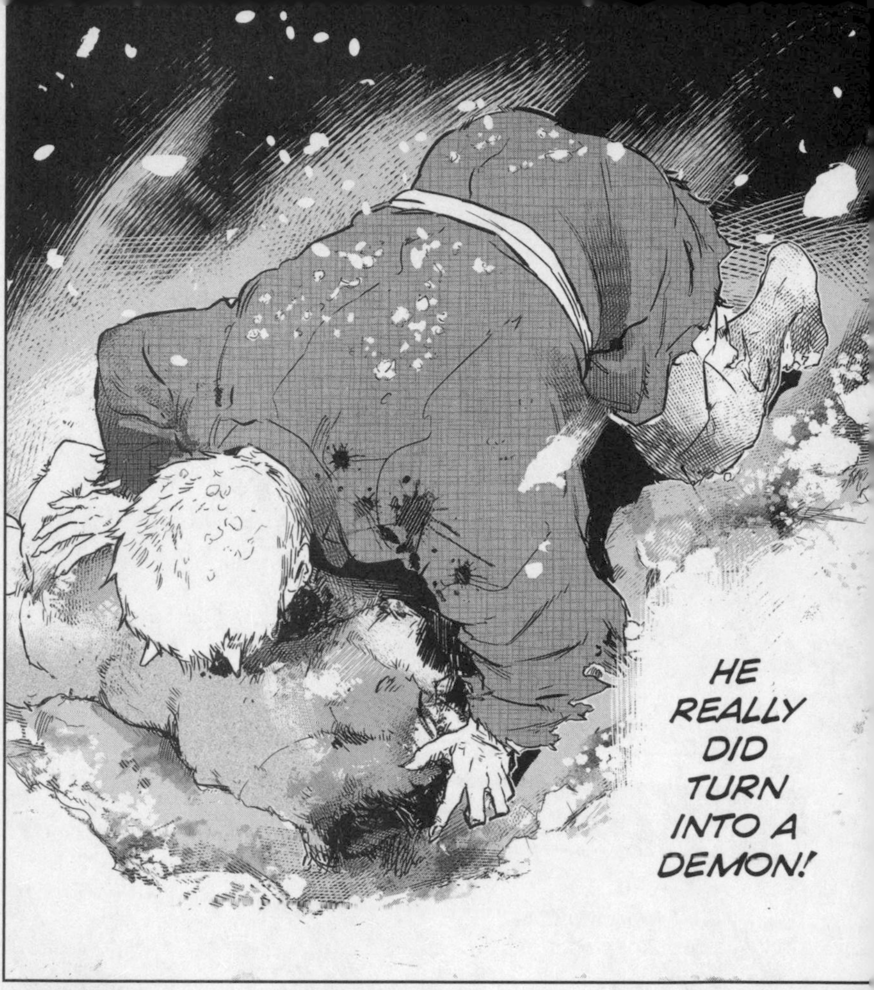
HE REALLY DID TURN INTO A DEMON!
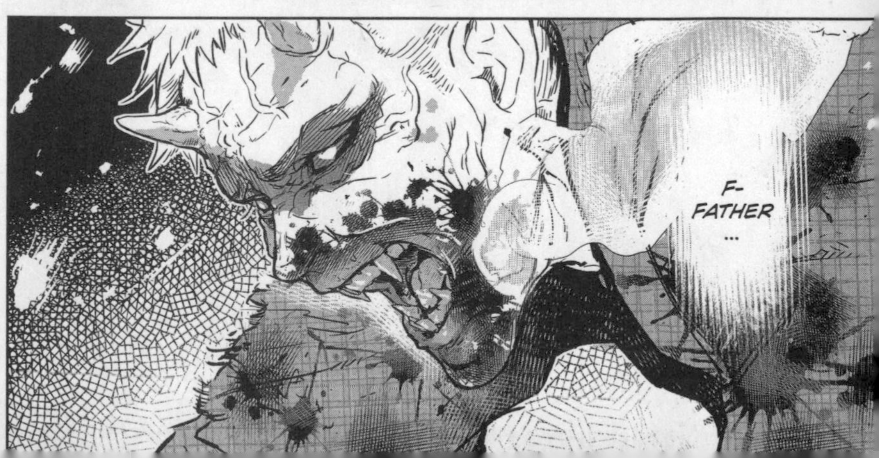
F- FATHER ...

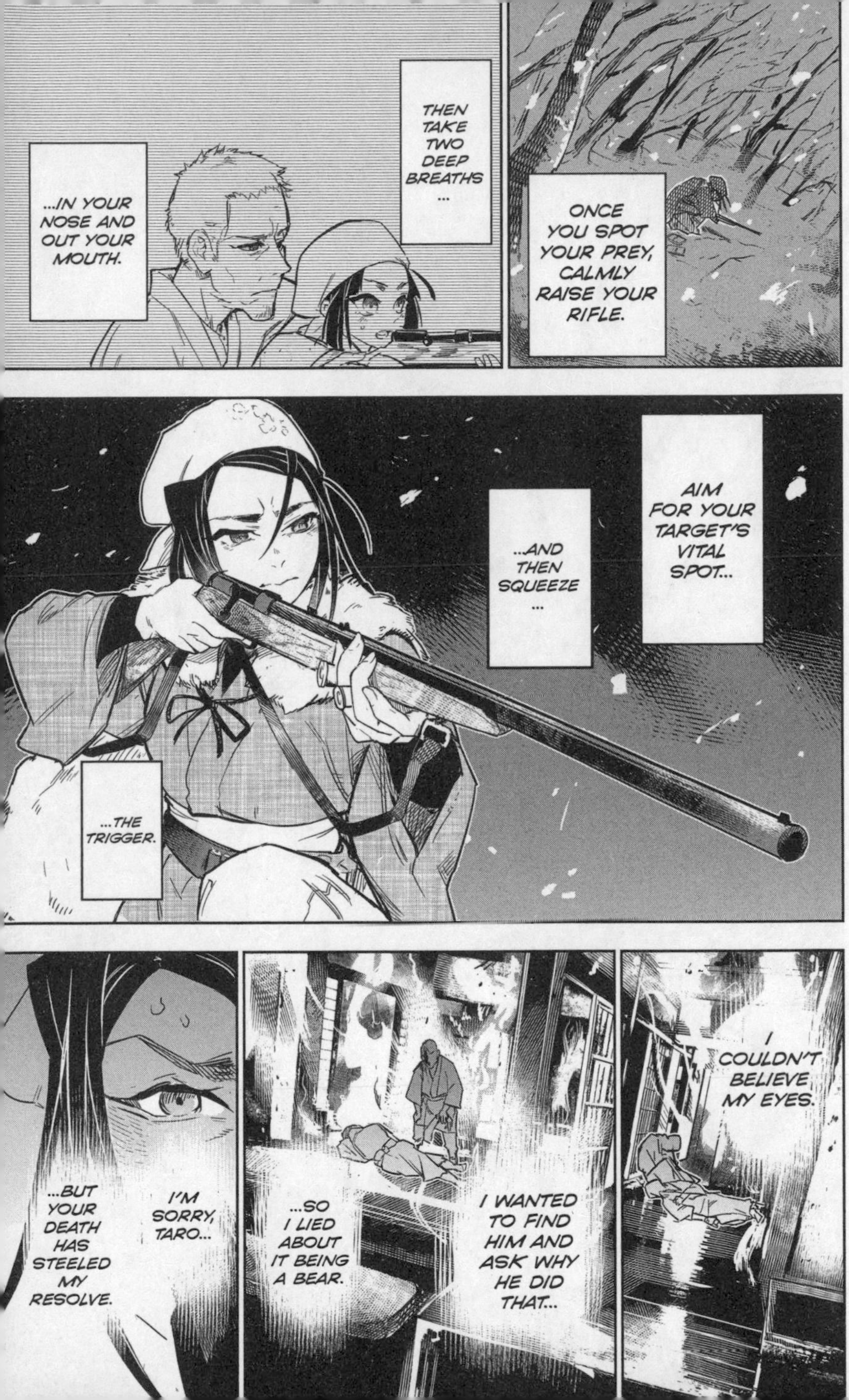
ONCE YOU SPOT YOUR PREY, CALMLY RAISE YOUR RIFLE.
THEN TAKE TWO DEEP BREATHS ...
...IN YOUR NOSE AND OUT YOUR MOUTH.
AIM FOR YOUR TARGET'S VITAL SPOT...
...AND THEN SQUEEZE ...
...THE TRIGGER.
I COULDN'T BELIEVE MY EYES.
I WANTED TO FIND HIM AND ASK WHY HE DID THAT...
...SO I LIED ABOUT IT BEING A BEAR.
I'M SORRY, TARO...
...BUT YOUR DEATH HAS STEELED MY RESOLVE.

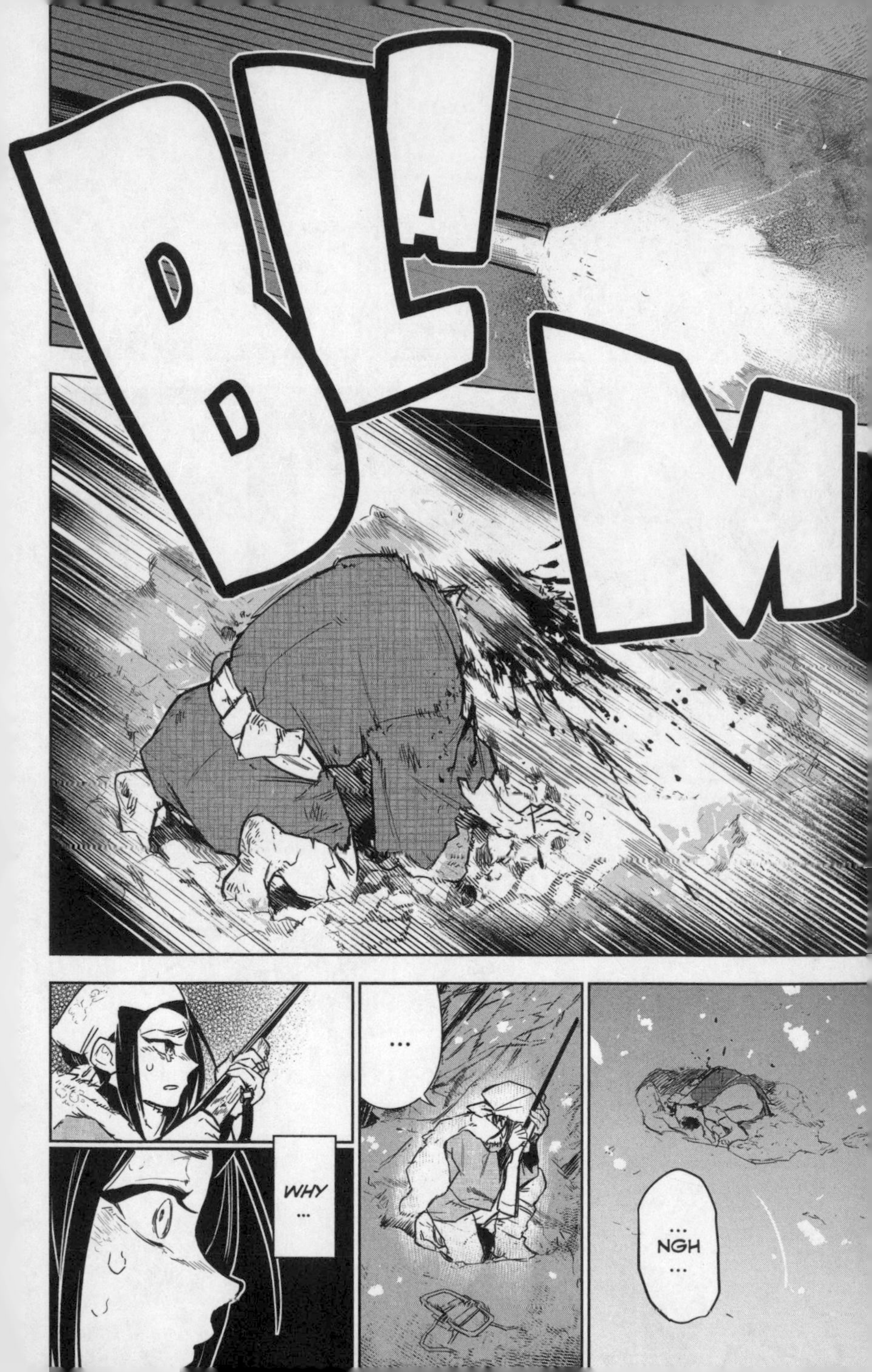
BLAM
... NGH ...
...
WHY ...

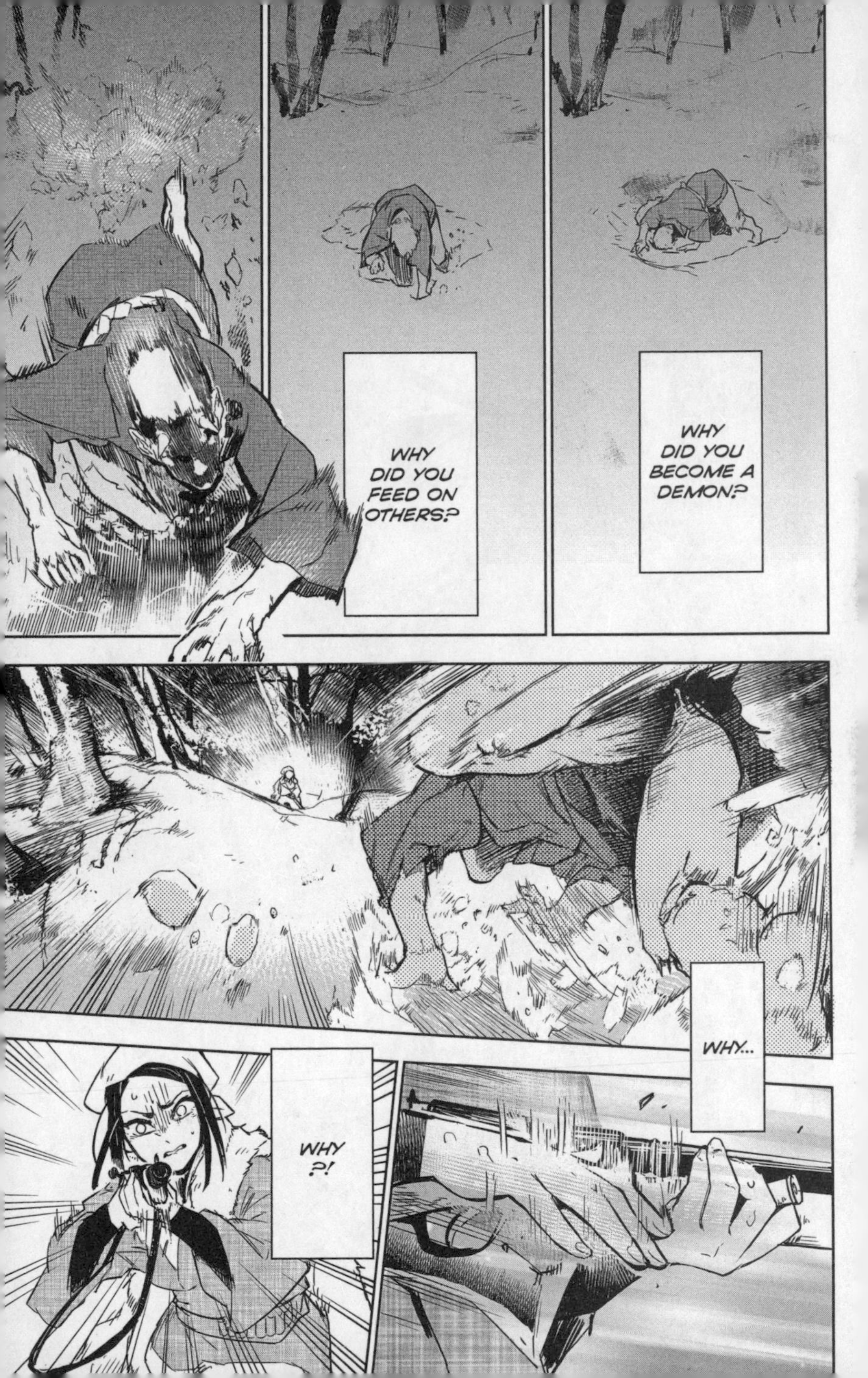
WHY DID YOU BECOME A DEMON?
WHY DID YOU FEED ON OTHERS?
WHY...
WHY ?!

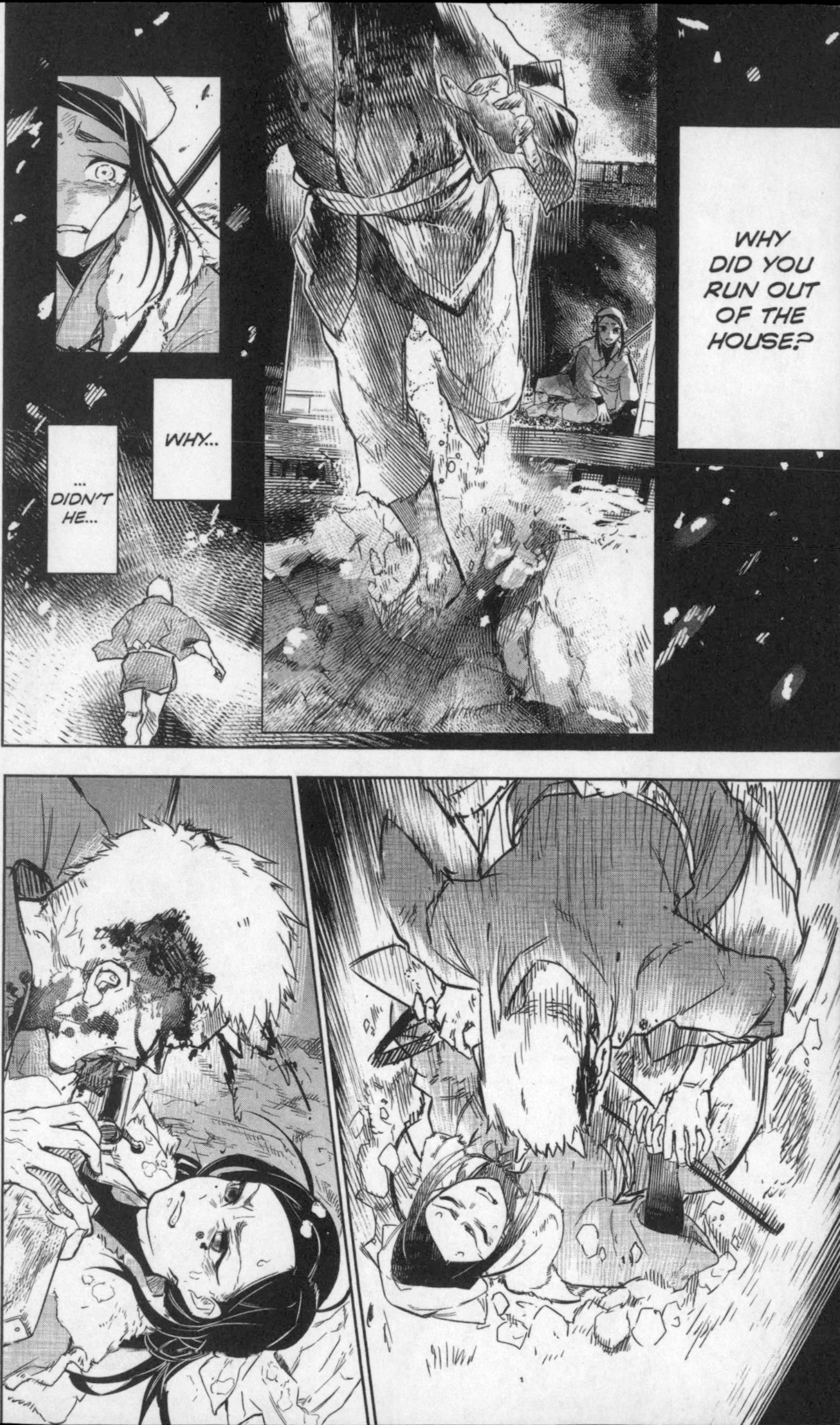
WHY DID YOU RUN OUT OF THE HOUSE?
WHY...
... DIDN'T HE...

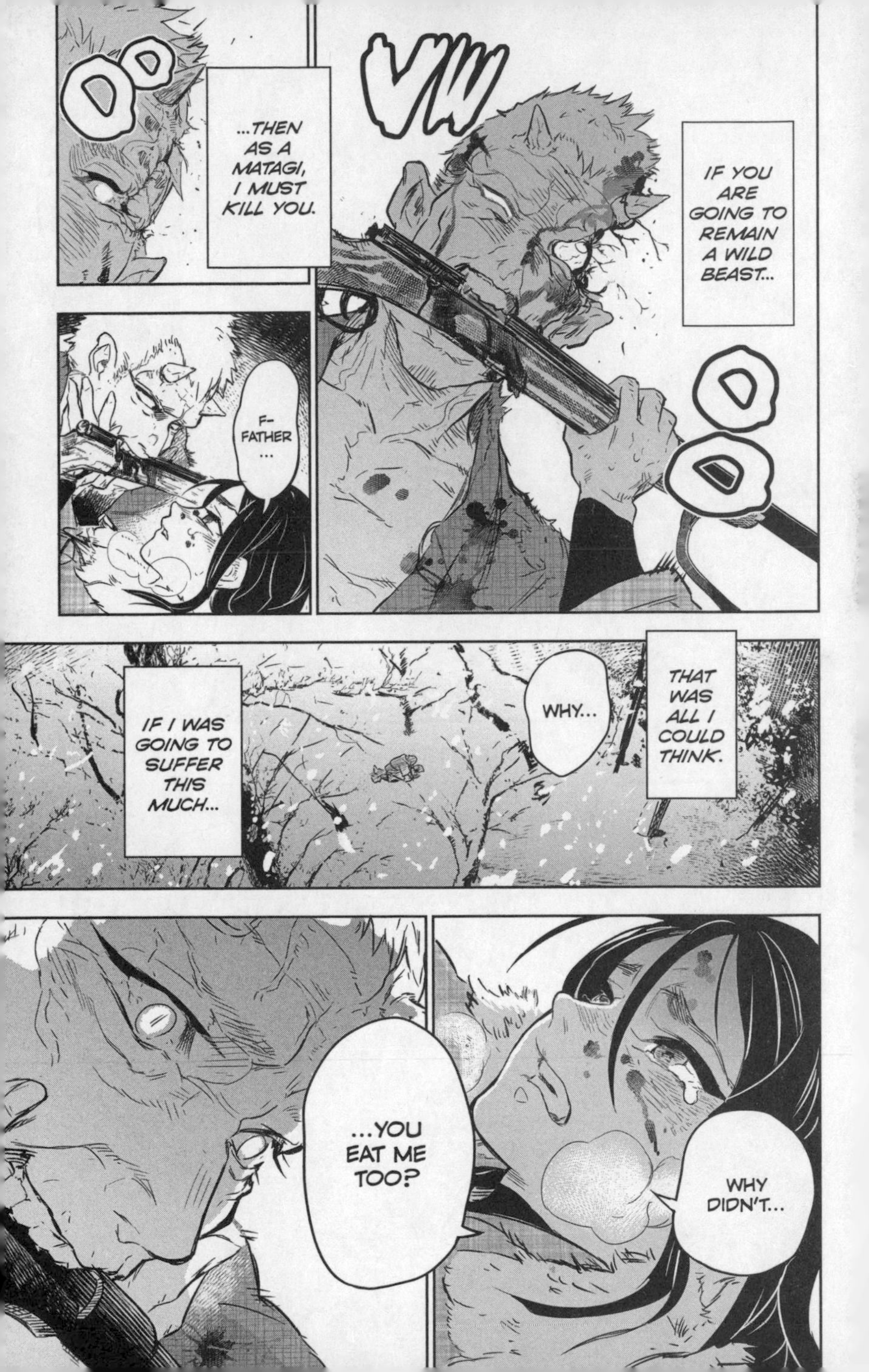
IF YOU ARE GOING TO REMAIN A WILD BEAST...
...THEN AS A MATAGI, I MUST KILL YOU.
F-FATHER...
THAT WAS ALL I COULD THINK.
WHY...
IF I WAS GOING TO SUFFER THIS MUCH...
WHY DIDN'T...
...YOU EAT ME TOO?

...E...
...E...
YA...

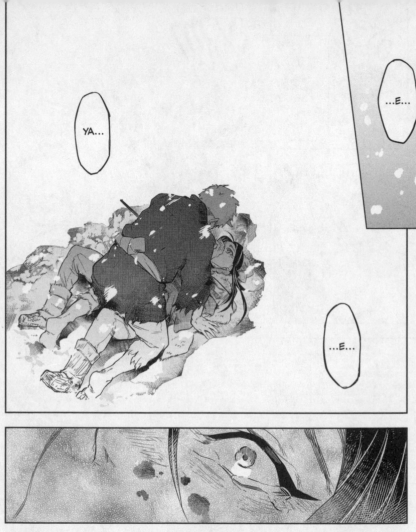

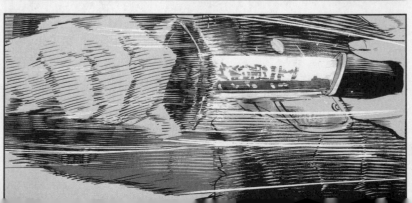

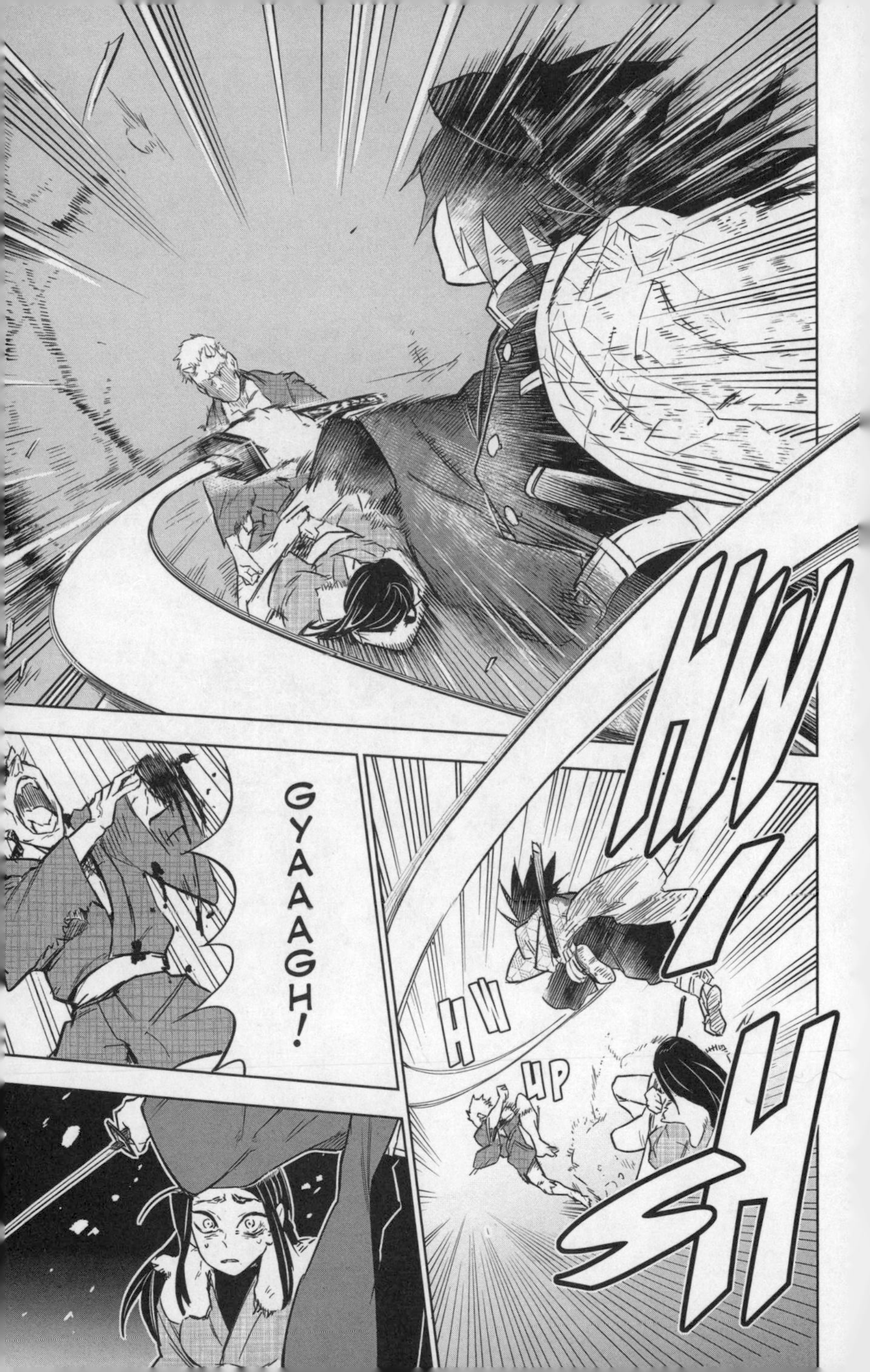
HWSH
HW
UP
GYAAAAGH!

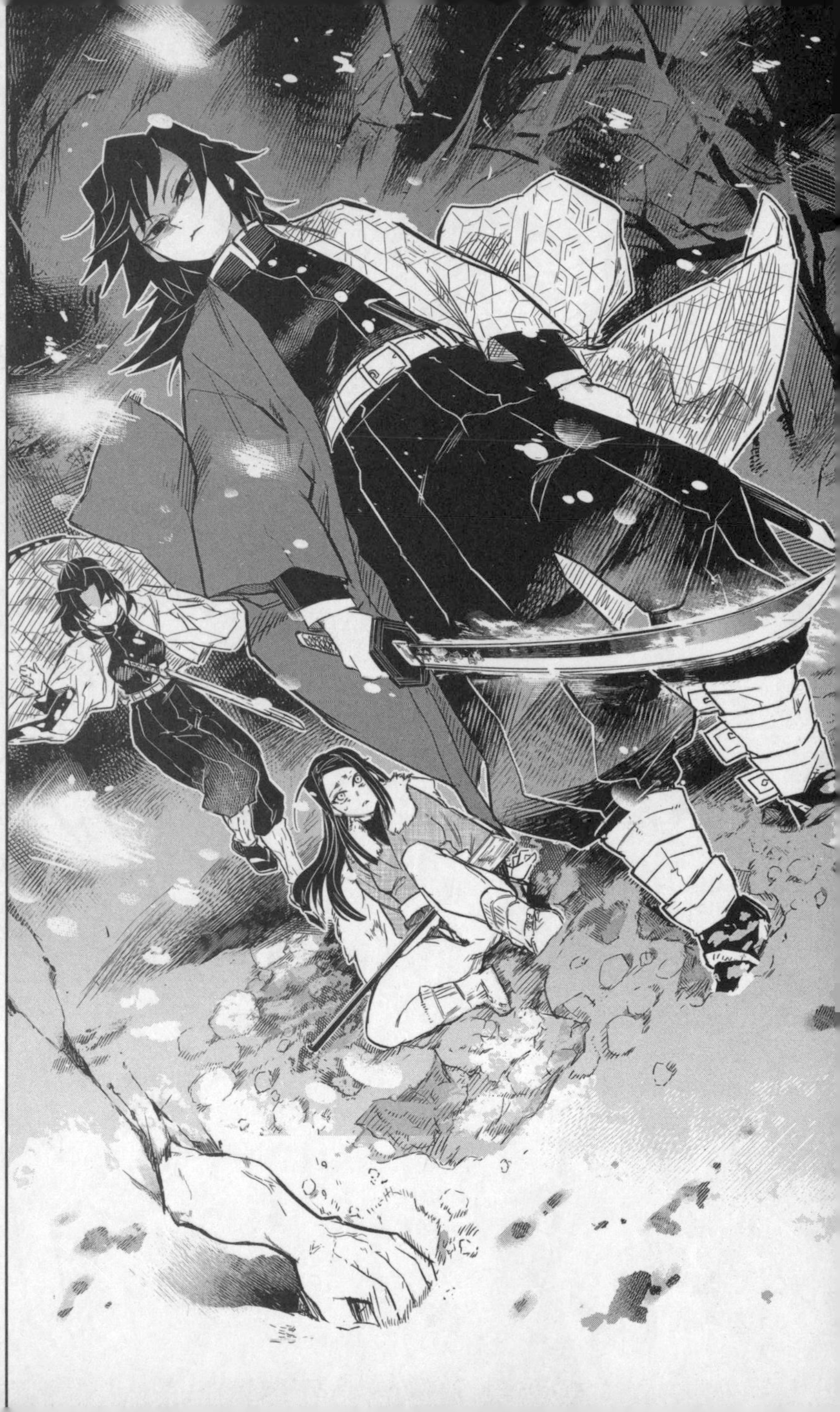

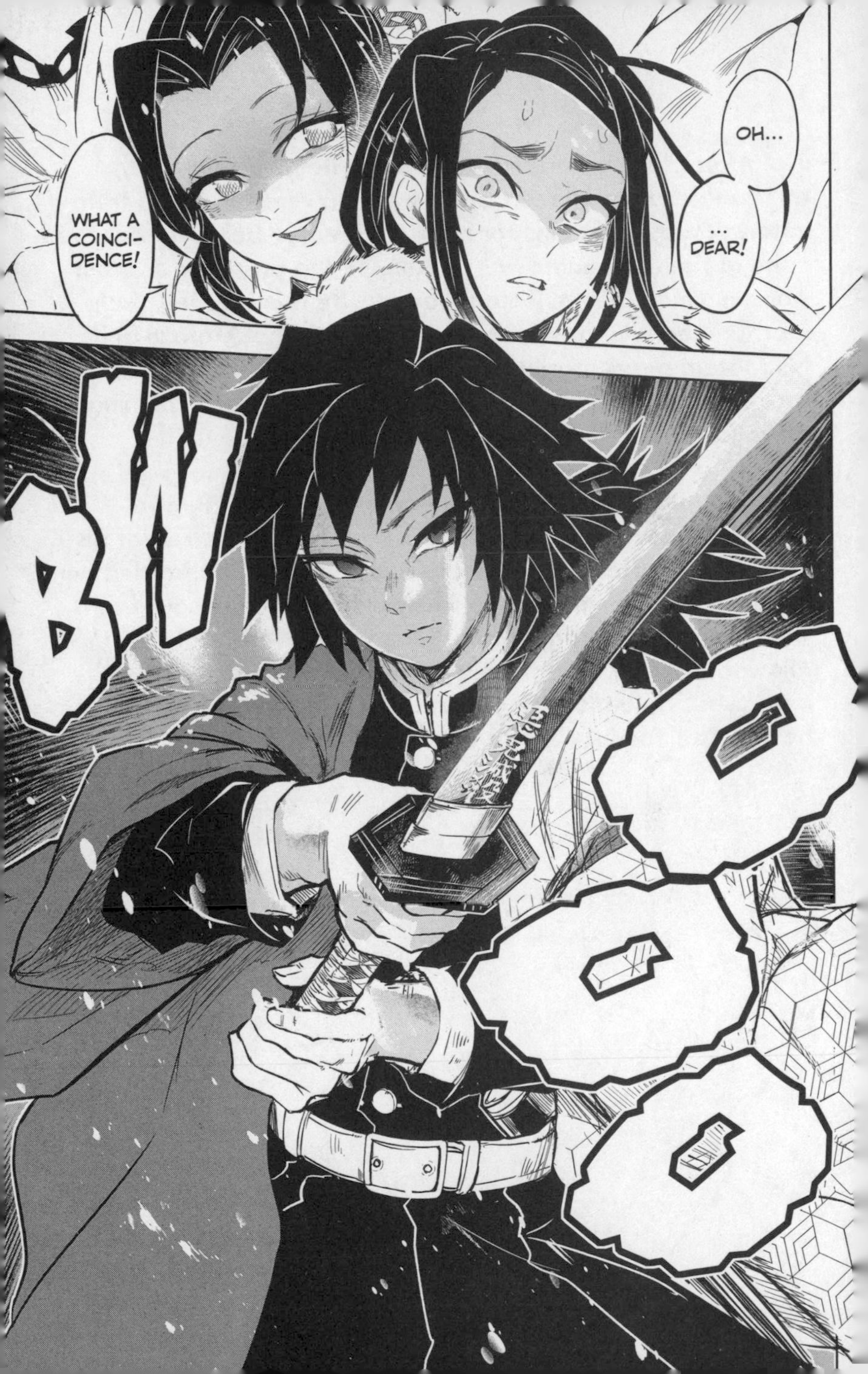
OH...
...DEAR!
WHAT A COINCIDENCE!
BWOOO

The *Matagi are* an organization of hunters. Traditionally, the hunters were all men, since women were forbidden from entering the mountains for hunting. (People believed that the deity of the mountains was female, so the presence of other women would inspire jealousy and invite misfortune.) Yae's mother died young, so out of concern for Yae, Matazo and his Matagi peers taught her how to shoot and hunt. However, they wouldn't take her hunting with them, so she often snuck off to hunt with Taro—and got in trouble for it.

Immediately after becoming a demon, Matazo ran away from Yae because he had regained a slight awareness of his human past after eating his comrades. When he throttled her in the forest, he was able to whisper her name because he was temporarily satiated from feasting on Taro, which allowed a single word to spill from what remained of his memories. If Tomioka and Kocho hadn't come, he would have eaten Yae just like he did Taro.

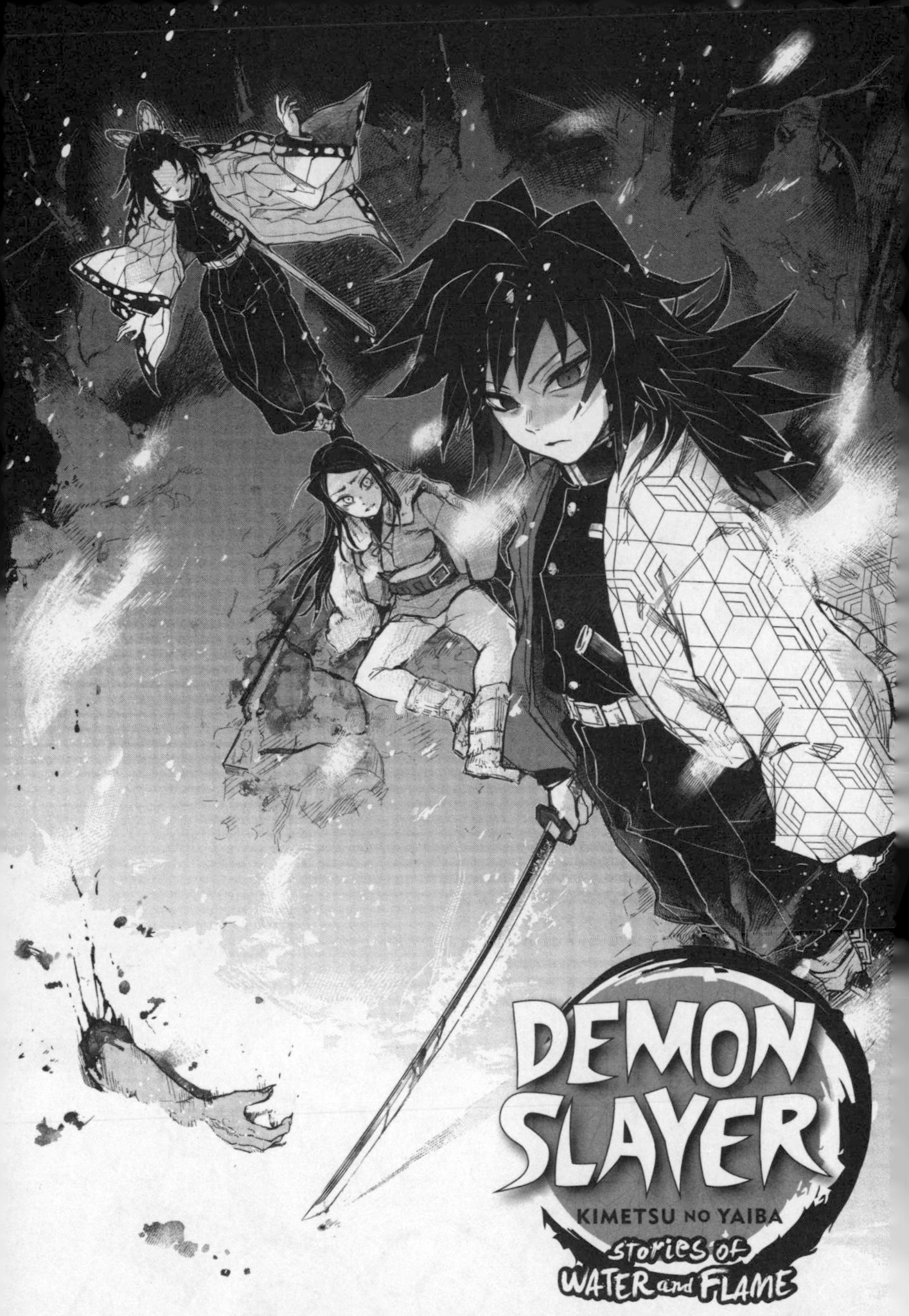
DEMON SLAYER
KIMETSU NO YAIBA
stories of
WATER and FLAME

# GIYU TOMIOKA'S STORY, PART 2

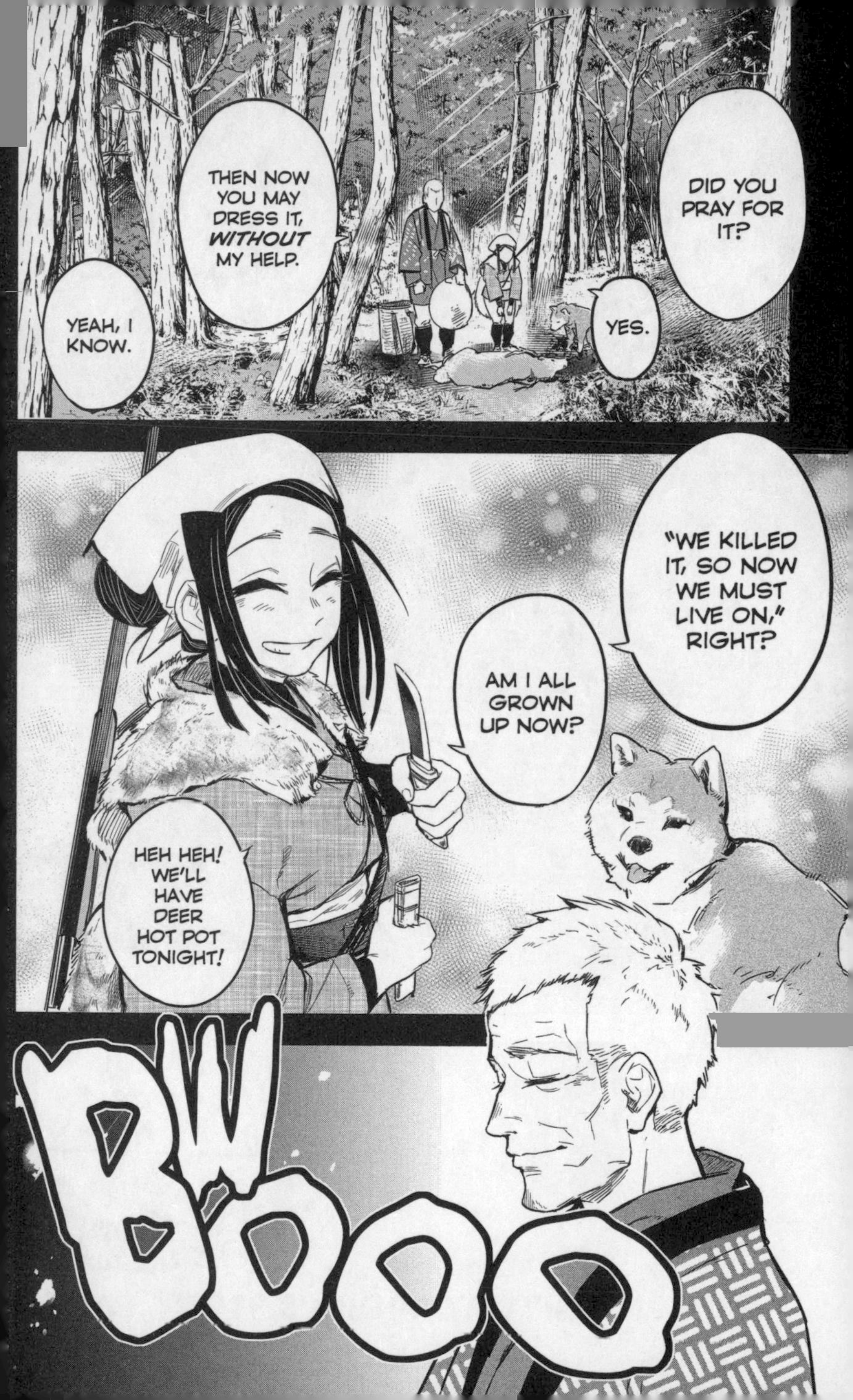
DID YOU PRAY FOR IT?
YES.
THEN NOW YOU MAY DRESS IT, *WITHOUT* MY HELP.
YEAH, I KNOW.
"WE KILLED IT, SO NOW WE MUST LIVE ON," RIGHT?
AM I ALL GROWN UP NOW?
HEH HEH! WE'LL HAVE DEER HOT POT TONIGHT!
BWOOO

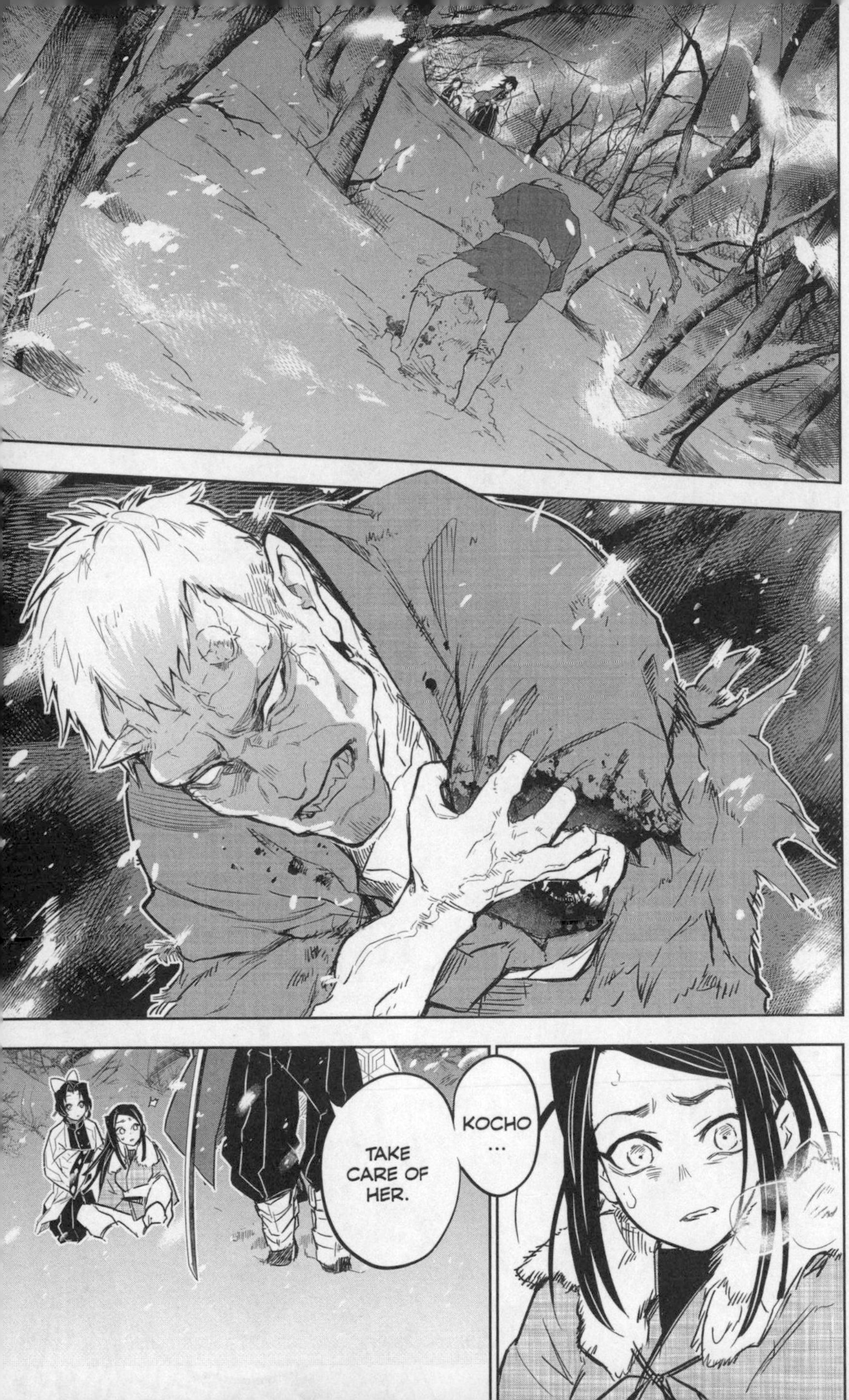
KOCHO...
TAKE CARE OF HER.

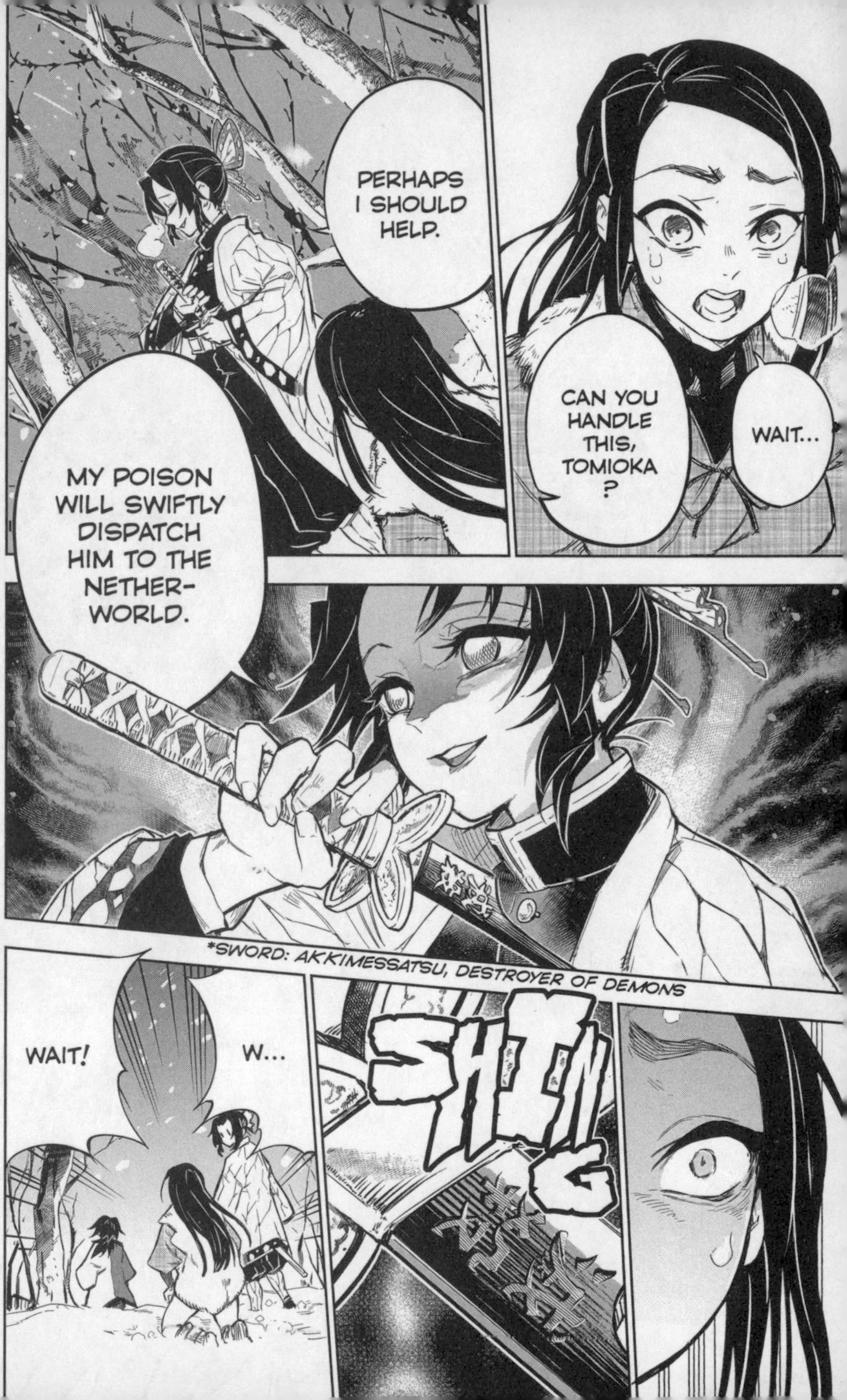
WAIT...
CAN YOU HANDLE THIS, TOMIOKA?
PERHAPS I SHOULD HELP.
MY POISON WILL SWIFTLY DISPATCH HIM TO THE NETHER-WORLD.
*SWORD: AKKIMESSATSU, DESTROYER OF DEMONS
SHING
W...
WAIT!

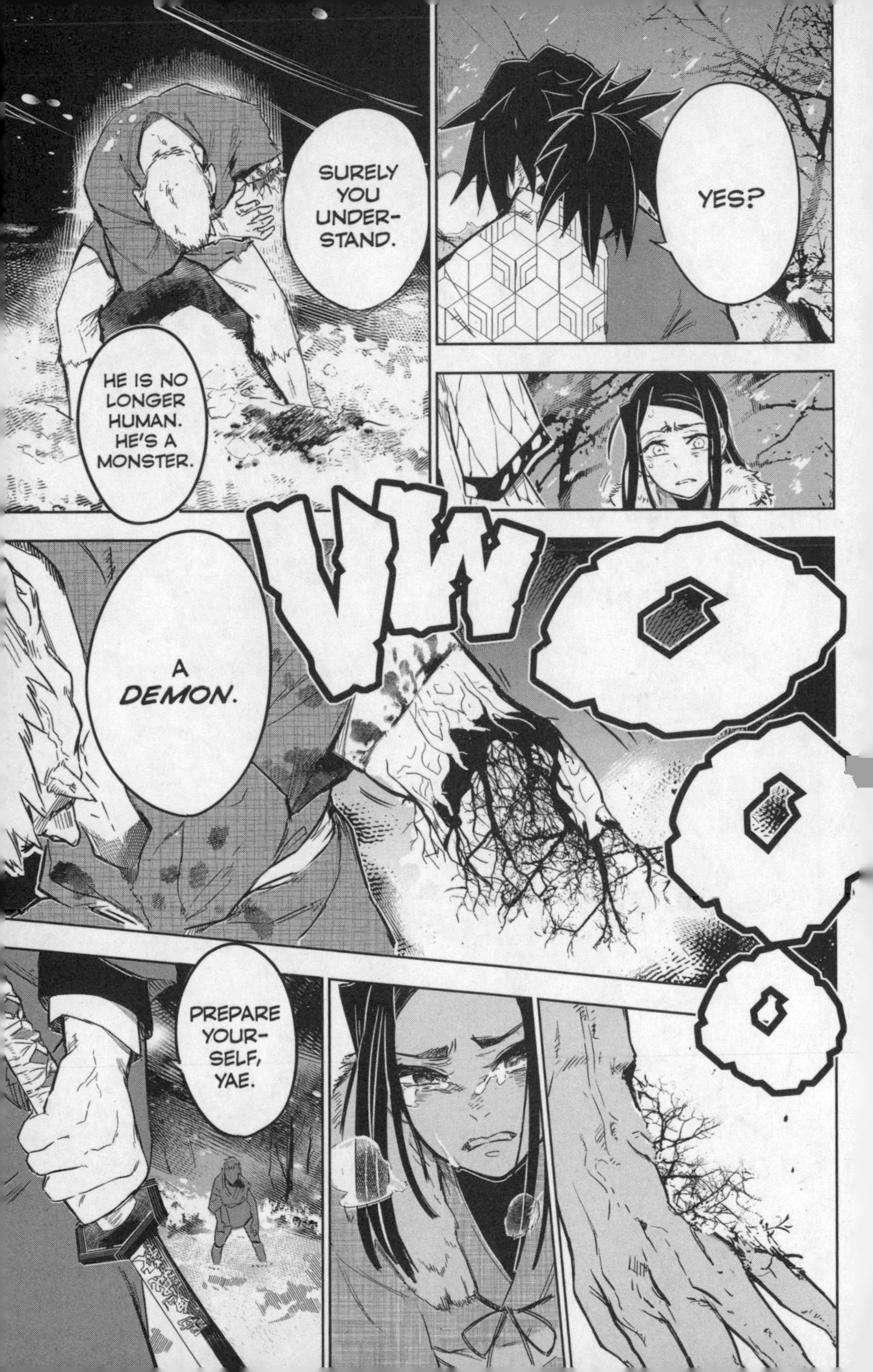
YES?
SURELY YOU UNDER-STAND.
HE IS NO LONGER HUMAN. HE'S A MONSTER.
A *DEMON*.
VWOOO
PREPARE YOUR-SELF, YAE.

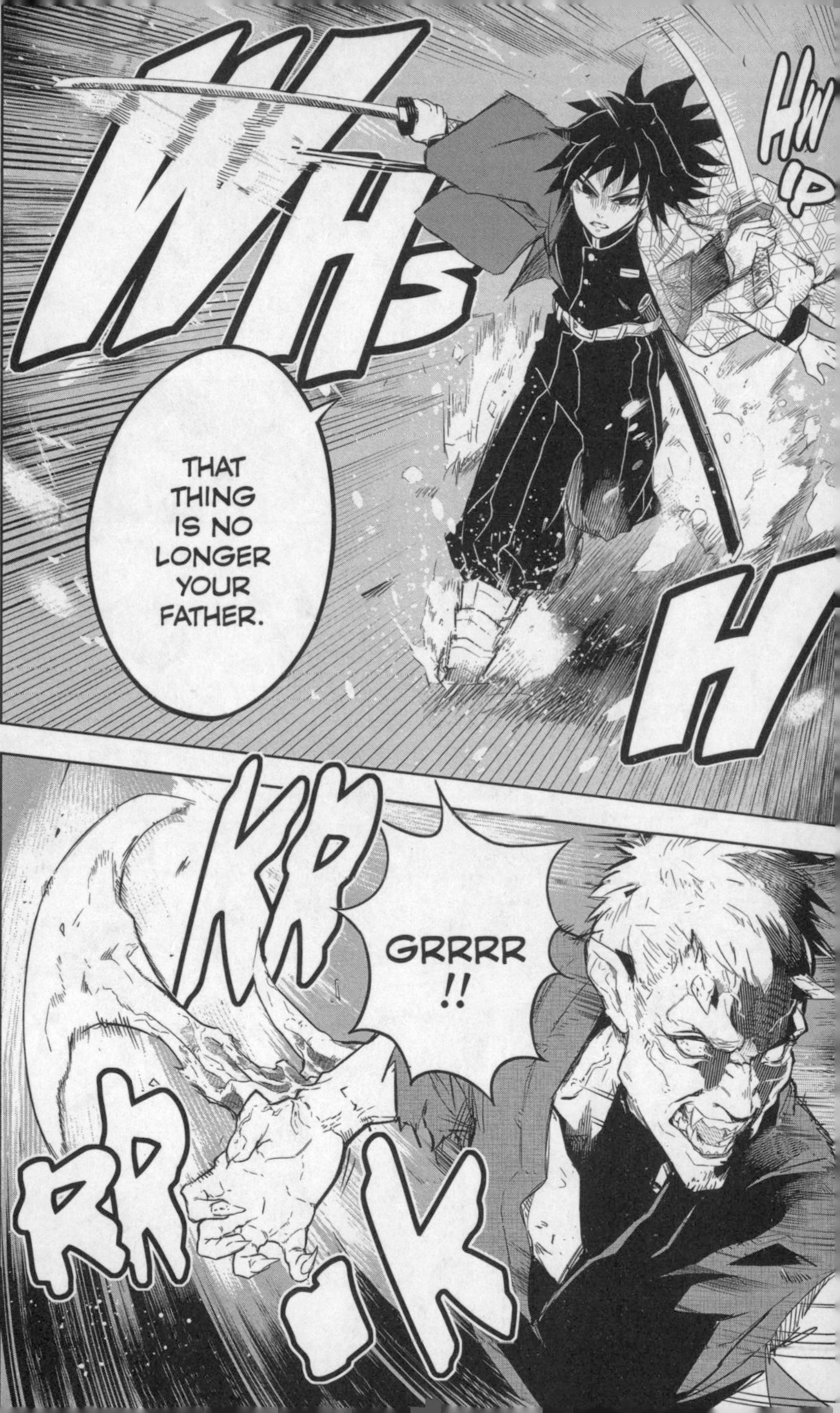
HWIP
WHAS
H
THAT THING IS NO LONGER YOUR FATHER.
KR
GRRRR !!
RR
K

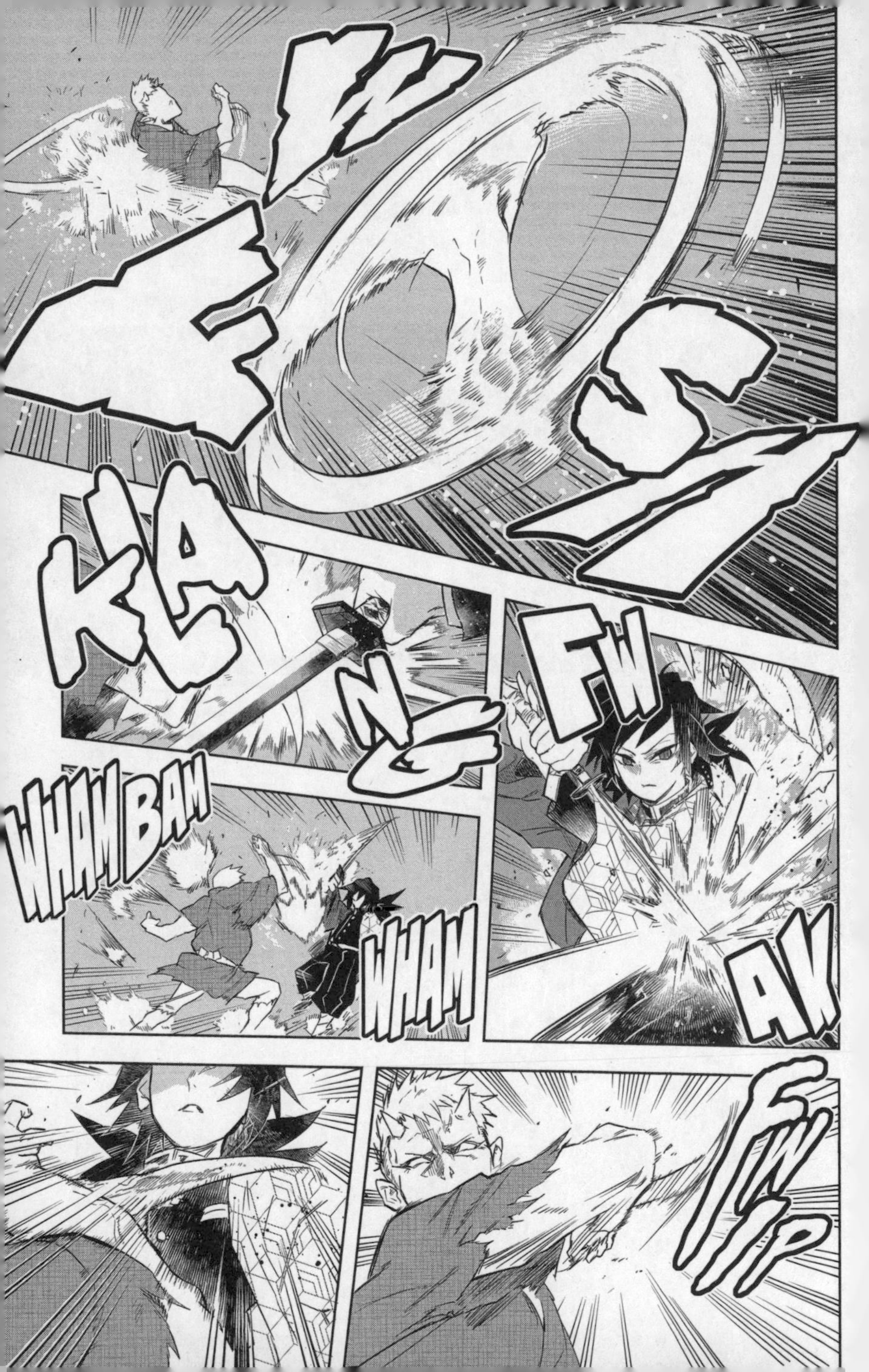
FW
KLANG
WHAM BAM
WHAM
FWIP

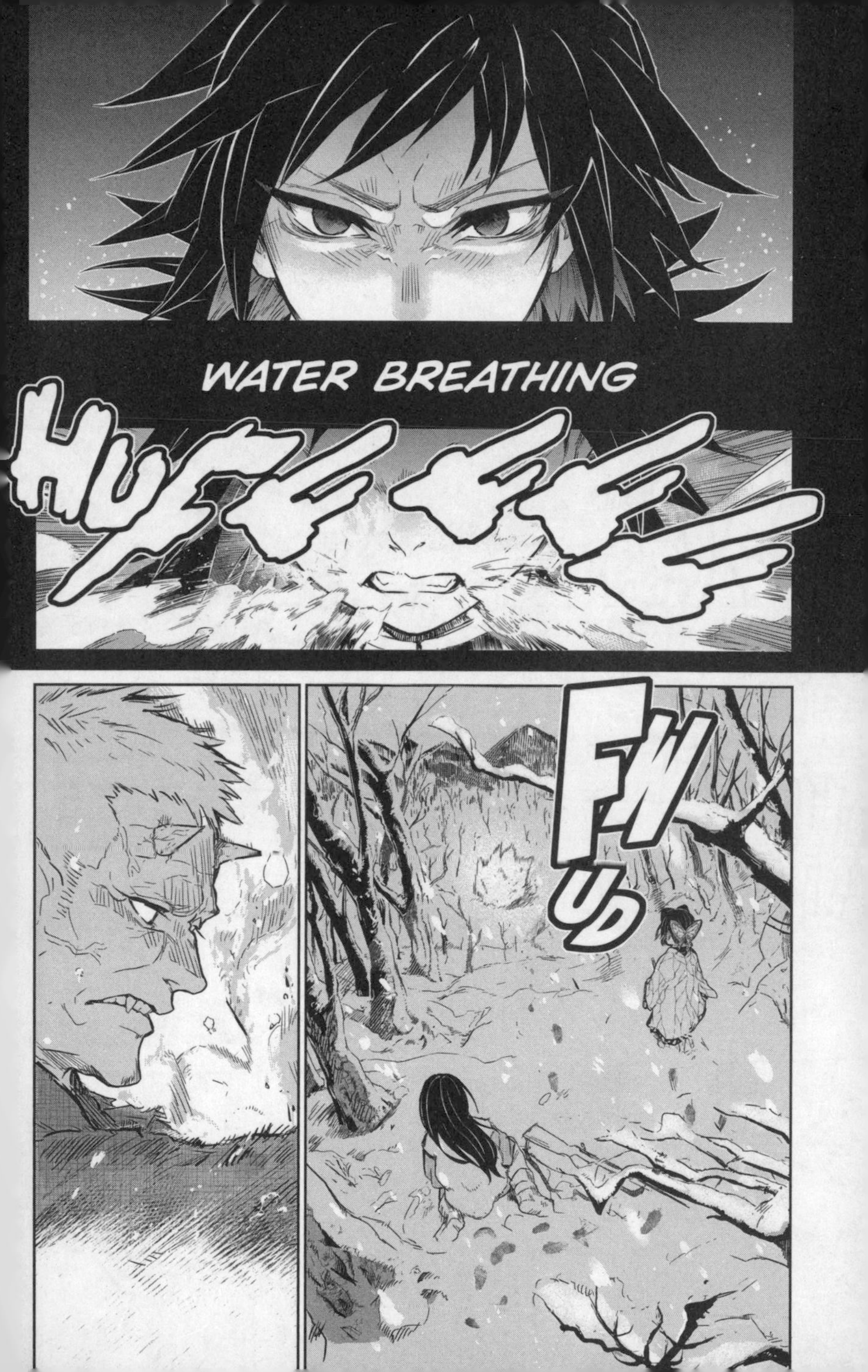
WATER BREATHING
FWUD

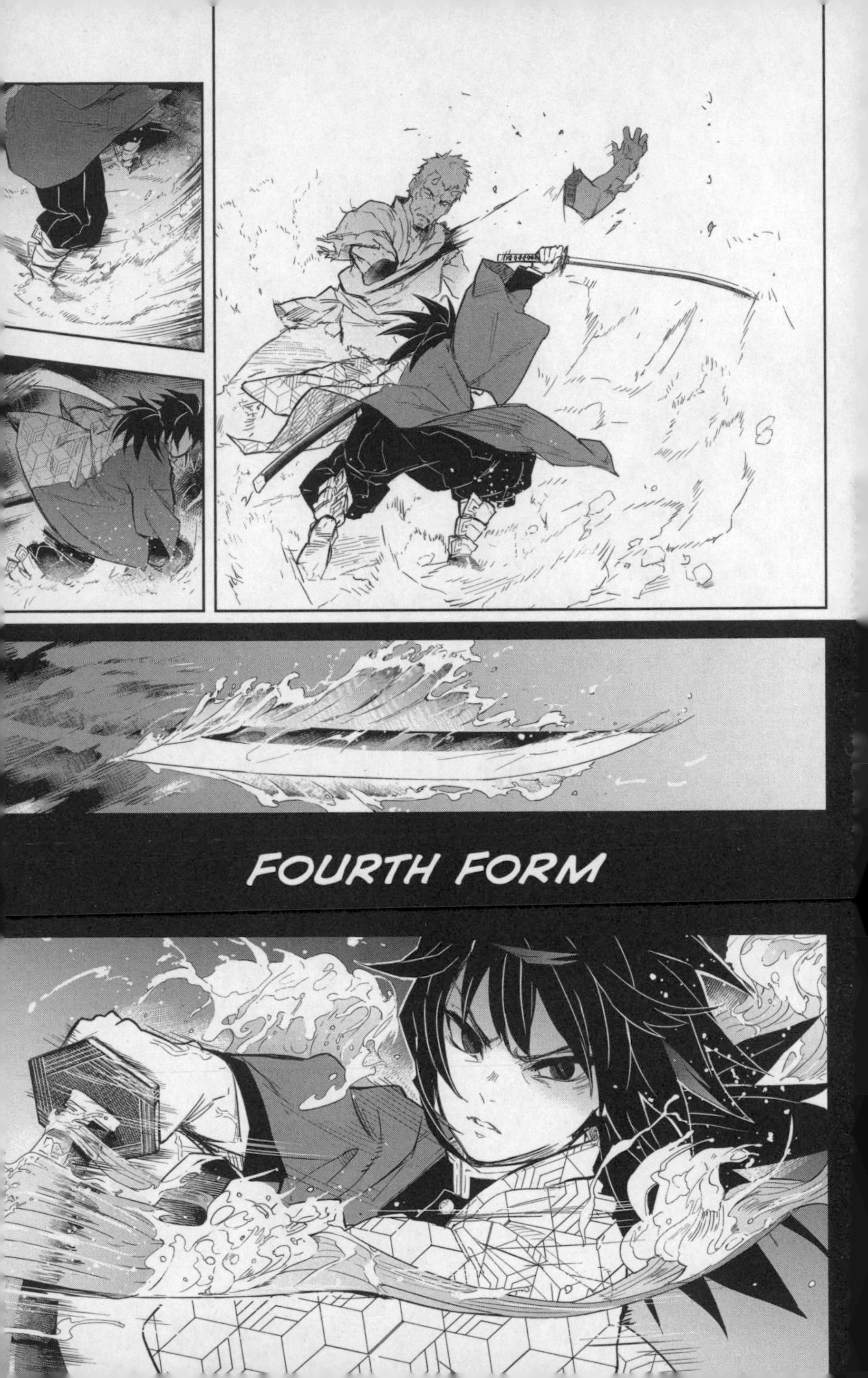
FOURTH FORM

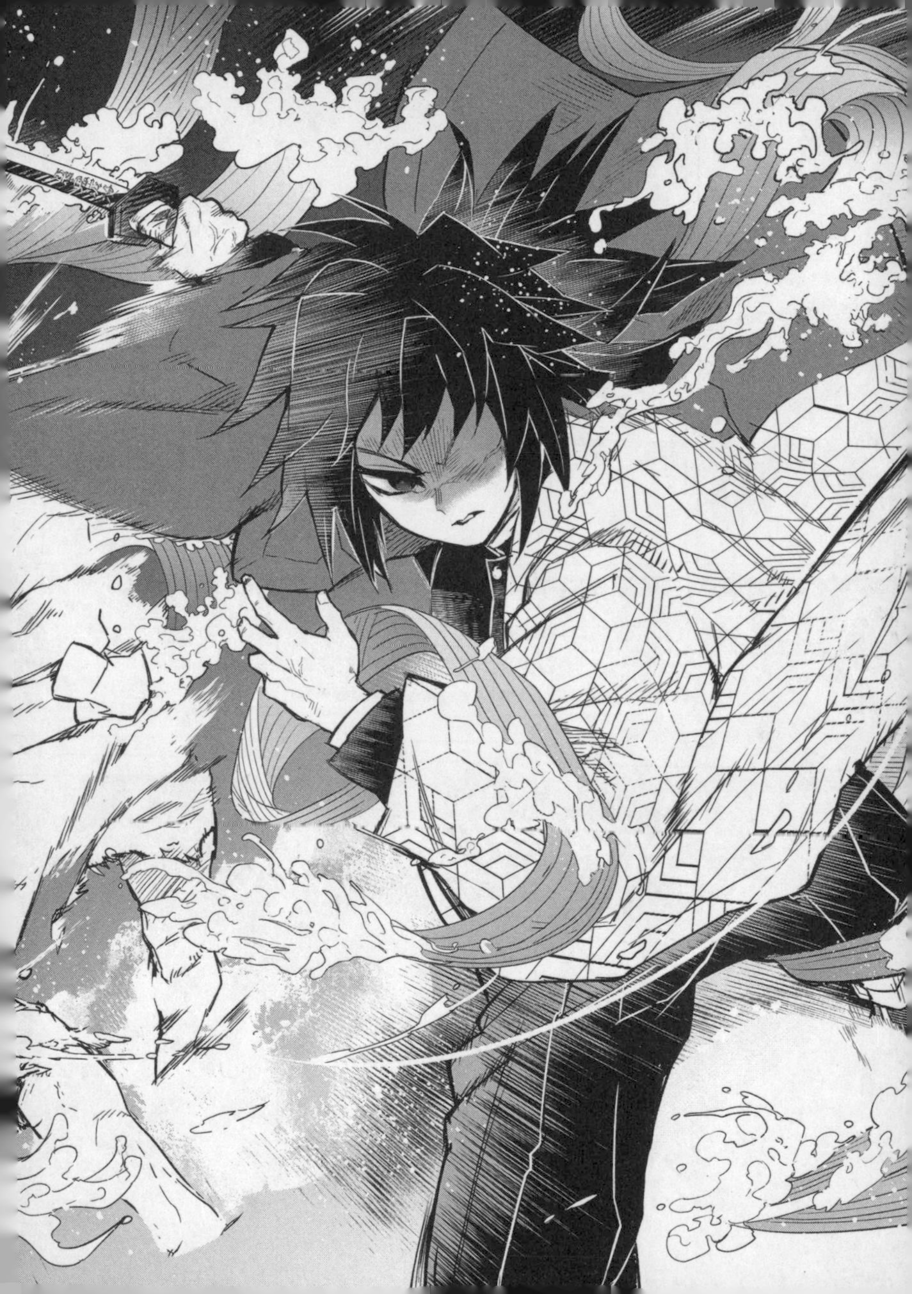

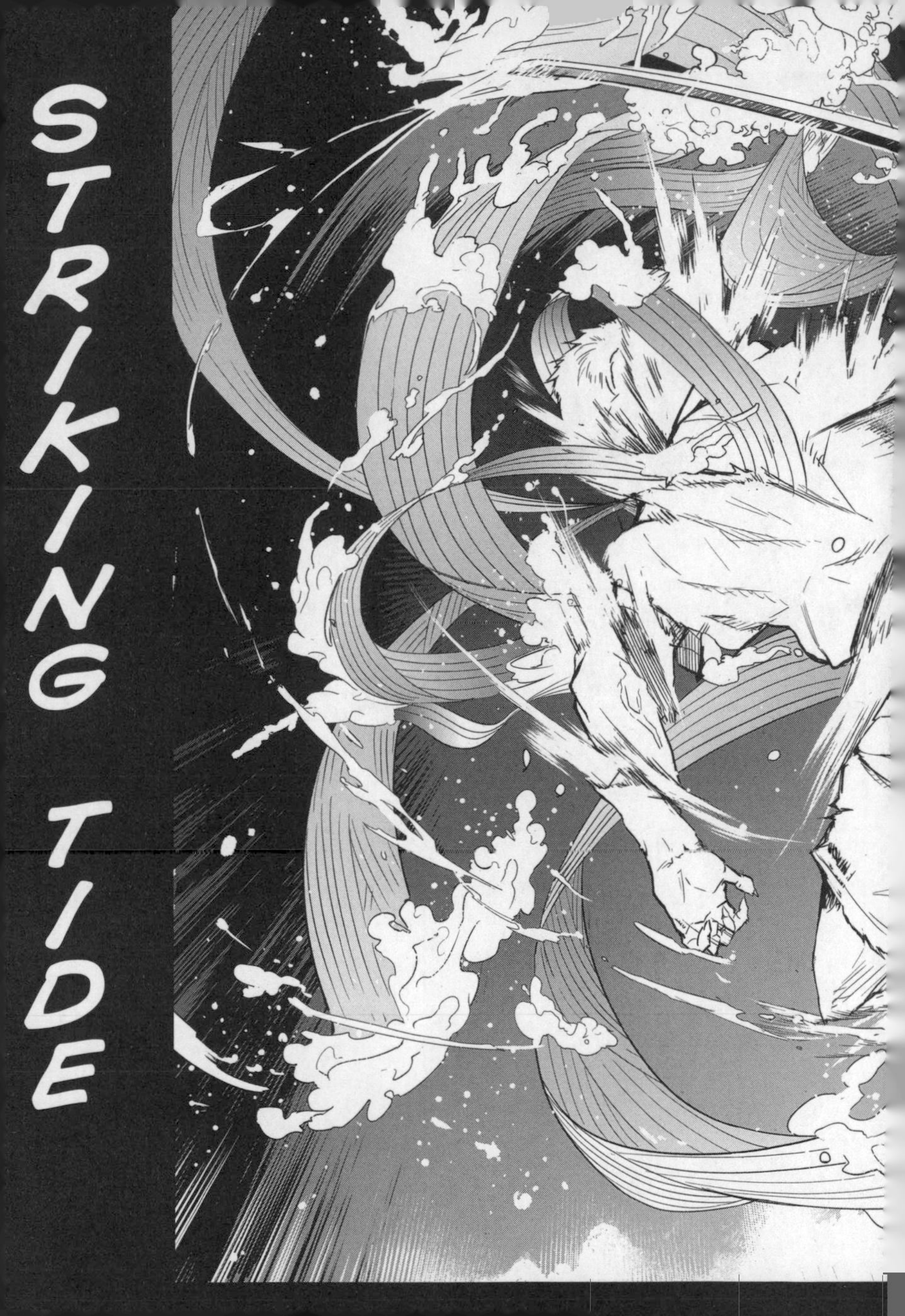
STRIKING TIDE

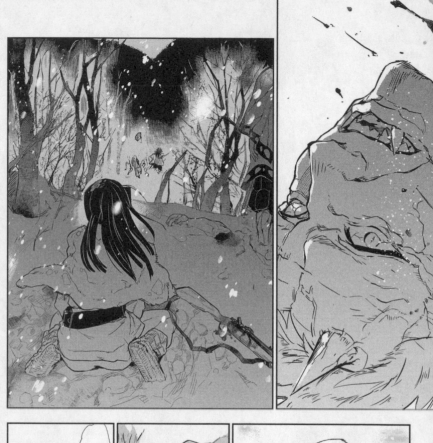

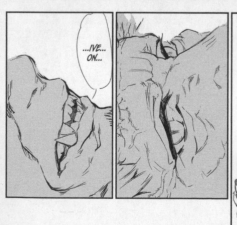

...IVE...
ON...

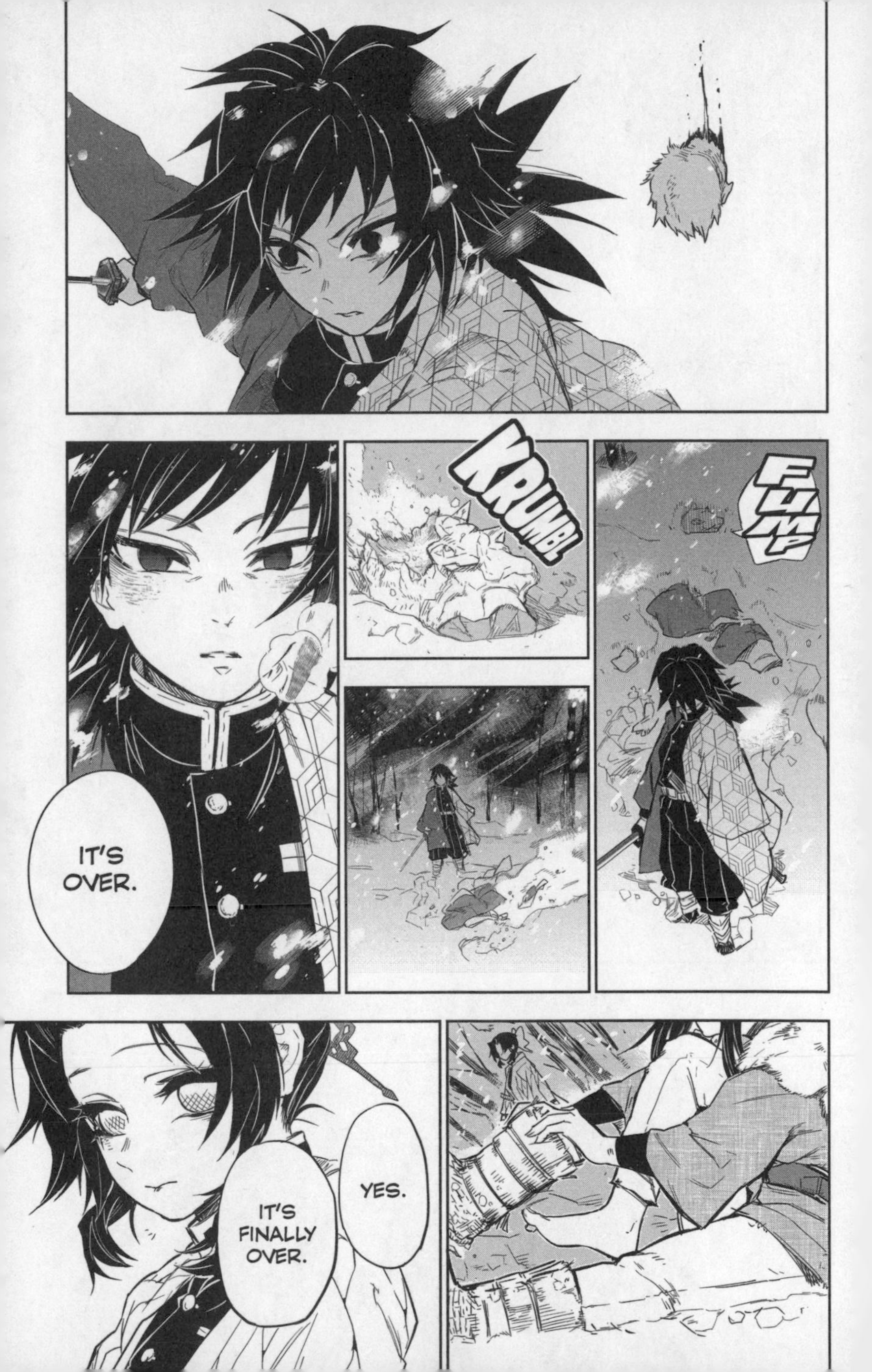
FUMP
KRUMBL
IT'S OVER.
YES.
IT'S FINALLY OVER.

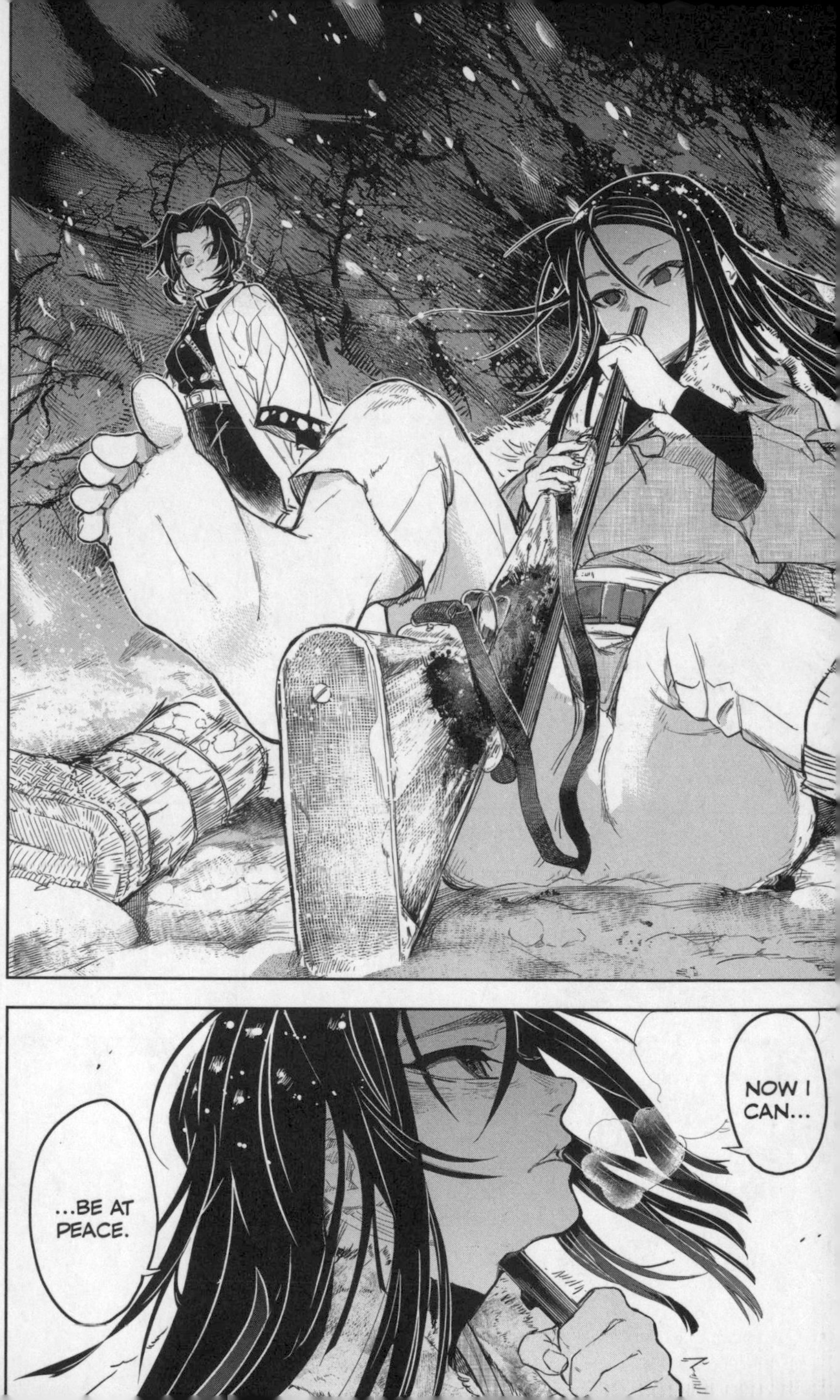
NOW I CAN...
...BE AT PEACE.

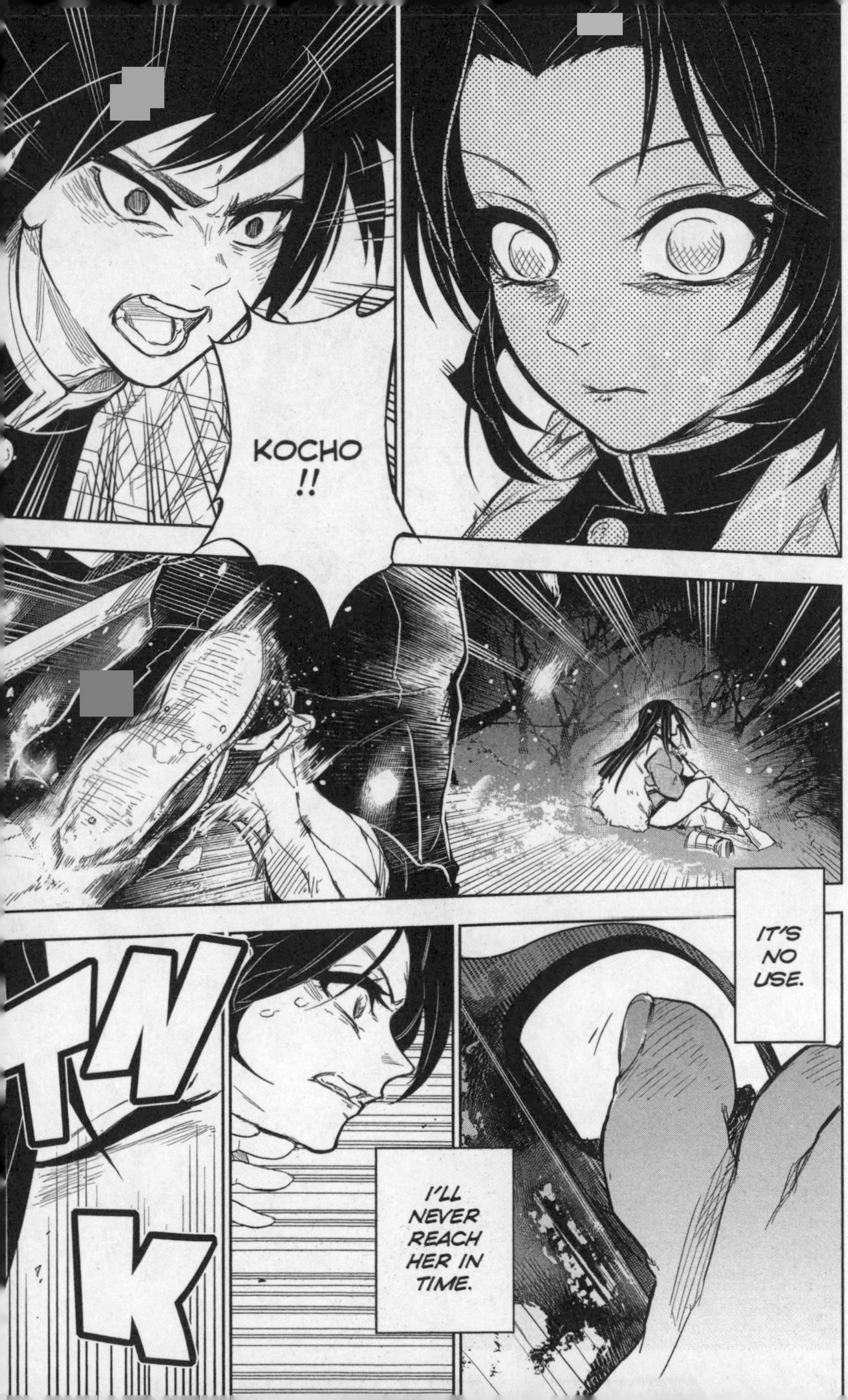
KOCHO !!
IT'S NO USE.
I'LL NEVER REACH HER IN TIME.

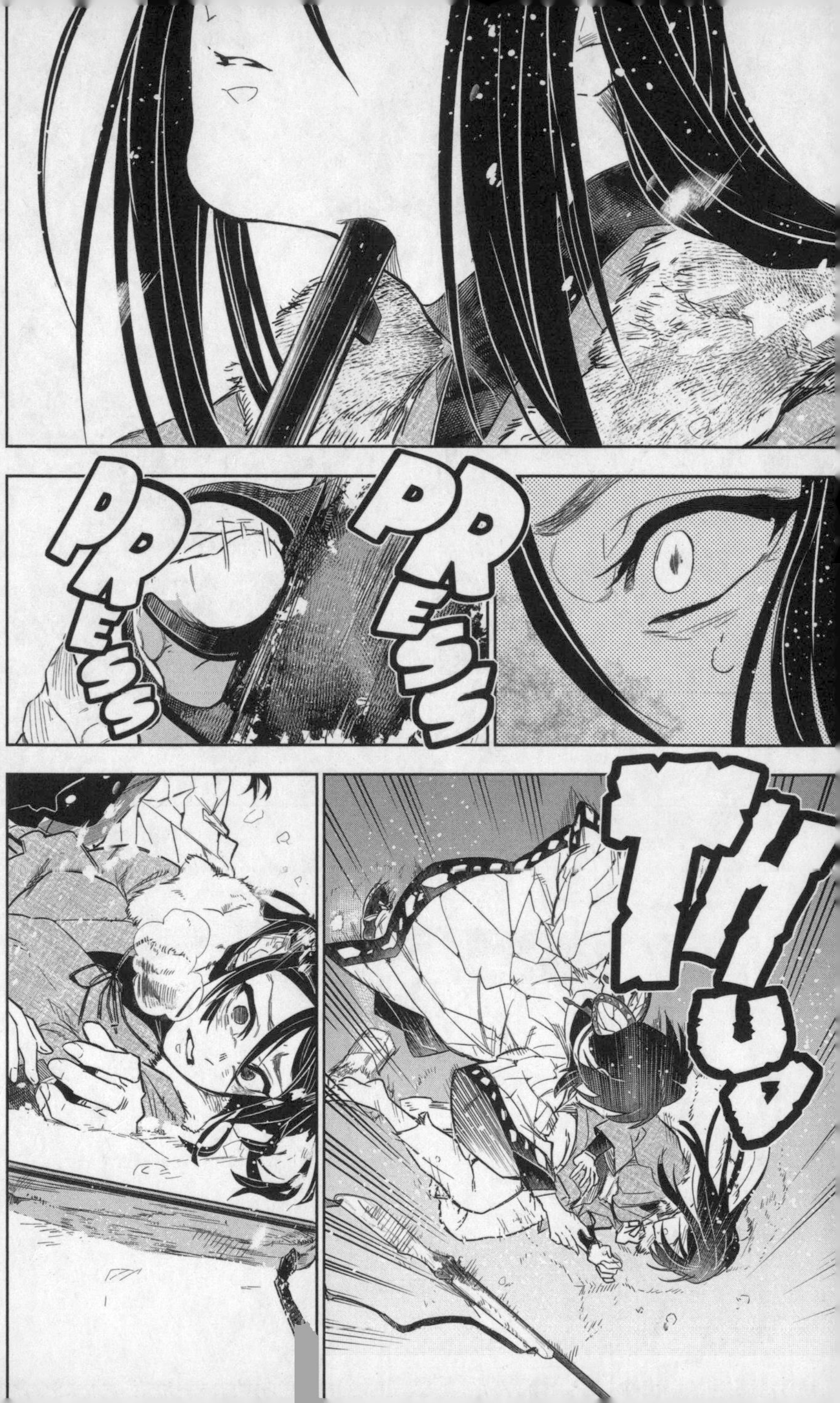
PRESS
PRESS
THUD

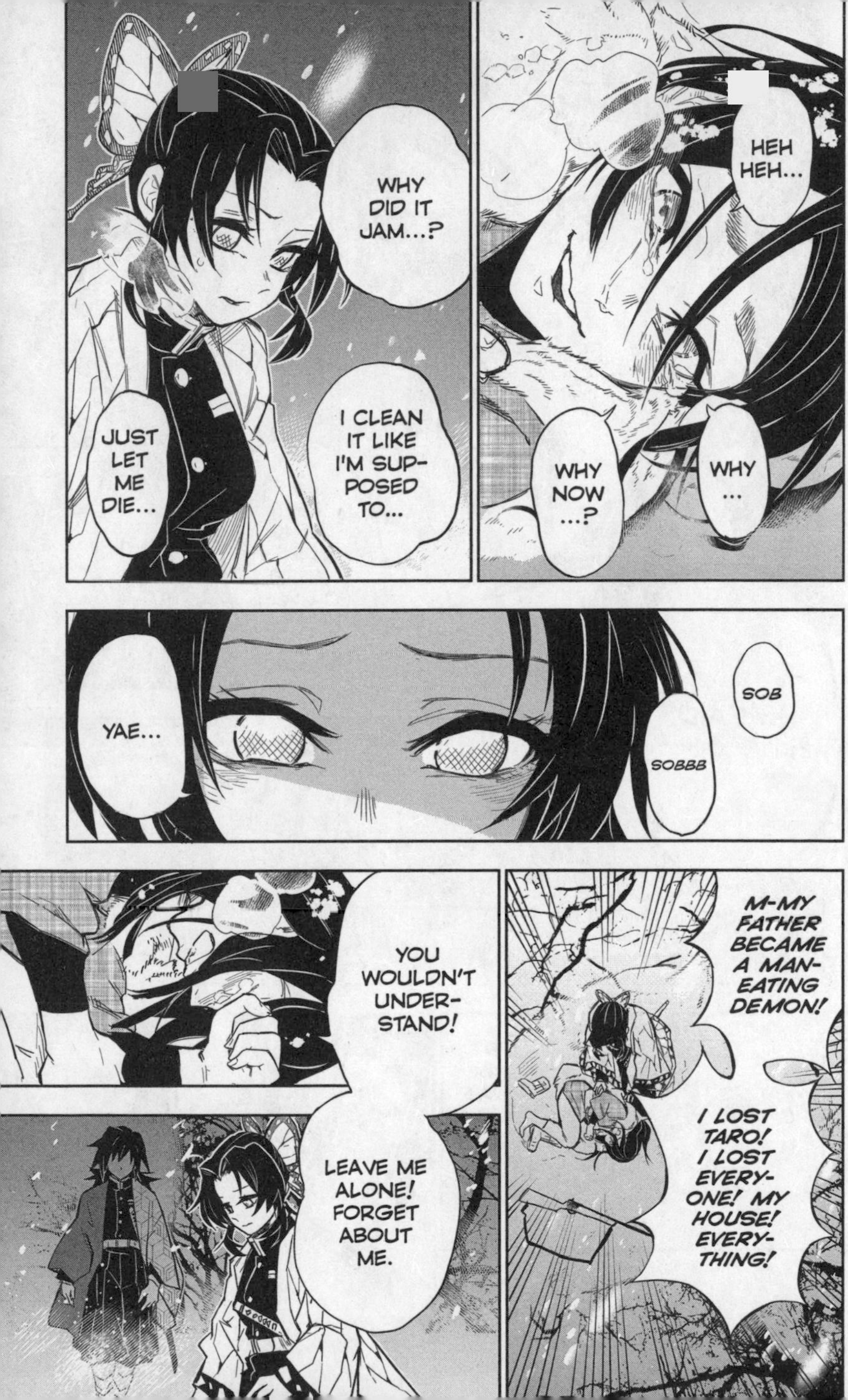
HEH HEH...
WHY ...
WHY NOW ...?
WHY DID IT JAM...?
I CLEAN IT LIKE I'M SUPPOSED TO...
JUST LET ME DIE...
SOB
SOBBB
YAE...
M-MY FATHER BECAME A MAN-EATING DEMON!
I LOST TARO! I LOST EVERYONE! MY HOUSE! EVERYTHING!
YOU WOULDN'T UNDERSTAND!
LEAVE ME ALONE! FORGET ABOUT ME.

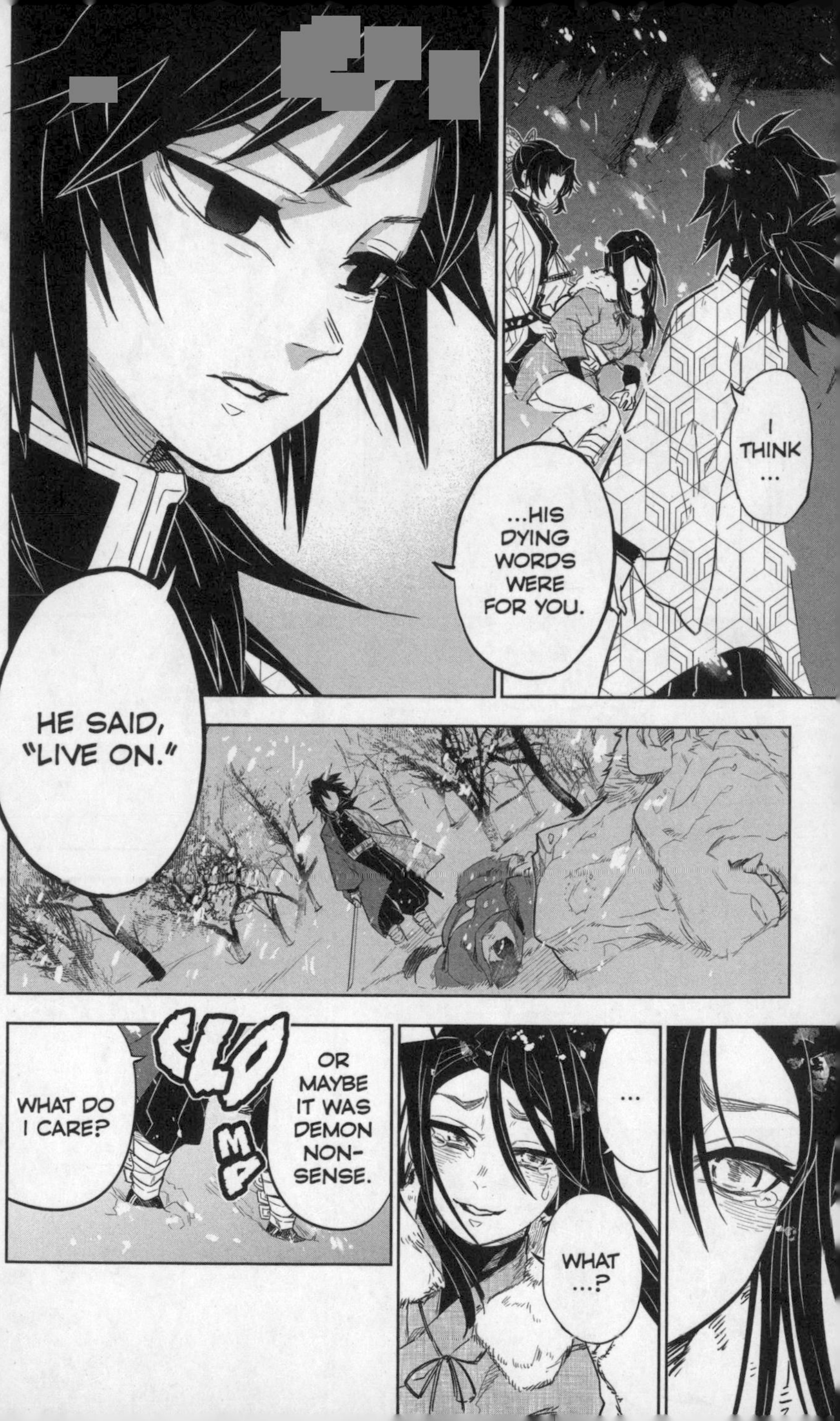
I THINK ...
...HIS DYING WORDS WERE FOR YOU.
HE SAID, "LIVE ON."
...
WHAT ...?
OR MAYBE IT WAS DEMON NON-SENSE.
CLOMP
WHAT DO I CARE?

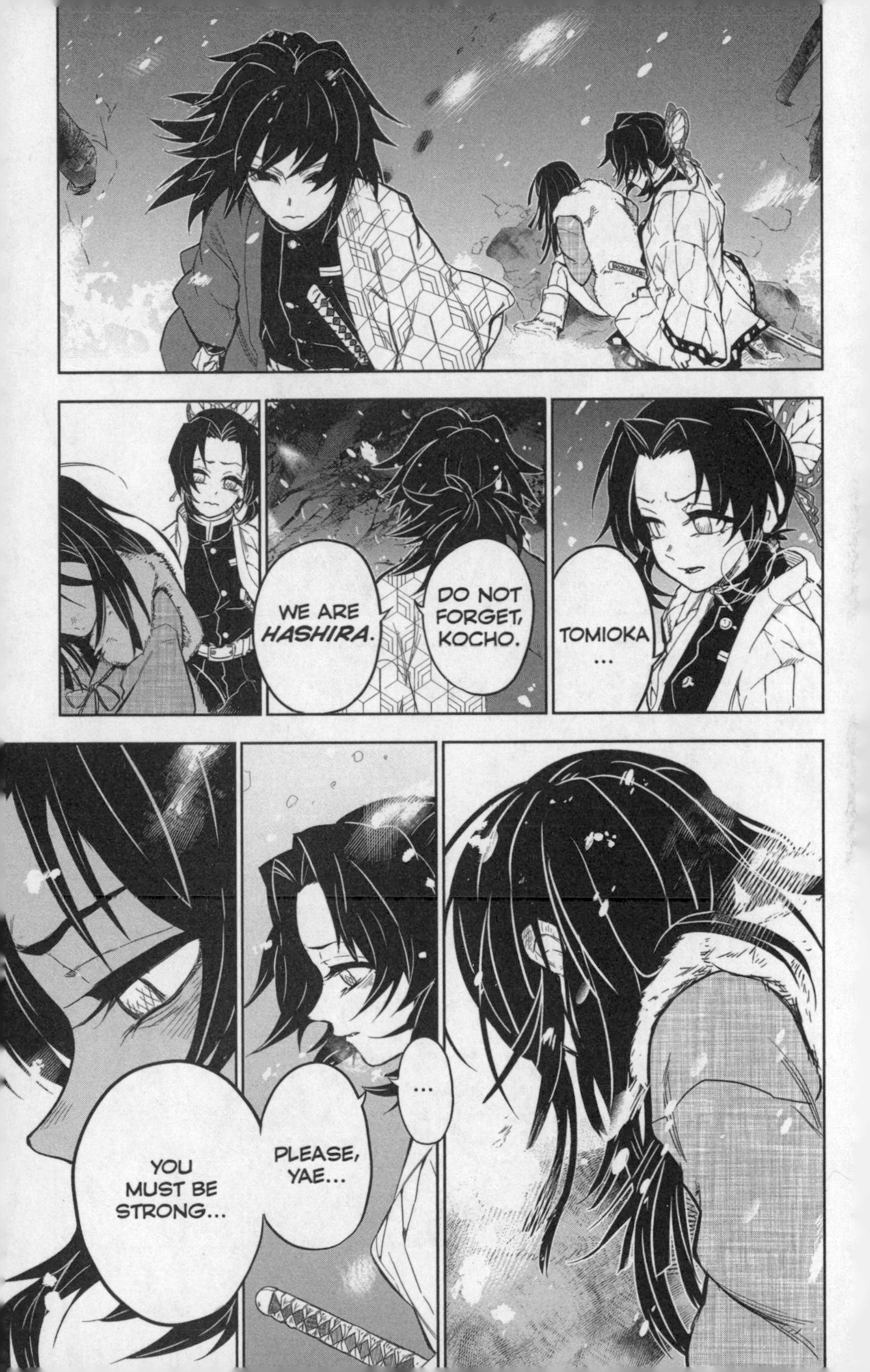
TOMIOKA ...
DO NOT FORGET, KOCHO.
WE ARE *HASHIRA*.
...
PLEASE, YAE...
YOU MUST BE STRONG...

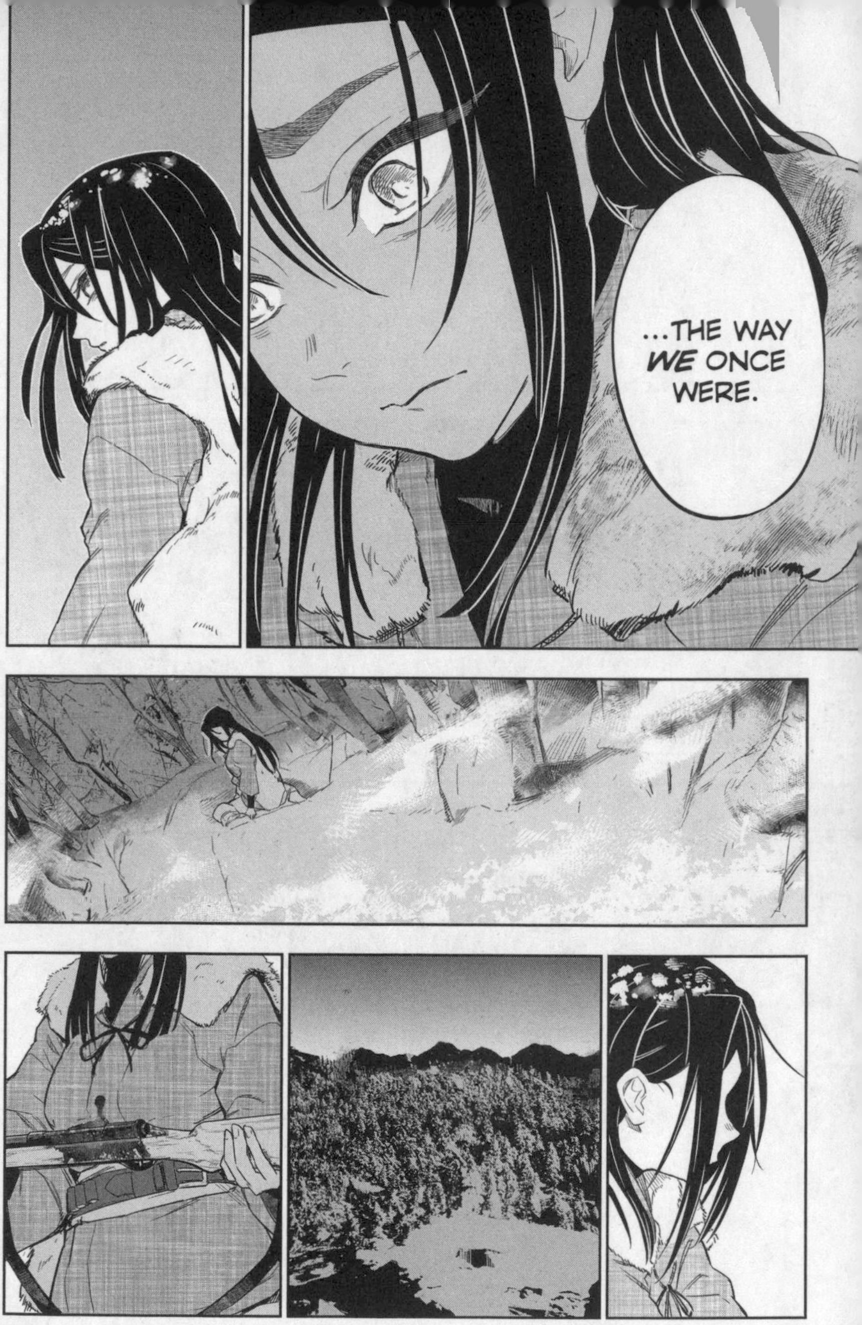
...THE WAY WE ONCE WERE.

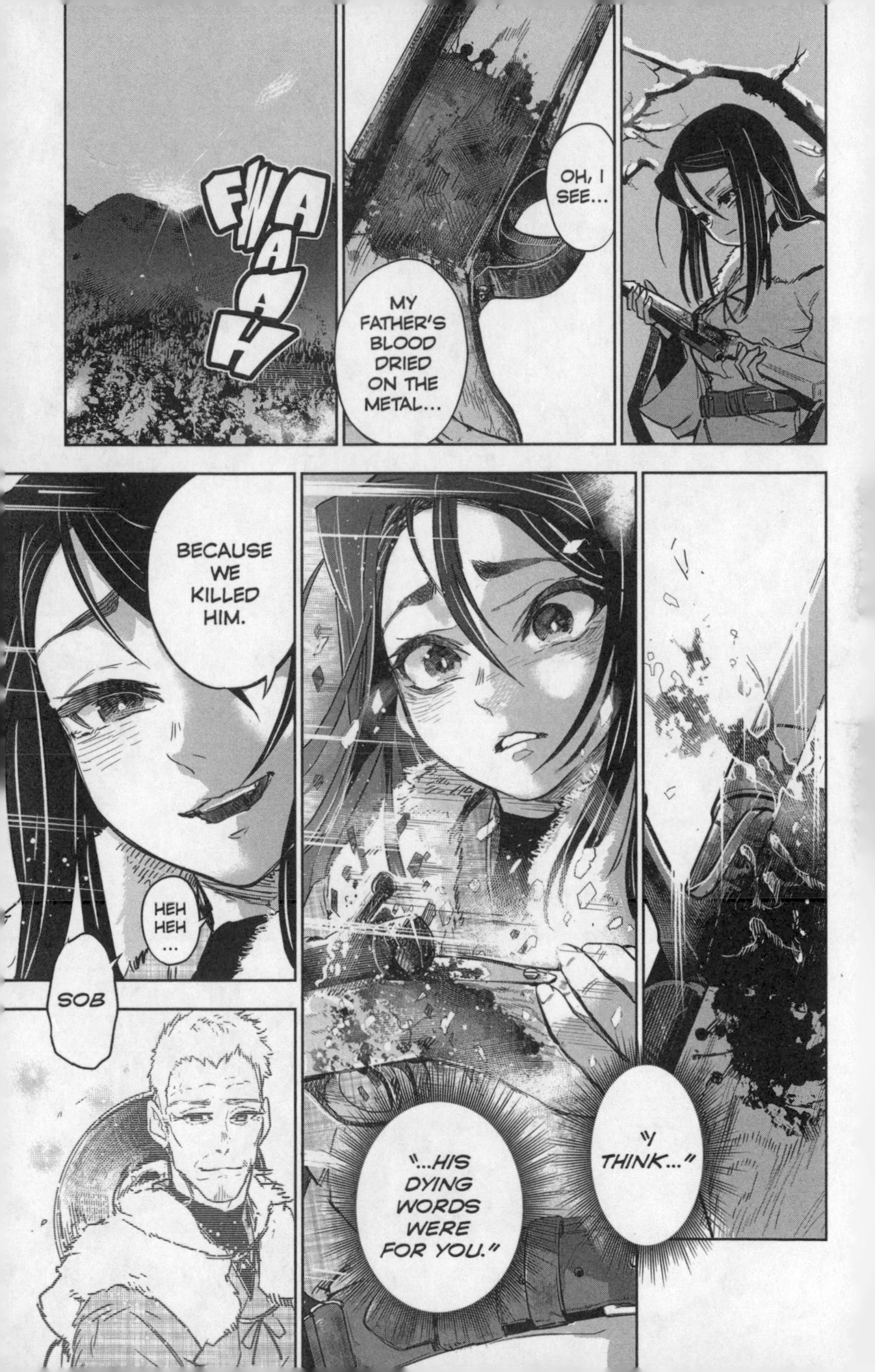
OH, I SEE...
MY FATHER'S BLOOD DRIED ON THE METAL...
FWAAAAH
"I THINK..."
"...HIS DYING WORDS WERE FOR YOU."
BECAUSE WE KILLED HIM.
HEH HEH ...
SOB

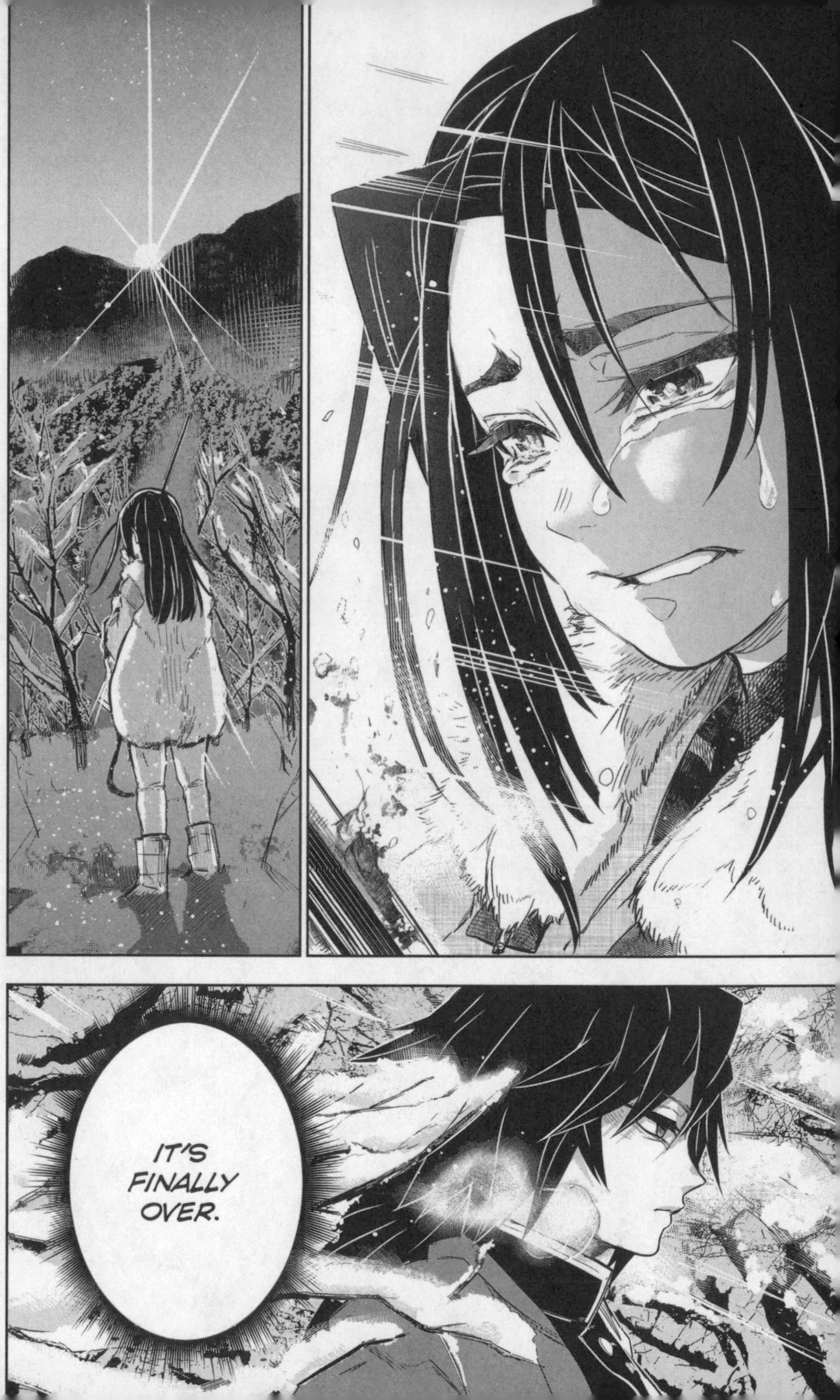
IT'S FINALLY OVER.

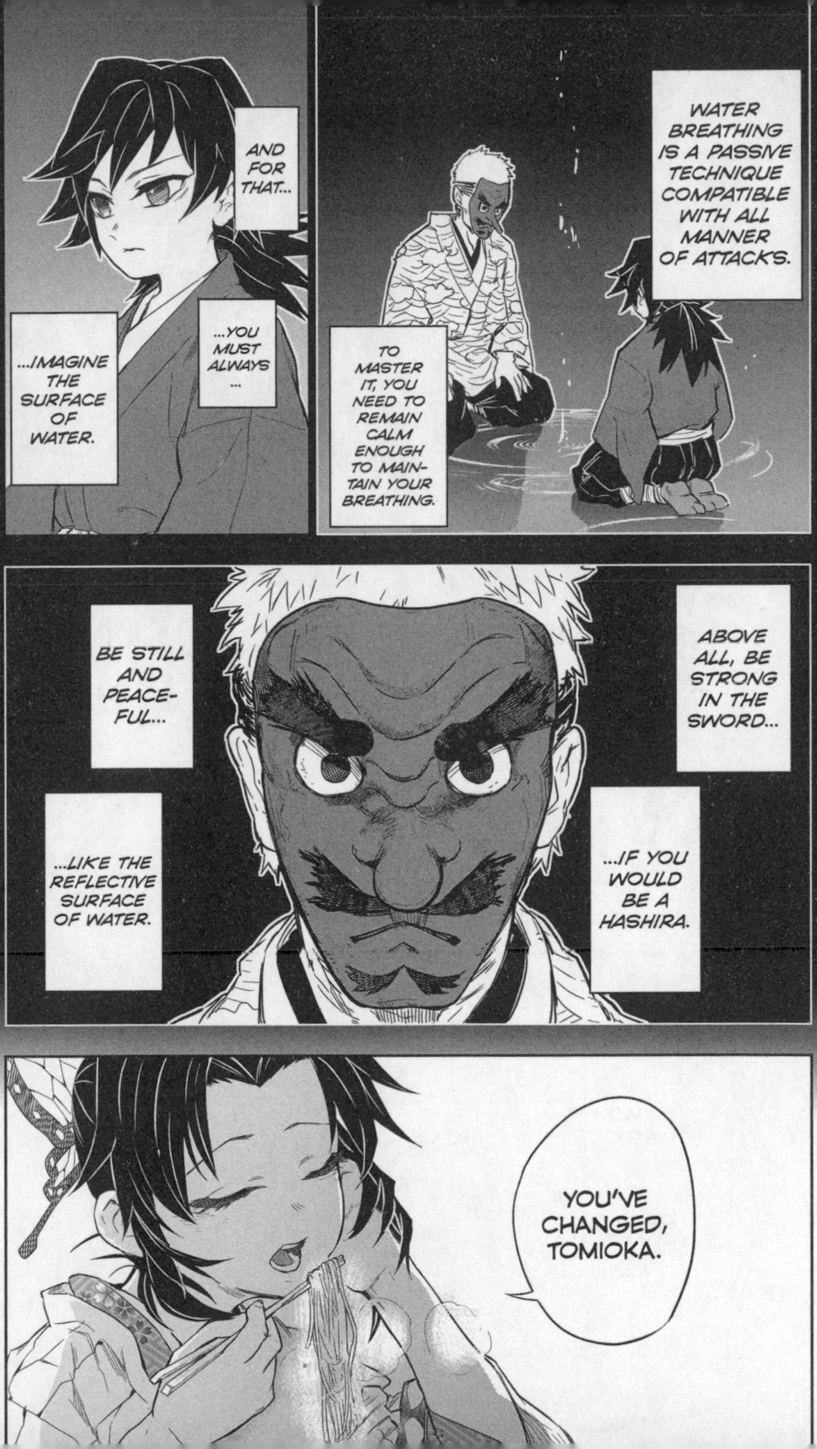
WATER BREATHING IS A PASSIVE TECHNIQUE COMPATIBLE WITH ALL MANNER OF ATTACKS.
TO MASTER IT, YOU NEED TO REMAIN CALM ENOUGH TO MAINTAIN YOUR BREATHING.
AND FOR THAT...
...YOU MUST ALWAYS ...
...IMAGINE THE SURFACE OF WATER.
ABOVE ALL, BE STRONG IN THE SWORD...
...IF YOU WOULD BE A HASHIRA.
BE STILL AND PEACEFUL...
...LIKE THE REFLECTIVE SURFACE OF WATER.
YOU'VE CHANGED, TOMIOKA.

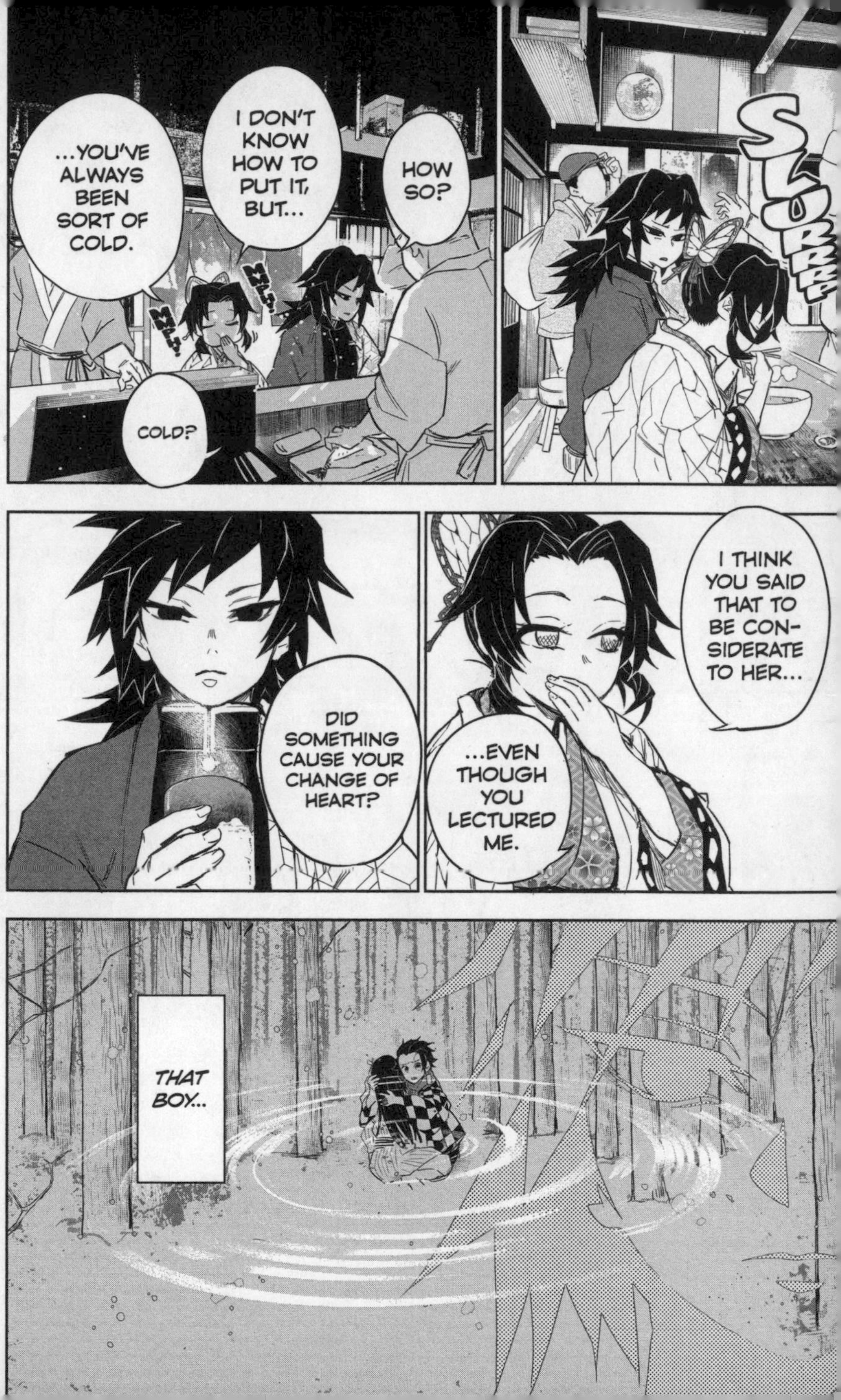
SLURRRP
HOW SO?
I DON'T KNOW HOW TO PUT IT, BUT...
...YOU'VE ALWAYS BEEN SORT OF COLD.
MMPH!
MMPH!
COLD?
I THINK YOU SAID THAT TO BE CONSIDERATE TO HER...
...EVEN THOUGH YOU LECTURED ME.
DID SOMETHING CAUSE YOUR CHANGE OF HEART?
THAT BOY...

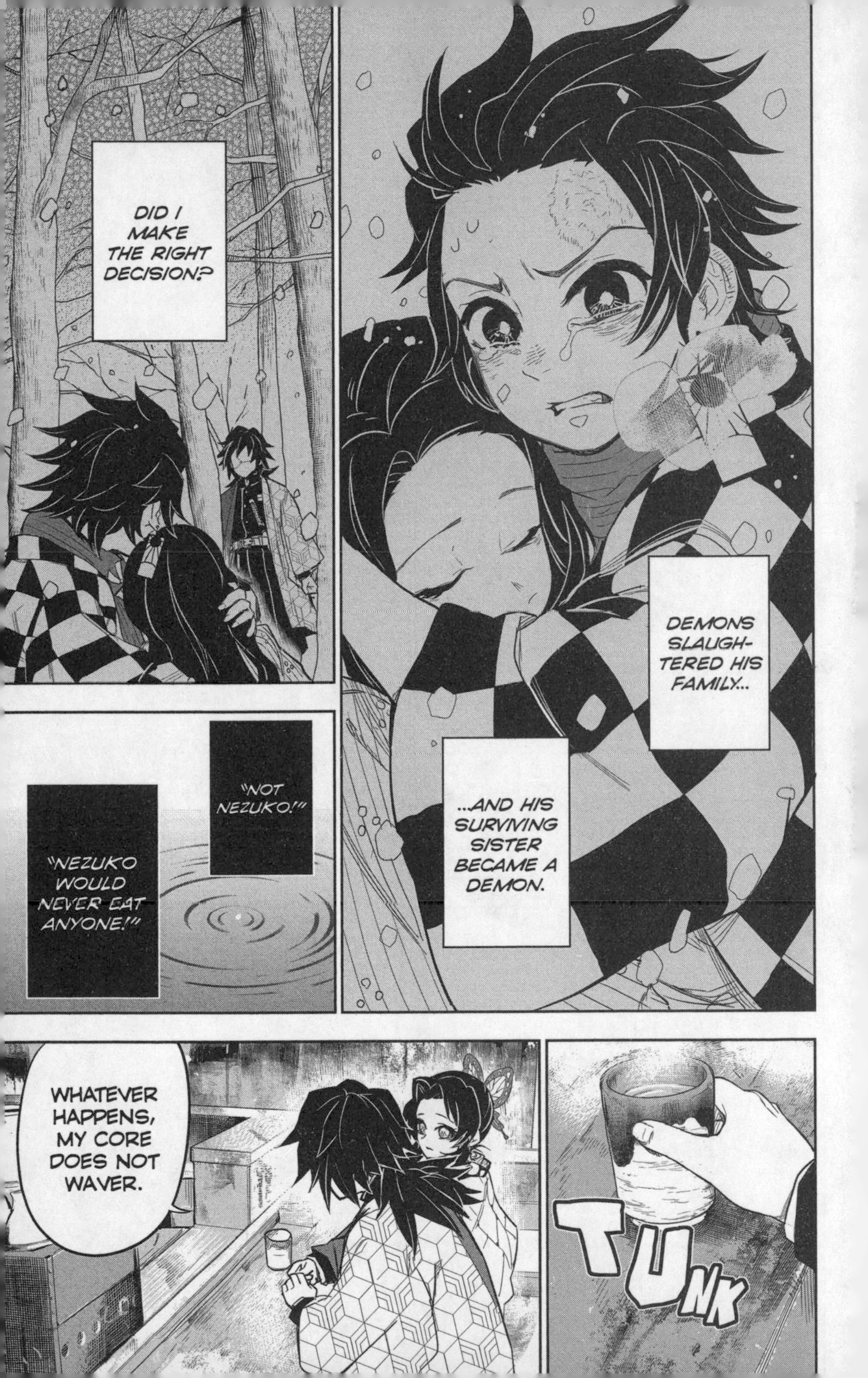
DEMONS SLAUGHTERED HIS FAMILY...
...AND HIS SURVIVING SISTER BECAME A DEMON.
DID I MAKE THE RIGHT DECISION?
"NOT NEZUKO!"
"NEZUKO WOULD NEVER EAT ANYONE!"
TUNK
WHATEVER HAPPENS, MY CORE DOES NOT WAVER.

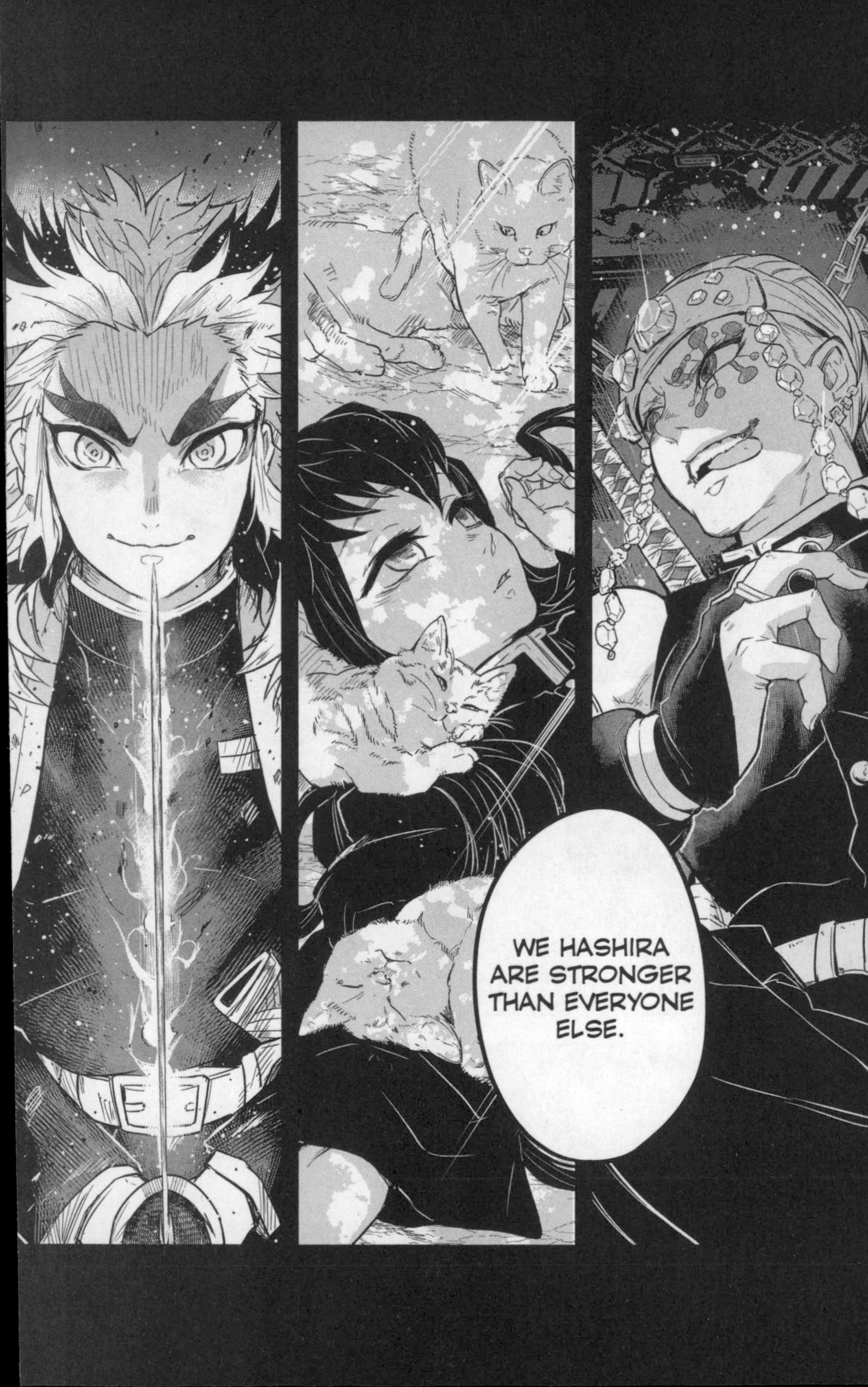
WE HASHIRA ARE STRONGER THAN EVERYONE ELSE.

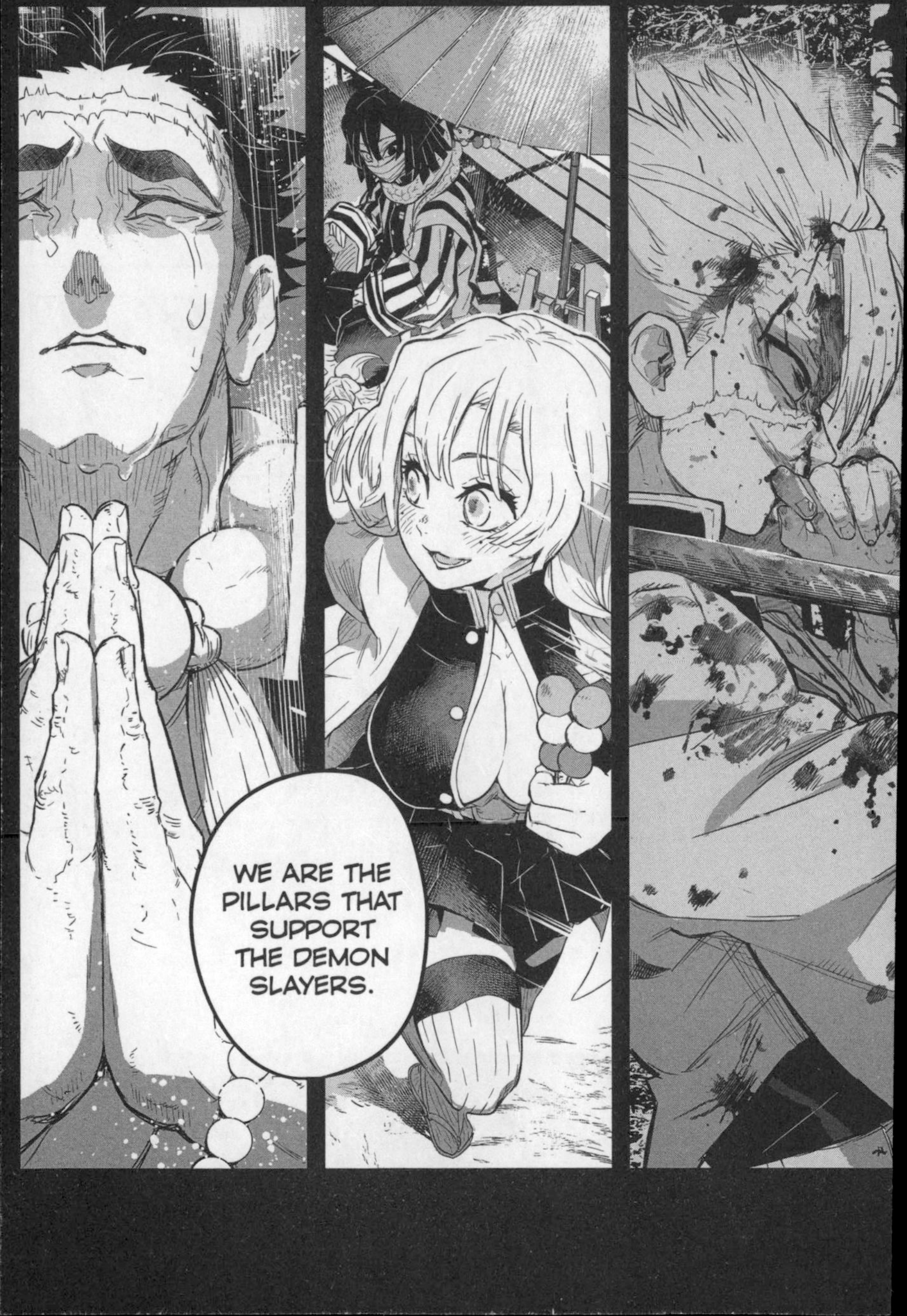
WE ARE THE PILLARS THAT SUPPORT THE DEMON SLAYERS.

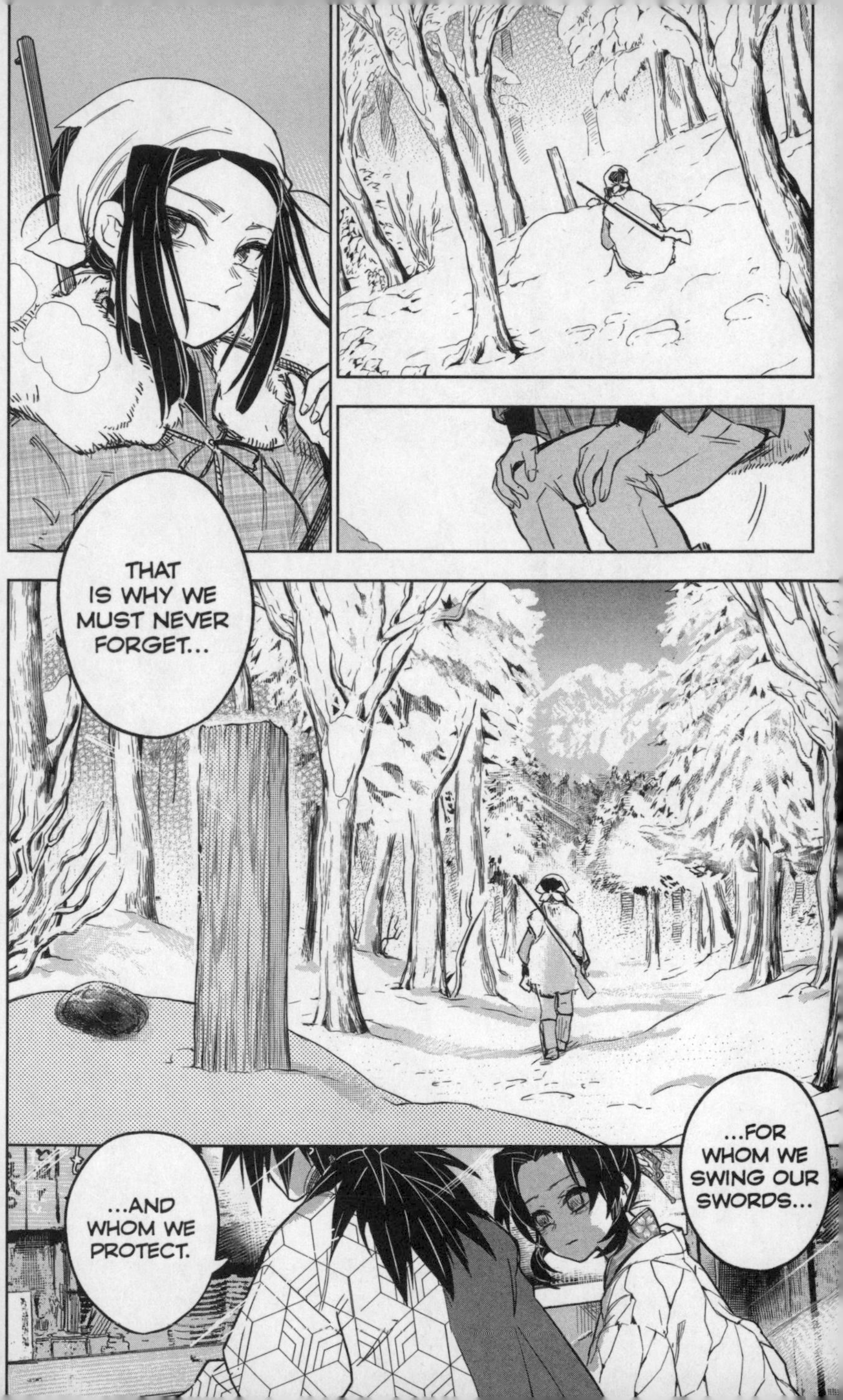
THAT IS WHY WE MUST NEVER FORGET...
...FOR WHOM WE SWING OUR SWORDS...
...AND WHOM WE PROTECT.

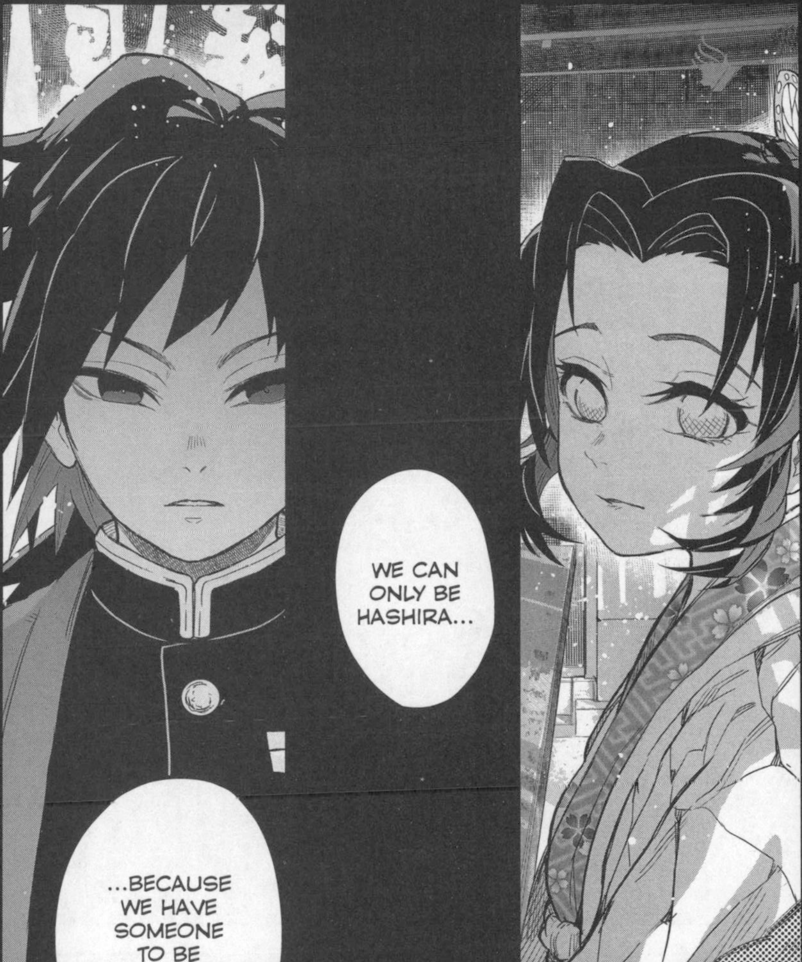
WE CAN ONLY BE HASHIRA...
...BECAUSE WE HAVE SOMEONE TO BE STRONG FOR.

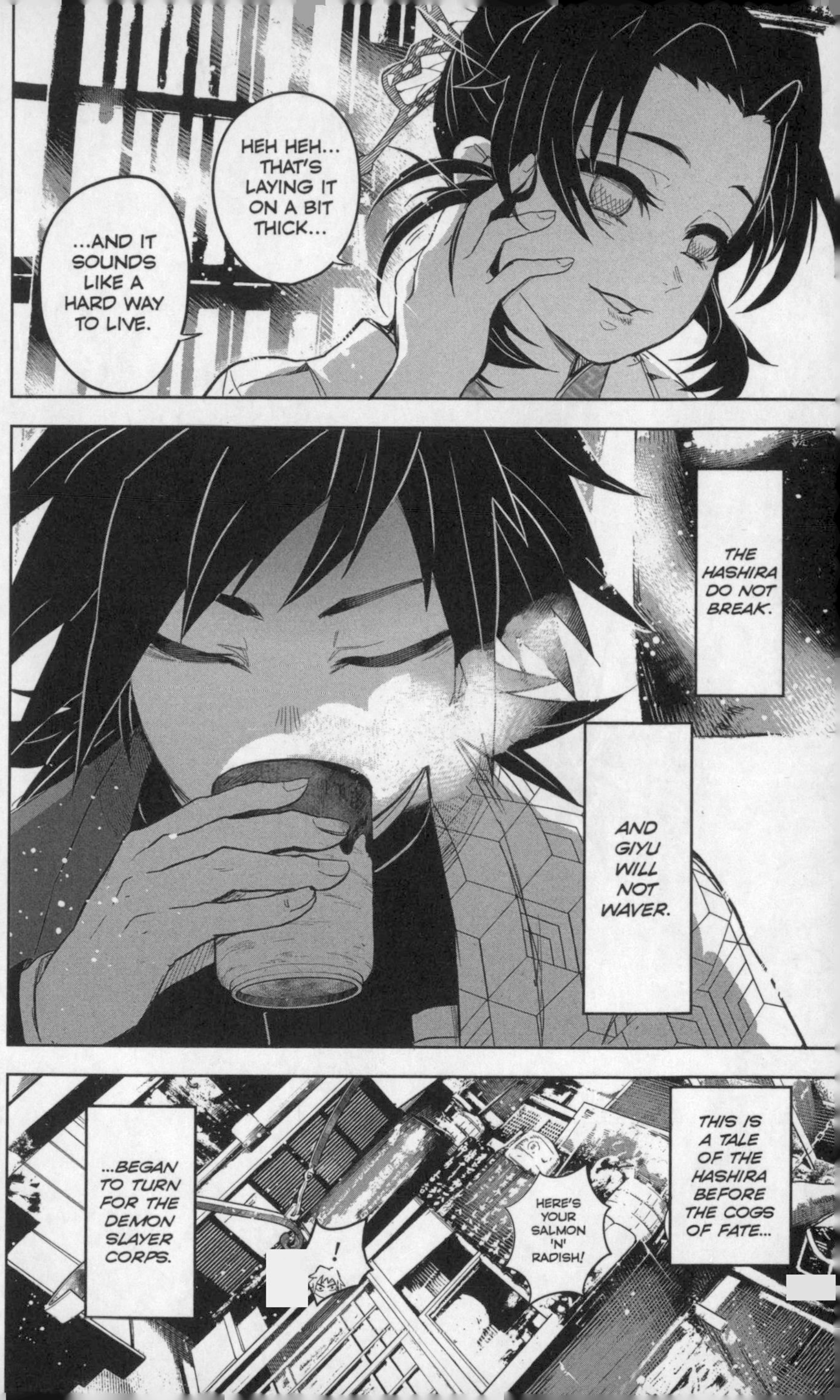
HEH HEH... THAT'S LAYING IT ON A BIT THICK...
...AND IT SOUNDS LIKE A HARD WAY TO LIVE.
THE HASHIRA DO NOT BREAK.
AND GIYU WILL NOT WAVER.
THIS IS A TALE OF THE HASHIRA BEFORE THE COGS OF FATE...
HERE'S YOUR SALMON 'N' RADISH!
!
...BEGAN TO TURN FOR THE DEMON SLAYER CORPS.

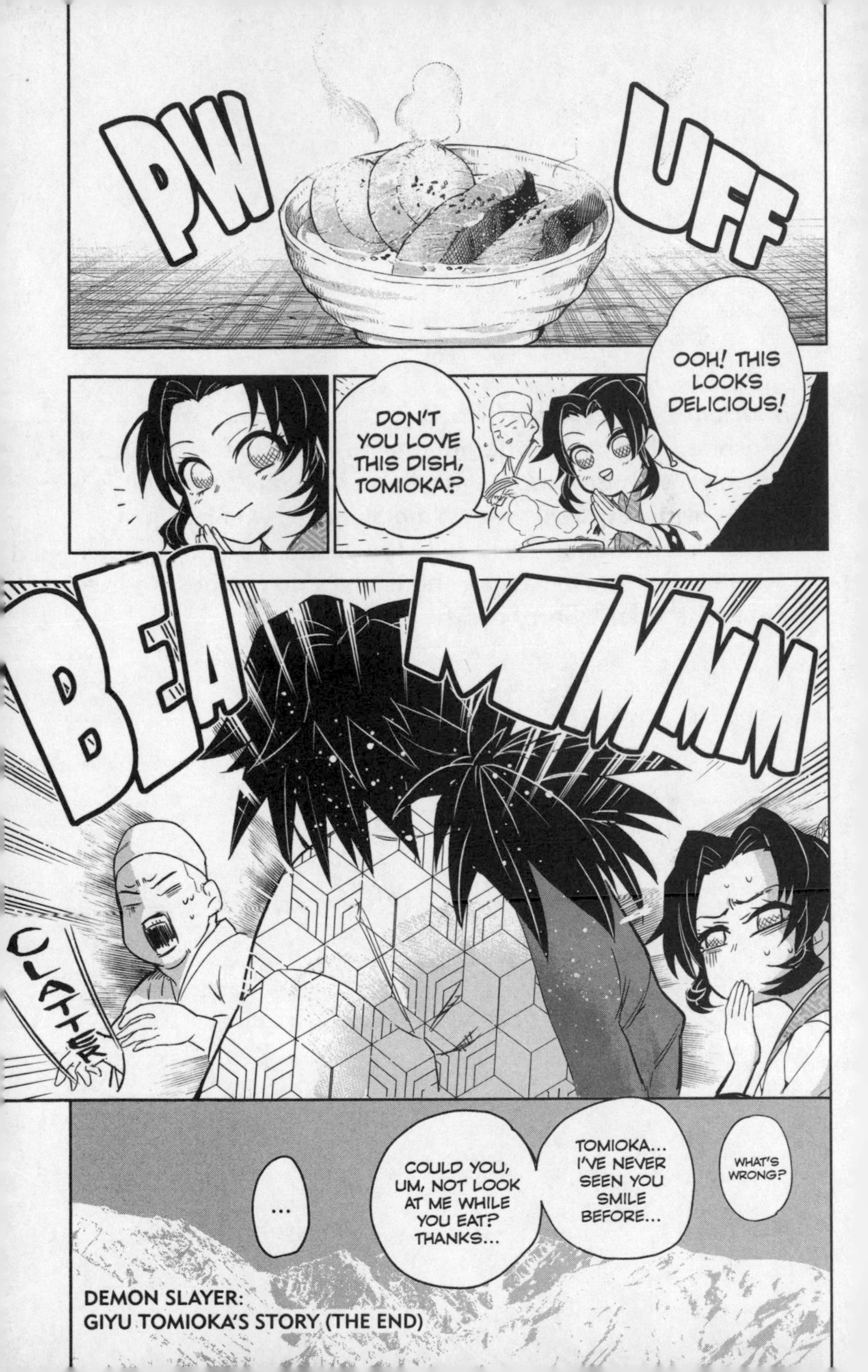
PW UFF
OOH! THIS LOOKS DELICIOUS!
DON'T YOU LOVE THIS DISH, TOMIOKA?
BEAMMMMM
CLATTER
WHAT'S WRONG?
TOMIOKA... I'VE NEVER SEEN YOU SMILE BEFORE...
COULD YOU, UM, NOT LOOK AT ME WHILE YOU EAT? THANKS...
...
DEMON SLAYER:
GIYU TOMIOKA'S STORY (THE END)

I included a scene in which Giyu tells Shinobu "We are Hashira," but in the original manga, he denies being a Hashira, so many people may have wondered which it is. In his own way, Giyu was telling Shinobu, who had just become a Hashira, "We are in the position of Hashira, which requires us to be strong (so let's do our best to live up to the title)." Sorry for the confusion!

*Maybe he's too silent?*

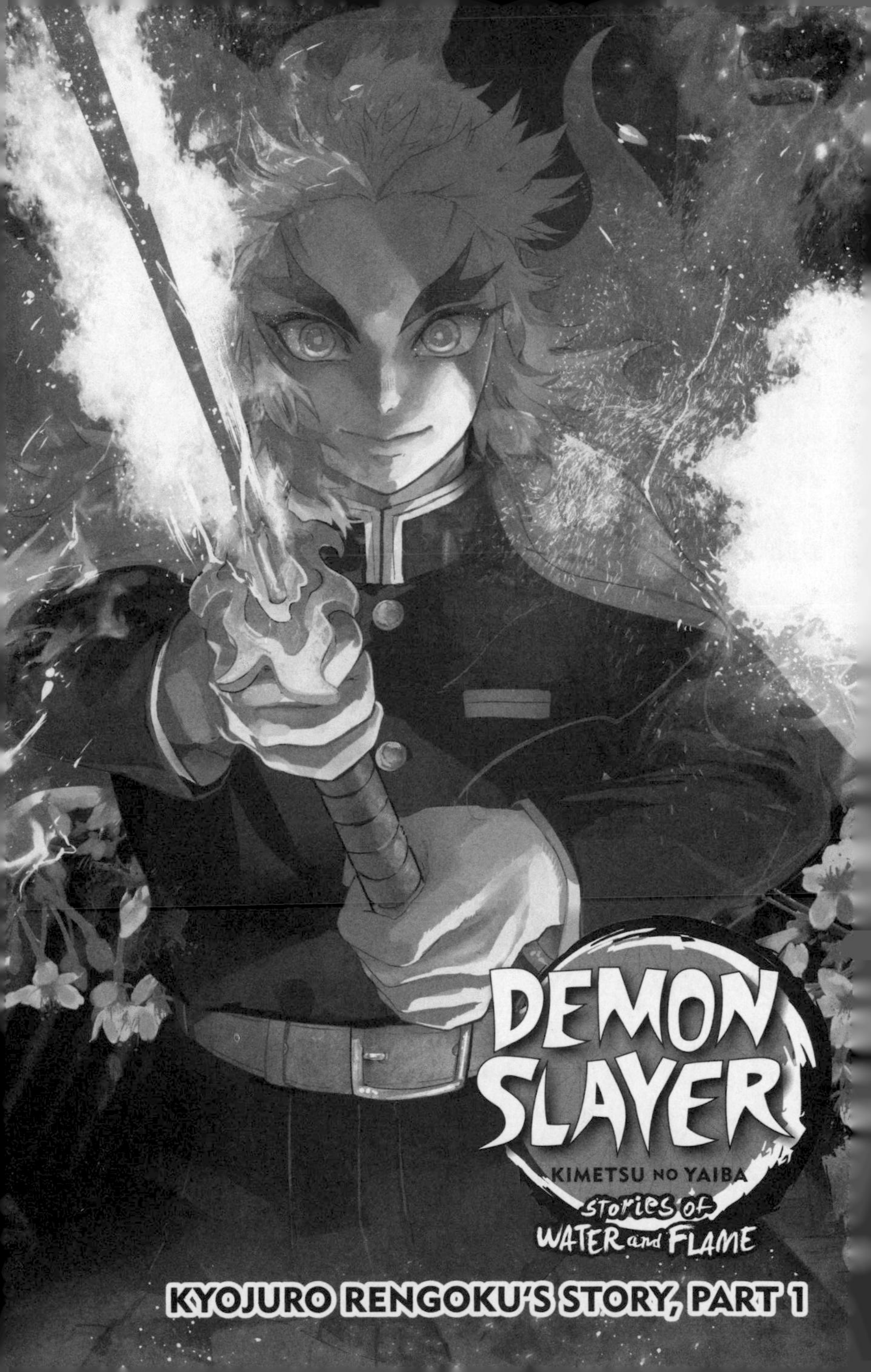
DEMON SLAYER
KIMETSU NO YAIBA
stories of
WATER and FLAME
KYOJURO RENGOKU'S STORY, PART 1

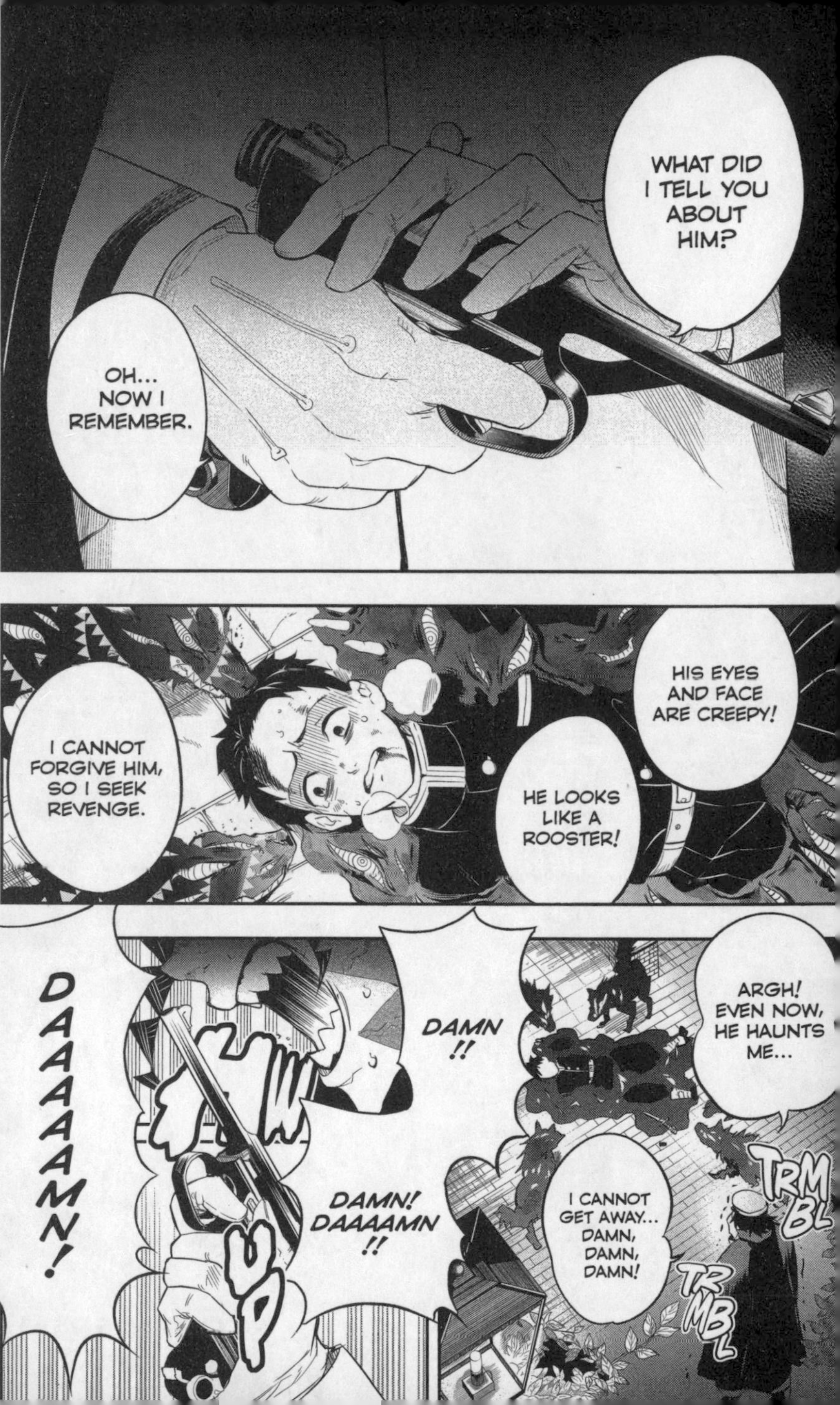
WHAT DID I TELL YOU ABOUT HIM?
OH... NOW I REMEMBER.
HIS EYES AND FACE ARE CREEPY!
HE LOOKS LIKE A ROOSTER!
I CANNOT FORGIVE HIM, SO I SEEK REVENGE.
ARGH! EVEN NOW, HE HAUNTS ME...
TRMBL
TRMBL
I CANNOT GET AWAY... DAMN, DAMN, DAMN!
DAMN!!
DAMN! DAAAAMN!!
DAAAAAAMN!

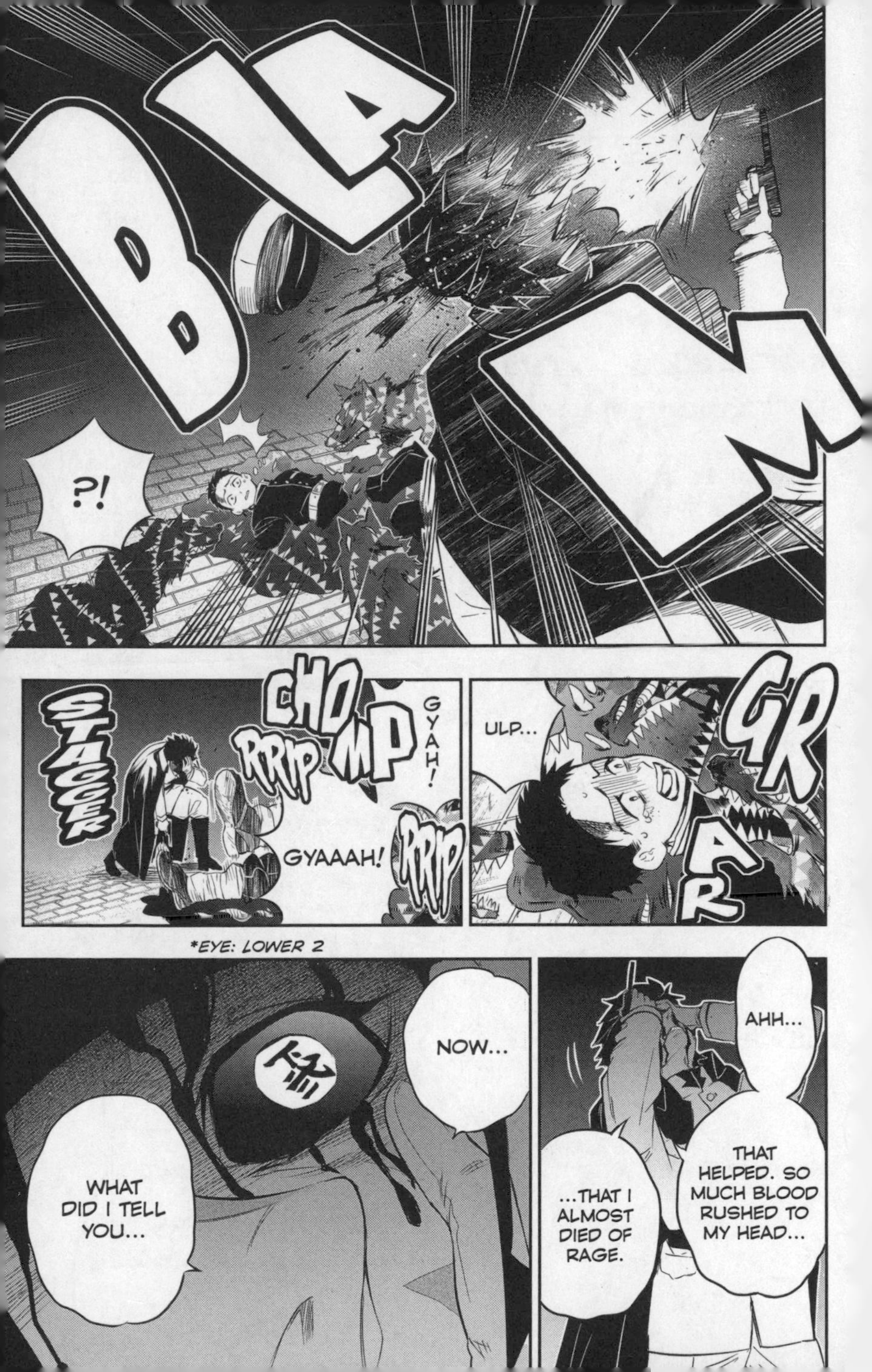
BLAM
?!
GRAR
ULP...
CHOMP
GYAH!
RRIP
STAGGER
GYAAAH!
RRIP
*EYE: LOWER 2
AHH...
THAT HELPED. SO MUCH BLOOD RUSHED TO MY HEAD...
...THAT I ALMOST DIED OF RAGE.
NOW...
下弐
WHAT DID I TELL YOU...

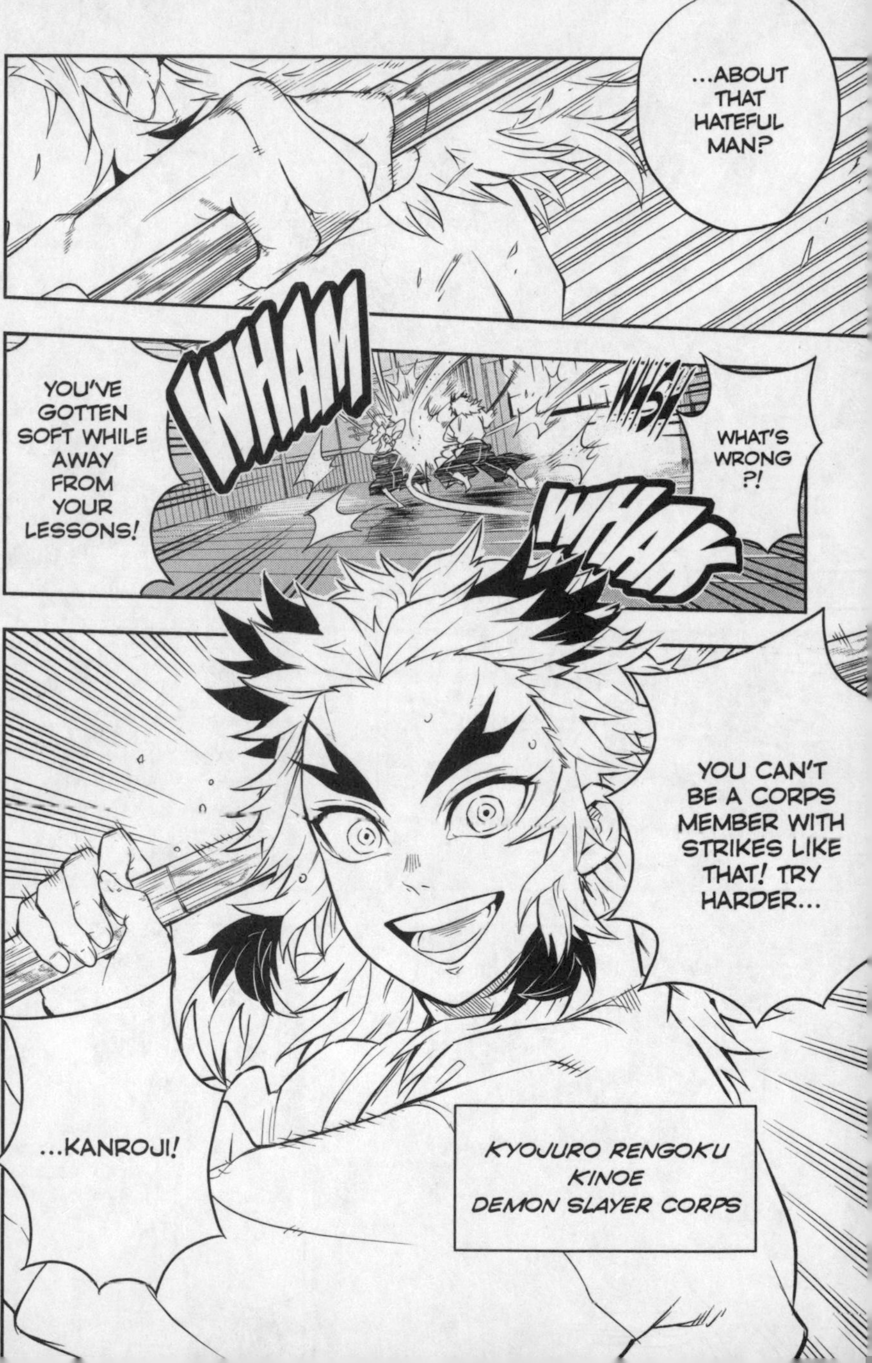
...ABOUT THAT HATEFUL MAN?
WHAT'S WRONG ?!
WHAM
YOU'VE GOTTEN SOFT WHILE AWAY FROM YOUR LESSONS!
YOU CAN'T BE A CORPS MEMBER WITH STRIKES LIKE THAT! TRY HARDER...
...KANROJI!
KYOJURO RENGOKU
KINOE
DEMON SLAYER CORPS

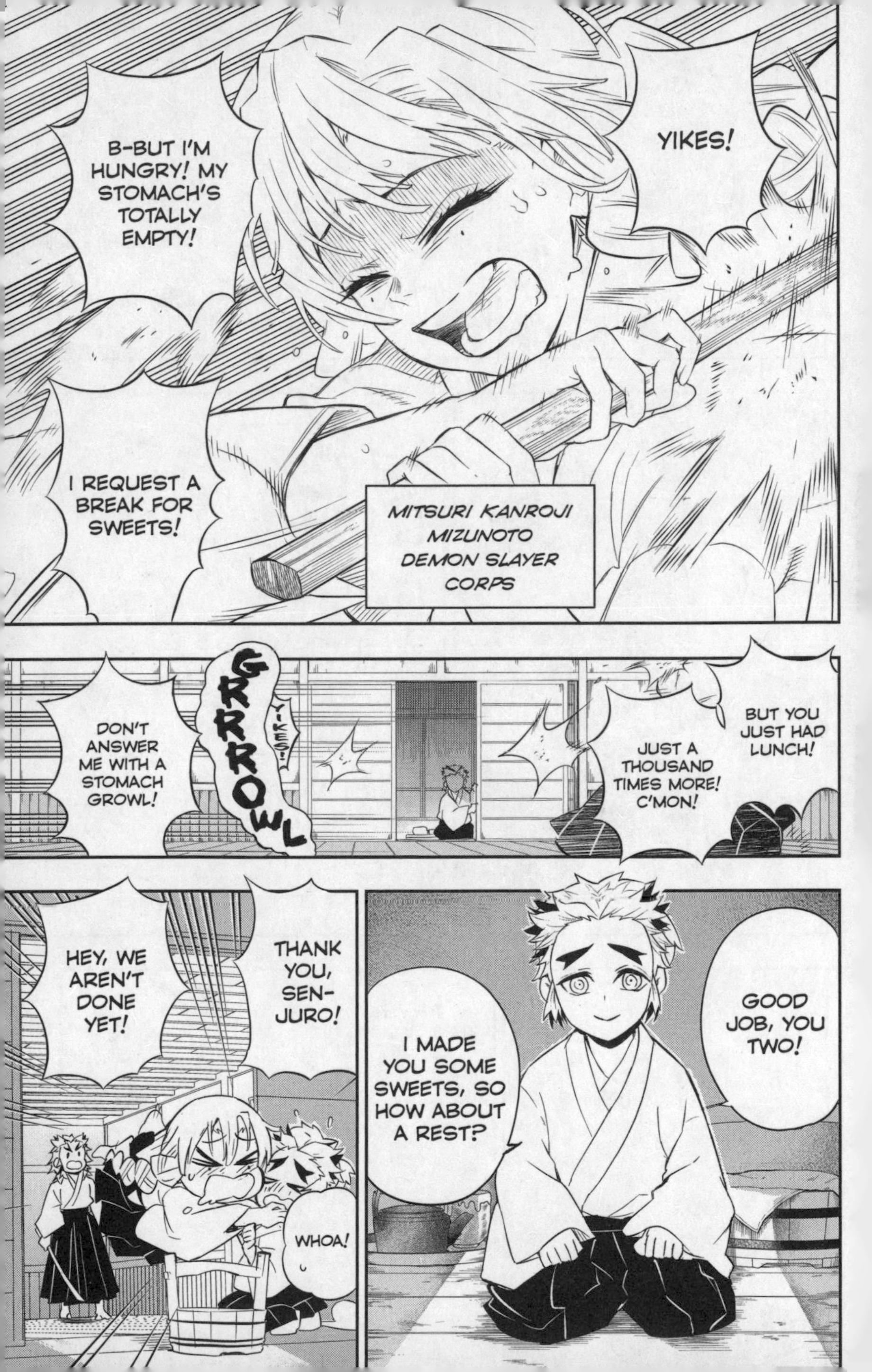
YIKES!
B-BUT I'M HUNGRY! MY STOMACH'S TOTALLY EMPTY!
MITSURI KANROJI
MIZUNOTO
DEMON SLAYER CORPS
I REQUEST A BREAK FOR SWEETS!
BUT YOU JUST HAD LUNCH!
JUST A THOUSAND TIMES MORE! C'MON!
YIKES!
GRRROWL
DON'T ANSWER ME WITH A STOMACH GROWL!
GOOD JOB, YOU TWO!
I MADE YOU SOME SWEETS, SO HOW ABOUT A REST?
THANK YOU, SEN-JURO!
HEY, WE AREN'T DONE YET!
WHOA!

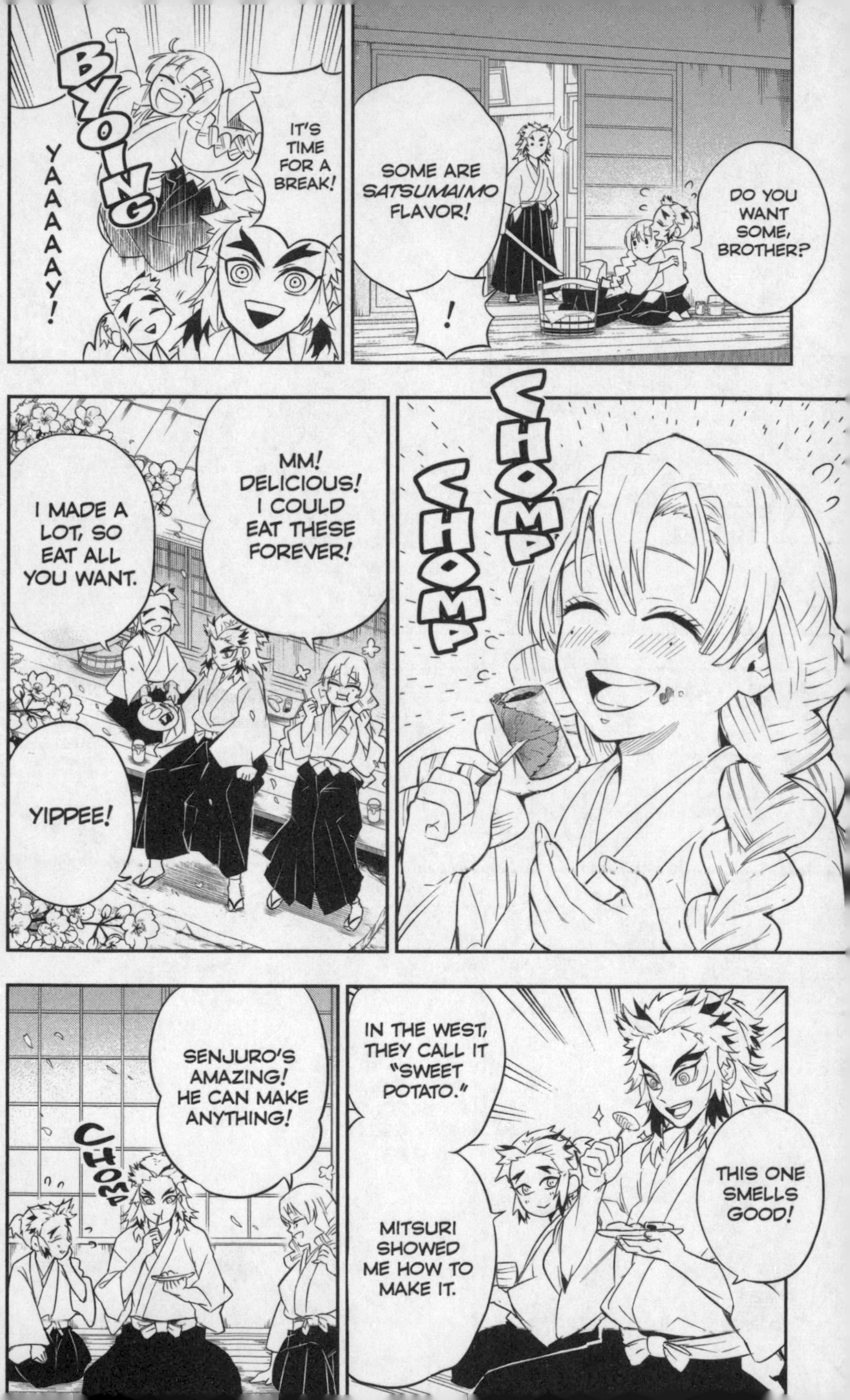
DO YOU WANT SOME, BROTHER?
SOME ARE SATSUMAIMO FLAVOR!
!
IT'S TIME FOR A BREAK!
BYOING
YAAAAAAY!
CHOMP
CHOMP
MM! DELICIOUS! I COULD EAT THESE FOREVER!
I MADE A LOT, SO EAT ALL YOU WANT.
YIPPEE!
THIS ONE SMELLS GOOD!
IN THE WEST, THEY CALL IT "SWEET POTATO."
MITSURI SHOWED ME HOW TO MAKE IT.
SENJURO'S AMAZING! HE CAN MAKE ANYTHING!
CHOMP

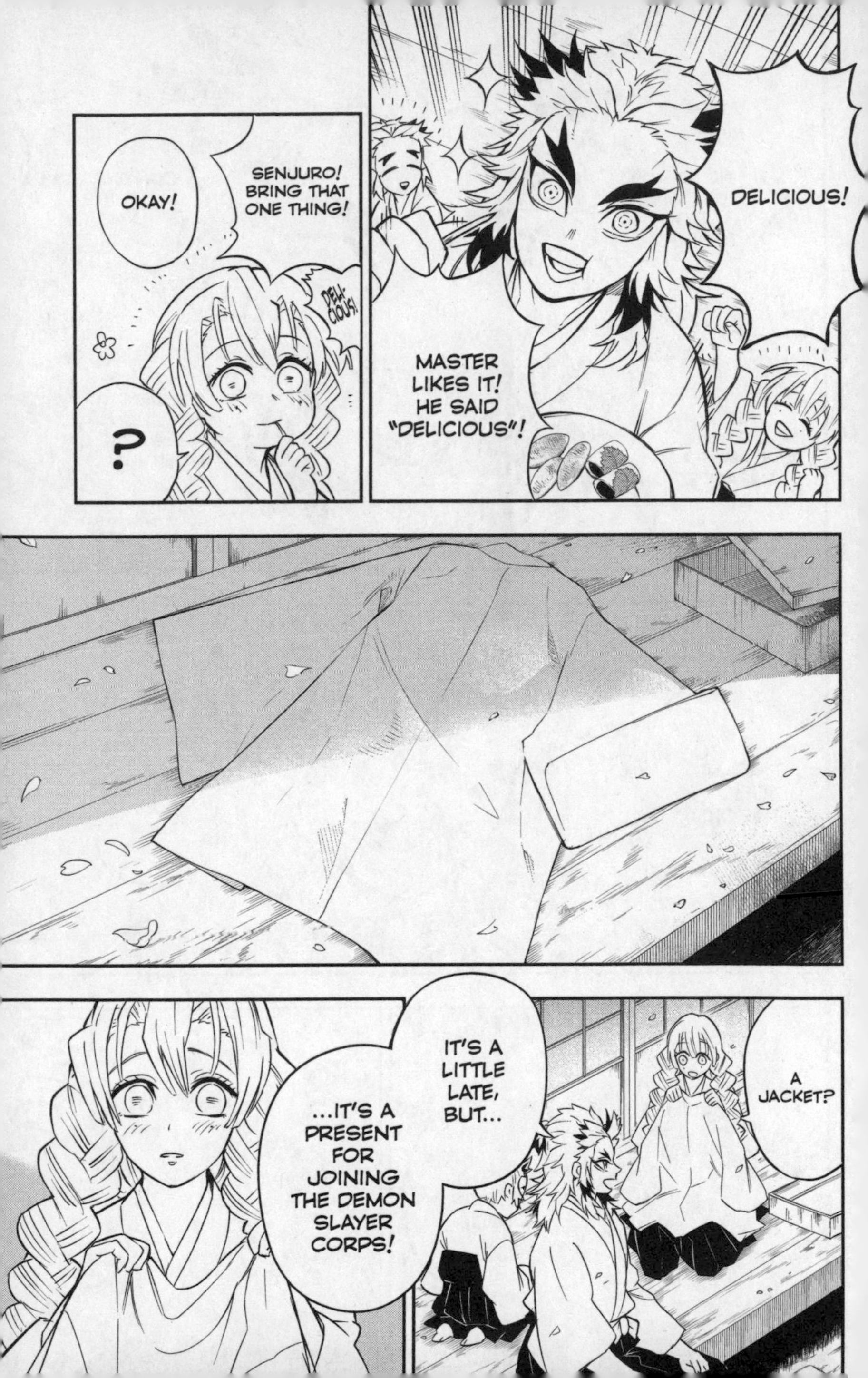
DELICIOUS!
MASTER LIKES IT! HE SAID "DELICIOUS"!
SENJURO! BRING THAT ONE THING!
OKAY!
DELI-CIOUS!
?
A JACKET?
IT'S A LITTLE LATE, BUT...
...IT'S A PRESENT FOR JOINING THE DEMON SLAYER CORPS!

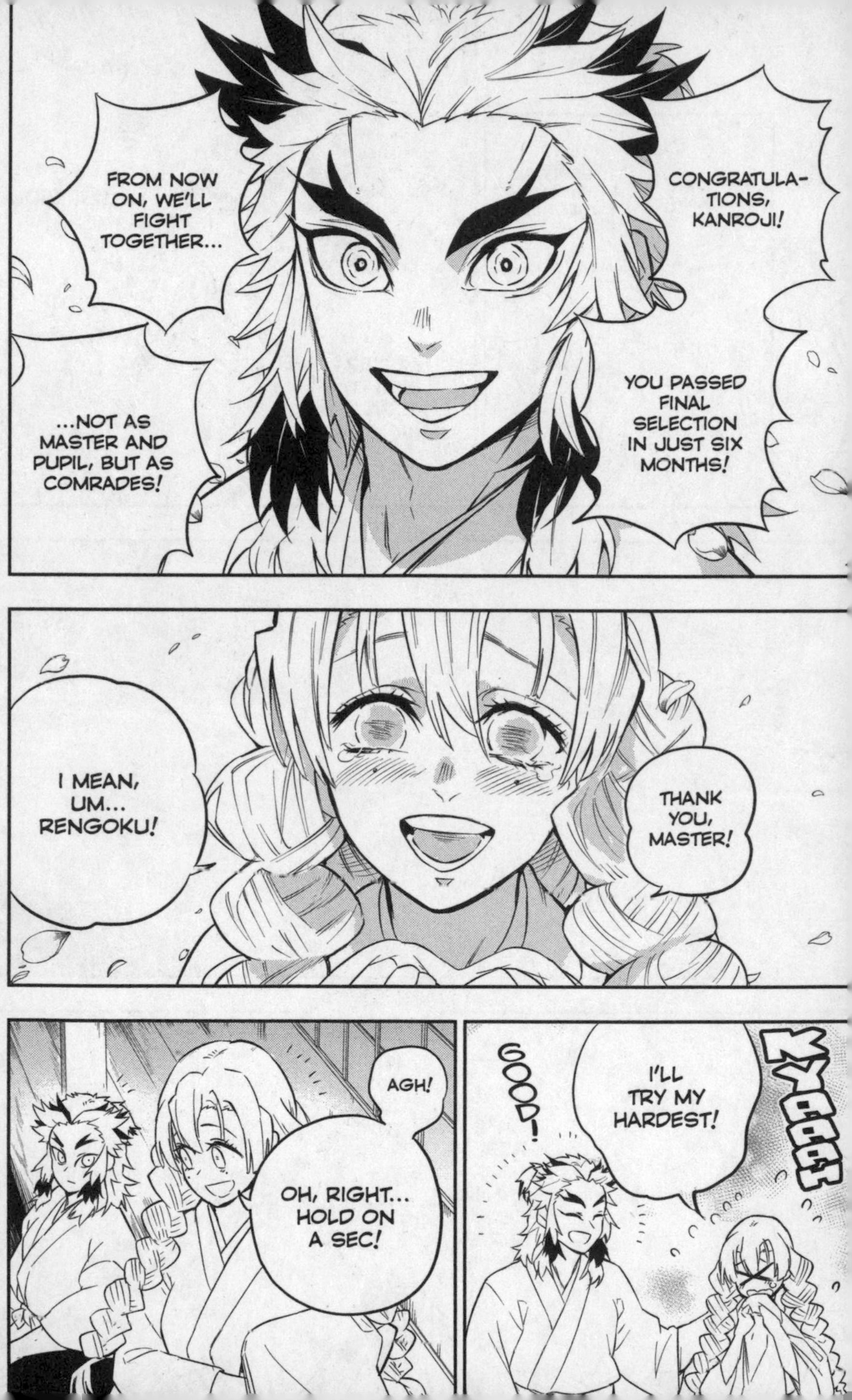
CONGRATULATIONS, KANROJI!
YOU PASSED FINAL SELECTION IN JUST SIX MONTHS!
FROM NOW ON, WE'LL FIGHT TOGETHER...
...NOT AS MASTER AND PUPIL, BUT AS COMRADES!
THANK YOU, MASTER!
I MEAN, UM... RENGOKU!
KYAAA!
I'LL TRY MY HARDEST!
GOOD!
AGH!
OH, RIGHT... HOLD ON A SEC!

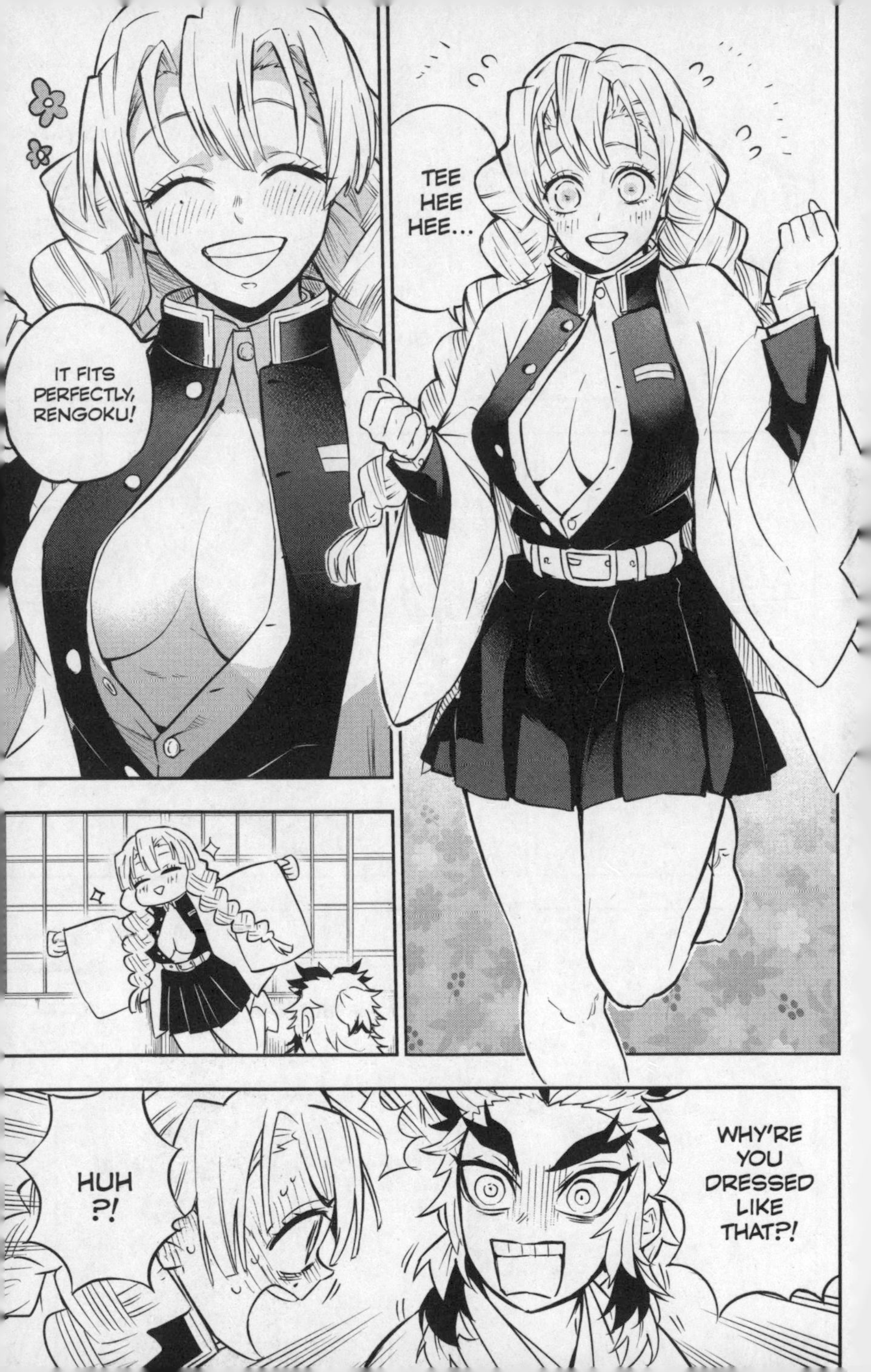
TEE HEE HEE...
IT FITS PERFECTLY, RENGOKU!
WHY'RE YOU DRESSED LIKE THAT?!
HUH ?!

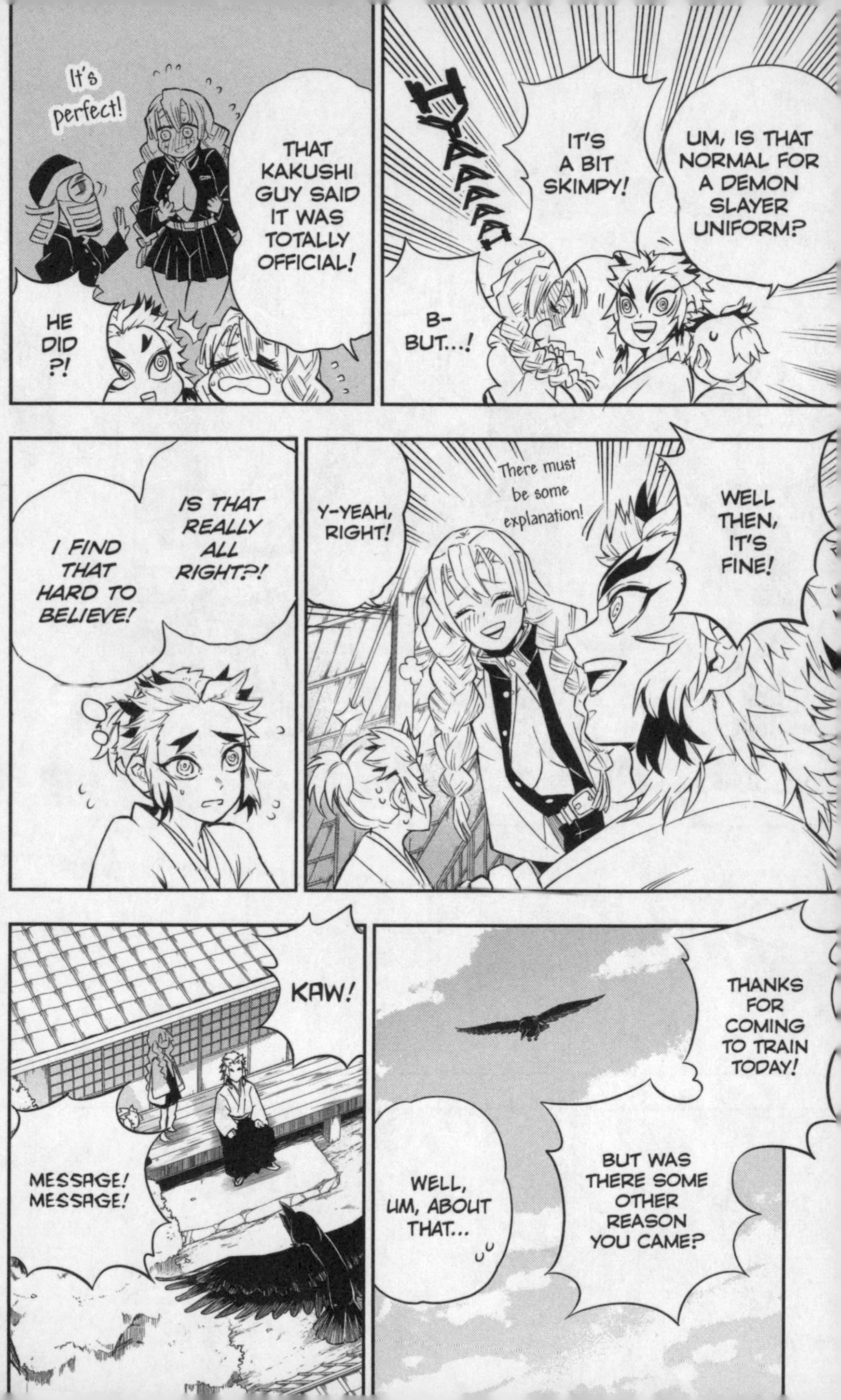
UM, IS THAT NORMAL FOR A DEMON SLAYER UNIFORM?
IT'S A BIT SKIMPY!
B-BUT...!
THAT KAKUSHI GUY SAID IT WAS TOTALLY OFFICIAL!
It's perfect!
HE DID?!
WELL THEN, IT'S FINE!
There must be some explanation!
Y-YEAH, RIGHT!
IS THAT REALLY ALL RIGHT?!
I FIND THAT HARD TO BELIEVE!
THANKS FOR COMING TO TRAIN TODAY!
BUT WAS THERE SOME OTHER REASON YOU CAME?
WELL, UM, ABOUT THAT...
KAW!
MESSAGE! MESSAGE!

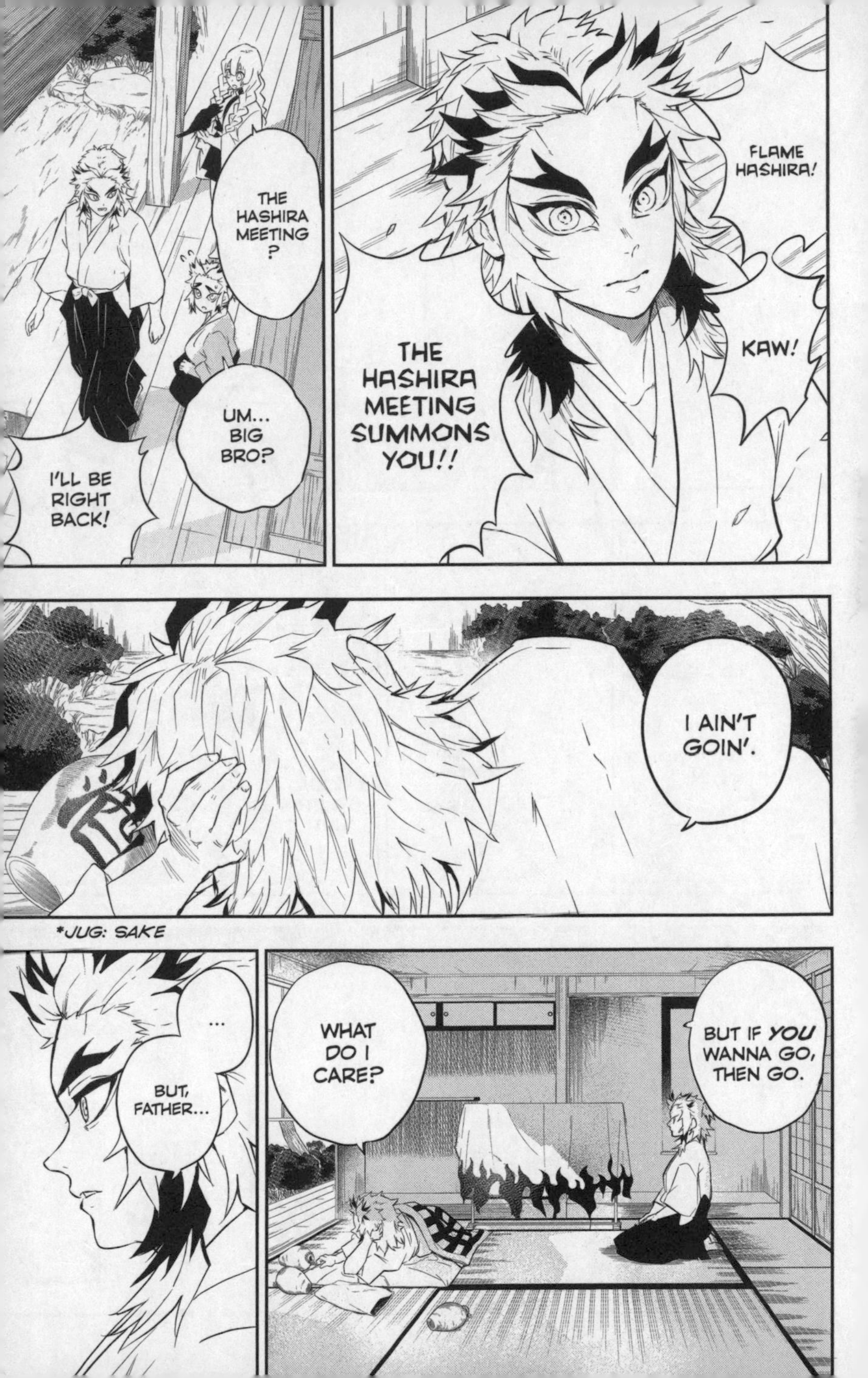
FLAME HASHIRA!
KAW!
THE HASHIRA MEETING SUMMONS YOU!!
THE HASHIRA MEETING?
UM... BIG BRO?
I'LL BE RIGHT BACK!
I AIN'T GOIN'.
*JUG: SAKE
BUT IF *YOU* WANNA GO, THEN GO.
WHAT DO I CARE?
...
BUT, FATHER...

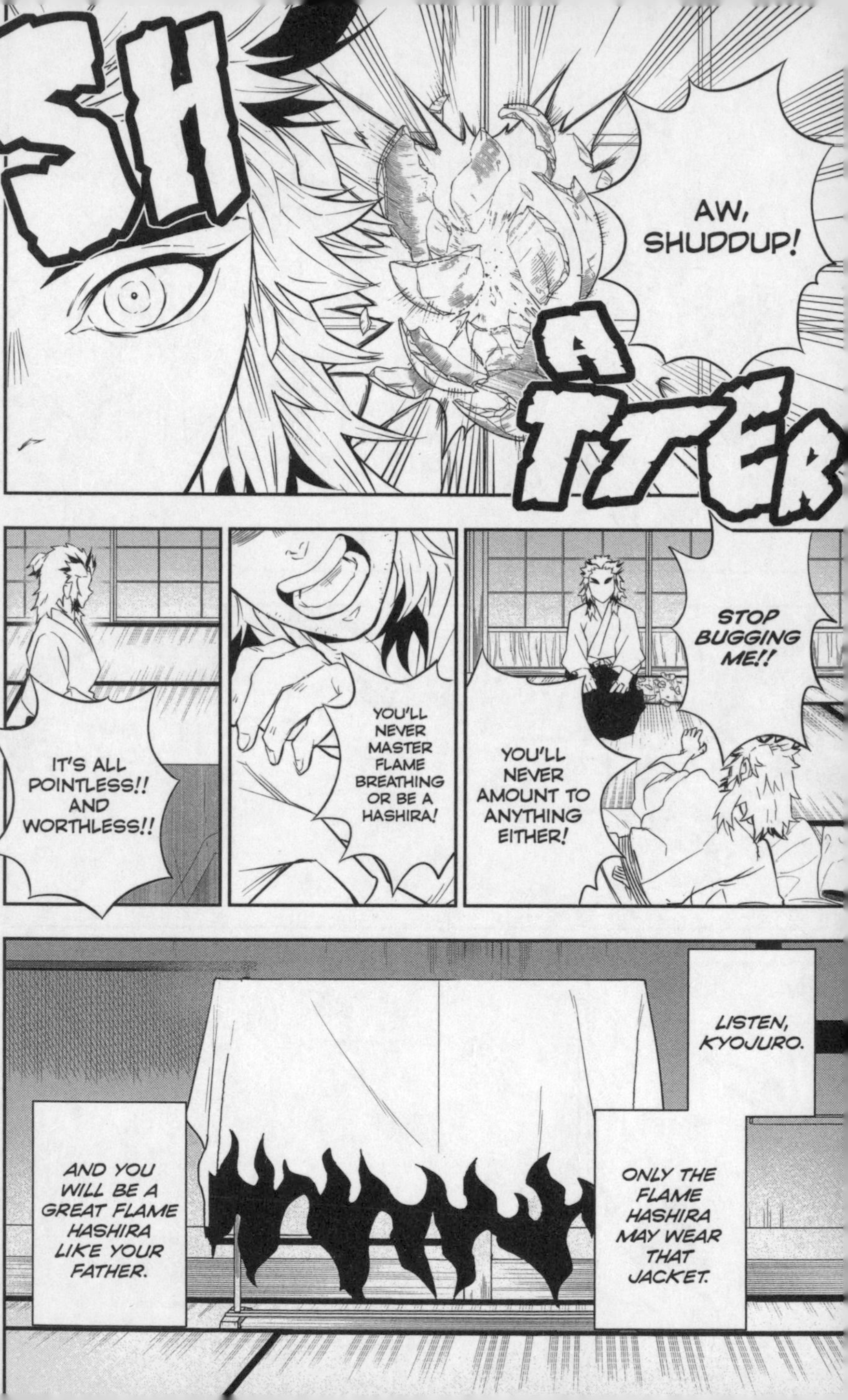
SHATTER
AW, SHUDDUP!
STOP BUGGING ME!!
YOU'LL NEVER AMOUNT TO ANYTHING EITHER!
YOU'LL NEVER MASTER FLAME BREATHING OR BE A HASHIRA!
IT'S ALL POINTLESS!! AND WORTHLESS!!
LISTEN, KYOJURO.
ONLY THE FLAME HASHIRA MAY WEAR THAT JACKET.
AND YOU WILL BE A GREAT FLAME HASHIRA LIKE YOUR FATHER.

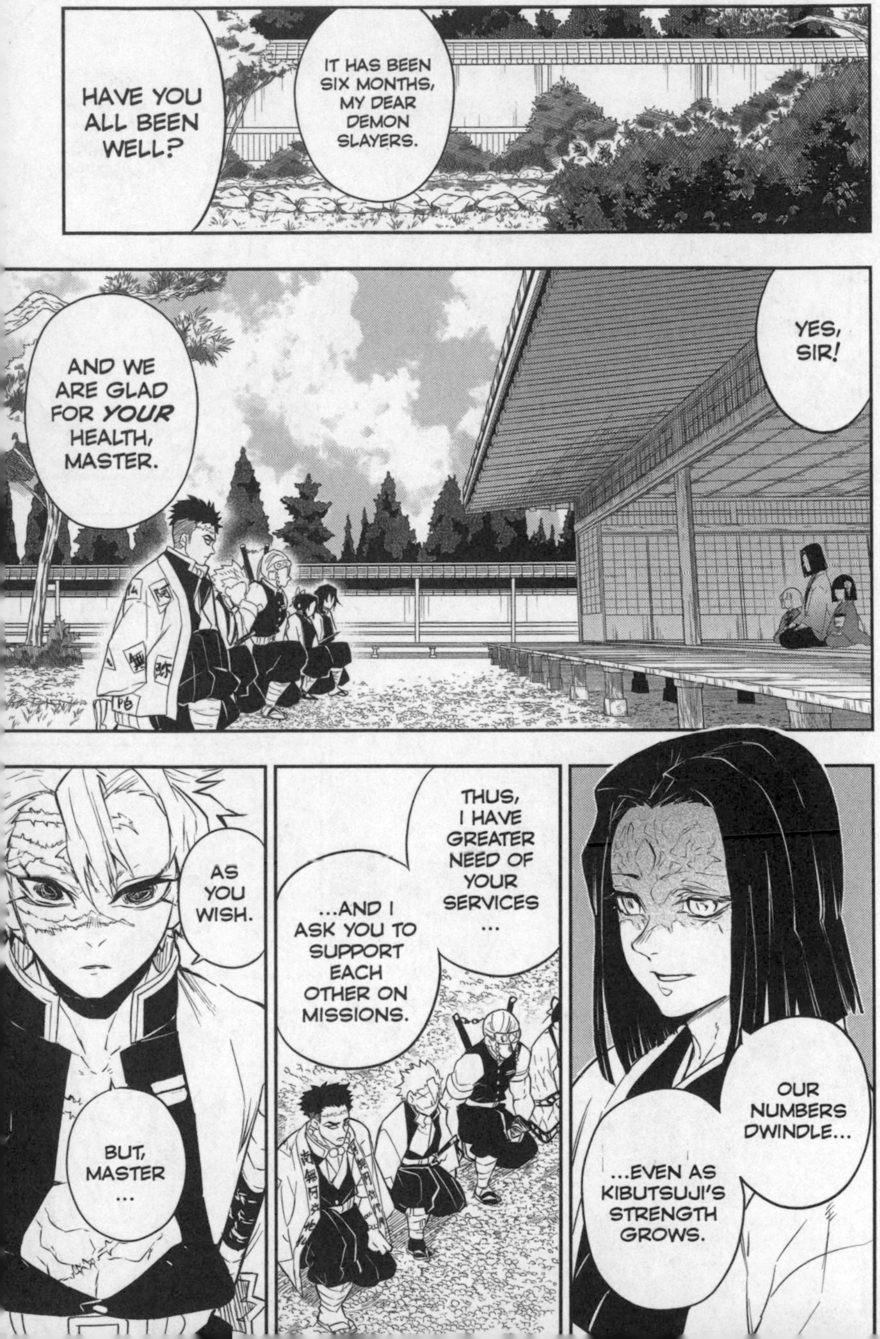
IT HAS BEEN SIX MONTHS, MY DEAR DEMON SLAYERS.
HAVE YOU ALL BEEN WELL?
YES, SIR!
AND WE ARE GLAD FOR *YOUR* HEALTH, MASTER.
OUR NUMBERS DWINDLE...
...EVEN AS KIBUTSUJI'S STRENGTH GROWS.
THUS, I HAVE GREATER NEED OF YOUR SERVICES ...
...AND I ASK YOU TO SUPPORT EACH OTHER ON MISSIONS.
AS YOU WISH.
BUT, MASTER ...

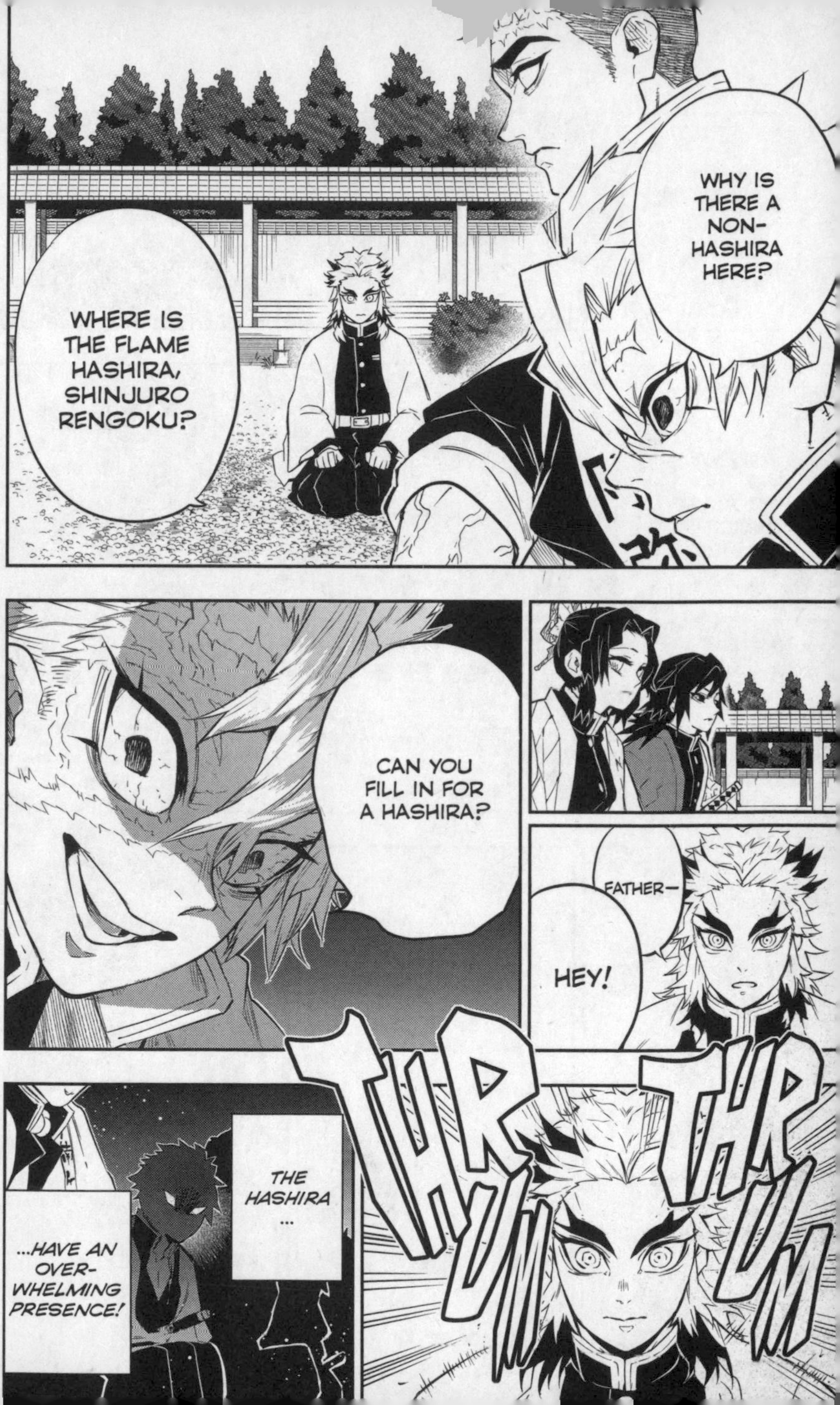
WHY IS THERE A NON-HASHIRA HERE?
WHERE IS THE FLAME HASHIRA, SHINJURO RENGOKU?
FATHER—
HEY!
CAN YOU FILL IN FOR A HASHIRA?
THRUM
THRUM
THE HASHIRA...
...HAVE AN OVERWHELMING PRESENCE!

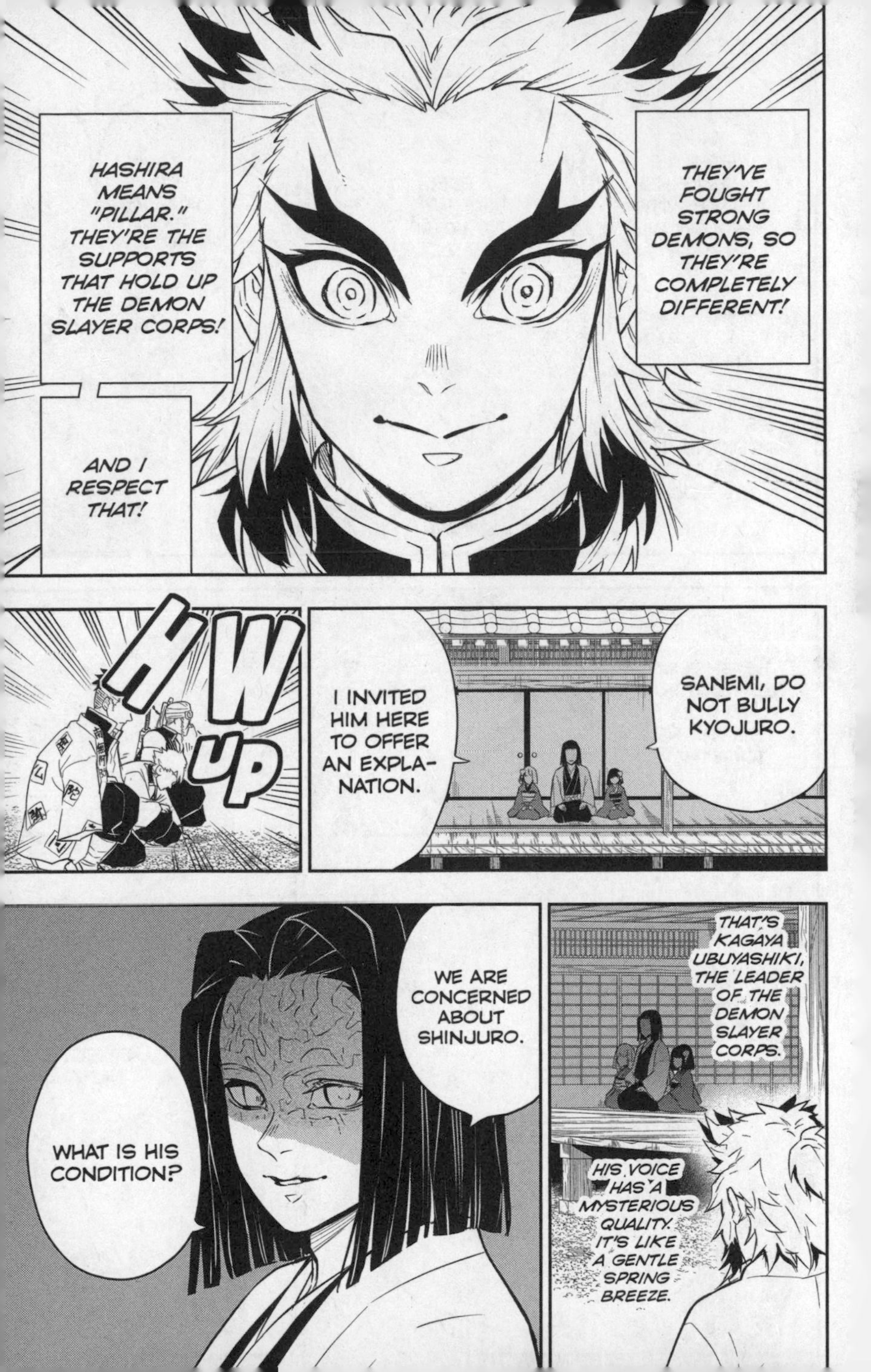
THEY'VE FOUGHT STRONG DEMONS, SO THEY'RE COMPLETELY DIFFERENT!
HASHIRA MEANS "PILLAR." THEY'RE THE SUPPORTS THAT HOLD UP THE DEMON SLAYER CORPS!
AND I RESPECT THAT!
SANEMI, DO NOT BULLY KYOJURO.
I INVITED HIM HERE TO OFFER AN EXPLA-NATION.
HWUP
THAT'S KAGAYA UBUYASHIKI, THE LEADER OF THE DEMON SLAYER CORPS.
HIS VOICE HAS A MYSTERIOUS QUALITY. IT'S LIKE A GENTLE SPRING BREEZE.
WE ARE CONCERNED ABOUT SHINJURO.
WHAT IS HIS CONDITION?

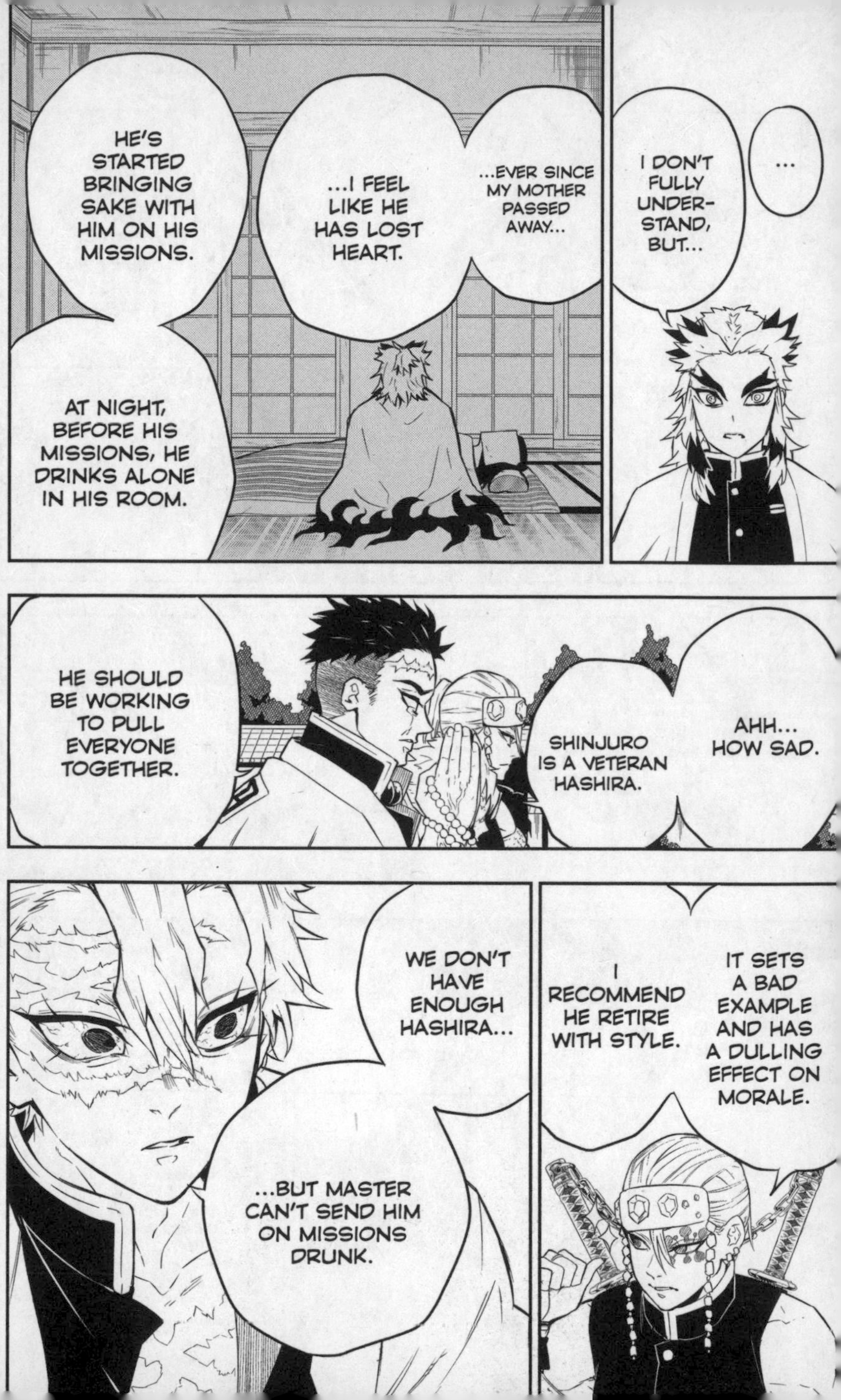
...
I DON'T FULLY UNDER-STAND, BUT...
...EVER SINCE MY MOTHER PASSED AWAY...
...I FEEL LIKE HE HAS LOST HEART.
HE'S STARTED BRINGING SAKE WITH HIM ON HIS MISSIONS.
AT NIGHT, BEFORE HIS MISSIONS, HE DRINKS ALONE IN HIS ROOM.
AHH... HOW SAD.
SHINJURO IS A VETERAN HASHIRA.
HE SHOULD BE WORKING TO PULL EVERYONE TOGETHER.
IT SETS A BAD EXAMPLE AND HAS A DULLING EFFECT ON MORALE.
I RECOMMEND HE RETIRE WITH STYLE.
WE DON'T HAVE ENOUGH HASHIRA...
...BUT MASTER CAN'T SEND HIM ON MISSIONS DRUNK.

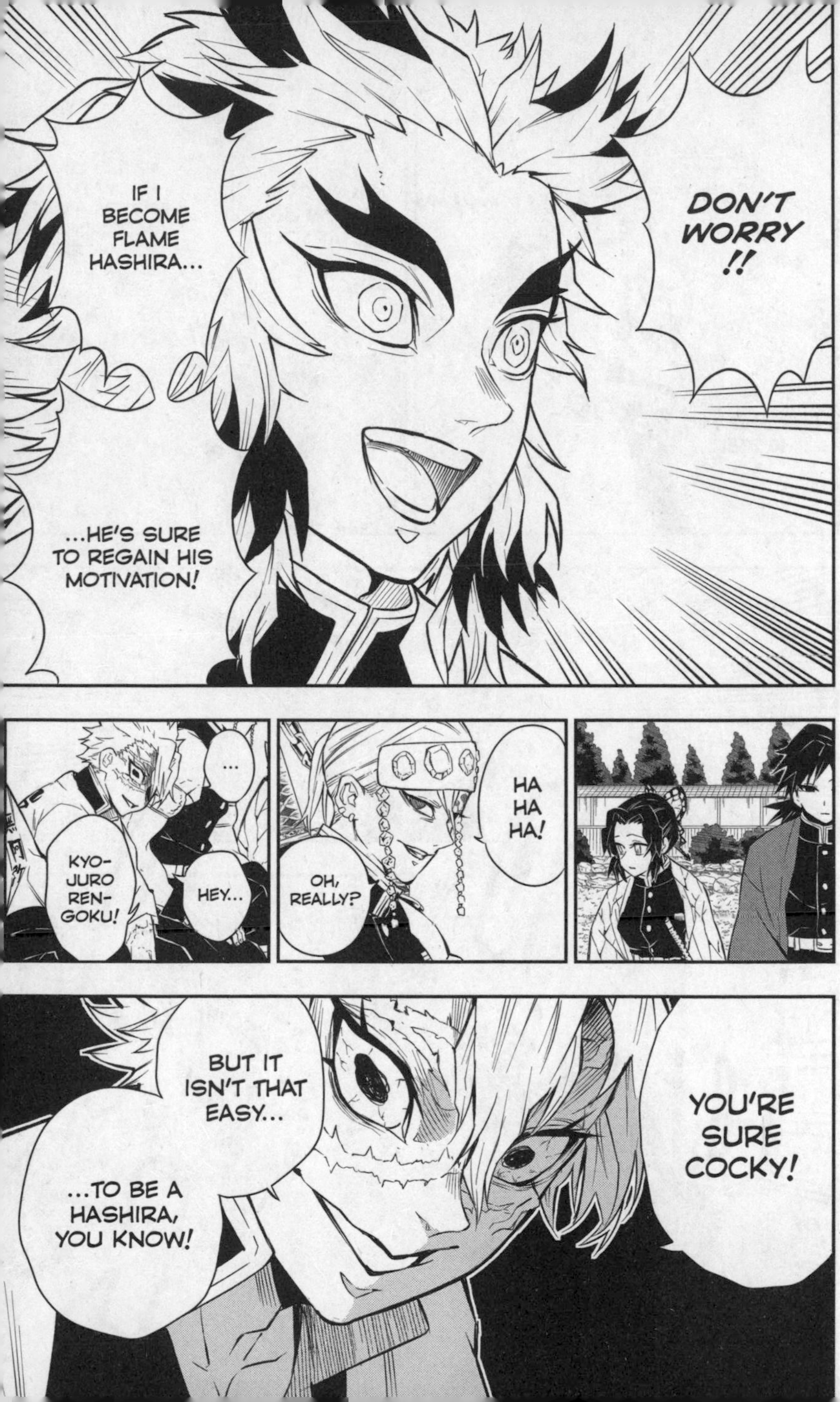
DON'T WORRY!!
IF I BECOME FLAME HASHIRA...
...HE'S SURE TO REGAIN HIS MOTIVATION!
HA HA HA!
OH, REALLY?
...
HEY...
KYO-JURO REN-GOKU!
YOU'RE SURE COCKY!
BUT IT ISN'T THAT EASY...
...TO BE A HASHIRA, YOU KNOW!

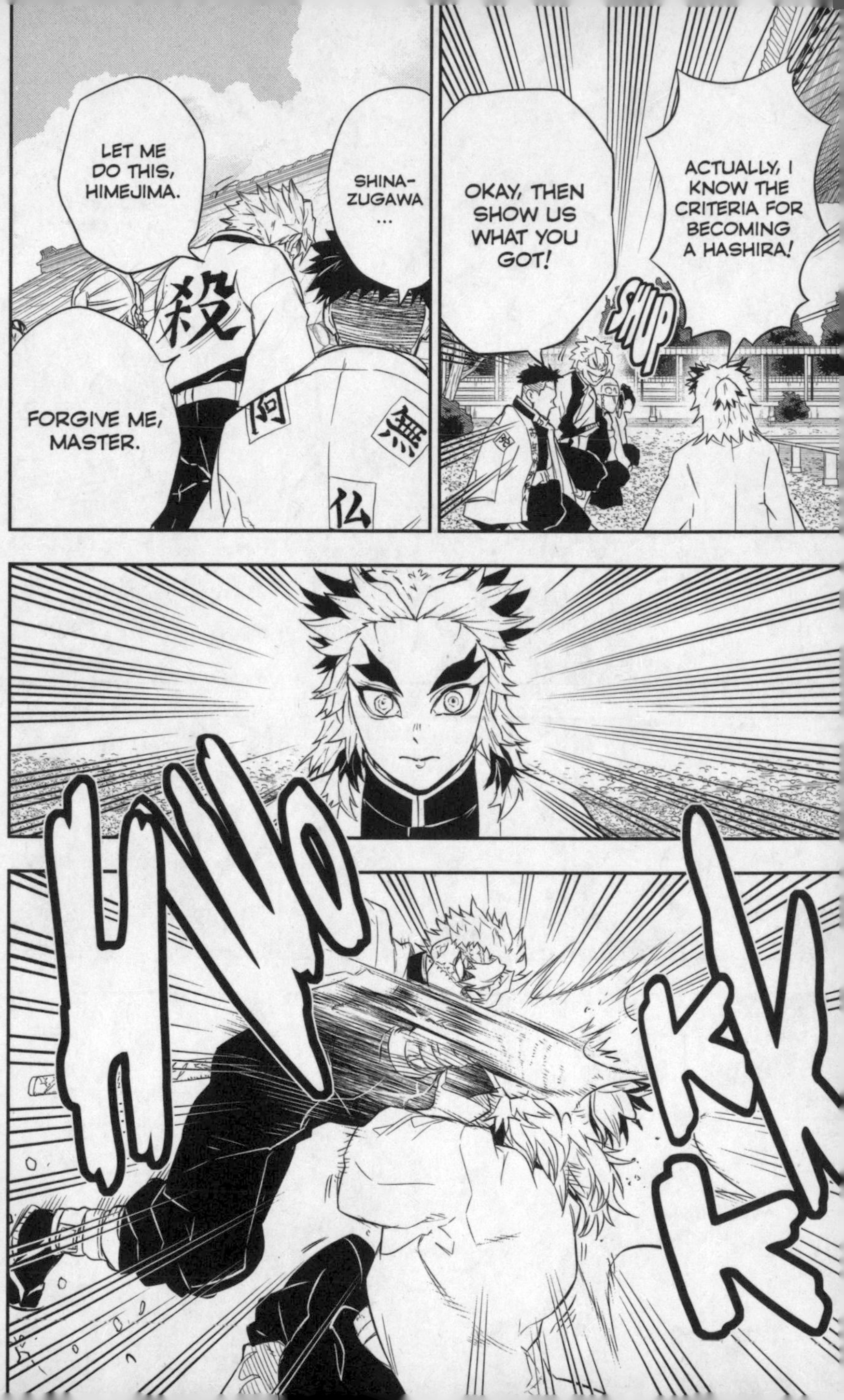
ACTUALLY, I KNOW THE CRITERIA FOR BECOMING A HASHIRA!
SHUP
OKAY, THEN SHOW US WHAT YOU GOT!
SHINA-ZUGAWA ...
LET ME DO THIS, HIMEJIMA.
FORGIVE ME, MASTER.

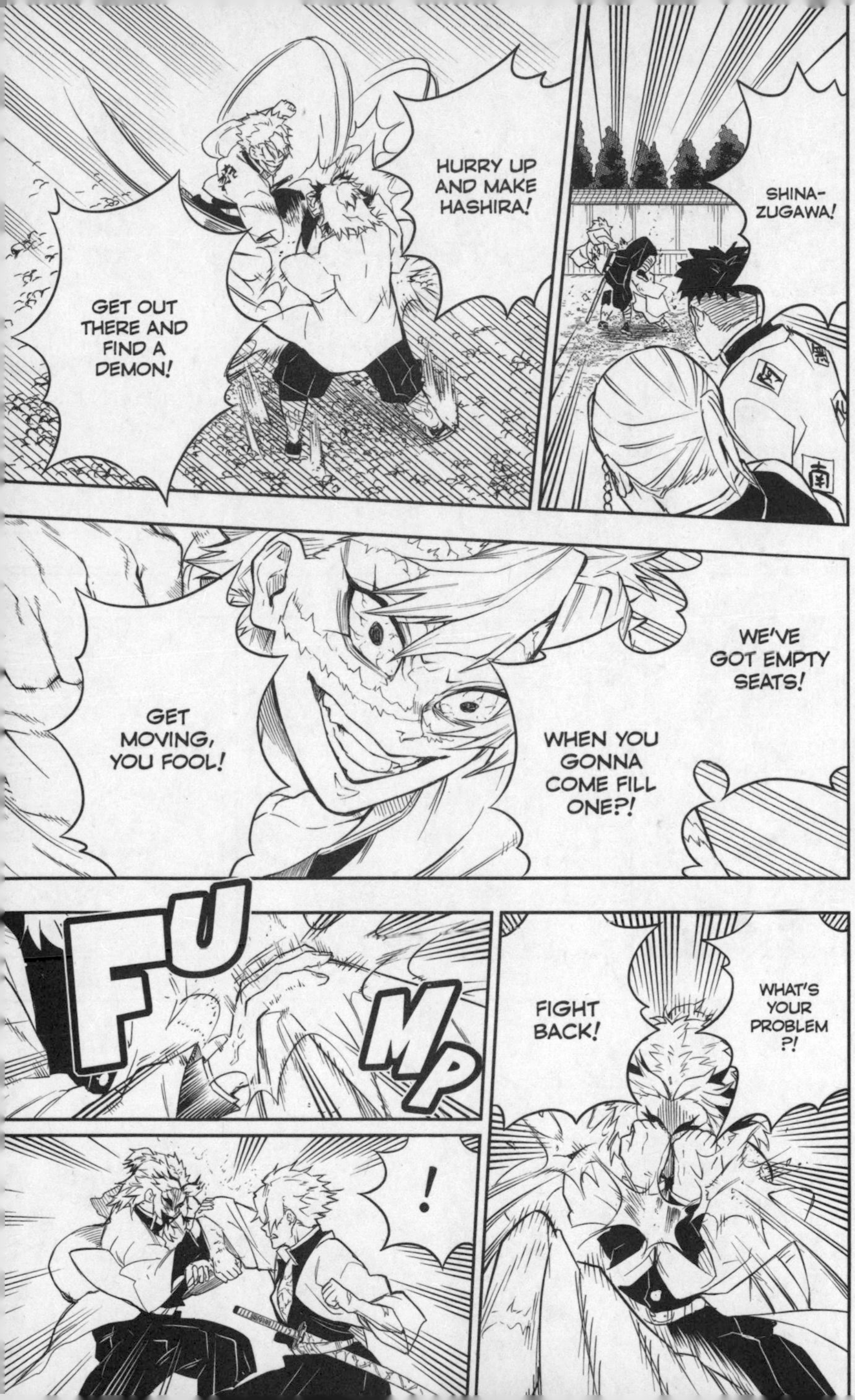
SHINA-
ZUGAWA!
HURRY UP AND MAKE HASHIRA!
GET OUT THERE AND FIND A DEMON!
WE'VE GOT EMPTY SEATS!
WHEN YOU GONNA COME FILL ONE?!
GET MOVING, YOU FOOL!
WHAT'S YOUR PROBLEM ?!
FIGHT BACK!
FUMP
!

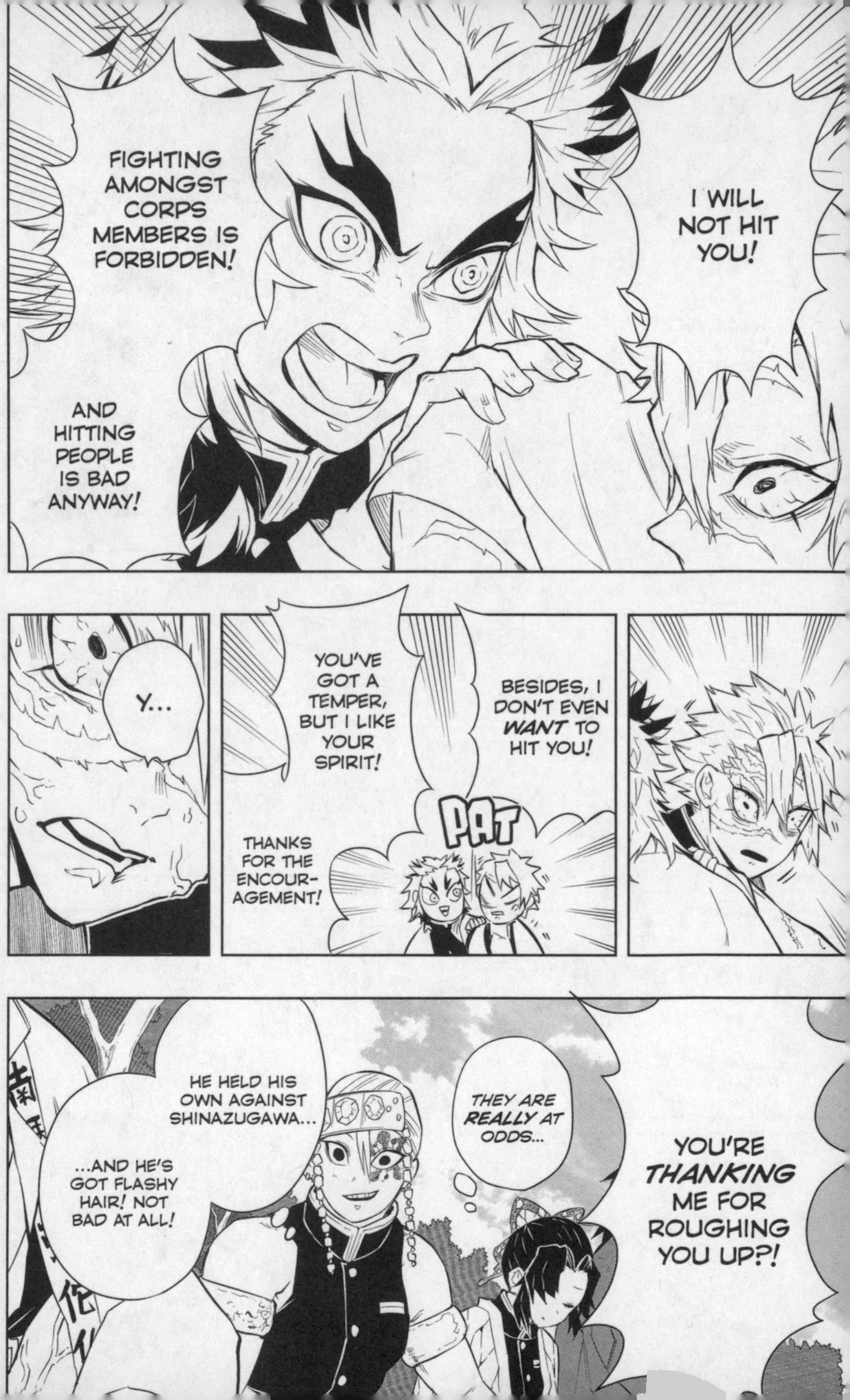
I WILL NOT HIT YOU!
FIGHTING AMONGST CORPS MEMBERS IS FORBIDDEN!
AND HITTING PEOPLE IS BAD ANYWAY!
BESIDES, I DON'T EVEN WANT TO HIT YOU!
YOU'VE GOT A TEMPER, BUT I LIKE YOUR SPIRIT!
PAT
THANKS FOR THE ENCOURAGEMENT!
Y...
YOU'RE THANKING ME FOR ROUGHING YOU UP?!
THEY ARE REALLY AT ODDS...
HE HELD HIS OWN AGAINST SHINAZUGAWA...
...AND HE'S GOT FLASHY HAIR! NOT BAD AT ALL!

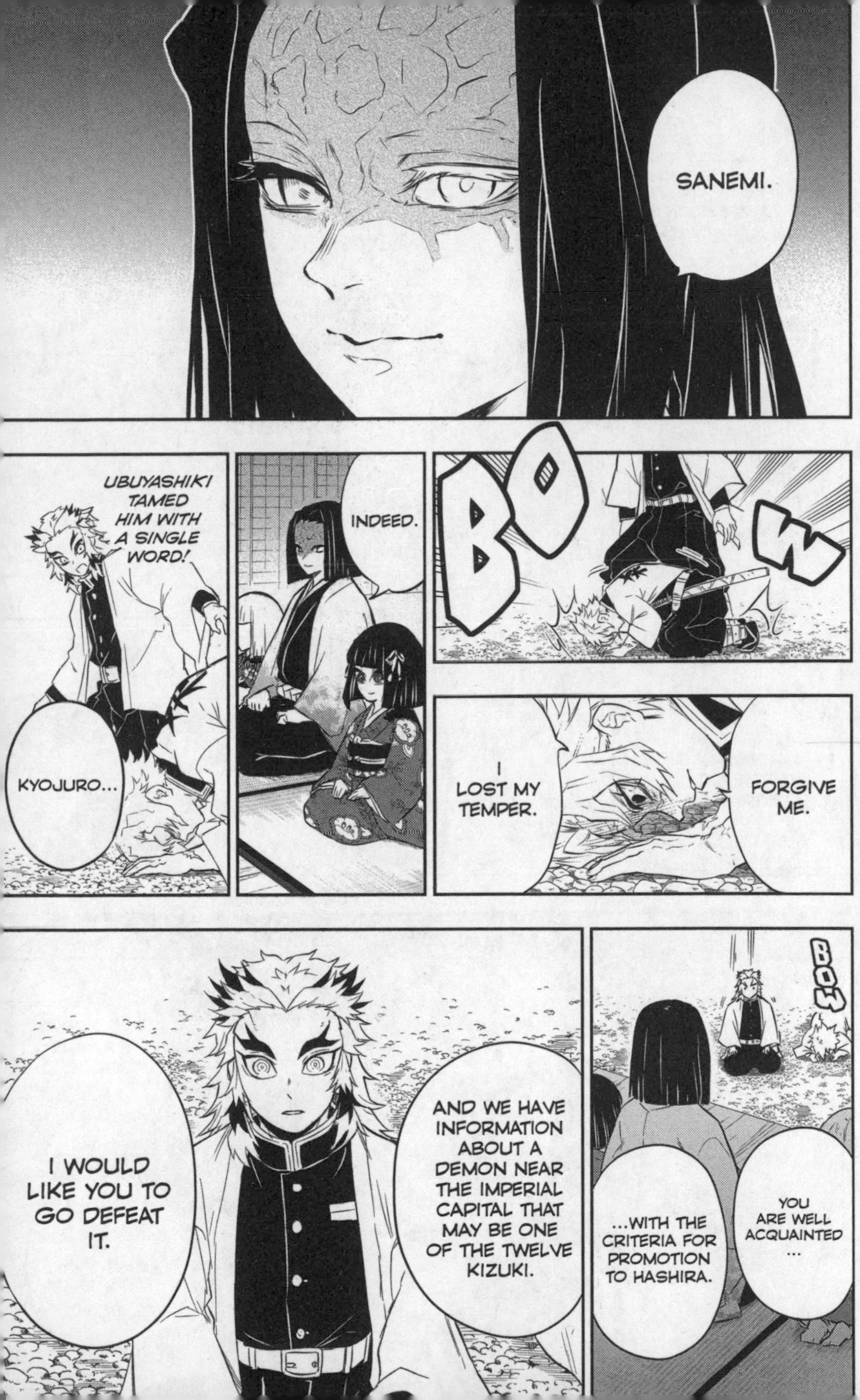
SANEMI.
BOW
FORGIVE ME.
I LOST MY TEMPER.
INDEED.
UBUYASHIKI TAMED HIM WITH A SINGLE WORD!
KYOJURO...
BOW
YOU ARE WELL ACQUAINTED ...
...WITH THE CRITERIA FOR PROMOTION TO HASHIRA.
AND WE HAVE INFORMATION ABOUT A DEMON NEAR THE IMPERIAL CAPITAL THAT MAY BE ONE OF THE TWELVE KIZUKI.
I WOULD LIKE YOU TO GO DEFEAT IT.

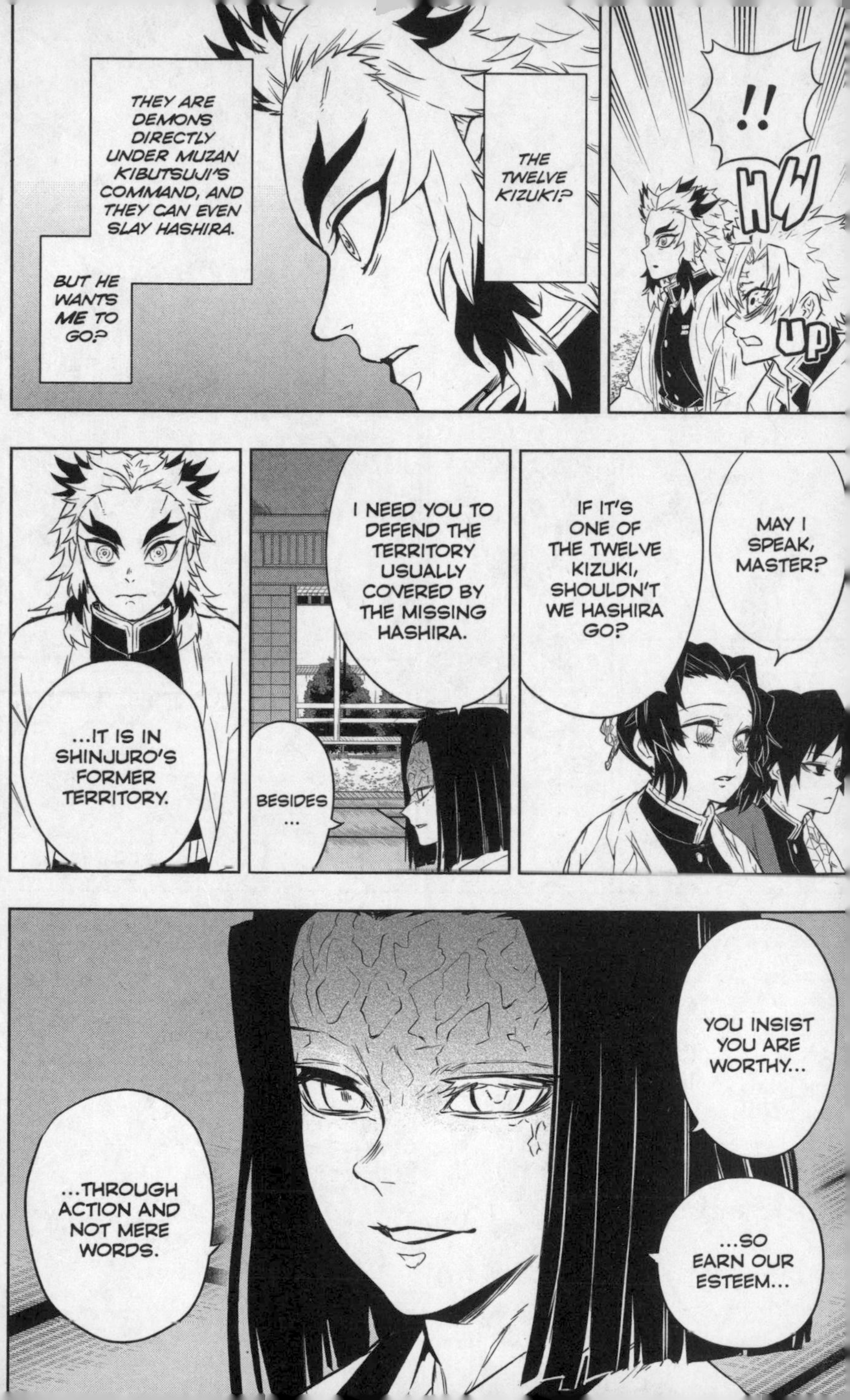
!!
HW
UP
THE TWELVE KIZUKI?
THEY ARE DEMONS DIRECTLY UNDER MUZAN KIBUTSUJI'S COMMAND, AND THEY CAN EVEN SLAY HASHIRA.
BUT HE WANTS ME TO GO?
MAY I SPEAK, MASTER?
IF IT'S ONE OF THE TWELVE KIZUKI, SHOULDN'T WE HASHIRA GO?
I NEED YOU TO DEFEND THE TERRITORY USUALLY COVERED BY THE MISSING HASHIRA.
BESIDES...
...IT IS IN SHINJURO'S FORMER TERRITORY.
YOU INSIST YOU ARE WORTHY...
...SO EARN OUR ESTEEM...
...THROUGH ACTION AND NOT MERE WORDS.

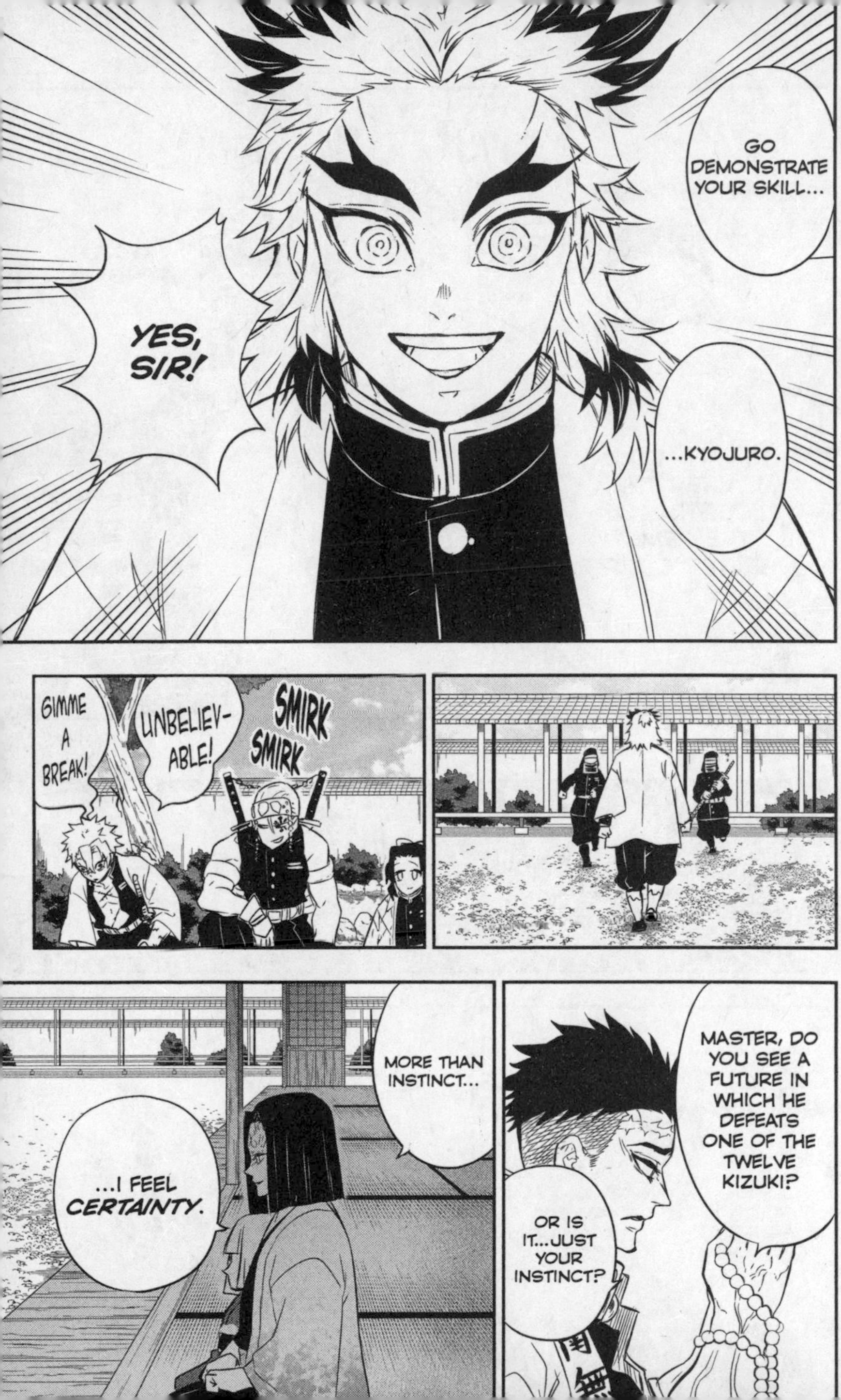
GO DEMONSTRATE YOUR SKILL...
...KYOJURO.
YES, SIR!
SMIRK SMIRK
UNBELIEV-ABLE!
GIMME A BREAK!
MASTER, DO YOU SEE A FUTURE IN WHICH HE DEFEATS ONE OF THE TWELVE KIZUKI?
OR IS IT...JUST YOUR INSTINCT?
MORE THAN INSTINCT...
...I FEEL CERTAINTY.

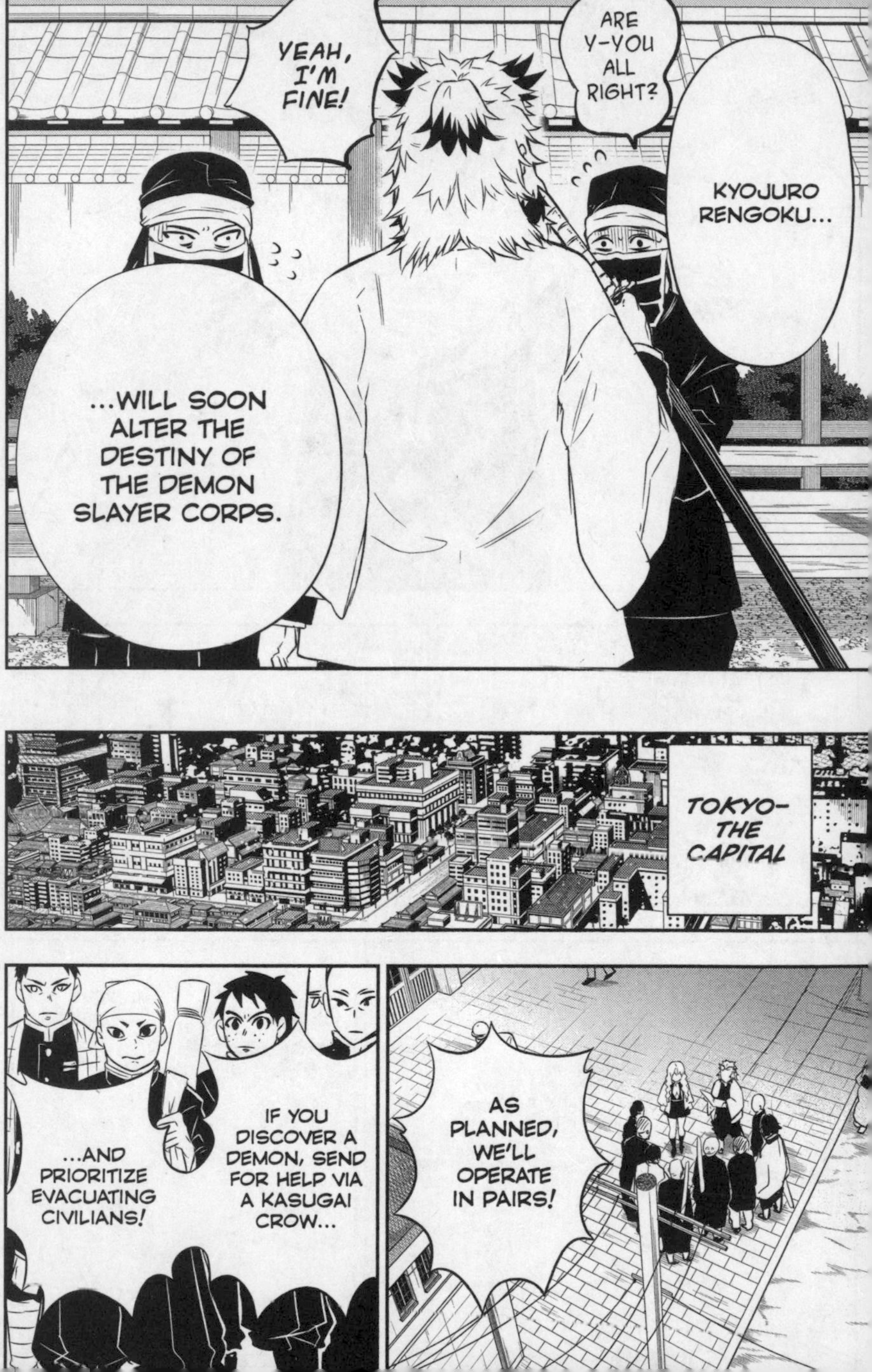
ARE Y-YOU ALL RIGHT?
YEAH, I'M FINE!
KYOJURO RENGOKU...
...WILL SOON ALTER THE DESTINY OF THE DEMON SLAYER CORPS.
TOKYO—THE CAPITAL
AS PLANNED, WE'LL OPERATE IN PAIRS!
IF YOU DISCOVER A DEMON, SEND FOR HELP VIA A KASUGAI CROW...
...AND PRIORITIZE EVACUATING CIVILIANS!

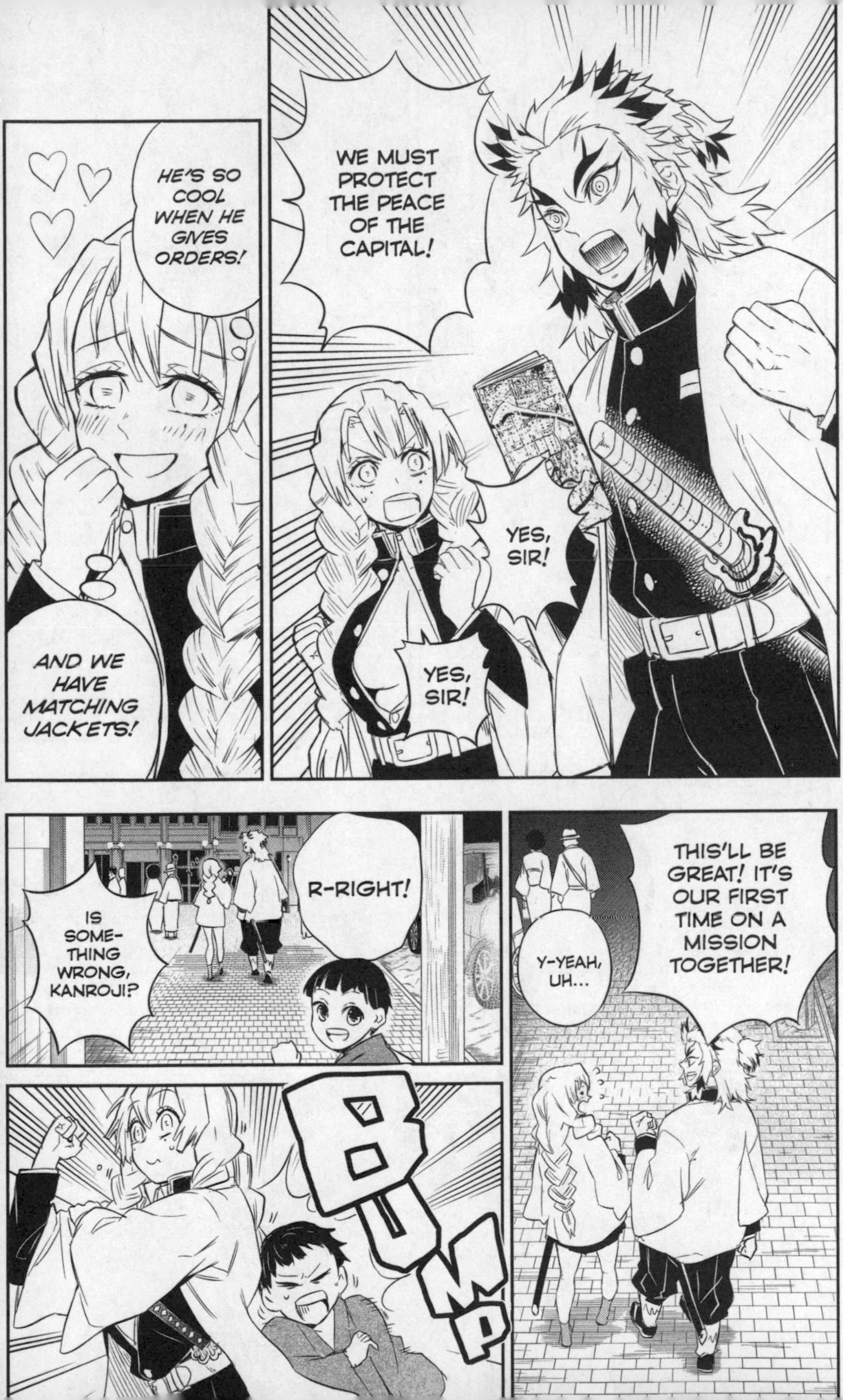
WE MUST PROTECT THE PEACE OF THE CAPITAL!
YES, SIR!
YES, SIR!
HE'S SO COOL WHEN HE GIVES ORDERS!
AND WE HAVE MATCHING JACKETS!
THIS'LL BE GREAT! IT'S OUR FIRST TIME ON A MISSION TOGETHER!
Y-YEAH, UH...
R-RIGHT!
IS SOMETHING WRONG, KANROJI?
BUMP

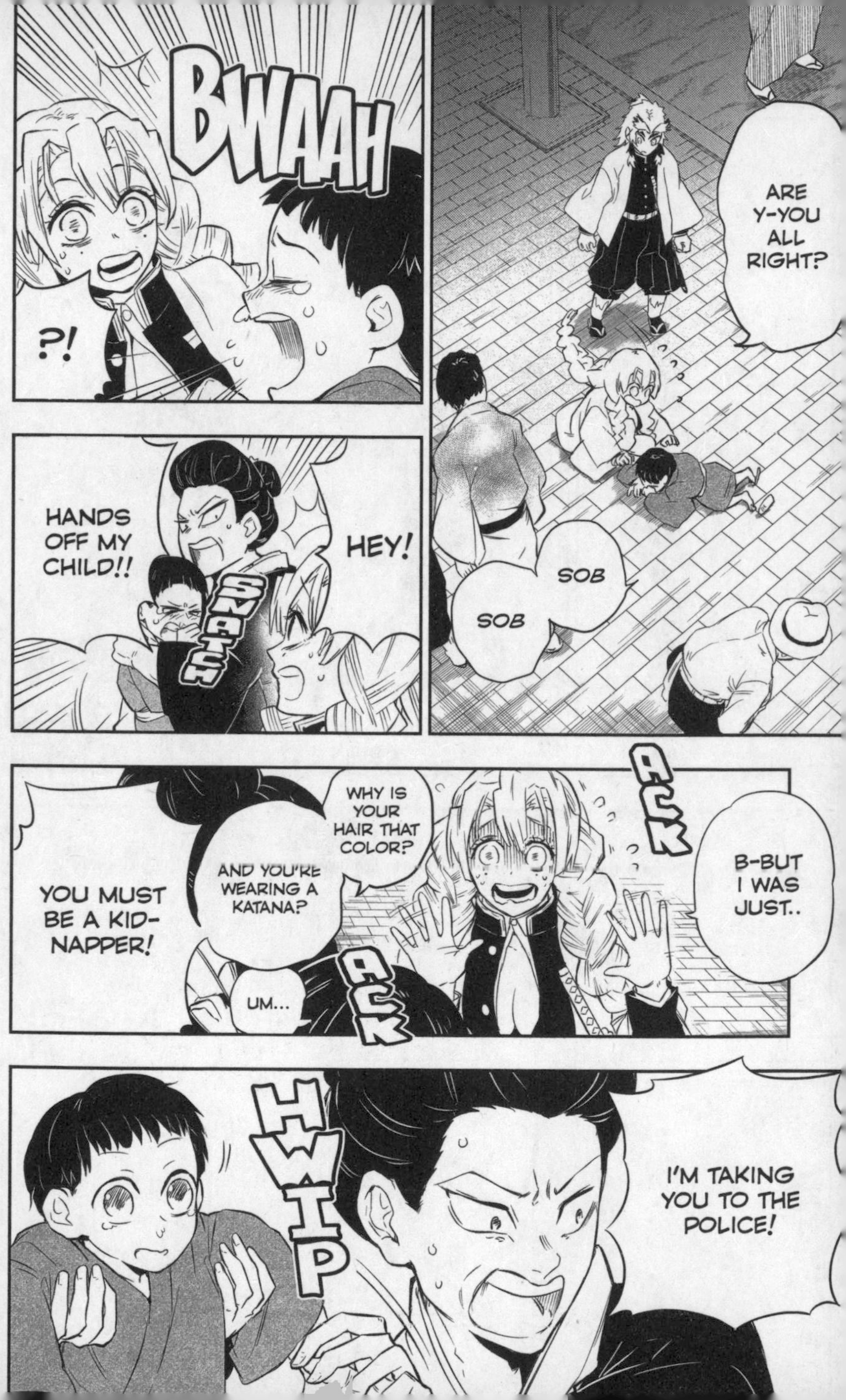
ARE Y-YOU ALL RIGHT?
SOB
SOB
BWAAH
?!
HEY!
SNATCH
HANDS OFF MY CHILD!!
ACK
B-BUT I WAS JUST..
WHY IS YOUR HAIR THAT COLOR?
AND YOU'RE WEARING A KATANA?
ACK
UM...
YOU MUST BE A KID-NAPPER!
I'M TAKING YOU TO THE POLICE!
HWIP

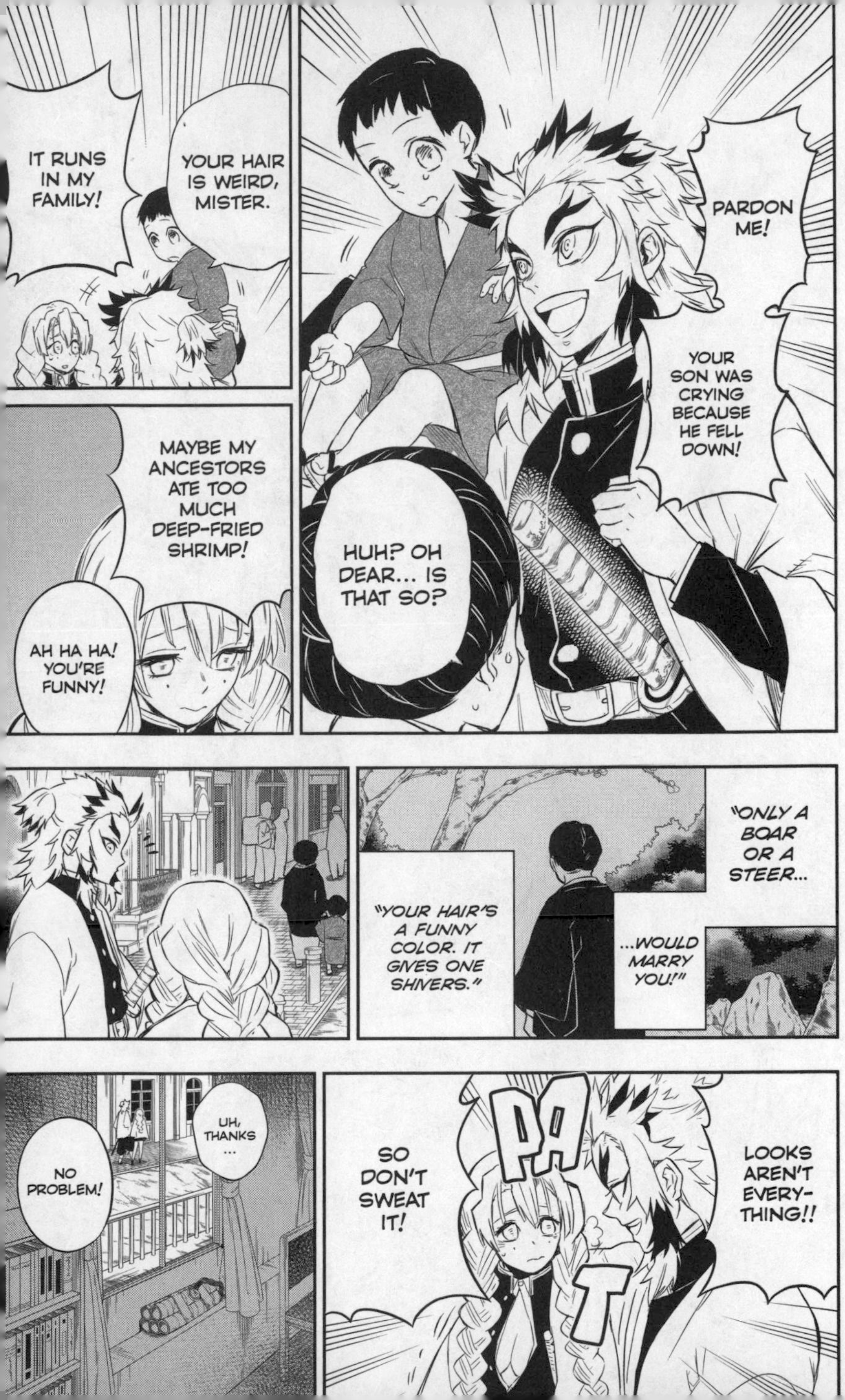
PARDON ME!
YOUR SON WAS CRYING BECAUSE HE FELL DOWN!
HUH? OH DEAR... IS THAT SO?
YOUR HAIR IS WEIRD, MISTER.
IT RUNS IN MY FAMILY!
MAYBE MY ANCESTORS ATE TOO MUCH DEEP-FRIED SHRIMP!
AH HA HA! YOU'RE FUNNY!
"ONLY A BOAR OR A STEER...
...WOULD MARRY YOU!"
"YOUR HAIR'S A FUNNY COLOR. IT GIVES ONE SHIVERS."
LOOKS AREN'T EVERY-THING!!
PAT
SO DON'T SWEAT IT!
UH, THANKS ...
NO PROBLEM!

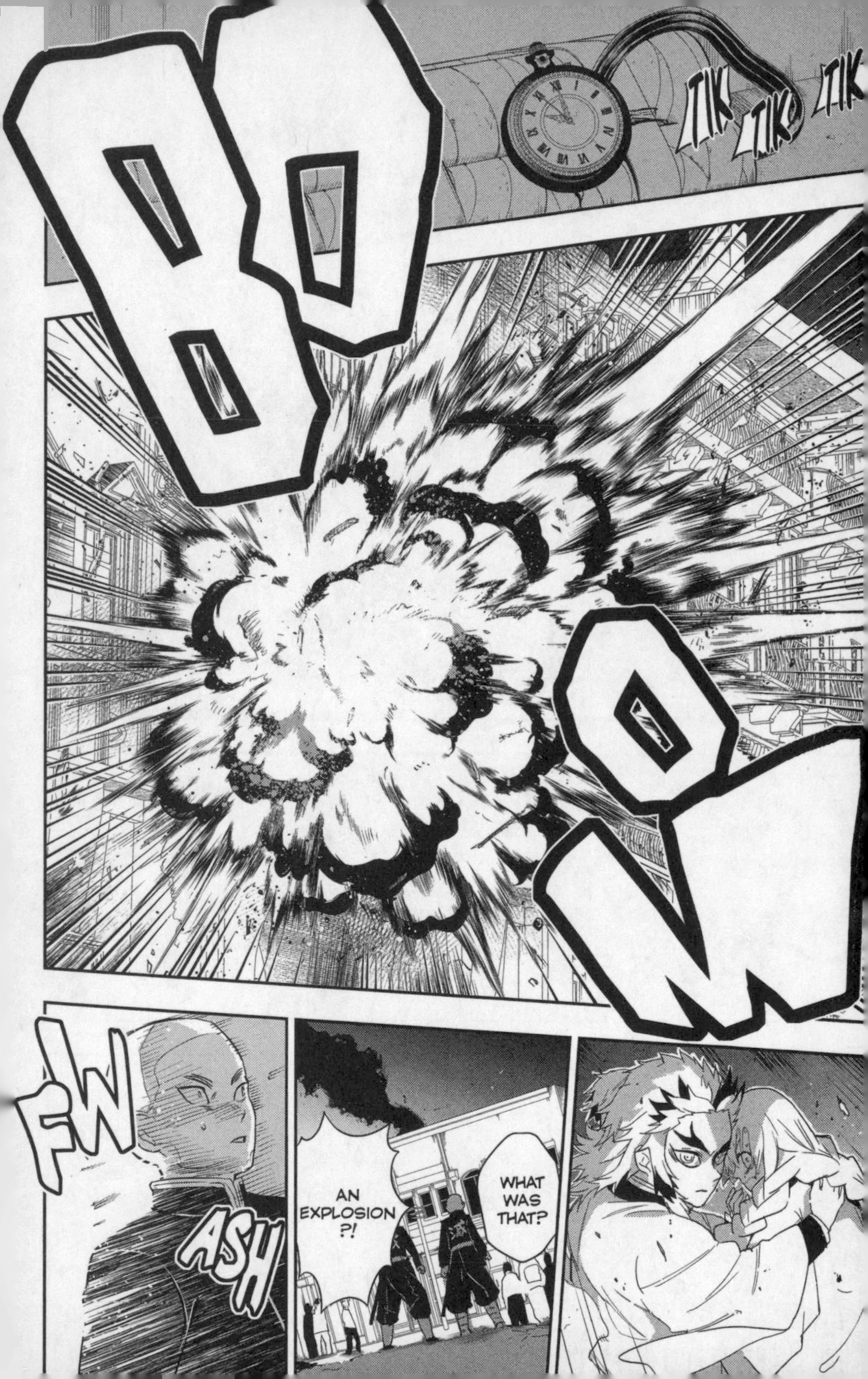
TIK
TIK
TIK
BOOM
WHAT WAS THAT?
AN EXPLOSION ?!
FWASH

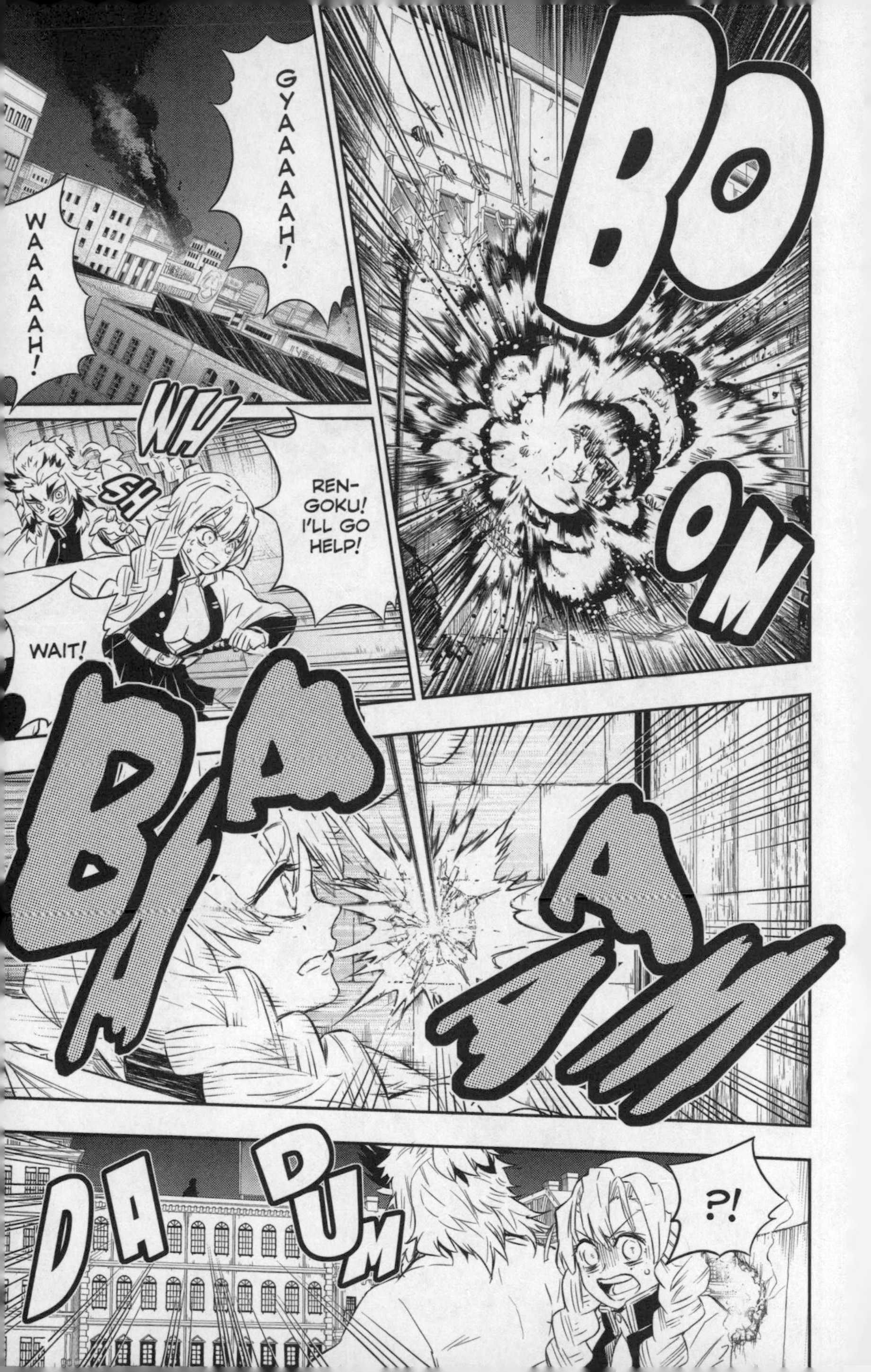
BOOM
GYAAAAAAH!
WAAAAAAH!
WHSH
REN-GOKU! I'LL GO HELP!
WAIT!
BAAM
?!
DADUM

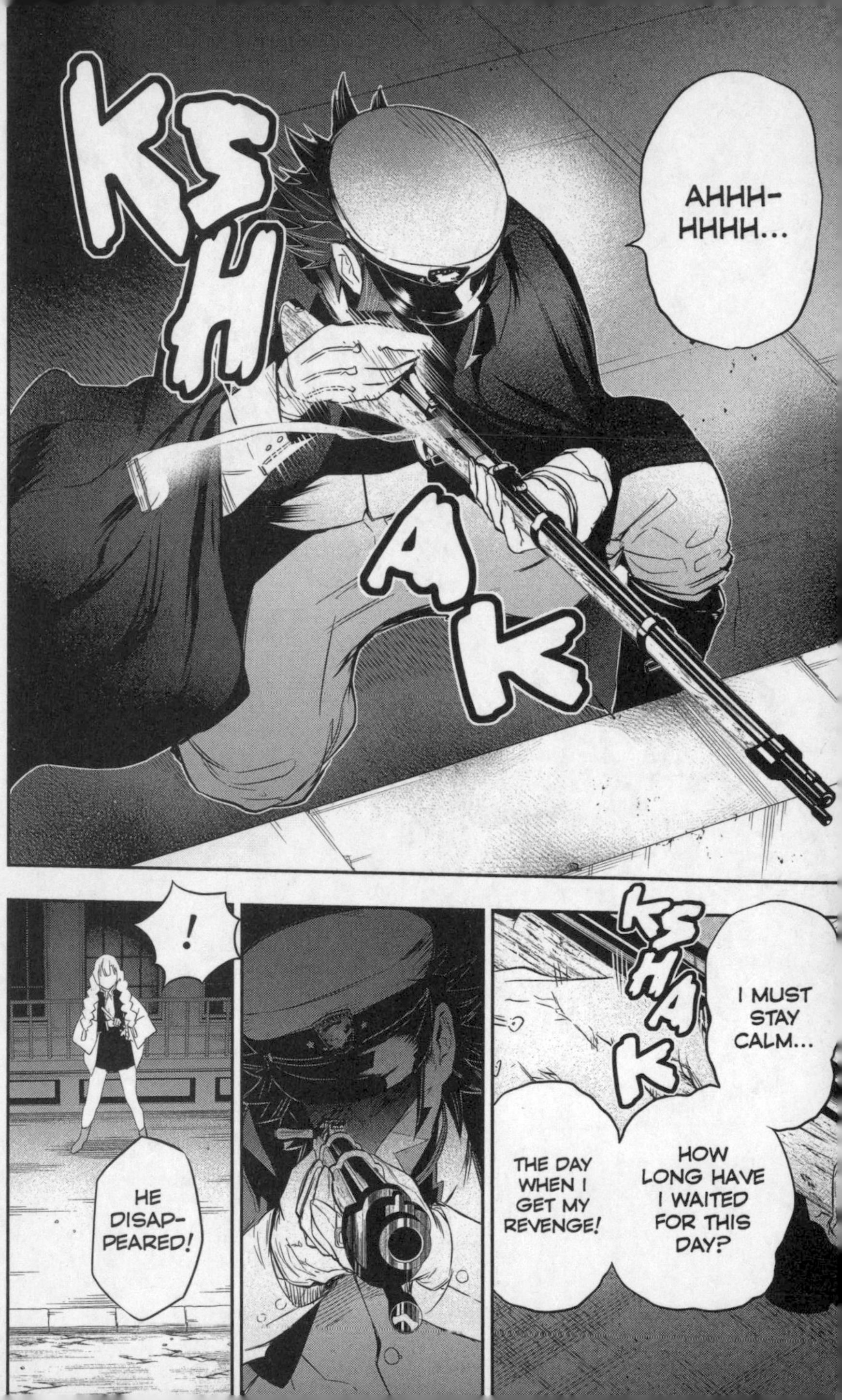
AHHH-HHHH...
KSHAK
I MUST STAY CALM...
KSHAK
HOW LONG HAVE I WAITED FOR THIS DAY?
THE DAY WHEN I GET MY REVENGE!
!
HE DISAPPEARED!

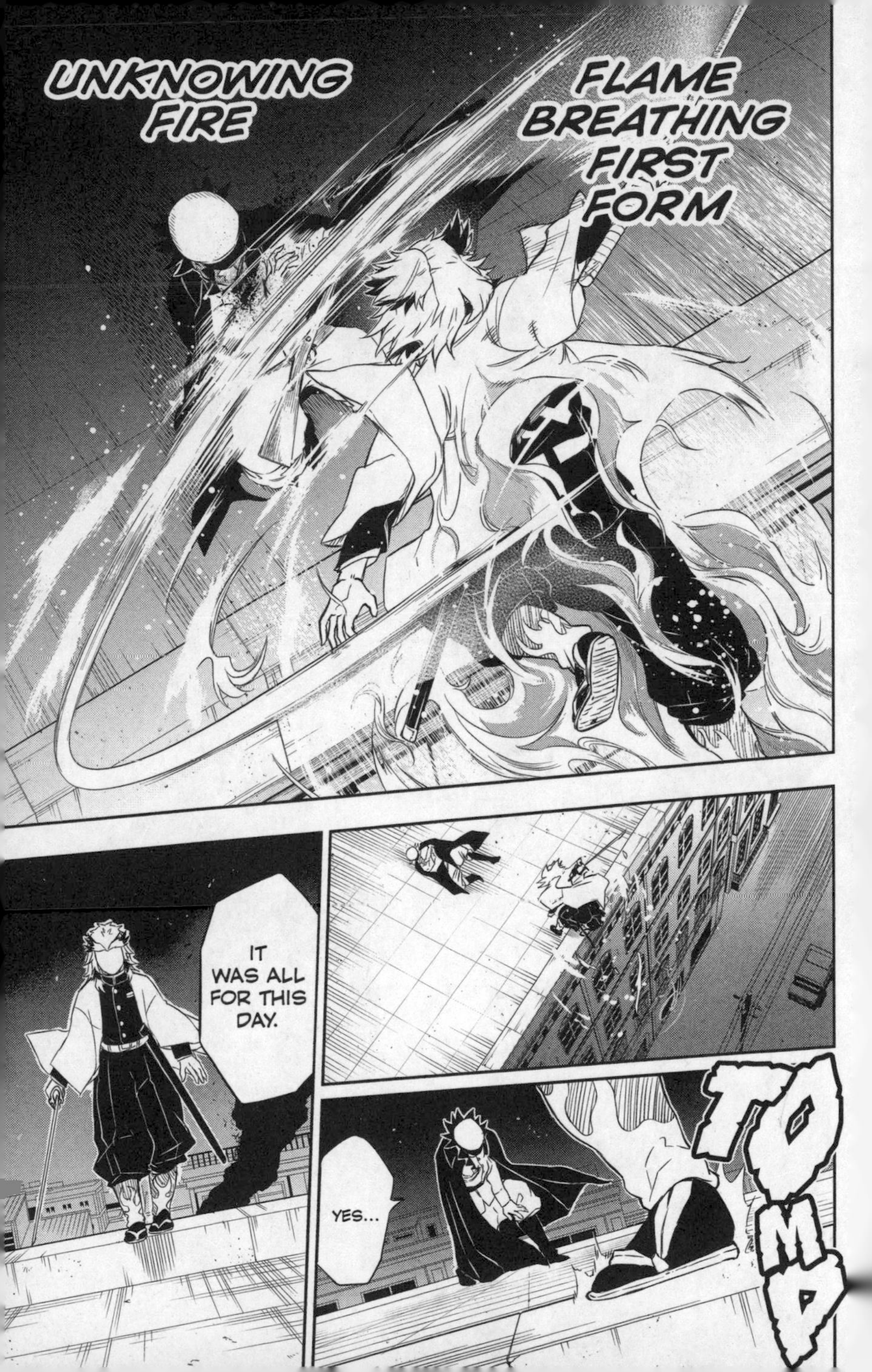
FLAME BREATHING FIRST FORM
UNKNOWING FIRE
YES...
TOMP
IT WAS ALL FOR THIS DAY.

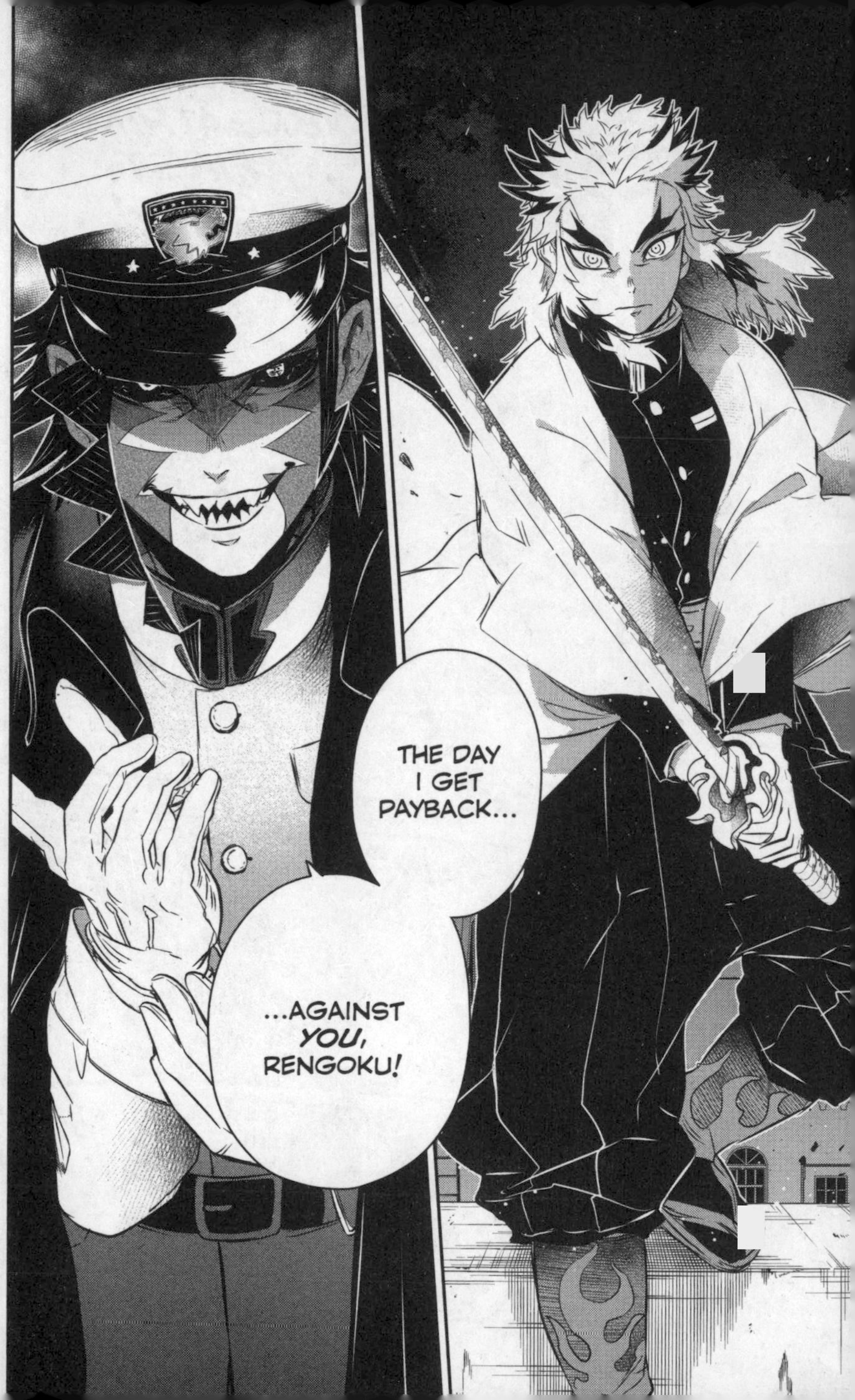
THE DAY I GET PAYBACK...
...AGAINST *YOU*, RENGOKU!

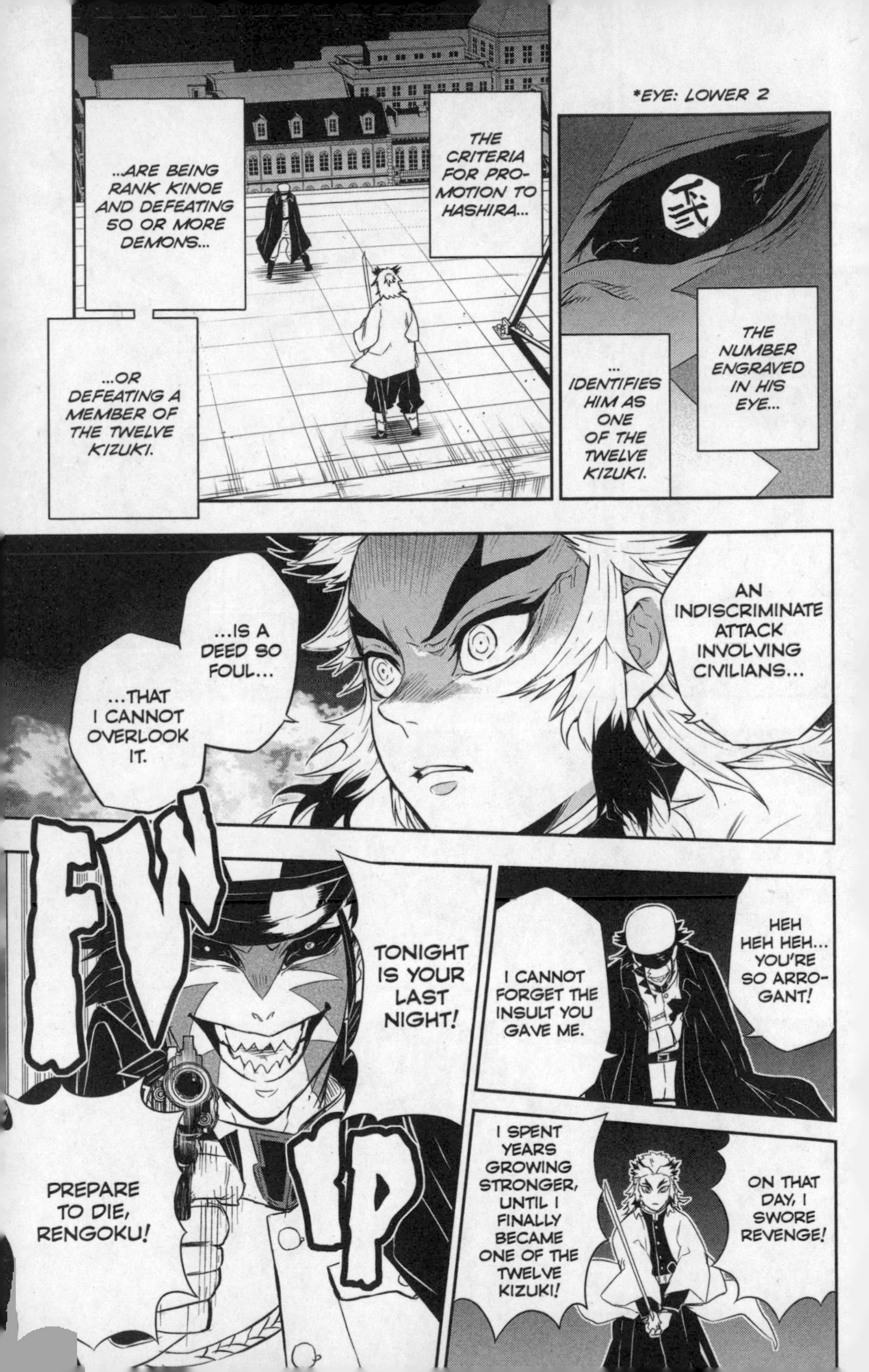
*EYE: LOWER 2
下弐
THE NUMBER ENGRAVED IN HIS EYE...
...IDENTIFIES HIM AS ONE OF THE TWELVE KIZUKI.
THE CRITERIA FOR PROMOTION TO HASHIRA...
...ARE BEING RANK KINOE AND DEFEATING 50 OR MORE DEMONS...
...OR DEFEATING A MEMBER OF THE TWELVE KIZUKI.
AN INDISCRIMINATE ATTACK INVOLVING CIVILIANS...
...IS A DEED SO FOUL...
...THAT I CANNOT OVERLOOK IT.
HEH HEH HEH... YOU'RE SO ARROGANT!
I CANNOT FORGET THE INSULT YOU GAVE ME.
ON THAT DAY, I SWORE REVENGE!
I SPENT YEARS GROWING STRONGER, UNTIL I FINALLY BECAME ONE OF THE TWELVE KIZUKI!
TONIGHT IS YOUR LAST NIGHT!
PREPARE TO DIE, RENGOKU!

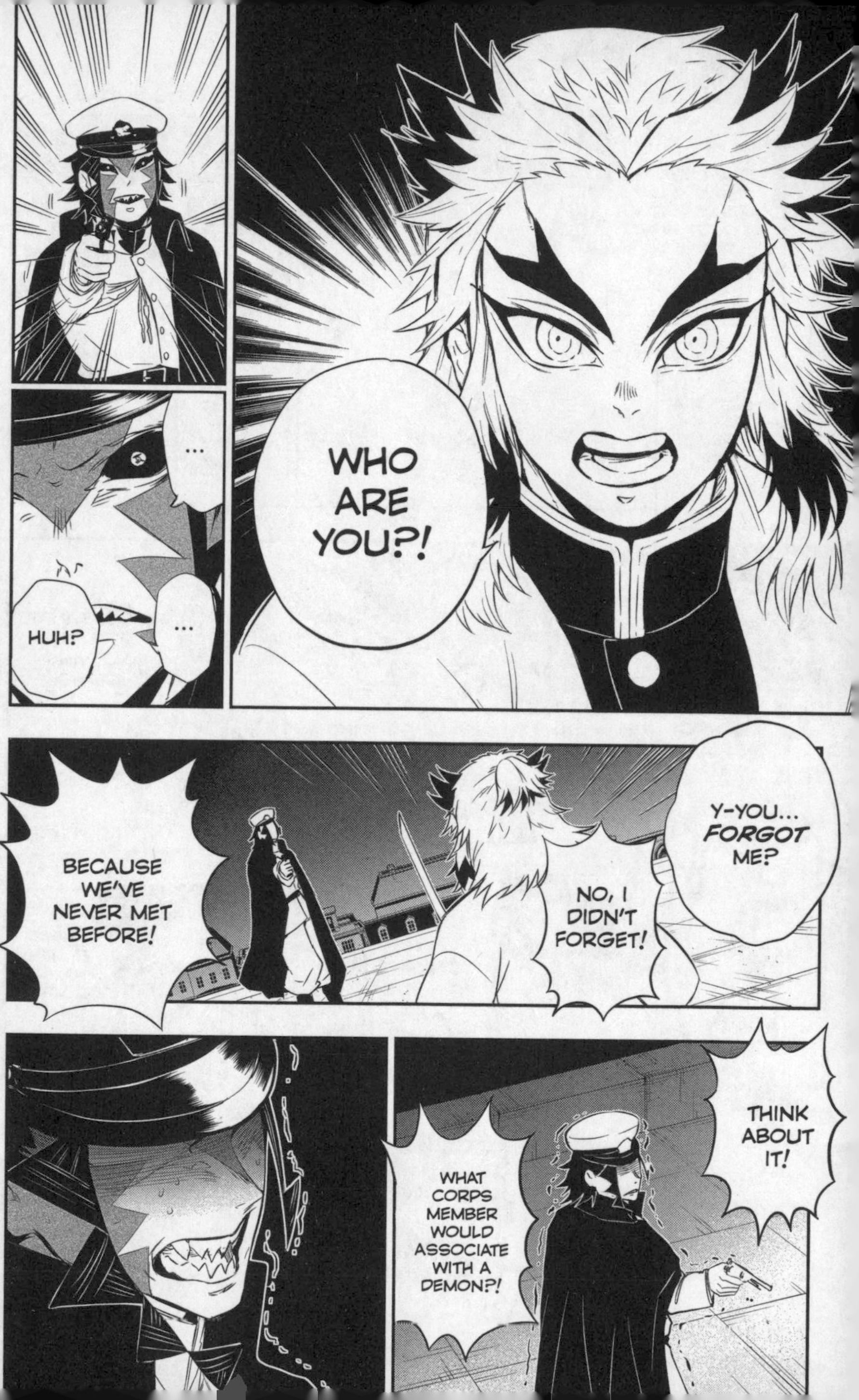
WHO ARE YOU?!
...
...
HUH?
Y-YOU... *FORGOT* ME?
NO, I DIDN'T FORGET!
BECAUSE WE'VE NEVER MET BEFORE!
THINK ABOUT IT!
WHAT CORPS MEMBER WOULD ASSOCIATE WITH A DEMON?!

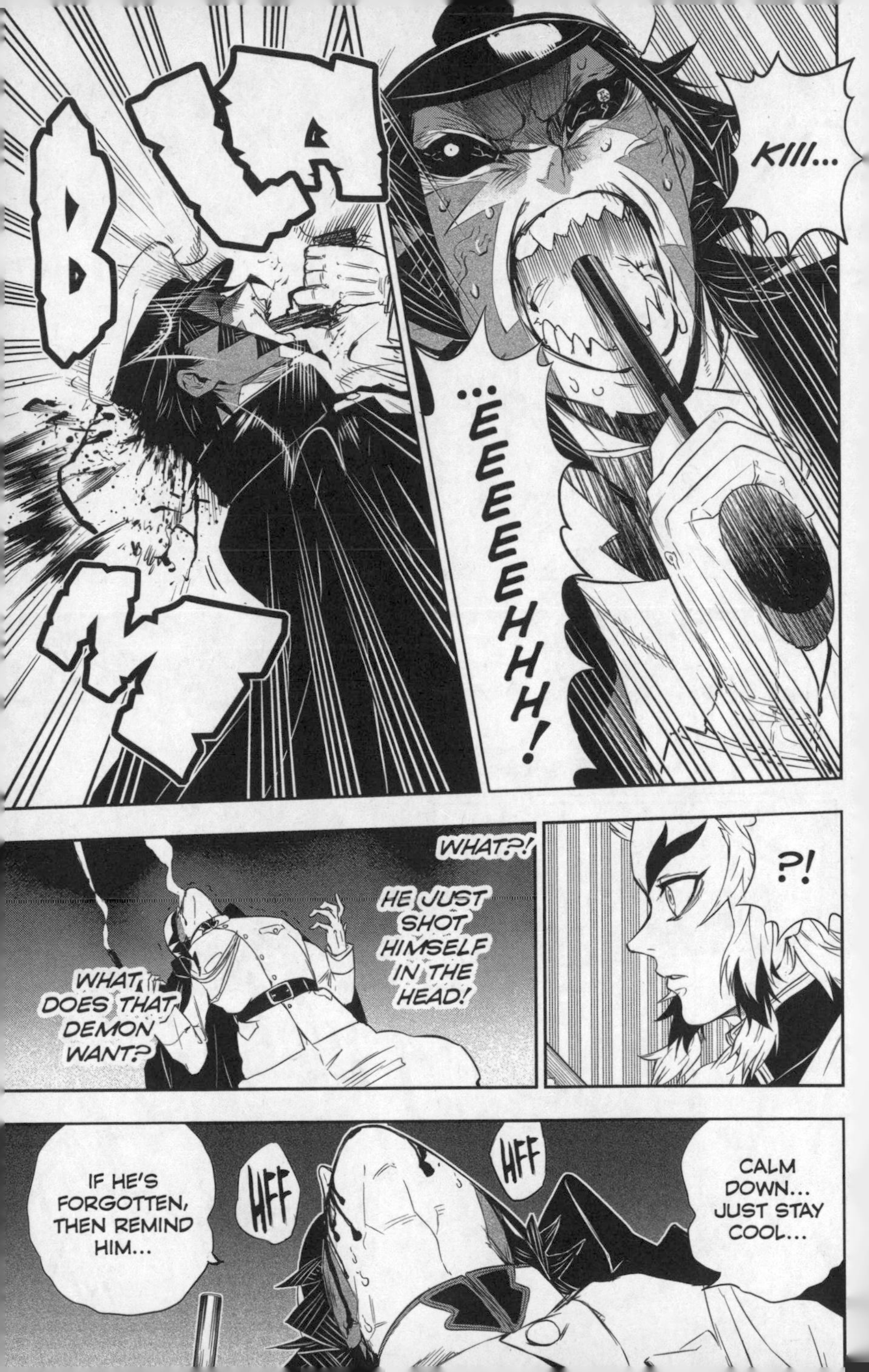
KIII...
...EEEEEEHHH!
BLAM
?!
WHAT?!
HE JUST SHOT HIMSELF IN THE HEAD!
WHAT DOES THAT DEMON WANT?
CALM DOWN... JUST STAY COOL...
HFF
HFF
IF HE'S FORGOTTEN, THEN REMIND HIM...

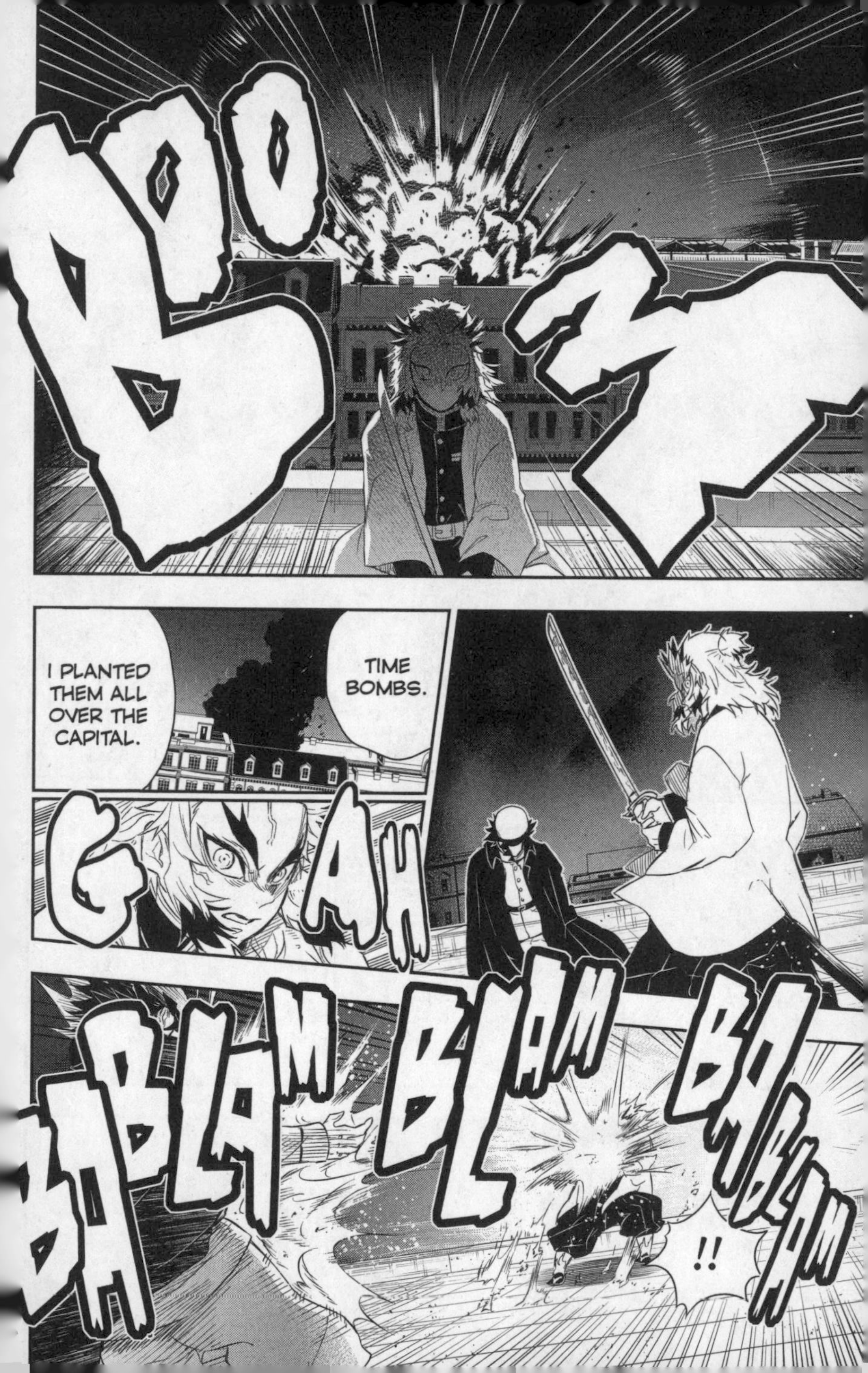
TIME BOMBS.
I PLANTED THEM ALL OVER THE CAPITAL.
GAH
B-BLAM
BLAM
BA-BLAM
!!

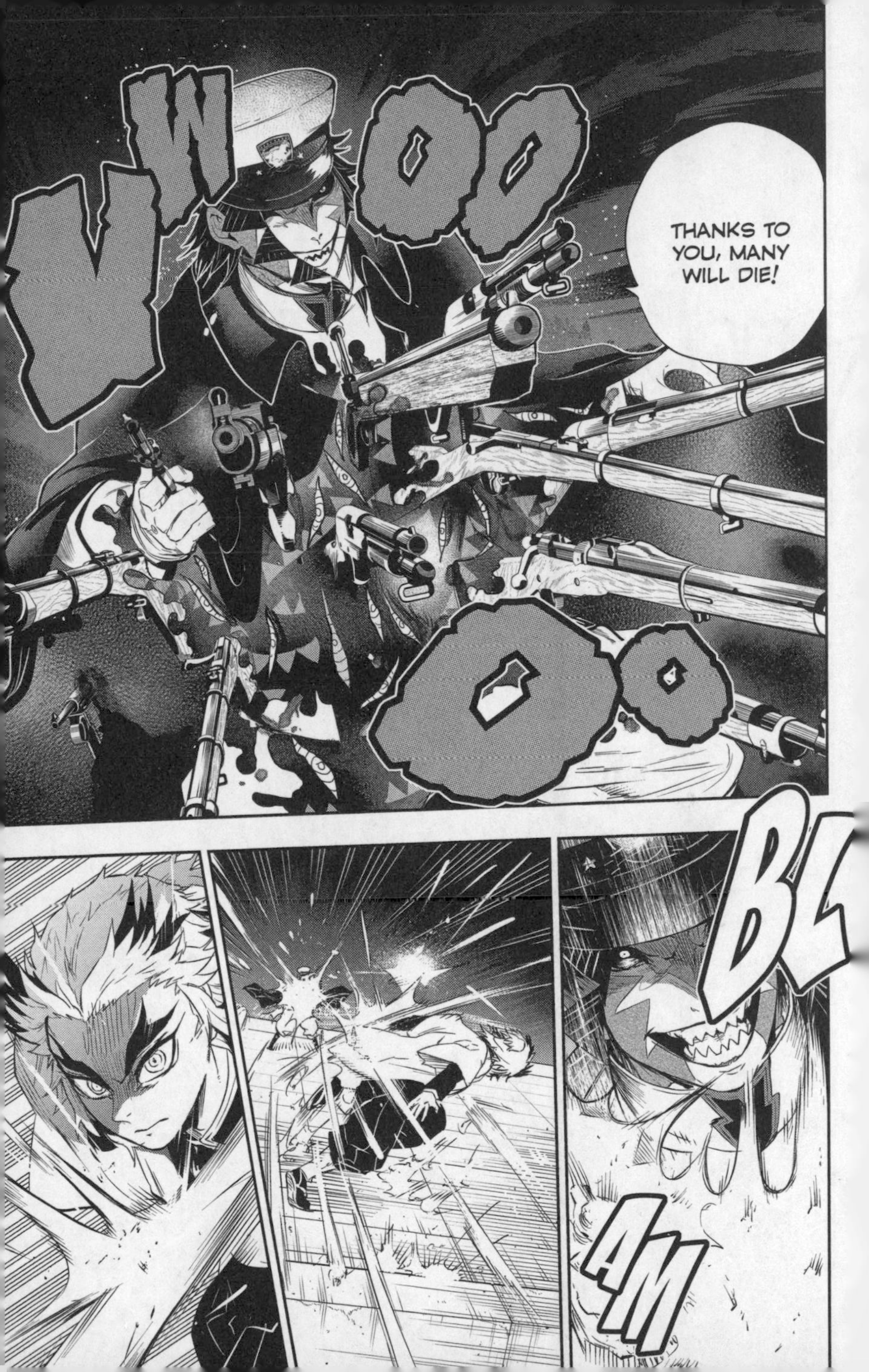
VWOOOO
THANKS TO YOU, MANY WILL DIE!
BLAM

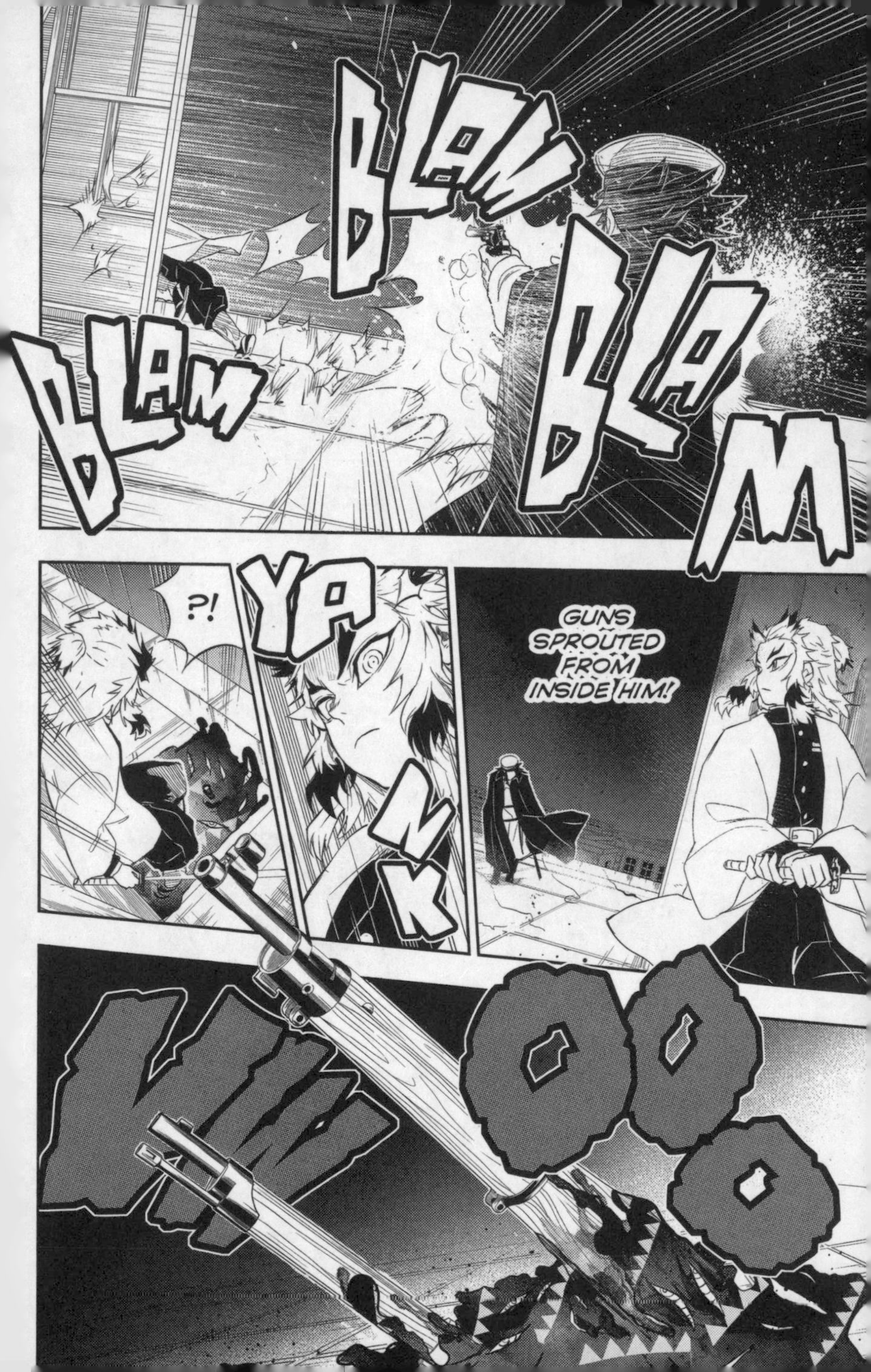
BLAM
BLAM
BLAM
GUNS SPROUTED FROM INSIDE HIM!
YANK
?!
WHOOO

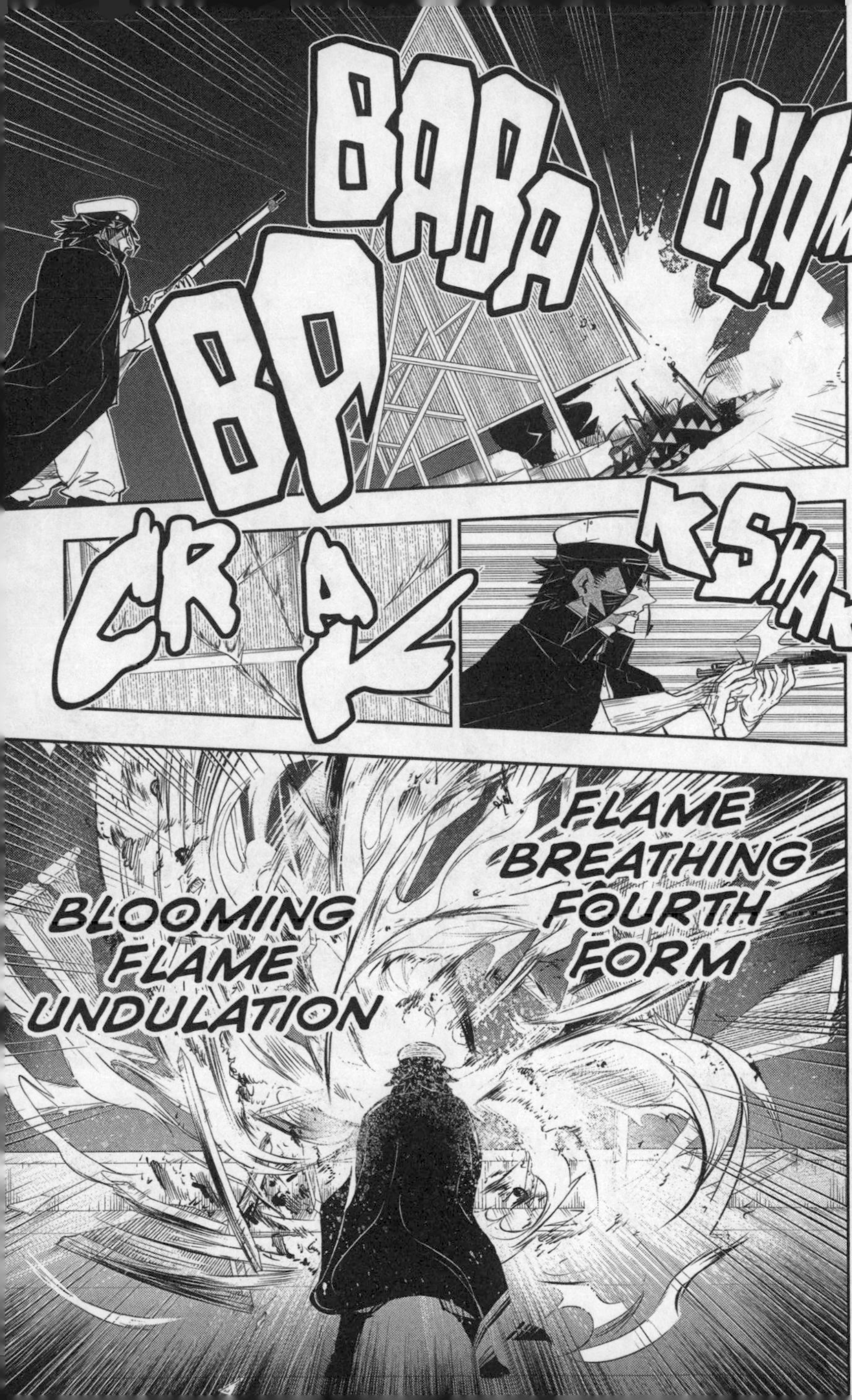
BLAM
BABA
BA
KSHAK
CRACK
FLAME BREATHING FOURTH FORM
BLOOMING FLAME UNDULATION

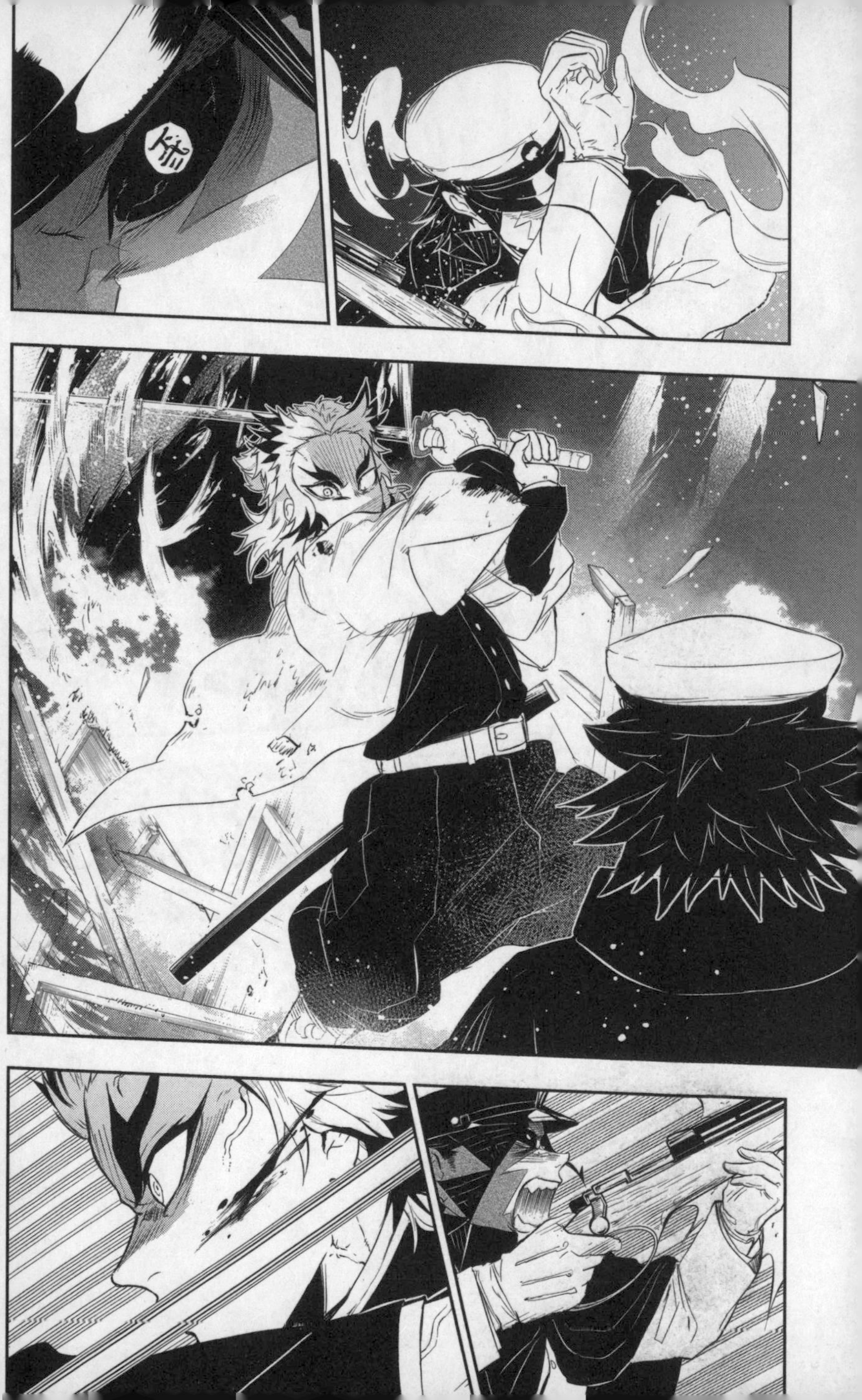

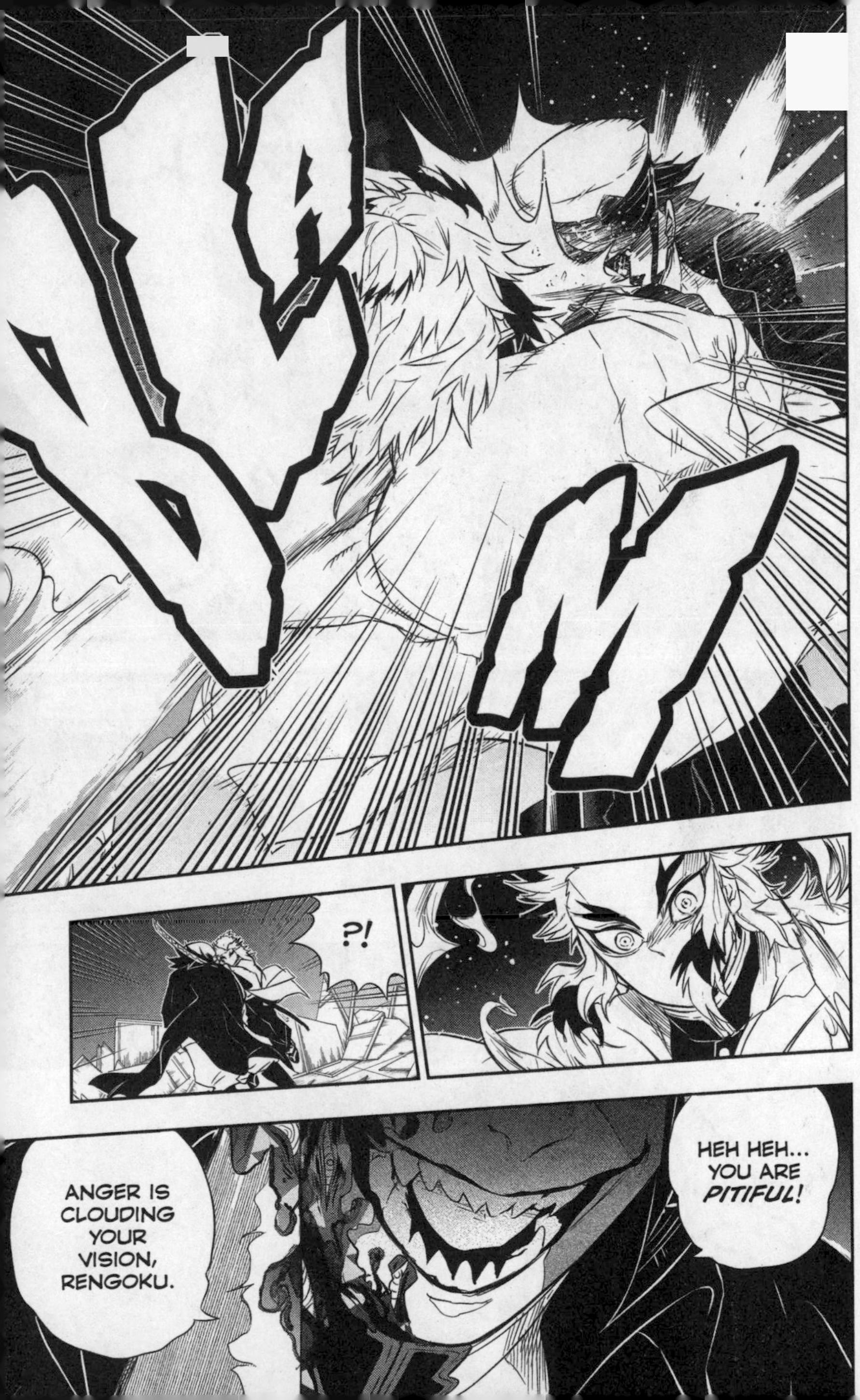
BAM
?!
HEH HEH... YOU ARE *PITIFUL!*
ANGER IS CLOUDING YOUR VISION, RENGOKU.

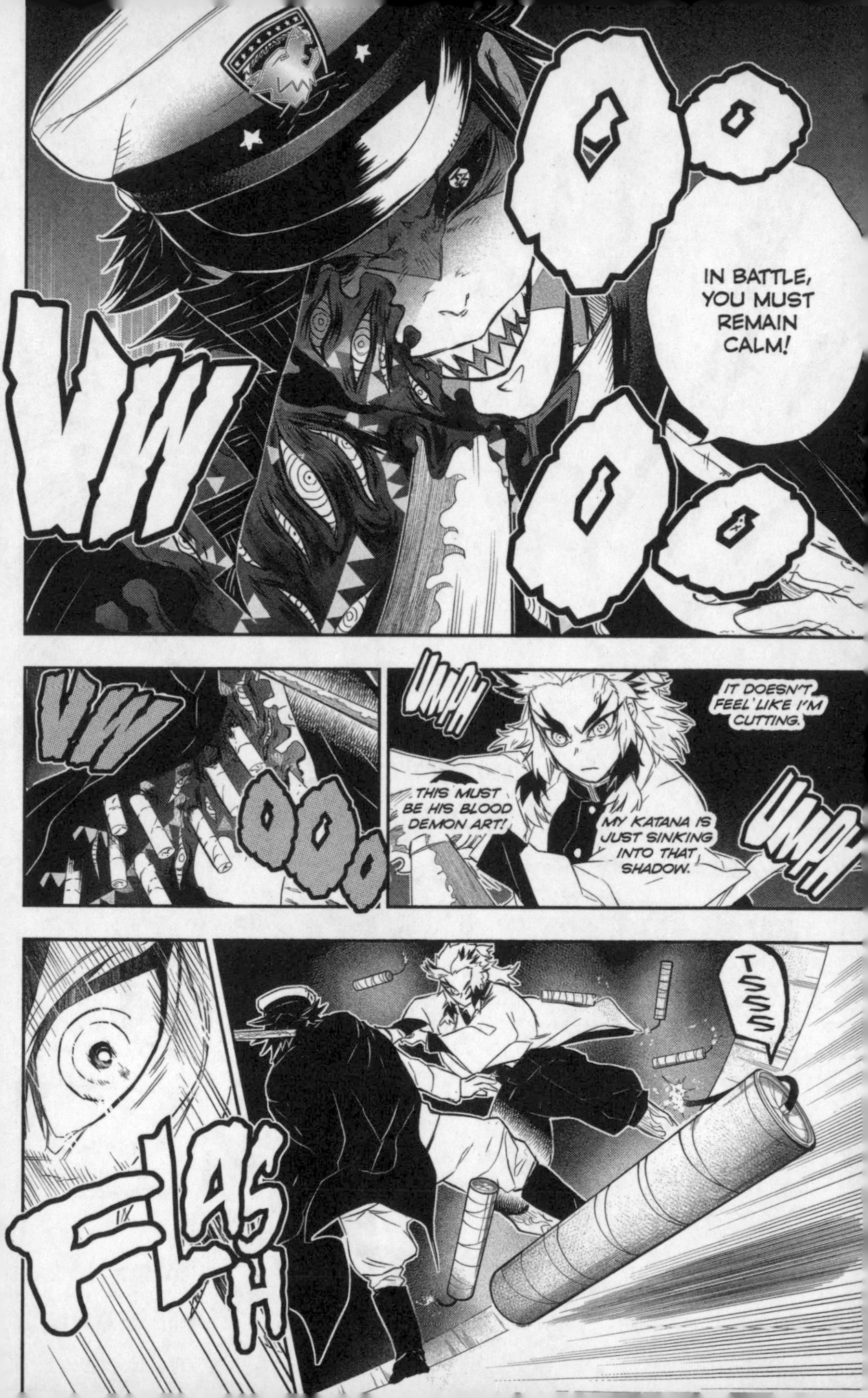
OOOO
IN BATTLE, YOU MUST REMAIN CALM!
VW
UMPH
IT DOESN'T FEEL LIKE I'M CUTTING.
UMPH
MY KATANA IS JUST SINKING INTO THAT SHADOW.
THIS MUST BE HIS BLOOD DEMON ART!
VW
OOOO
TSSS
FLASH

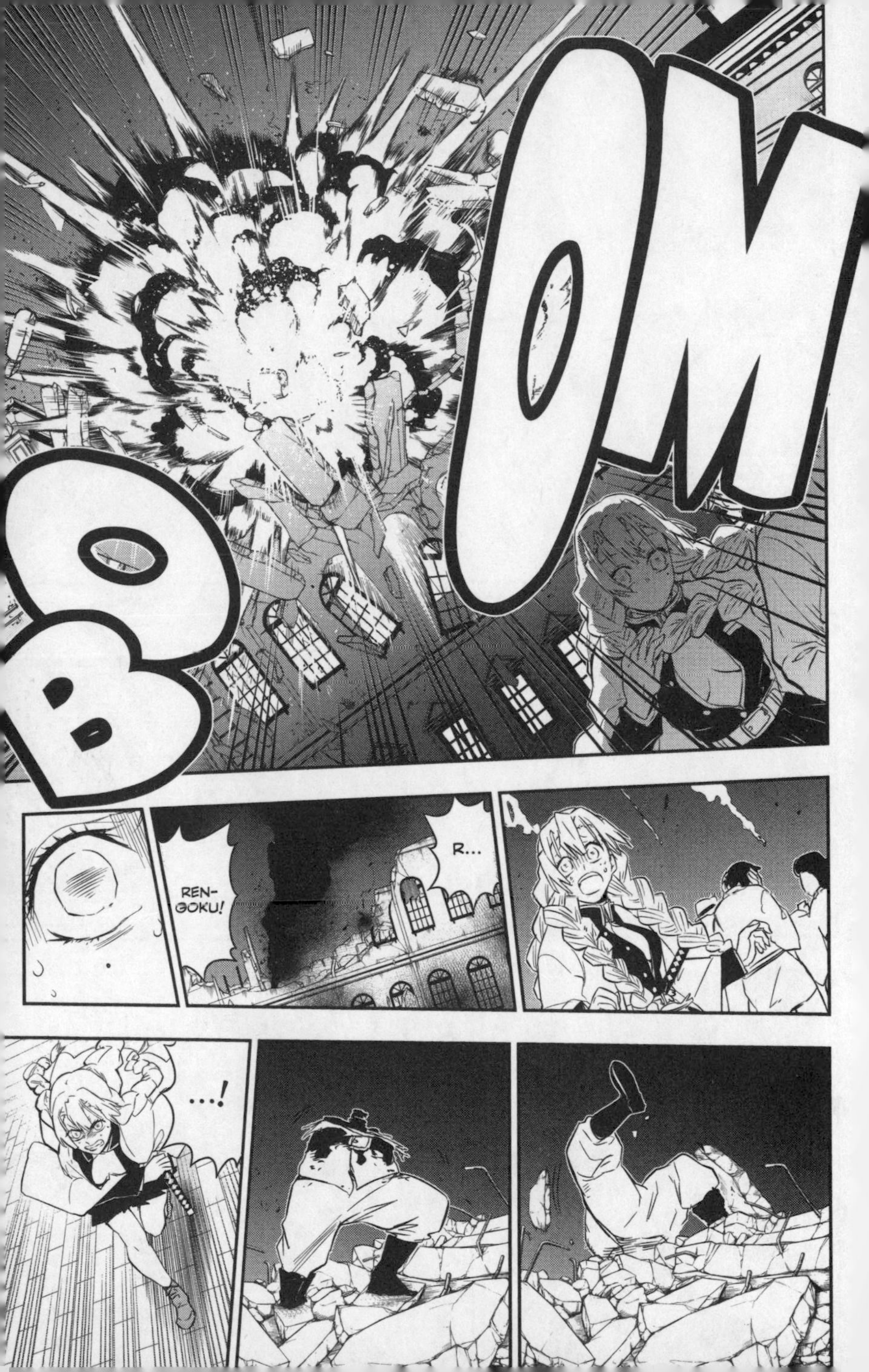
BOOM
R...
REN-GOKU!
...!

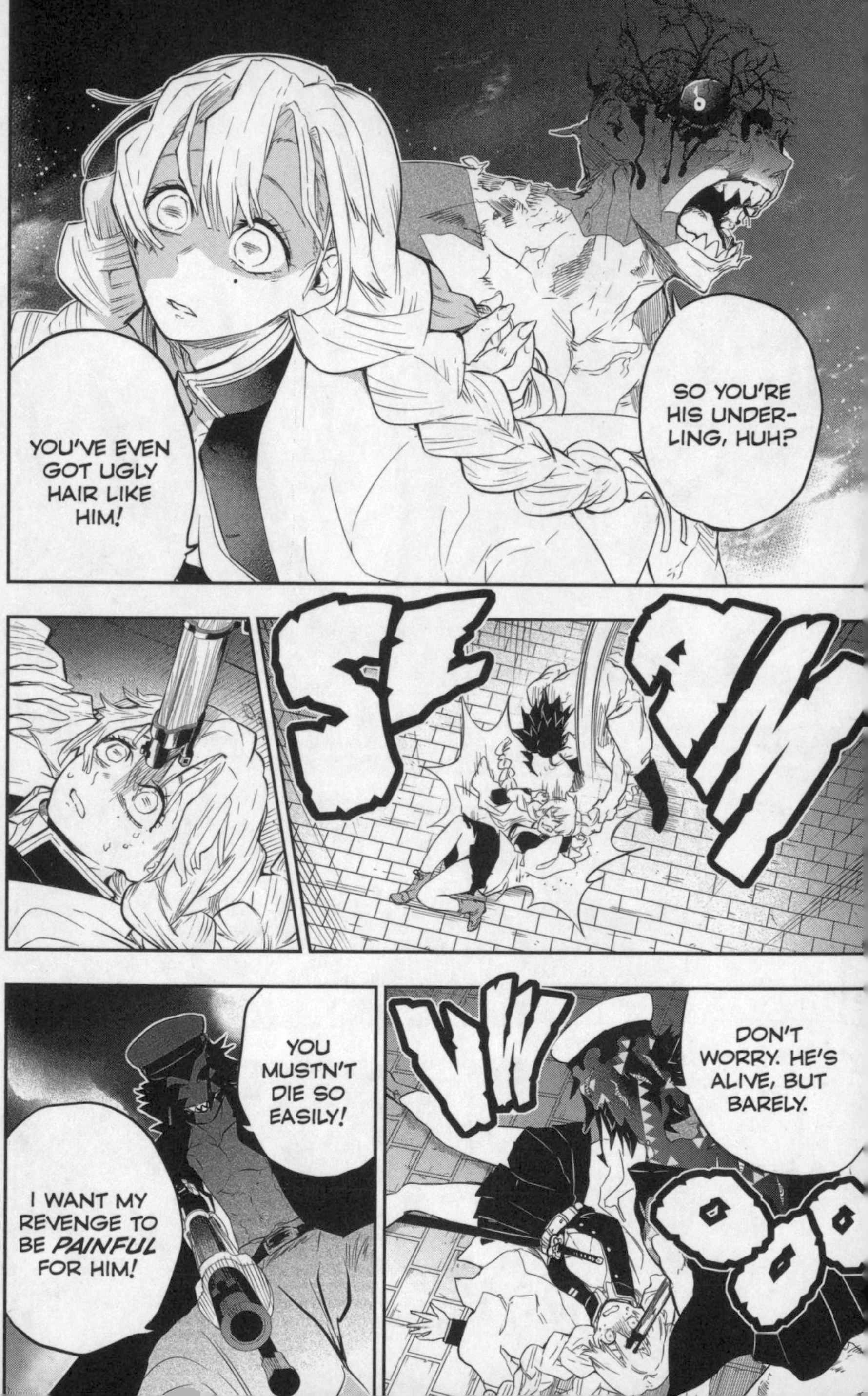
SO YOU'RE HIS UNDERLING, HUH?
YOU'VE EVEN GOT UGLY HAIR LIKE HIM!
DON'T WORRY. HE'S ALIVE, BUT BARELY.
YOU MUSTN'T DIE SO EASILY!
I WANT MY REVENGE TO BE *PAINFUL* FOR HIM!

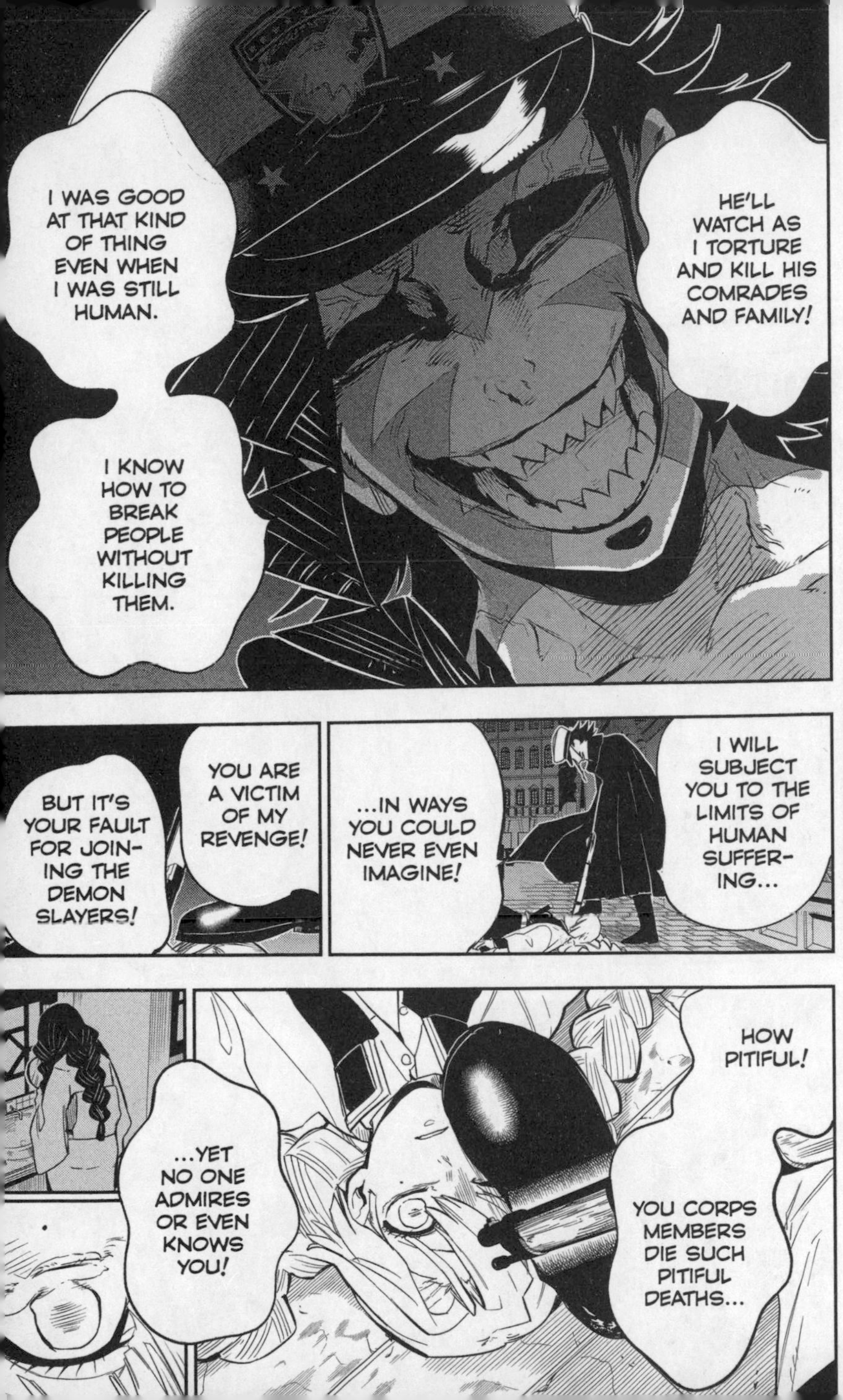
HE'LL WATCH AS I TORTURE AND KILL HIS COMRADES AND FAMILY!
I WAS GOOD AT THAT KIND OF THING EVEN WHEN I WAS STILL HUMAN.
I KNOW HOW TO BREAK PEOPLE WITHOUT KILLING THEM.
I WILL SUBJECT YOU TO THE LIMITS OF HUMAN SUFFER-ING...
...IN WAYS YOU COULD NEVER EVEN IMAGINE!
YOU ARE A VICTIM OF MY REVENGE!
BUT IT'S YOUR FAULT FOR JOIN-ING THE DEMON SLAYERS!
HOW PITIFUL!
YOU CORPS MEMBERS DIE SUCH PITIFUL DEATHS...
...YET NO ONE ADMIRES OR EVEN KNOWS YOU!

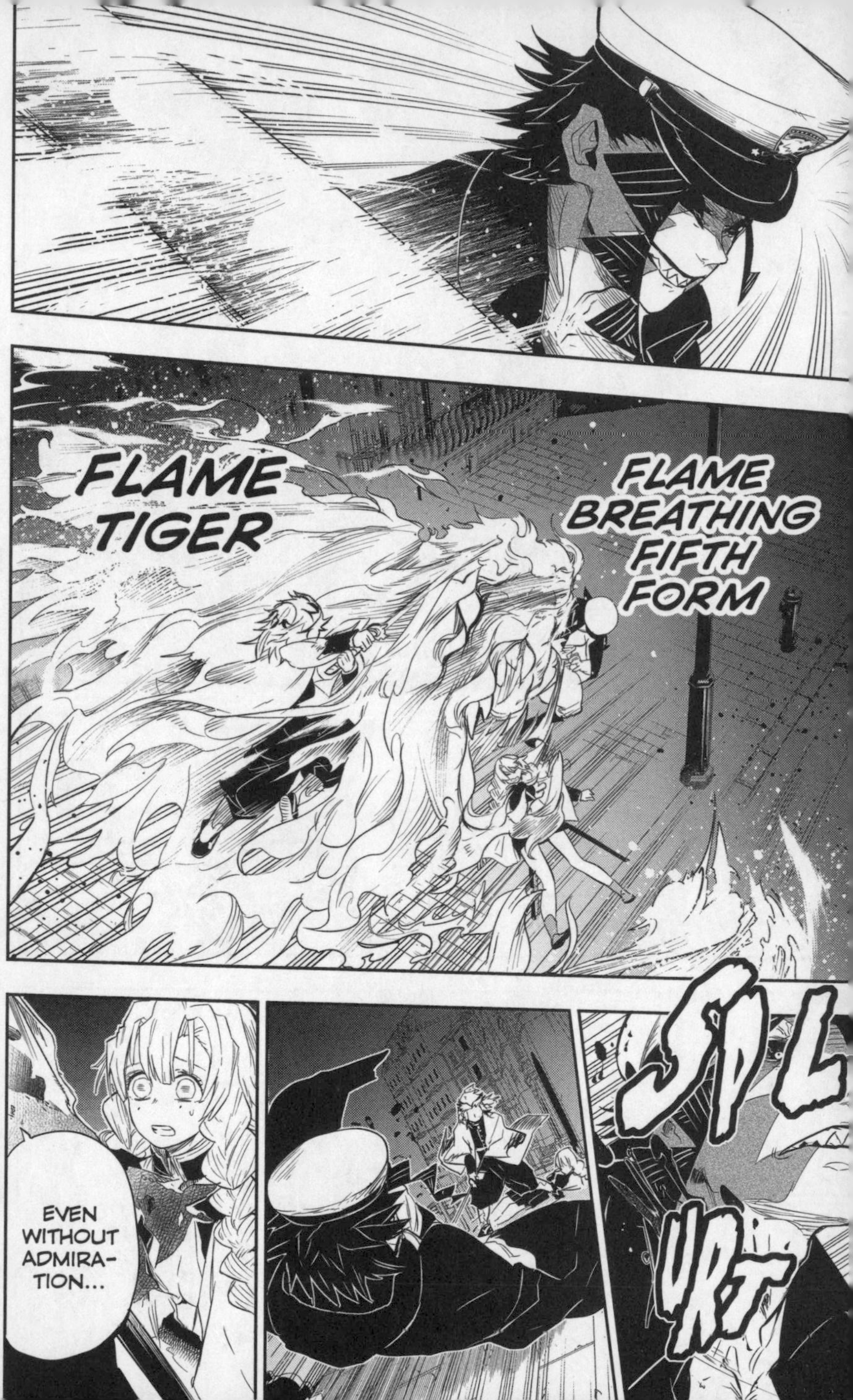
FLAME BREATHING FIFTH FORM
FLAME TIGER
SPLURT
EVEN WITHOUT ADMIRA-TION...

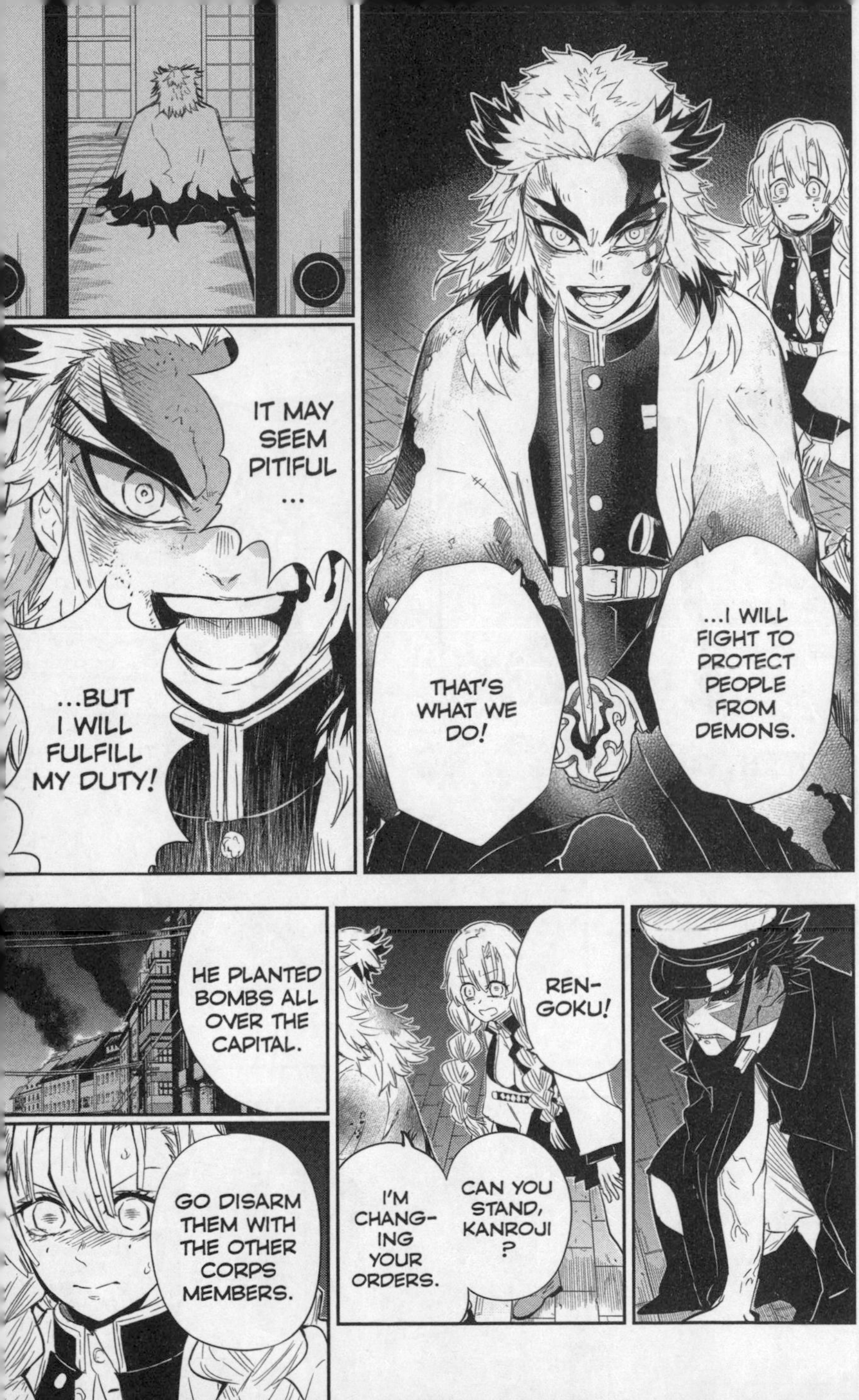
...I WILL FIGHT TO PROTECT PEOPLE FROM DEMONS.
THAT'S WHAT WE DO!
IT MAY SEEM PITIFUL ...
...BUT I WILL FULFILL MY DUTY!
REN-GOKU!
CAN YOU STAND, KANROJI ?
I'M CHANG-ING YOUR ORDERS.
HE PLANTED BOMBS ALL OVER THE CAPITAL.
GO DISARM THEM WITH THE OTHER CORPS MEMBERS.

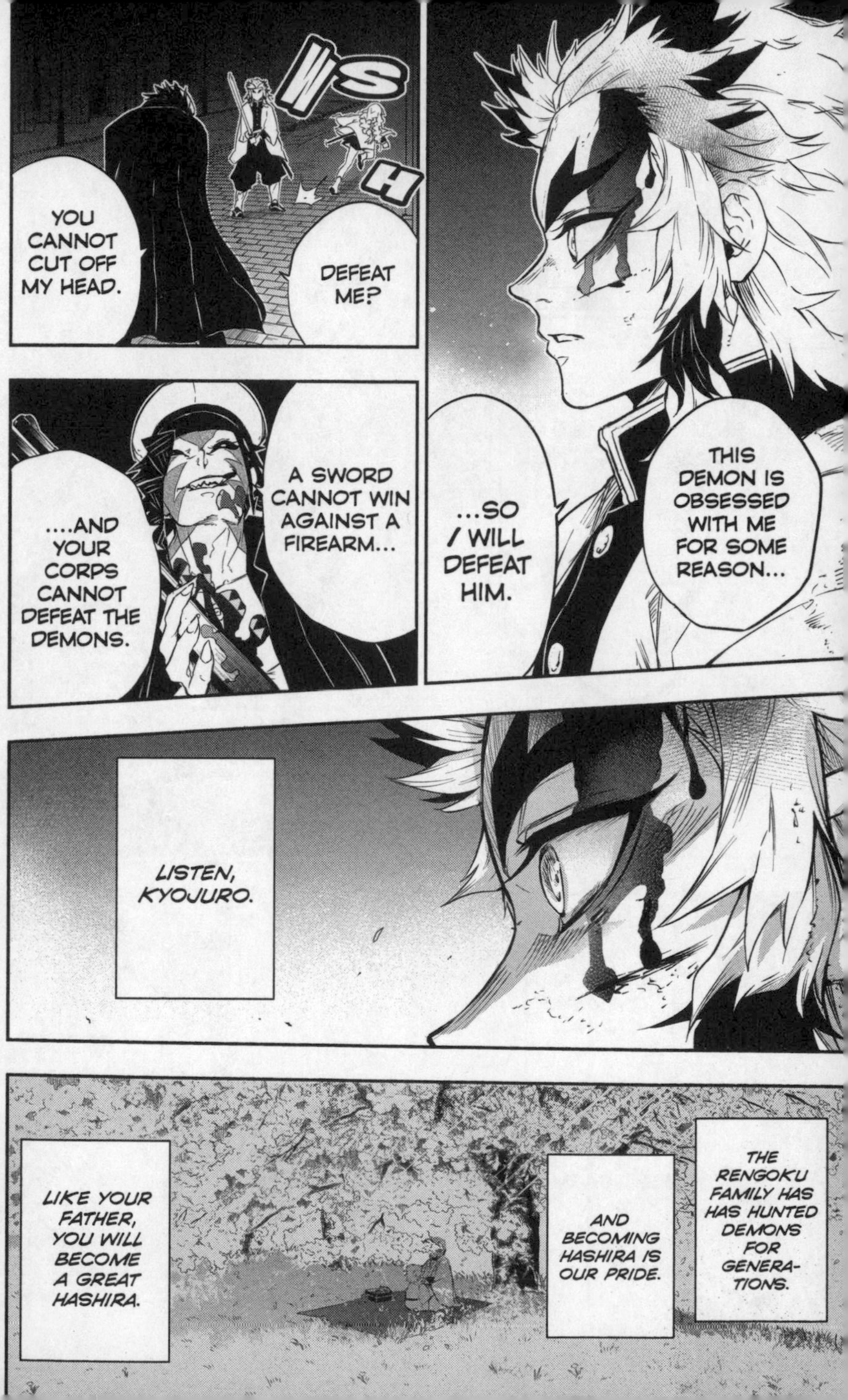
THIS DEMON IS OBSESSED WITH ME FOR SOME REASON...
...SO I WILL DEFEAT HIM.
DEFEAT ME?
YOU CANNOT CUT OFF MY HEAD.
A SWORD CANNOT WIN AGAINST A FIREARM...
....AND YOUR CORPS CANNOT DEFEAT THE DEMONS.
LISTEN, KYOJURO.
THE RENGOKU FAMILY HAS HAS HUNTED DEMONS FOR GENERATIONS.
AND BECOMING HASHIRA IS OUR PRIDE.
LIKE YOUR FATHER, YOU WILL BECOME A GREAT HASHIRA.

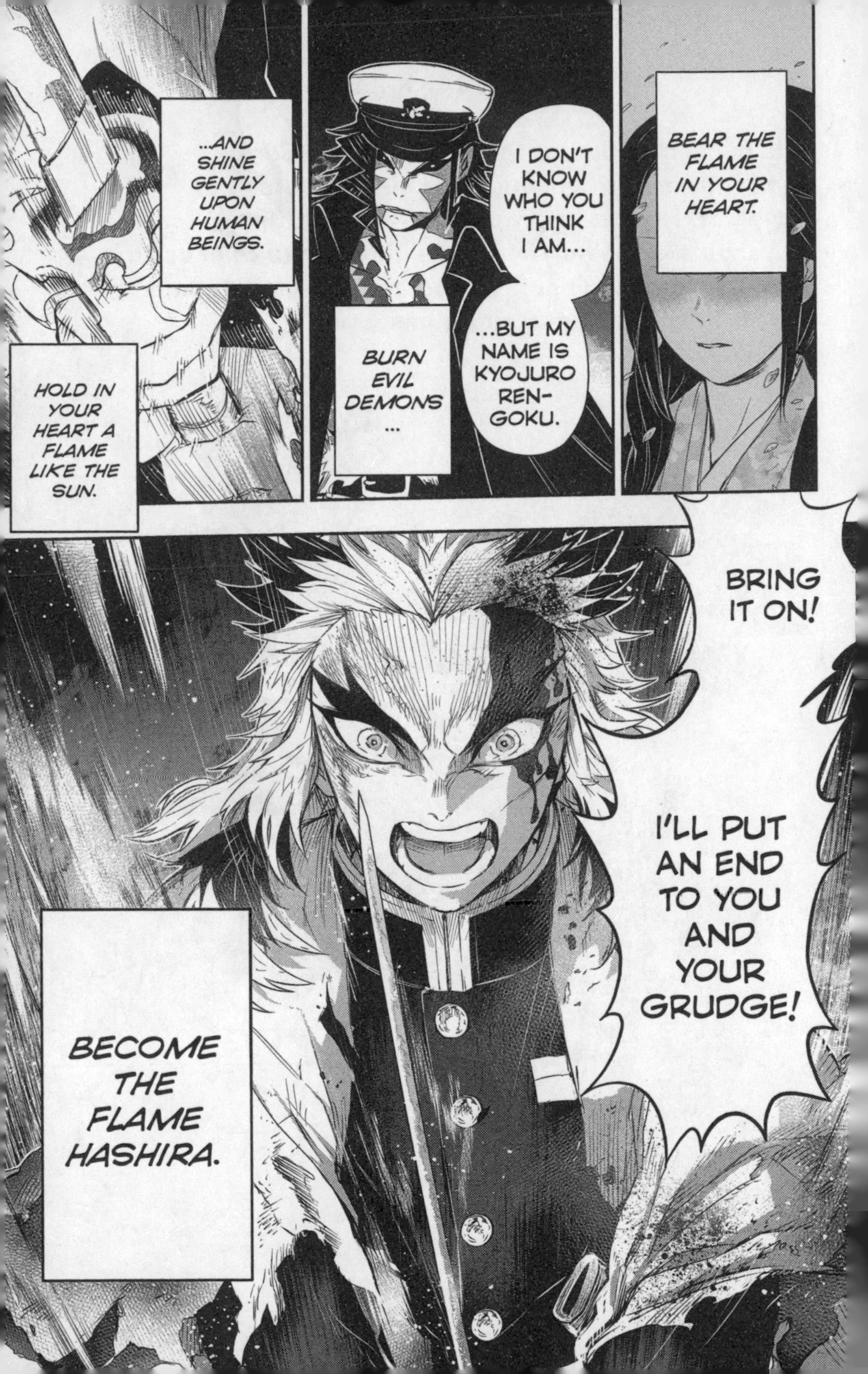
BEAR THE FLAME IN YOUR HEART.
I DON'T KNOW WHO YOU THINK I AM...
...BUT MY NAME IS KYOJURO REN-GOKU.
BURN EVIL DEMONS ...
...AND SHINE GENTLY UPON HUMAN BEINGS.
HOLD IN YOUR HEART A FLAME LIKE THE SUN.
BRING IT ON!
I'LL PUT AN END TO YOU AND YOUR GRUDGE!
BECOME THE FLAME HASHIRA.

## THE LOWER RANK 2 DEMON

He hunts members of the Demon Slayer Corps and collects the handguards from their katana as trophies. He gets angry over the slightest things, and he shoots himself in the head with a gun to calm down. However, he hasn't noticed that the repeated trauma to his brain has damaged his memory.

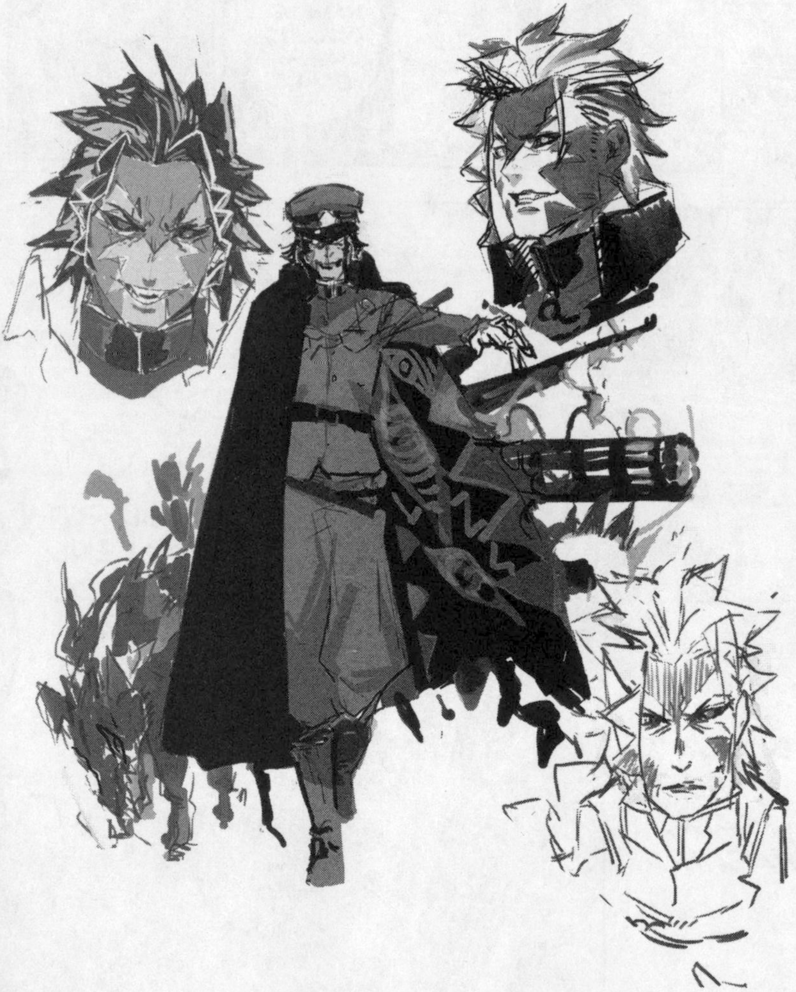

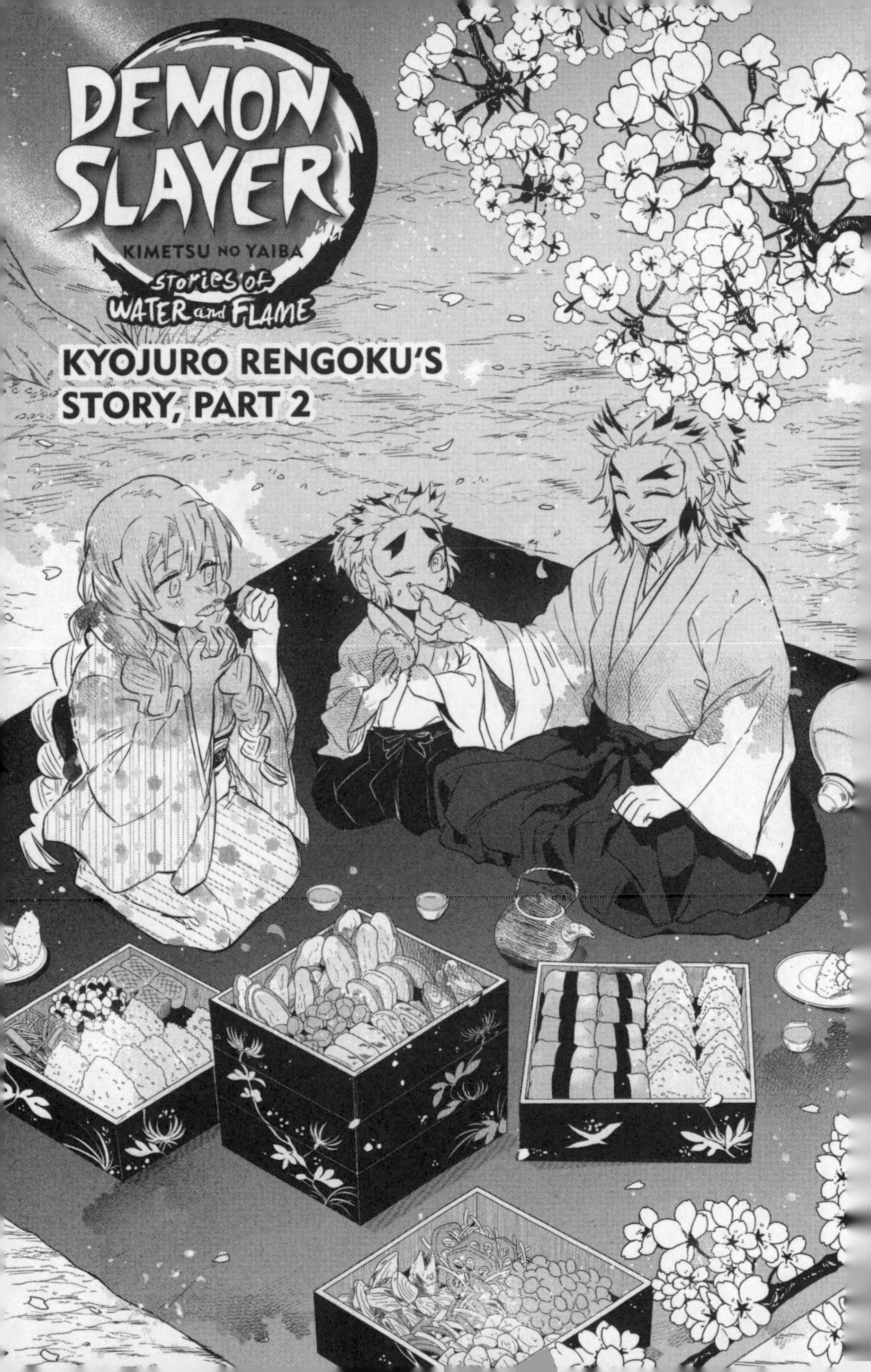
DEMON SLAYER
KIMETSU NO YAIBA
stories of WATER and FLAME
KYOJURO RENGOKU'S STORY, PART 2

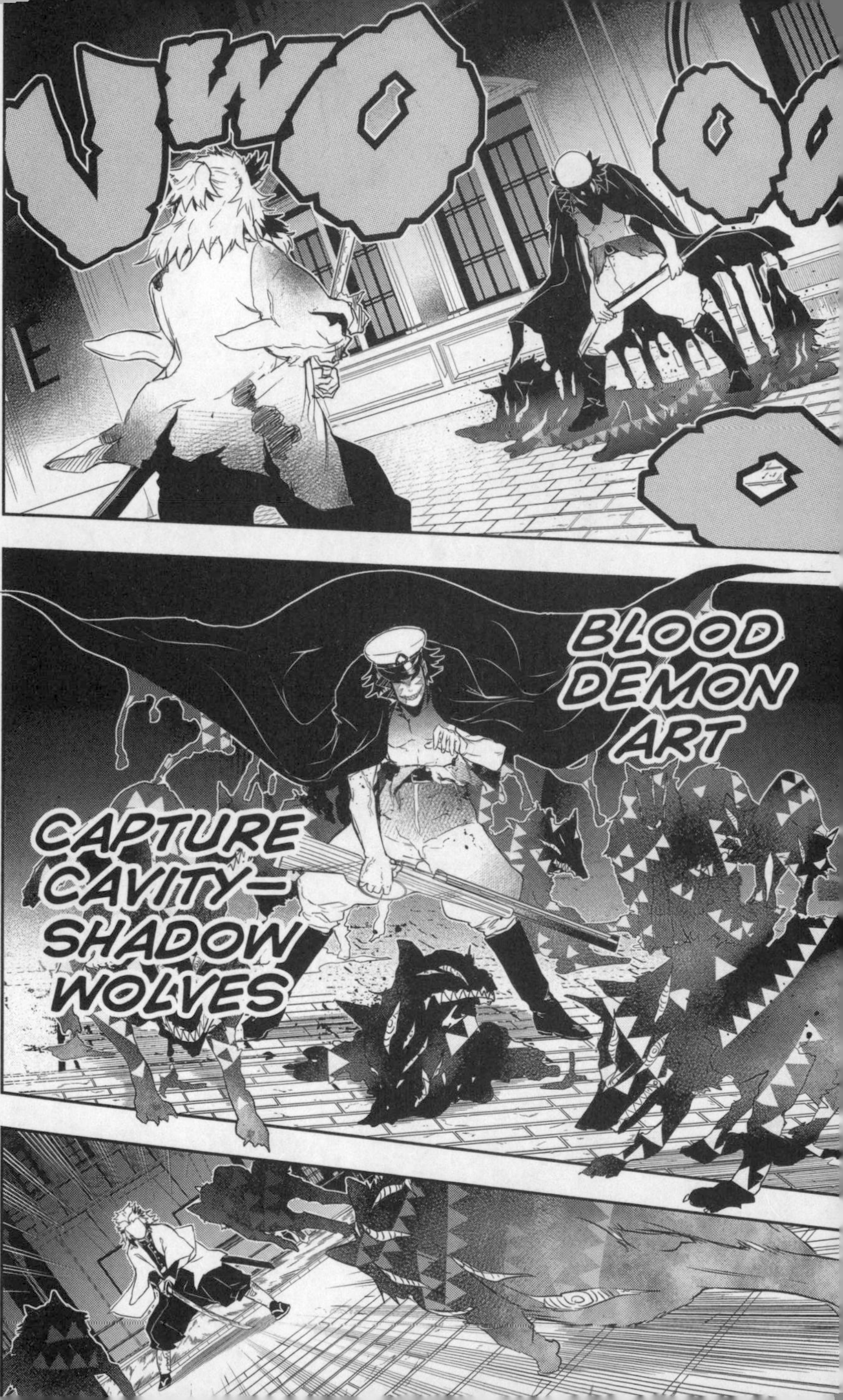
UWOOOO
BLOOD DEMON ART
CAPTURE CAVITY— SHADOW WOLVES

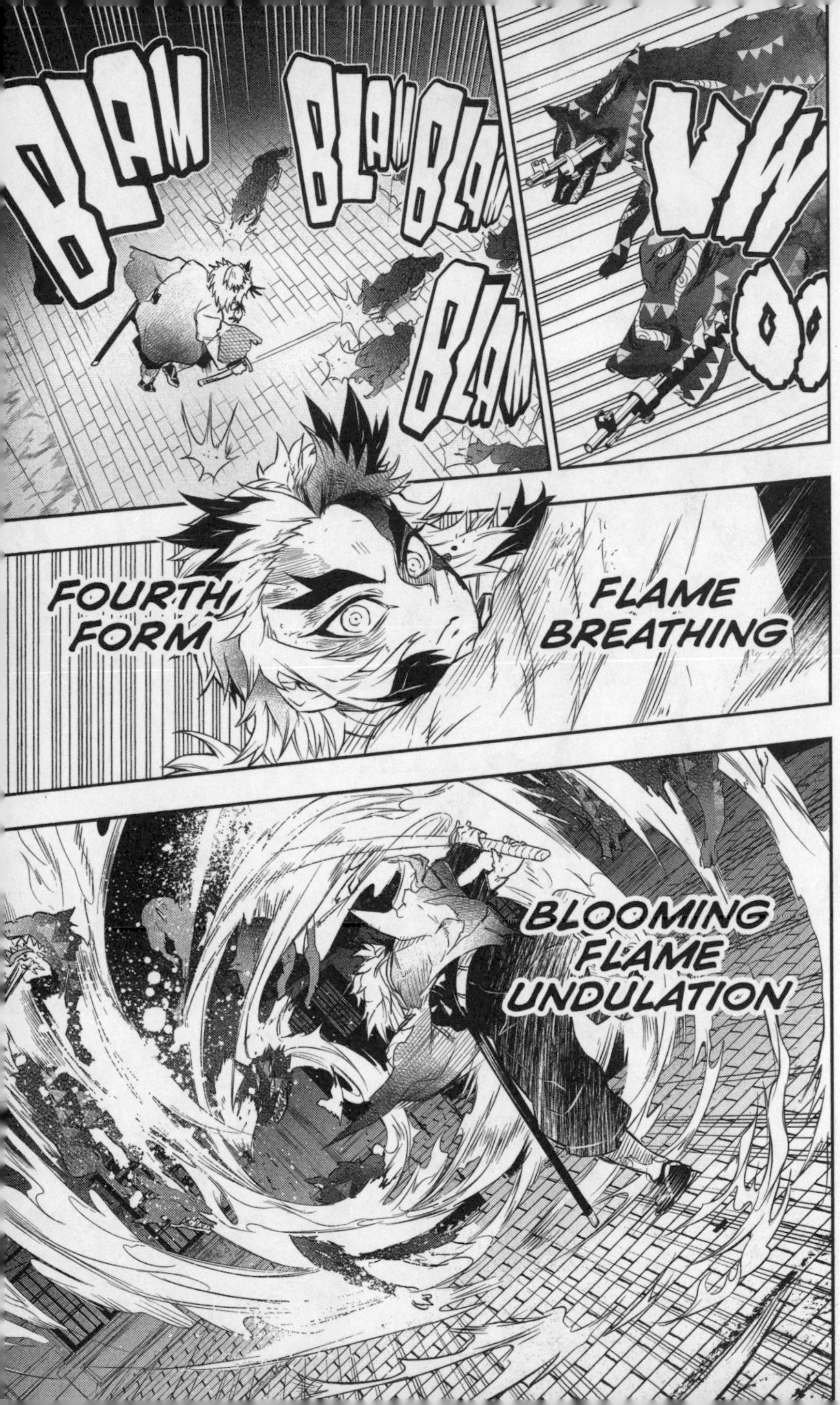
VWOO
BLAM BLAM
BLAM
BLAM
BLAM
FLAME BREATHING
FOURTH FORM
BLOOMING FLAME UNDULATION

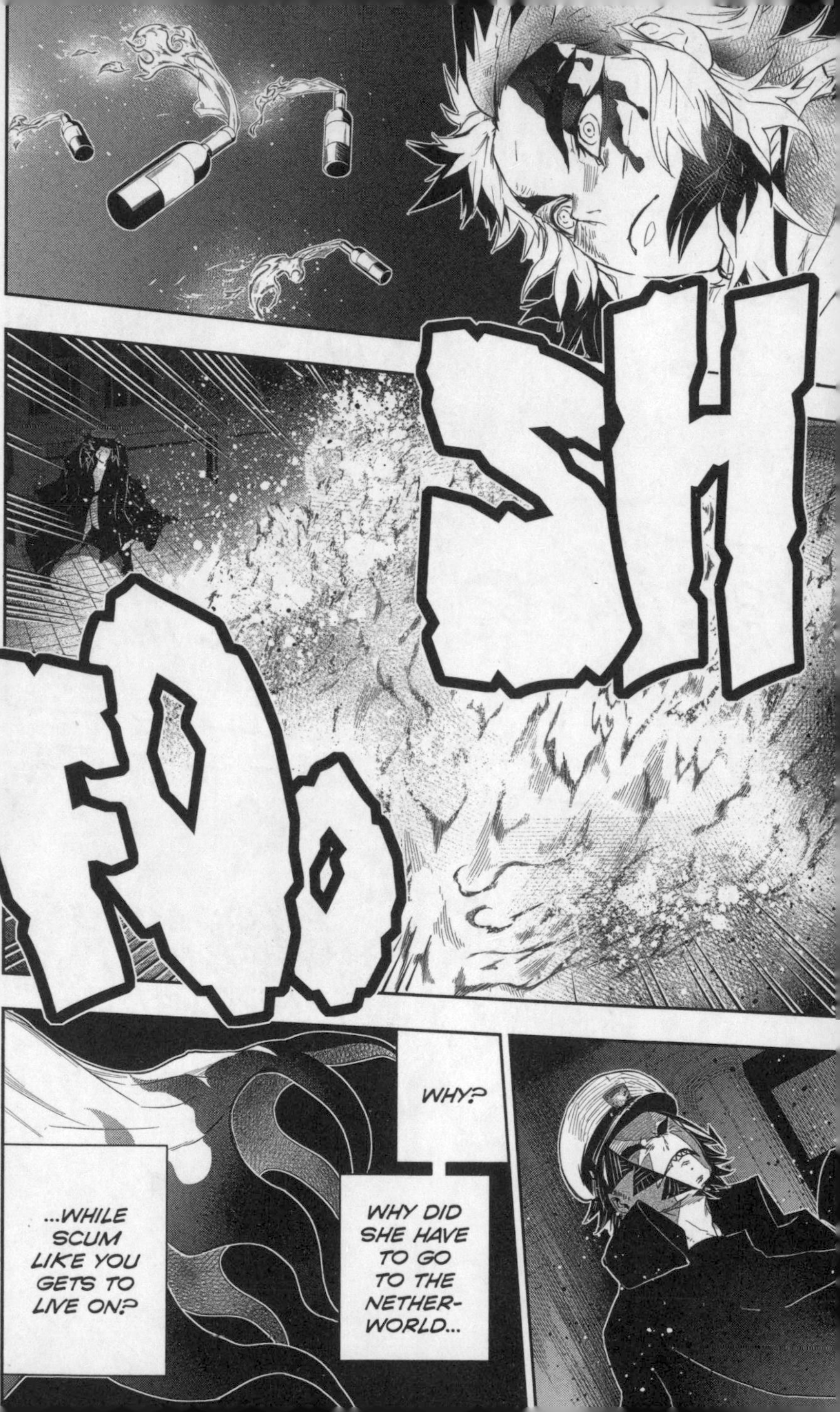
FOOSH
WHY?
WHY DID SHE HAVE TO GO TO THE NETHER-WORLD...
...WHILE SCUM LIKE YOU GETS TO LIVE ON?

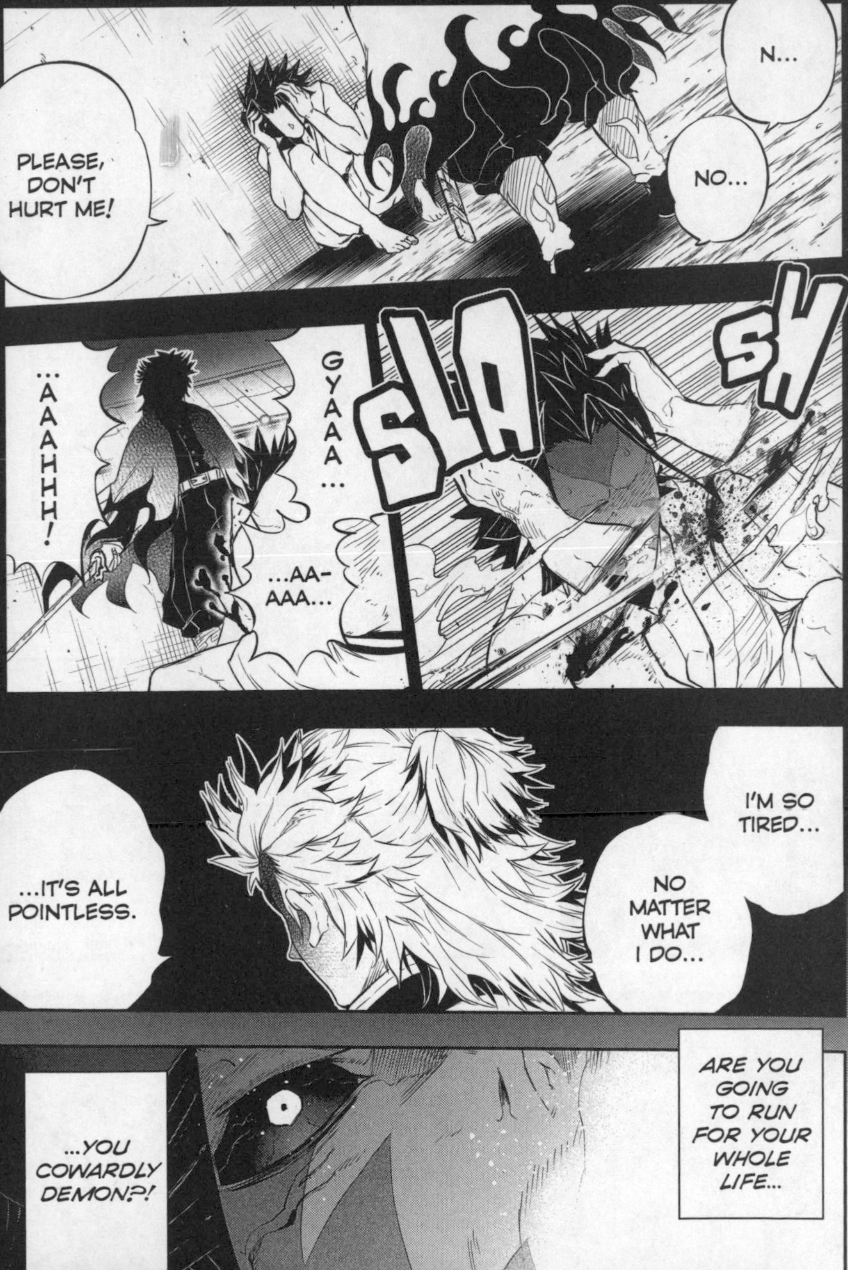
N...
NO...
PLEASE, DON'T HURT ME!
SLASH
GYAAA...
...AA-AAA...
...AAAAHHH!
I'M SO TIRED...
NO MATTER WHAT I DO...
...IT'S ALL POINTLESS.
ARE YOU GOING TO RUN FOR YOUR WHOLE LIFE...
...YOU COWARDLY DEMON?!

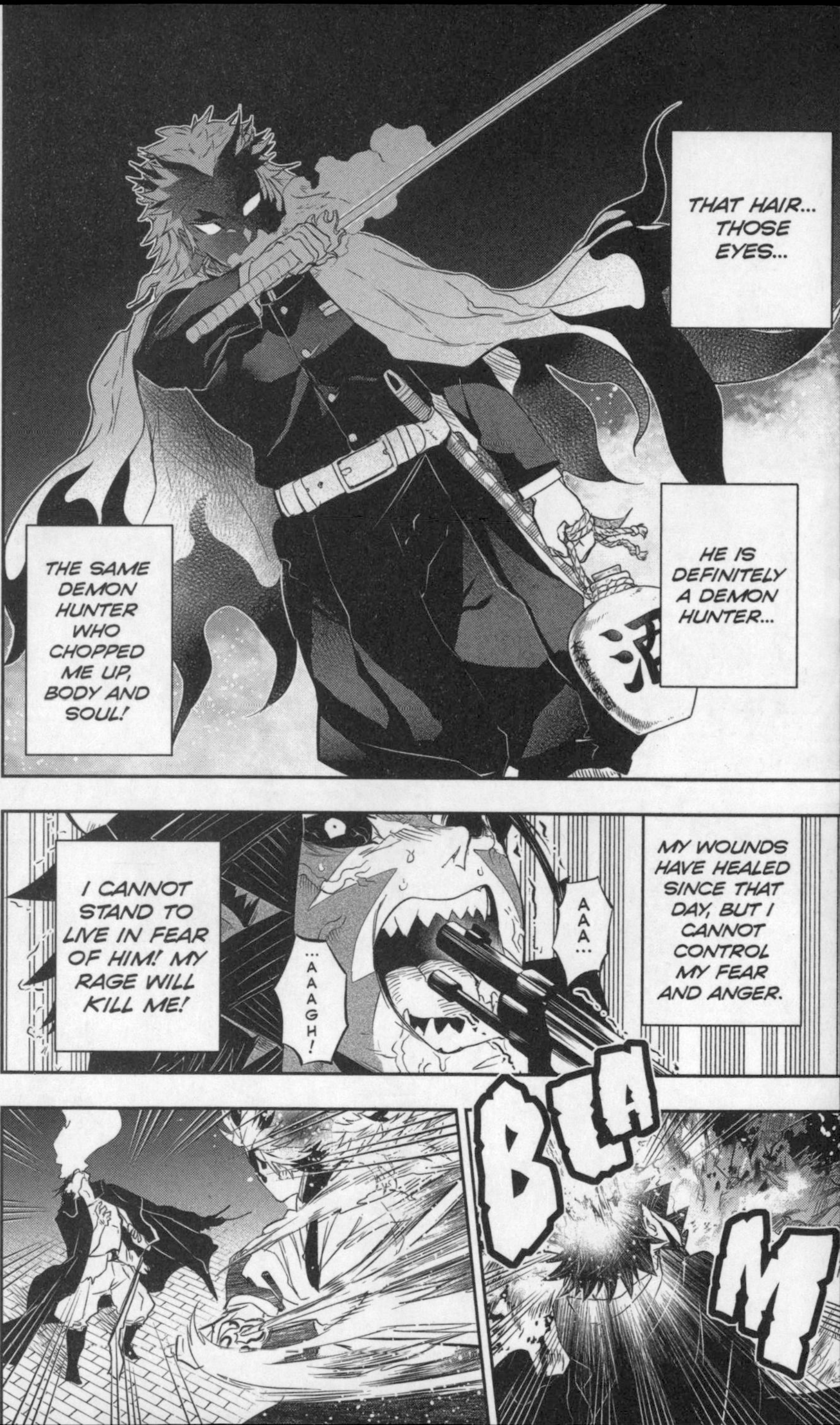
THAT HAIR... THOSE EYES...
HE IS DEFINITELY A DEMON HUNTER...
THE SAME DEMON HUNTER WHO CHOPPED ME UP, BODY AND SOUL!
MY WOUNDS HAVE HEALED SINCE THAT DAY, BUT I CANNOT CONTROL MY FEAR AND ANGER.
AAA...
...AAAAGH!
I CANNOT STAND TO LIVE IN FEAR OF HIM! MY RAGE WILL KILL ME!
BLAM

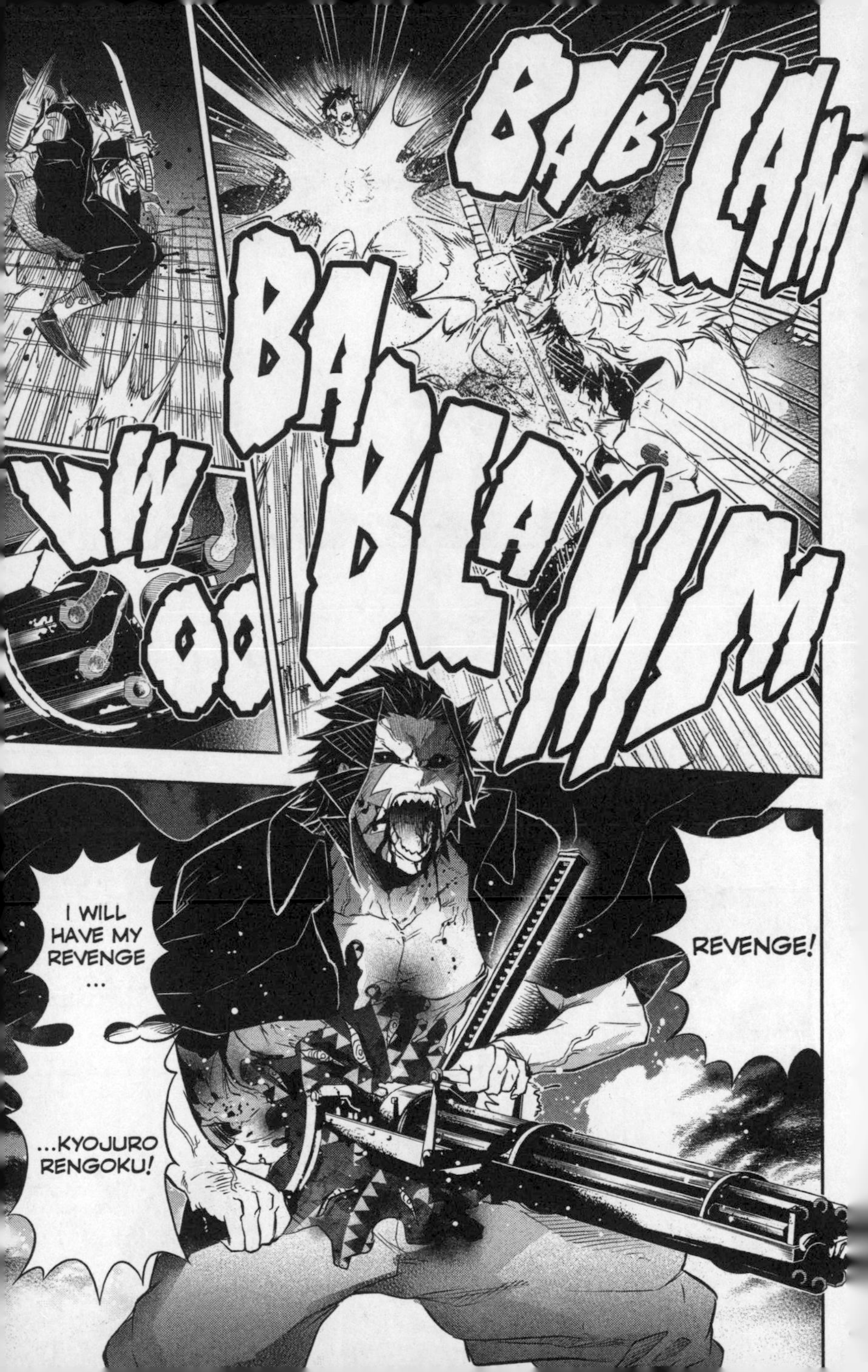
BABLAM
BA BLAMMM
VWOO
REVENGE!
I WILL HAVE MY REVENGE ...
...KYOJURO RENGOKU!

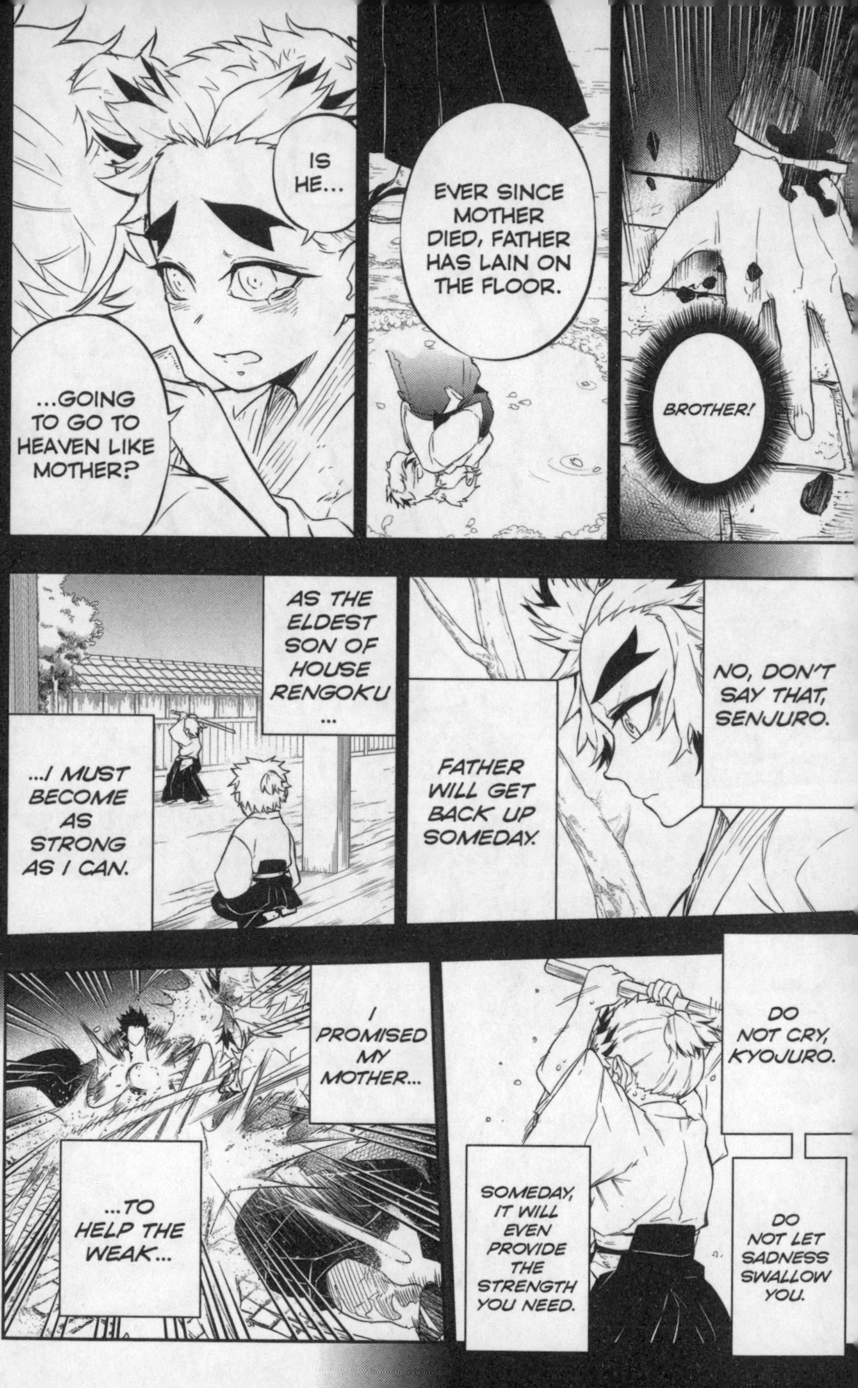
BROTHER!
EVER SINCE MOTHER DIED, FATHER HAS LAIN ON THE FLOOR.
IS HE...
...GOING TO GO TO HEAVEN LIKE MOTHER?
NO, DON'T SAY THAT, SENJURO.
FATHER WILL GET BACK UP SOMEDAY.
AS THE ELDEST SON OF HOUSE RENGOKU ...
...I MUST BECOME AS STRONG AS I CAN.
DO NOT CRY, KYOJURO.
DO NOT LET SADNESS SWALLOW YOU.
SOMEDAY, IT WILL EVEN PROVIDE THE STRENGTH YOU NEED.
I PROMISED MY MOTHER...
...TO HELP THE WEAK...

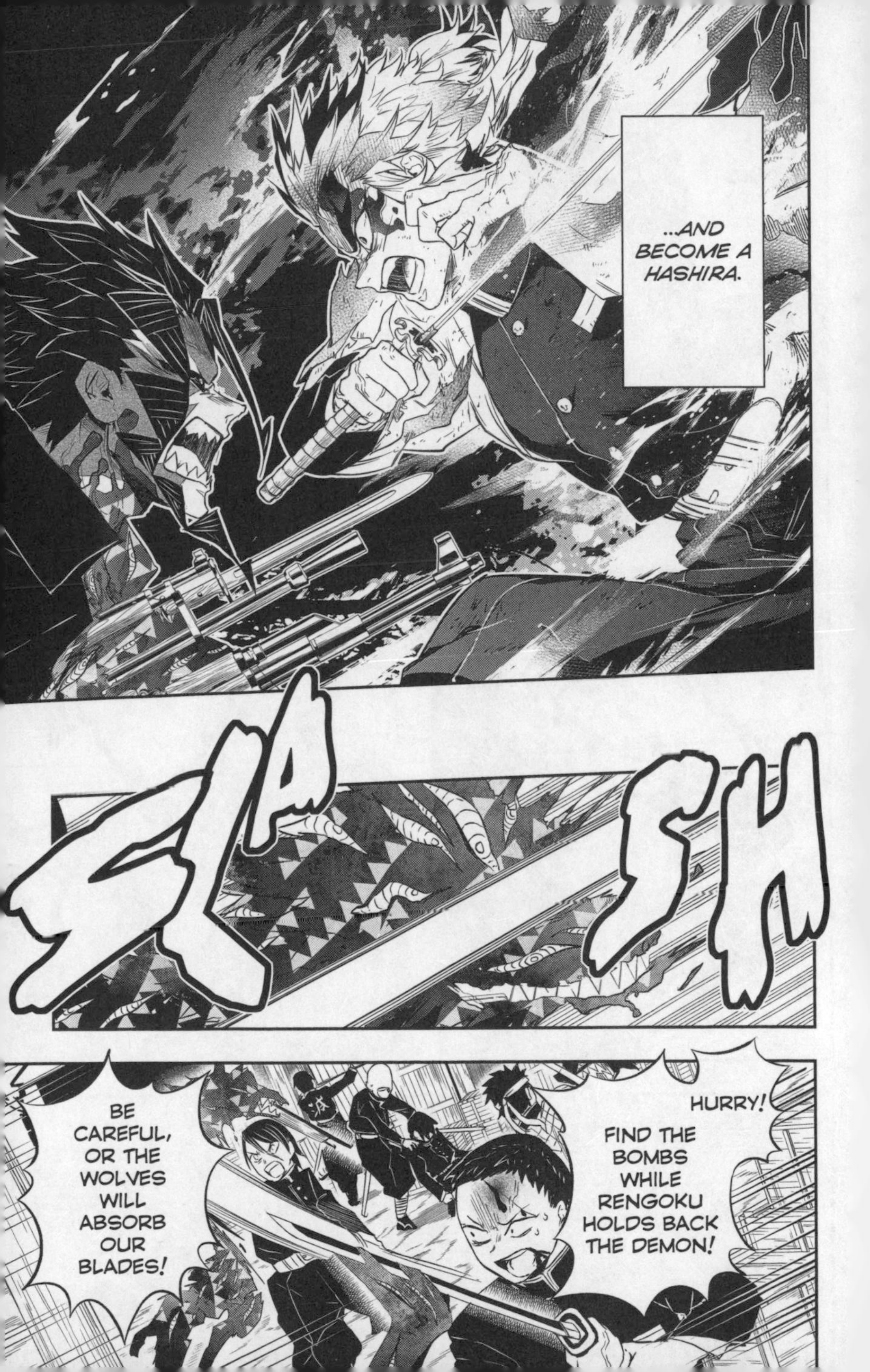
...AND BECOME A HASHIRA.
SLASH
HURRY!
FIND THE BOMBS WHILE RENGOKU HOLDS BACK THE DEMON!
BE CAREFUL, OR THE WOLVES WILL ABSORB OUR BLADES!

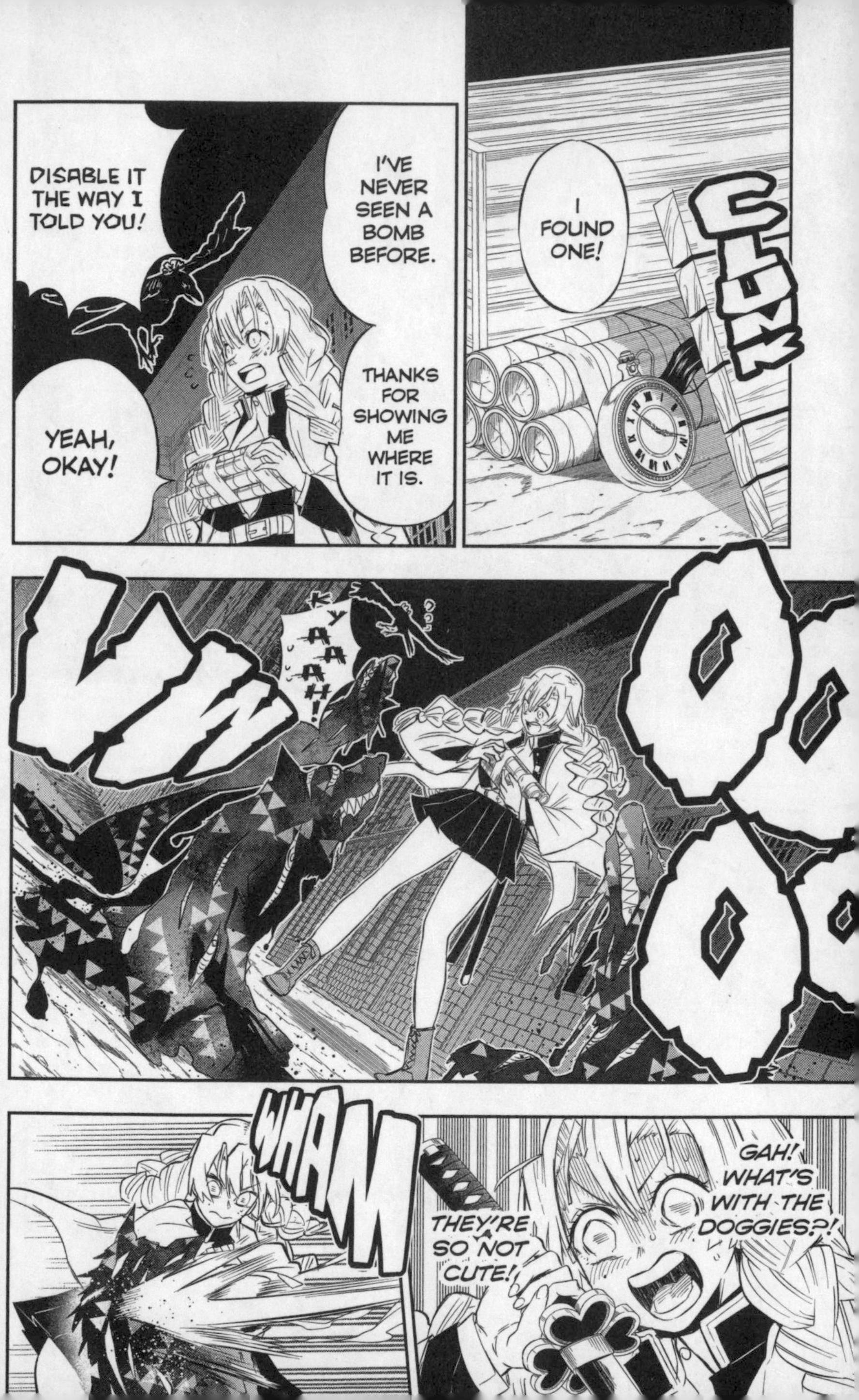
I FOUND ONE!
CLUNK
I'VE NEVER SEEN A BOMB BEFORE.
THANKS FOR SHOWING ME WHERE IT IS.
DISABLE IT THE WAY I TOLD YOU!
YEAH, OKAY!
KYAAAAH!
WOO
GAH! WHAT'S WITH THE DOGGIES?!
THEY'RE SO NOT CUTE!
WHAM

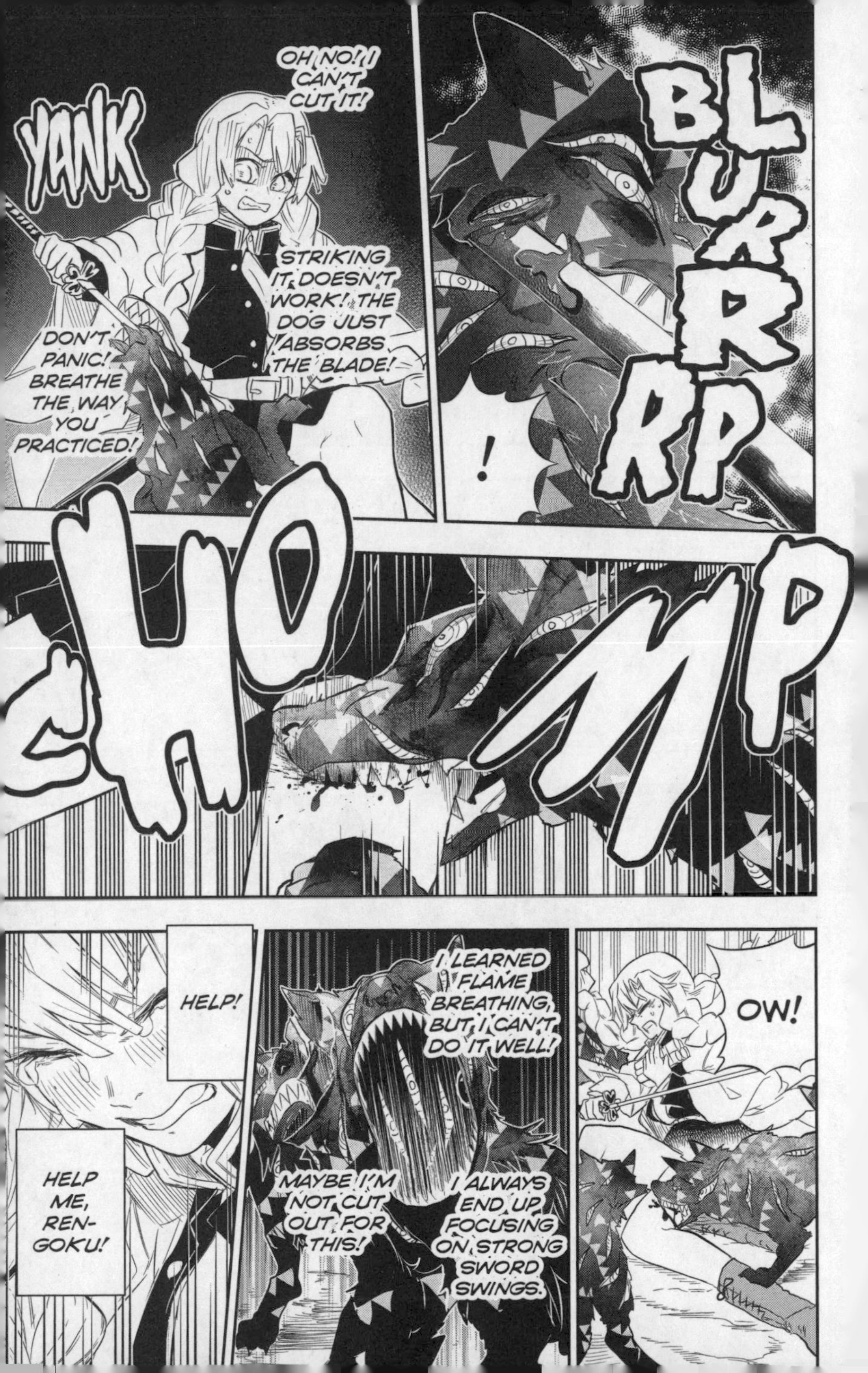
BLURRP
!
OH NO! I CAN'T CUT IT!
YANK
STRIKING IT DOESN'T WORK! THE DOG JUST ABSORBS THE BLADE!
DON'T PANIC! BREATHE THE WAY YOU PRACTICED!
CHOMP
OW!
I LEARNED FLAME BREATHING, BUT I CAN'T DO IT WELL!
I ALWAYS END UP FOCUSING ON STRONG SWORD SWINGS.
MAYBE I'M NOT CUT OUT FOR THIS!
HELP!
HELP ME, REN-GOKU!

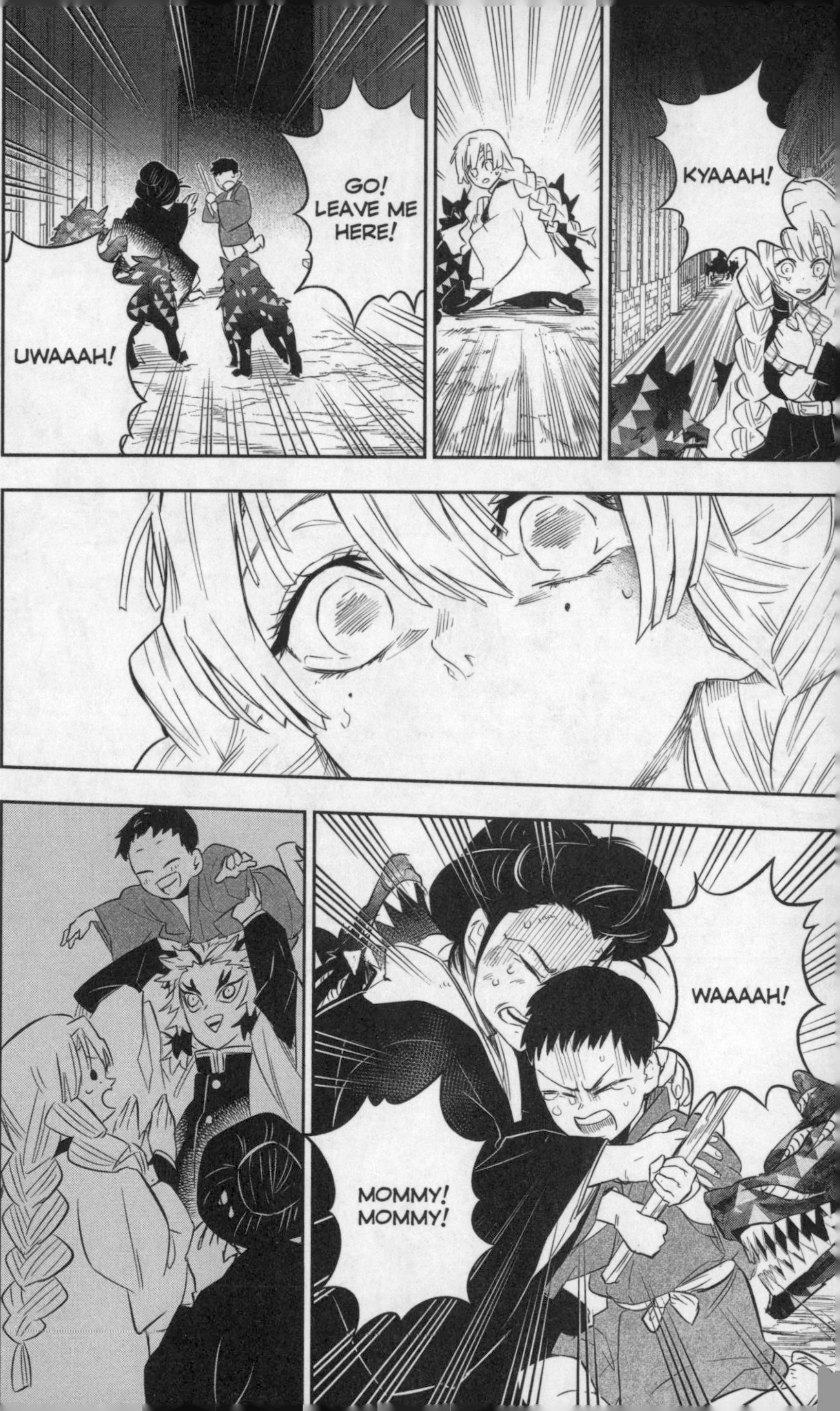
KYAAAH!
GO! LEAVE ME HERE!
UWAAAH!
WAAAAH!
MOMMY! MOMMY!

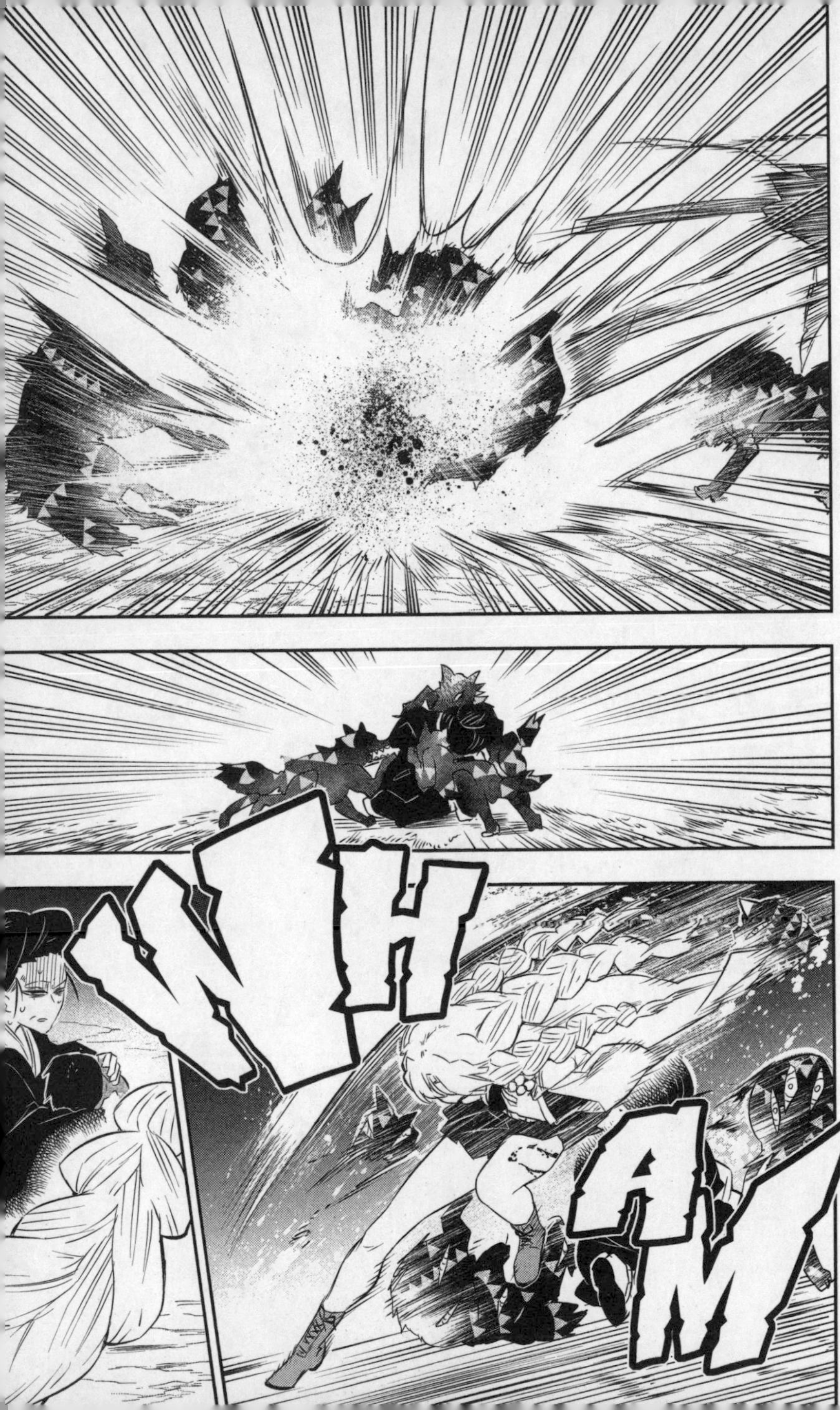
WHAM!

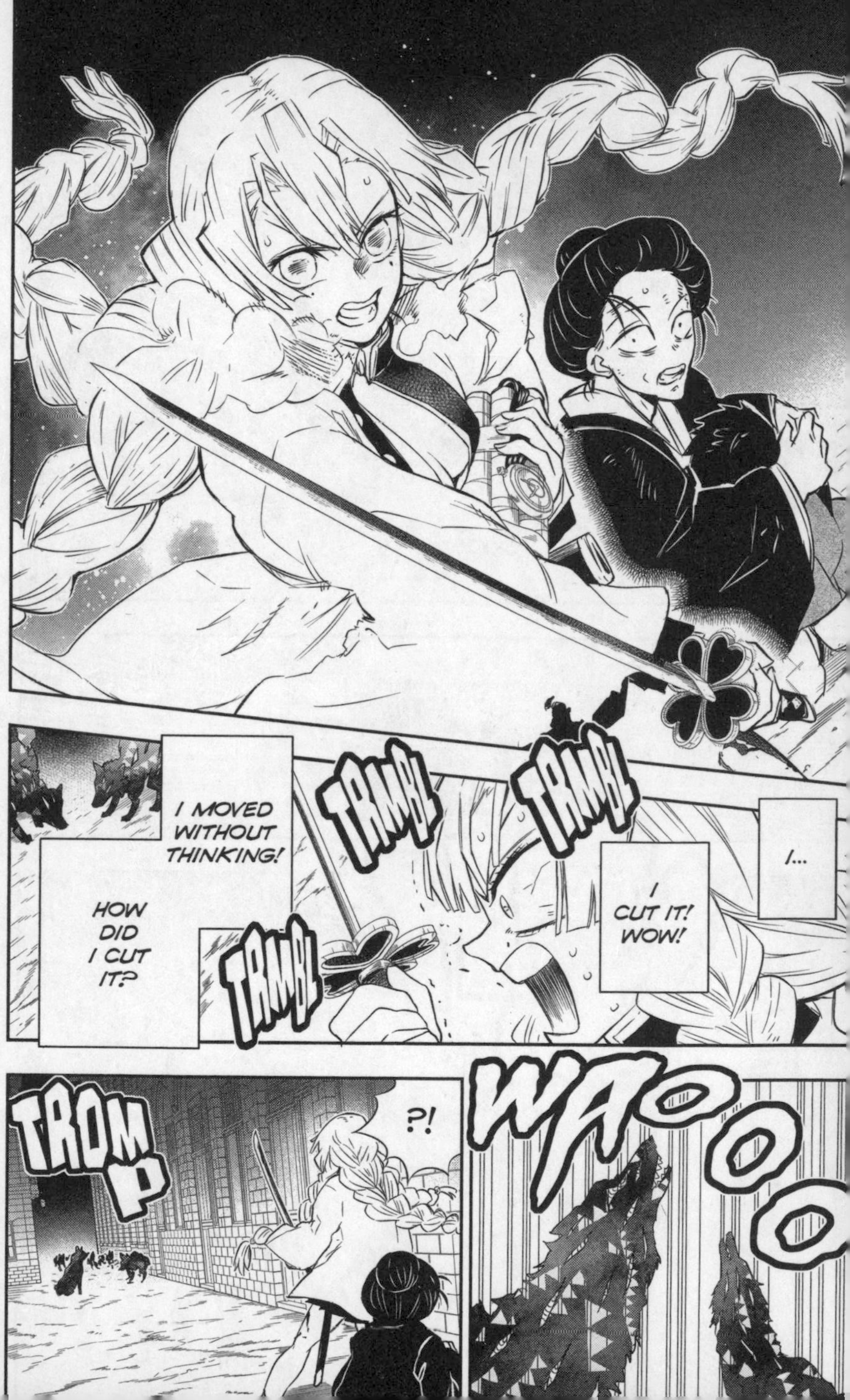
I...
TRAMBL
I CUT IT! WOW!
TRAMBL
I MOVED WITHOUT THINKING!
HOW DID I CUT IT?
TRAMBL
WAOOOO
?!
TROMP

ULP...!

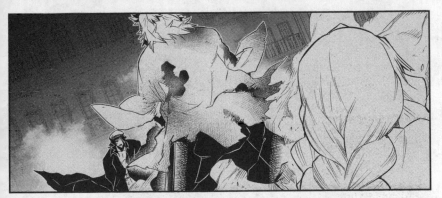

GOOD JOB STICKING BY YOUR MOTHER!

HEY, KID...

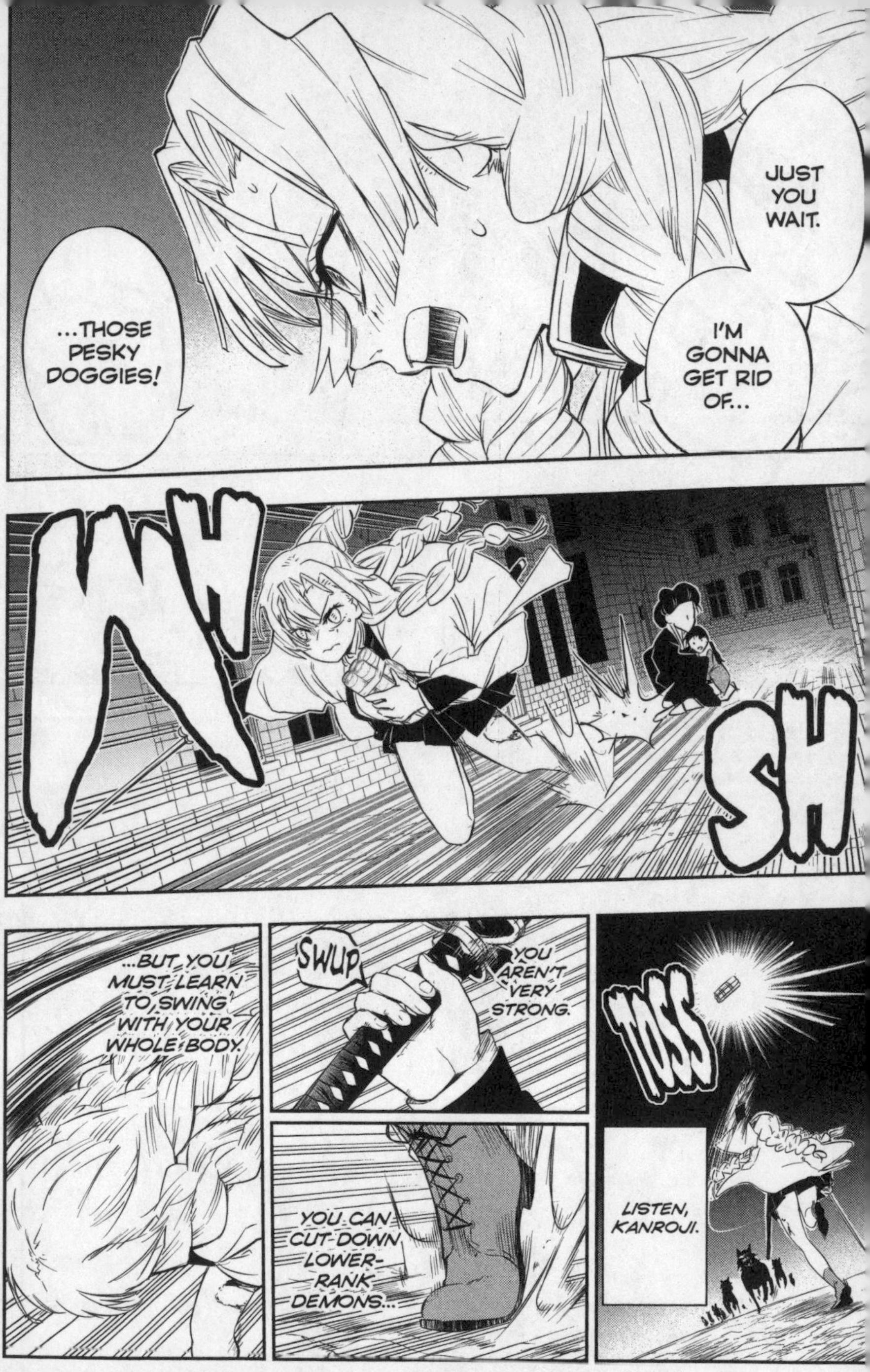
JUST YOU WAIT.
I'M GONNA GET RID OF...
...THOSE PESKY DOGGIES!
WH
SH
TOSS
LISTEN, KANROJI.
YOU AREN'T VERY STRONG.
SWUP
YOU CAN CUT DOWN LOWER-RANK DEMONS...
...BUT YOU MUST LEARN TO SWING WITH YOUR WHOLE BODY.

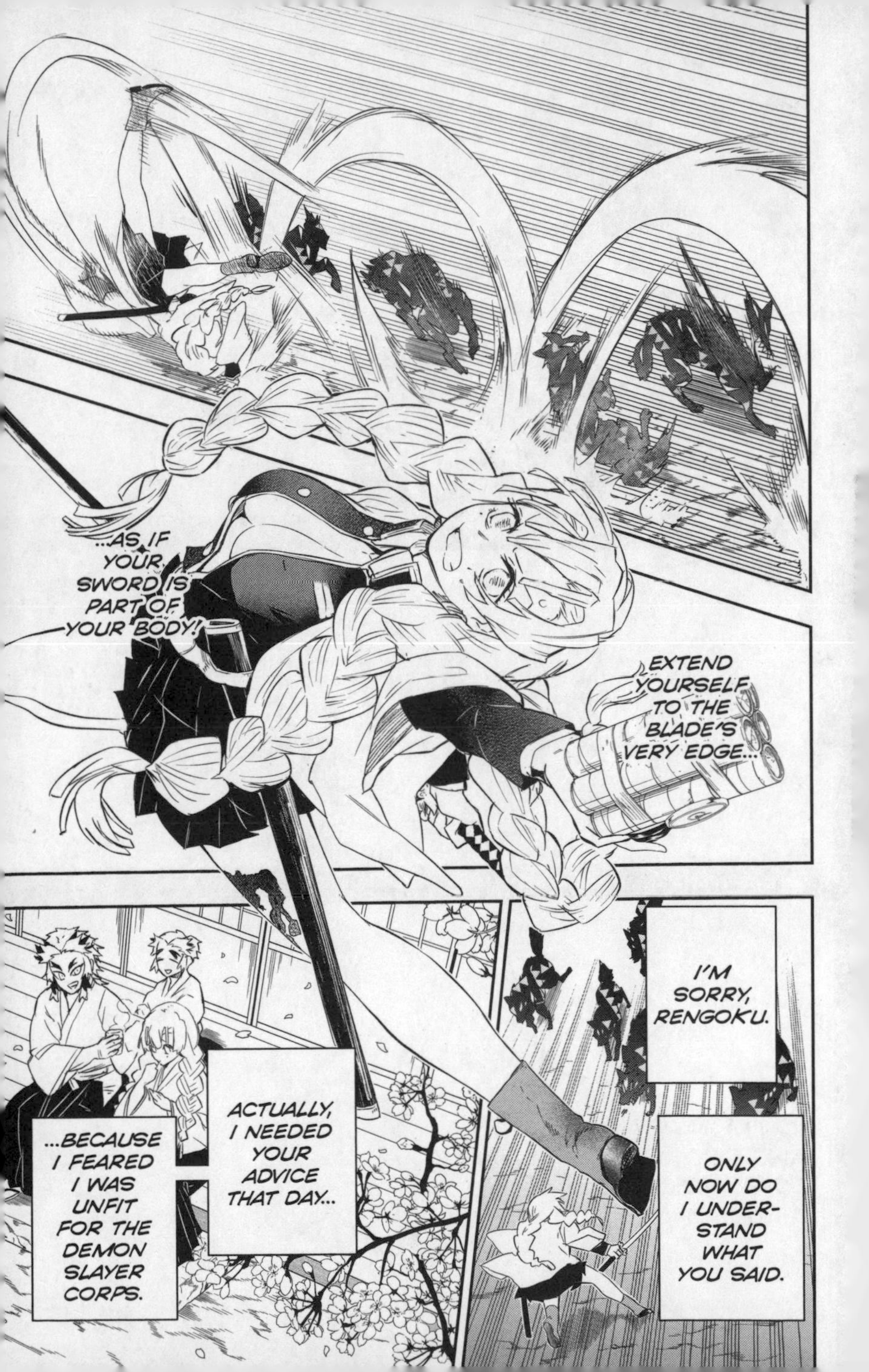
EXTEND YOURSELF TO THE BLADE'S VERY EDGE...
...AS IF YOUR SWORD IS PART OF YOUR BODY!
I'M SORRY, RENGOKU.
ONLY NOW DO I UNDER-STAND WHAT YOU SAID.
ACTUALLY, I NEEDED YOUR ADVICE THAT DAY...
...BECAUSE I FEARED I WAS UNFIT FOR THE DEMON SLAYER CORPS.

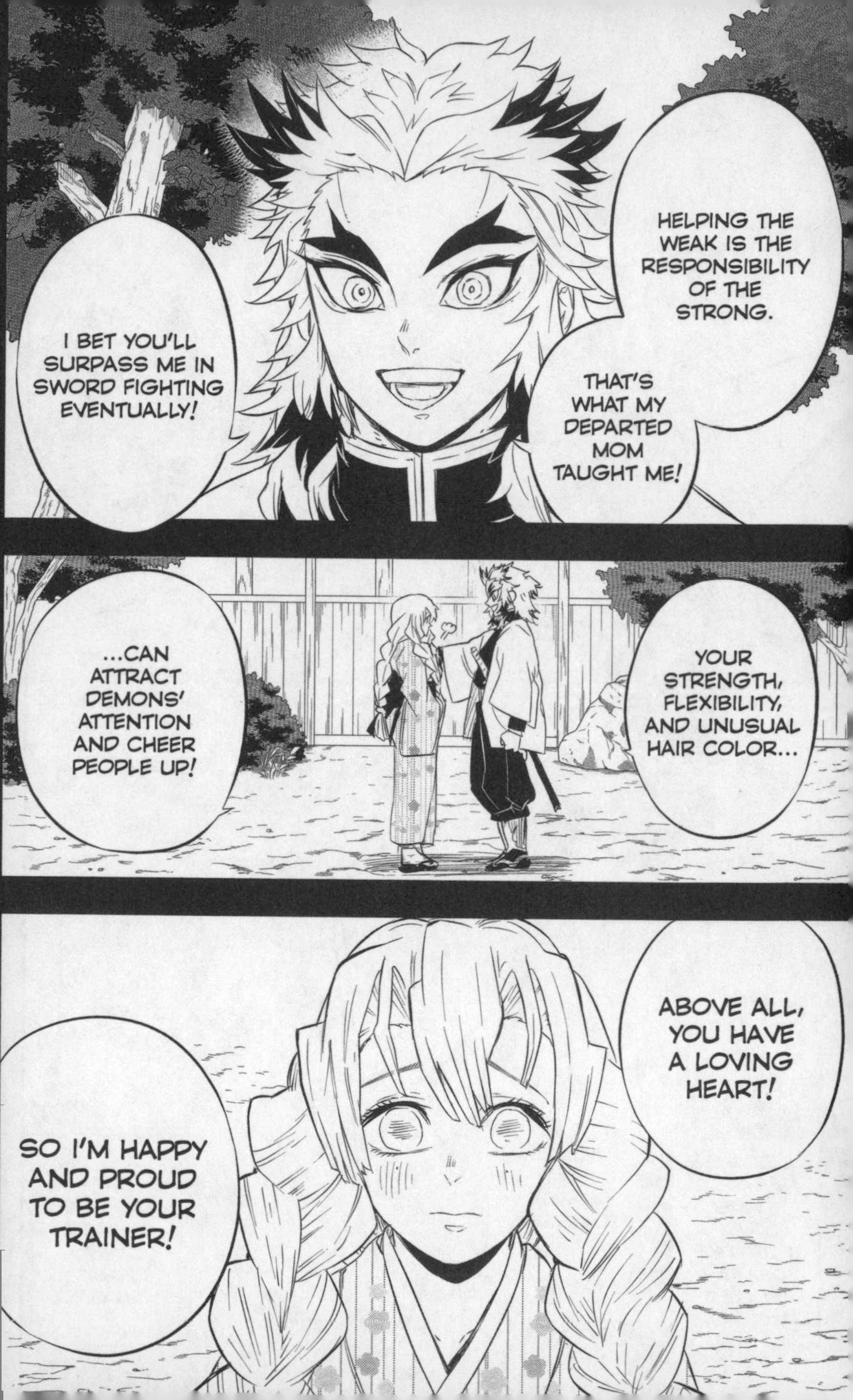
HELPING THE WEAK IS THE RESPONSIBILITY OF THE STRONG.
THAT'S WHAT MY DEPARTED MOM TAUGHT ME!
I BET YOU'LL SURPASS ME IN SWORD FIGHTING EVENTUALLY!
YOUR STRENGTH, FLEXIBILITY, AND UNUSUAL HAIR COLOR...
...CAN ATTRACT DEMONS' ATTENTION AND CHEER PEOPLE UP!
ABOVE ALL, YOU HAVE A LOVING HEART!
SO I'M HAPPY AND PROUD TO BE YOUR TRAINER!

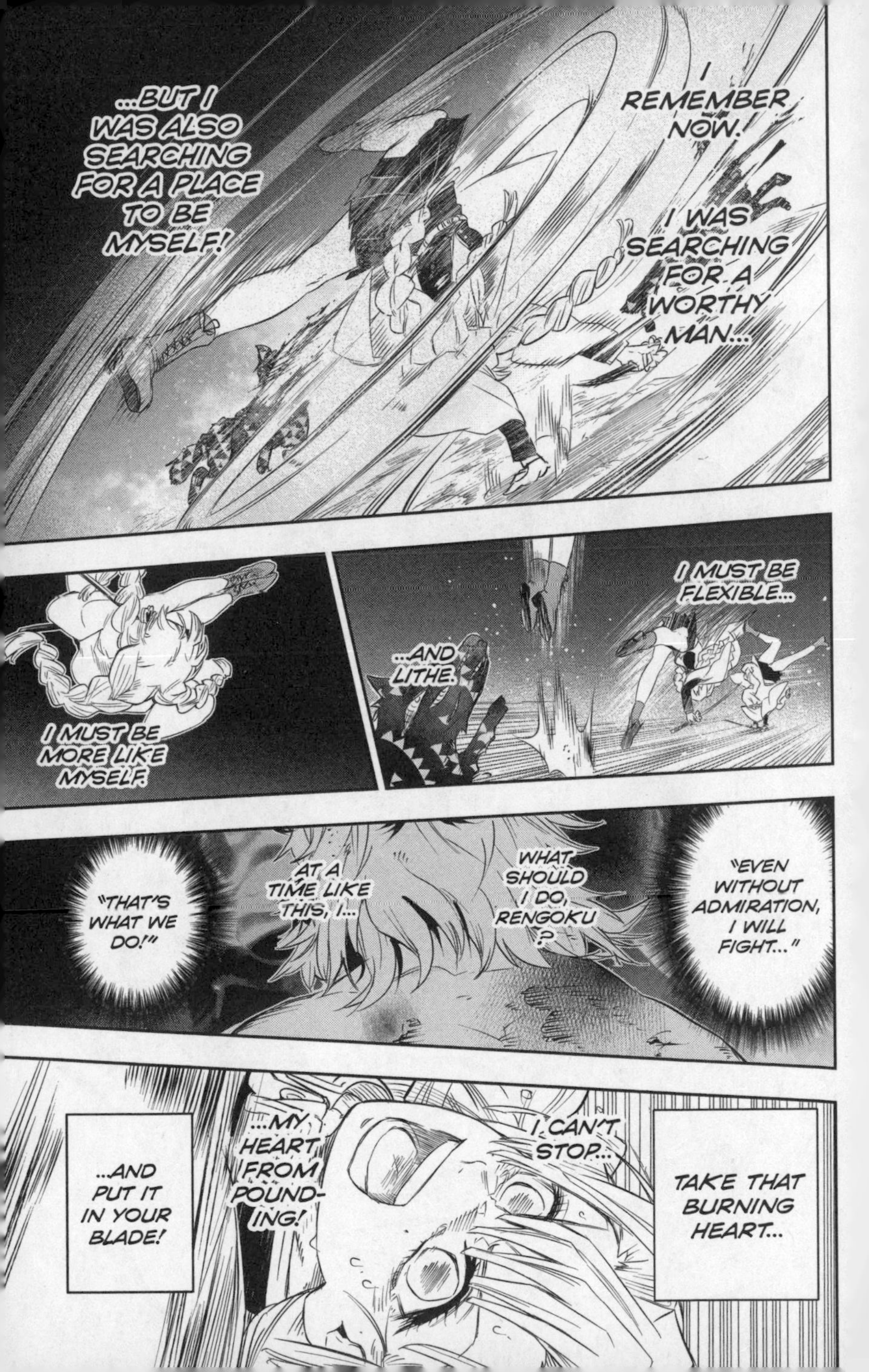
I REMEMBER NOW.
I WAS SEARCHING FOR A WORTHY MAN...
...BUT I WAS ALSO SEARCHING FOR A PLACE TO BE MYSELF!
I MUST BE FLEXIBLE...
...AND LITHE.
I MUST BE MORE LIKE MYSELF.
"EVEN WITHOUT ADMIRATION, I WILL FIGHT..."
WHAT SHOULD I DO, RENGOKU?
AT A TIME LIKE THIS, I...
"THAT'S WHAT WE DO!"
TAKE THAT BURNING HEART...
I CAN'T STOP...
...MY HEART FROM POUND-ING!
...AND PUT IT IN YOUR BLADE!

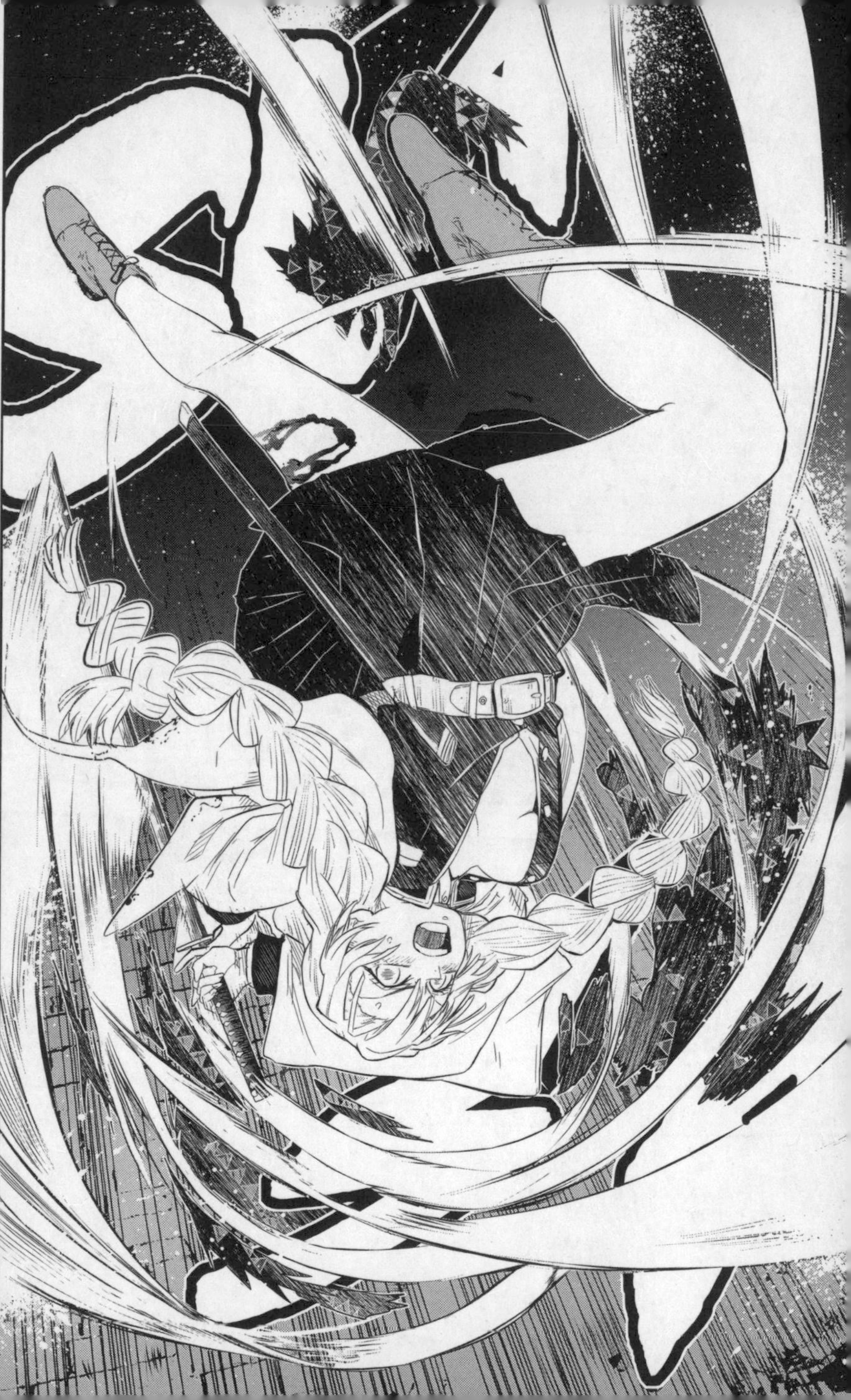

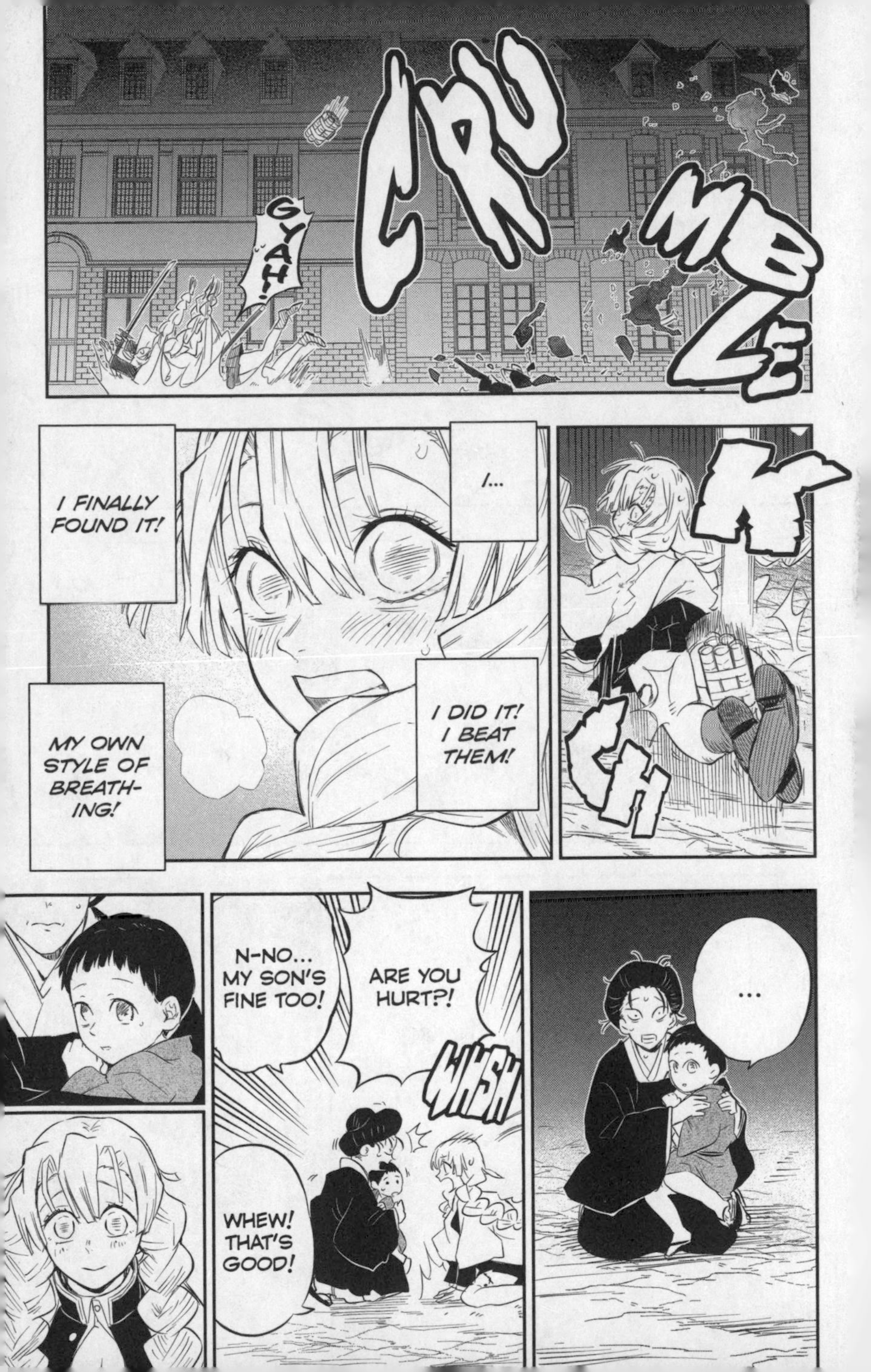
CRUMBLE
GYAH!
KCH
I...
I FINALLY FOUND IT!
I DID IT! I BEAT THEM!
MY OWN STYLE OF BREATH-ING!
...
WHSH
ARE YOU HURT?!
N-NO... MY SON'S FINE TOO!
WHEW! THAT'S GOOD!

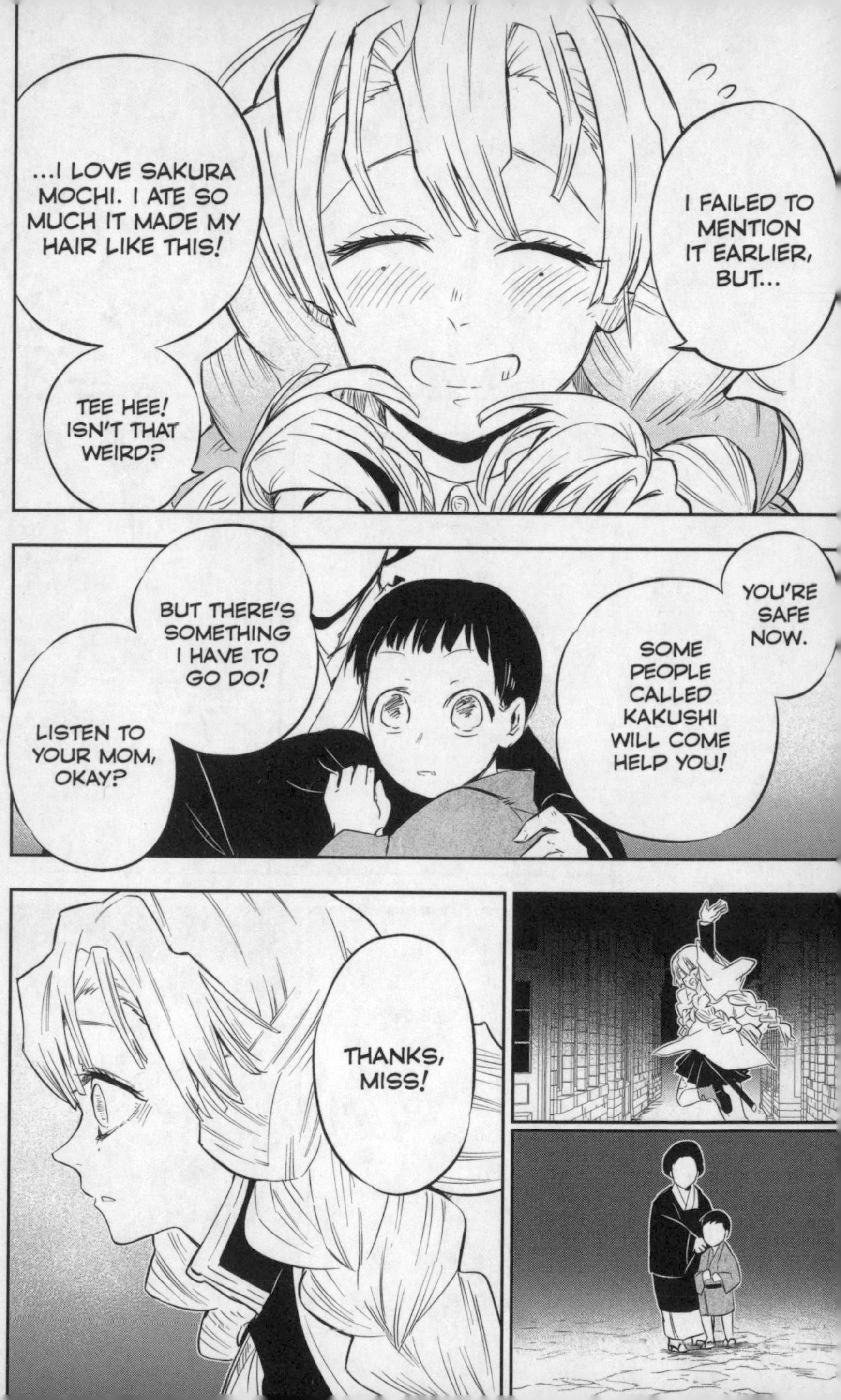
I FAILED TO MENTION IT EARLIER, BUT...
...I LOVE SAKURA MOCHI. I ATE SO MUCH IT MADE MY HAIR LIKE THIS!
TEE HEE! ISN'T THAT WEIRD?
YOU'RE SAFE NOW.
SOME PEOPLE CALLED KAKUSHI WILL COME HELP YOU!
BUT THERE'S SOMETHING I HAVE TO GO DO!
LISTEN TO YOUR MOM, OKAY?
THANKS, MISS!

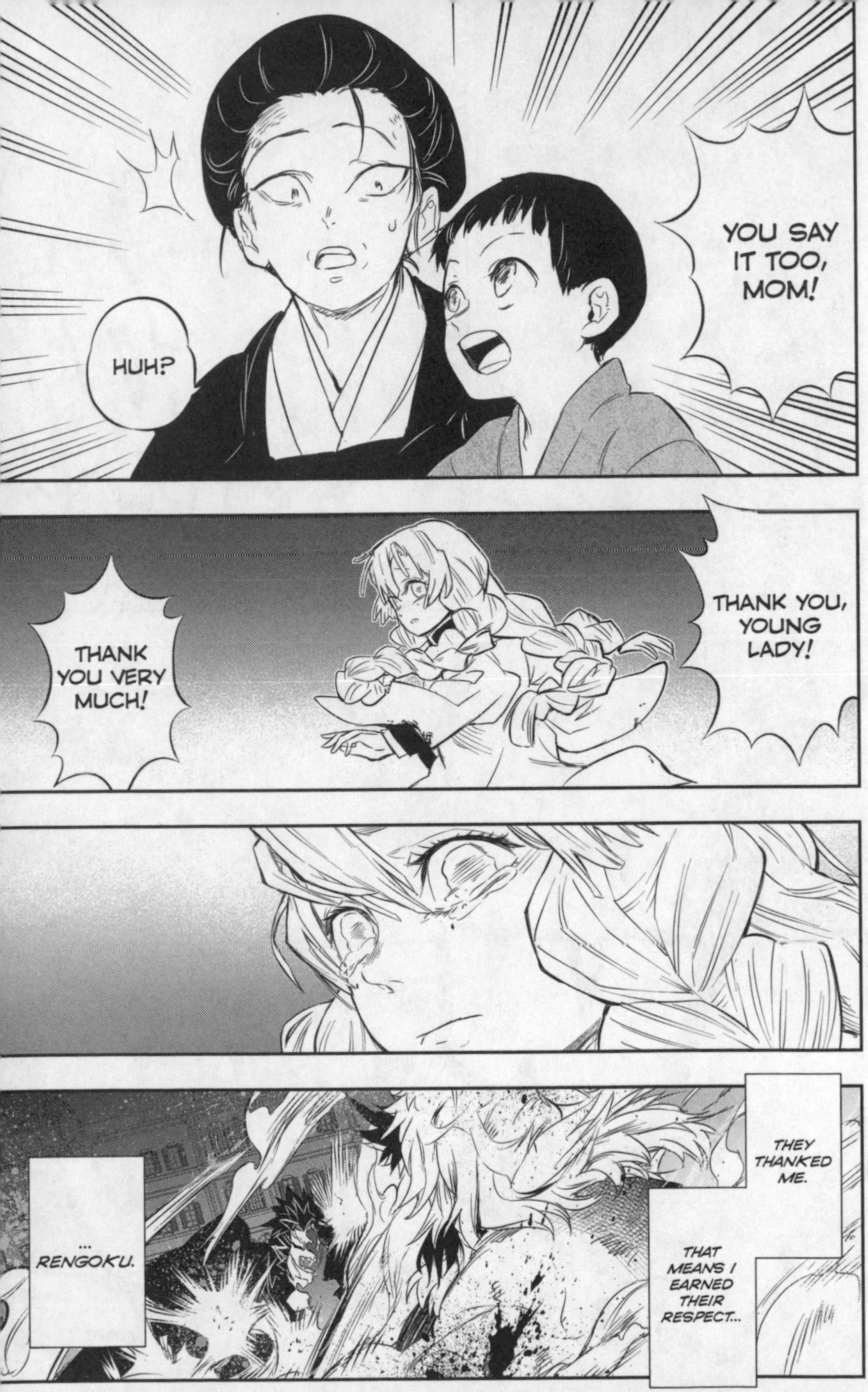
YOU SAY IT TOO, MOM!
HUH?
THANK YOU, YOUNG LADY!
THANK YOU VERY MUCH!
THEY THANKED ME.
THAT MEANS I EARNED THEIR RESPECT...
... RENGOKU.

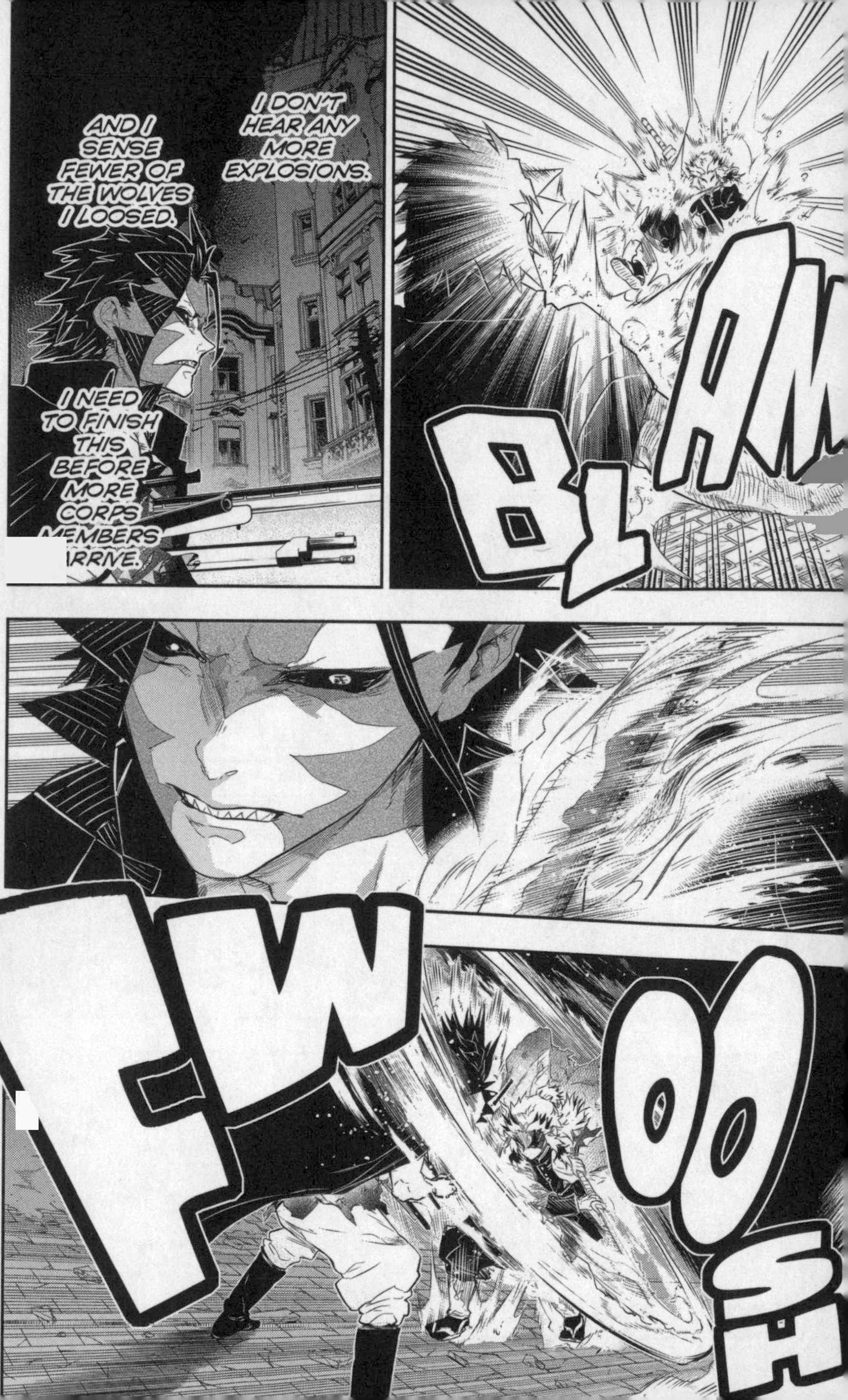
BLAM
I DON'T HEAR ANY MORE EXPLOSIONS.
AND I SENSE FEWER OF THE WOLVES I LOOSED.
I NEED TO FINISH THIS BEFORE MORE CORPS MEMBERS ARRIVE.
F-WOOSH

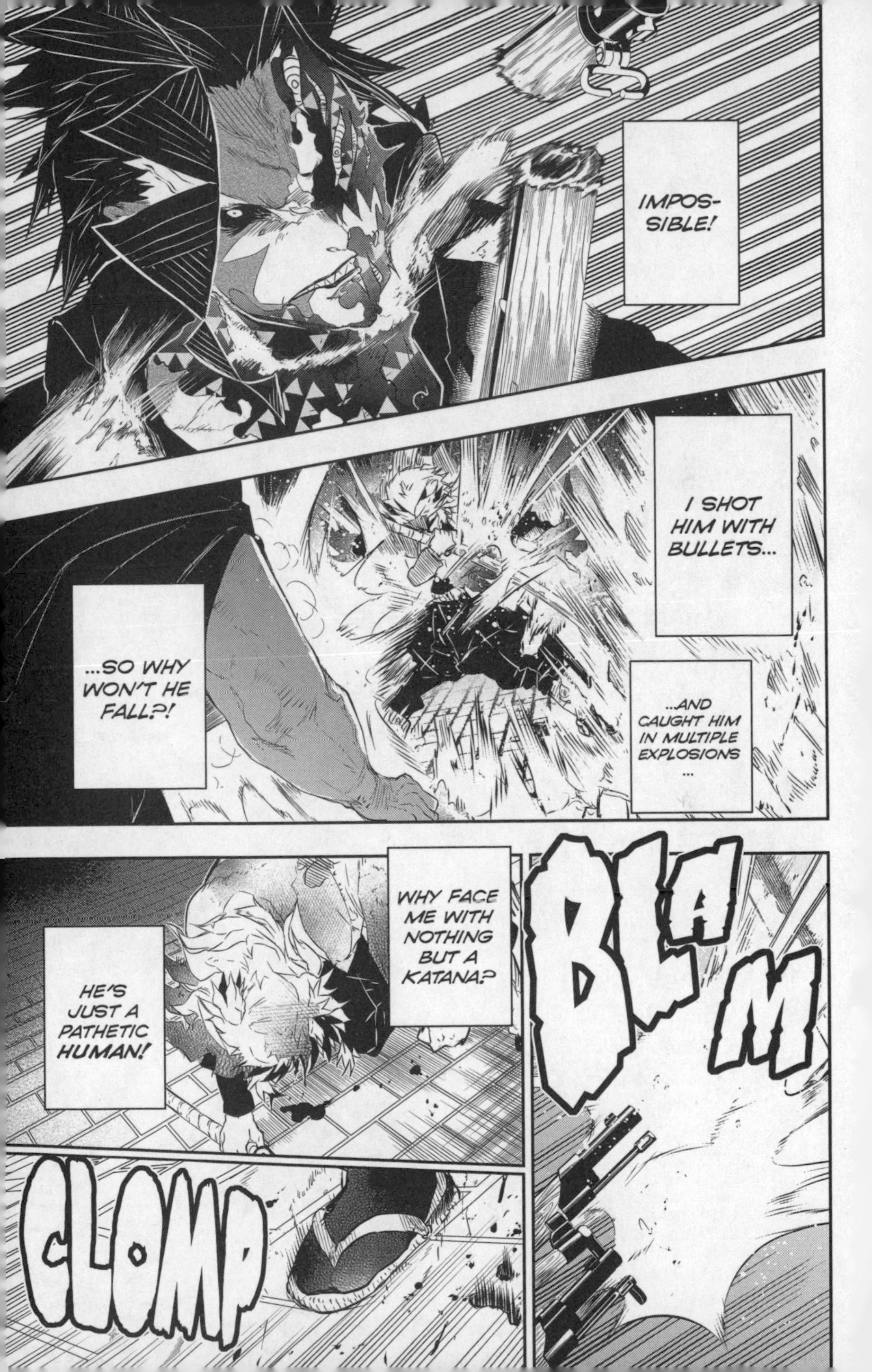
IMPOS-
SIBLE!
I SHOT HIM WITH BULLETS...
...AND CAUGHT HIM IN MULTIPLE EXPLOSIONS ...
...SO WHY WON'T HE FALL?!
BLAM
WHY FACE ME WITH NOTHING BUT A KATANA?
HE'S JUST A PATHETIC HUMAN!
CLOMP

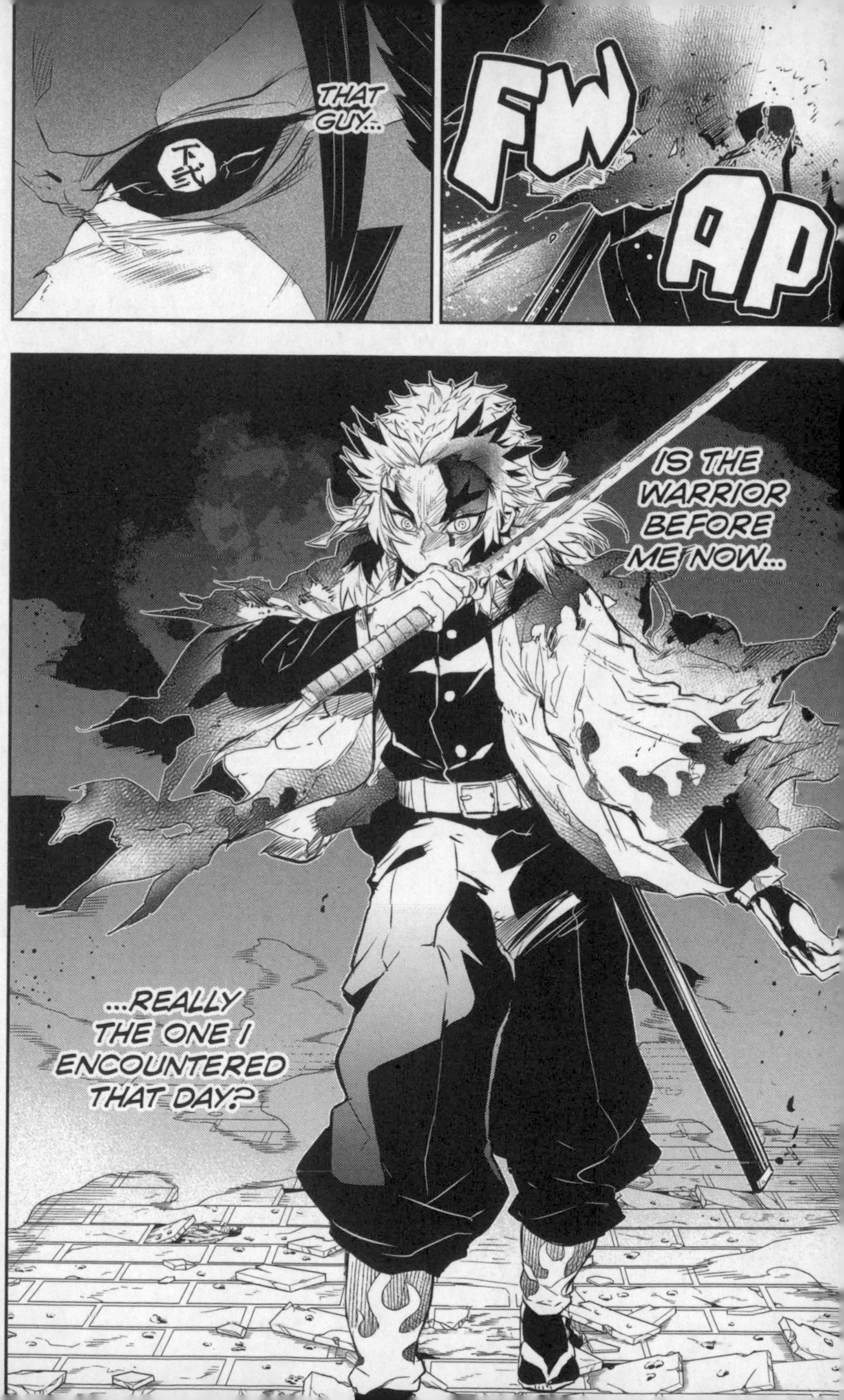
FWAP
THAT GUY...
下弐
IS THE WARRIOR BEFORE ME NOW...
...REALLY THE ONE I ENCOUNTERED THAT DAY?

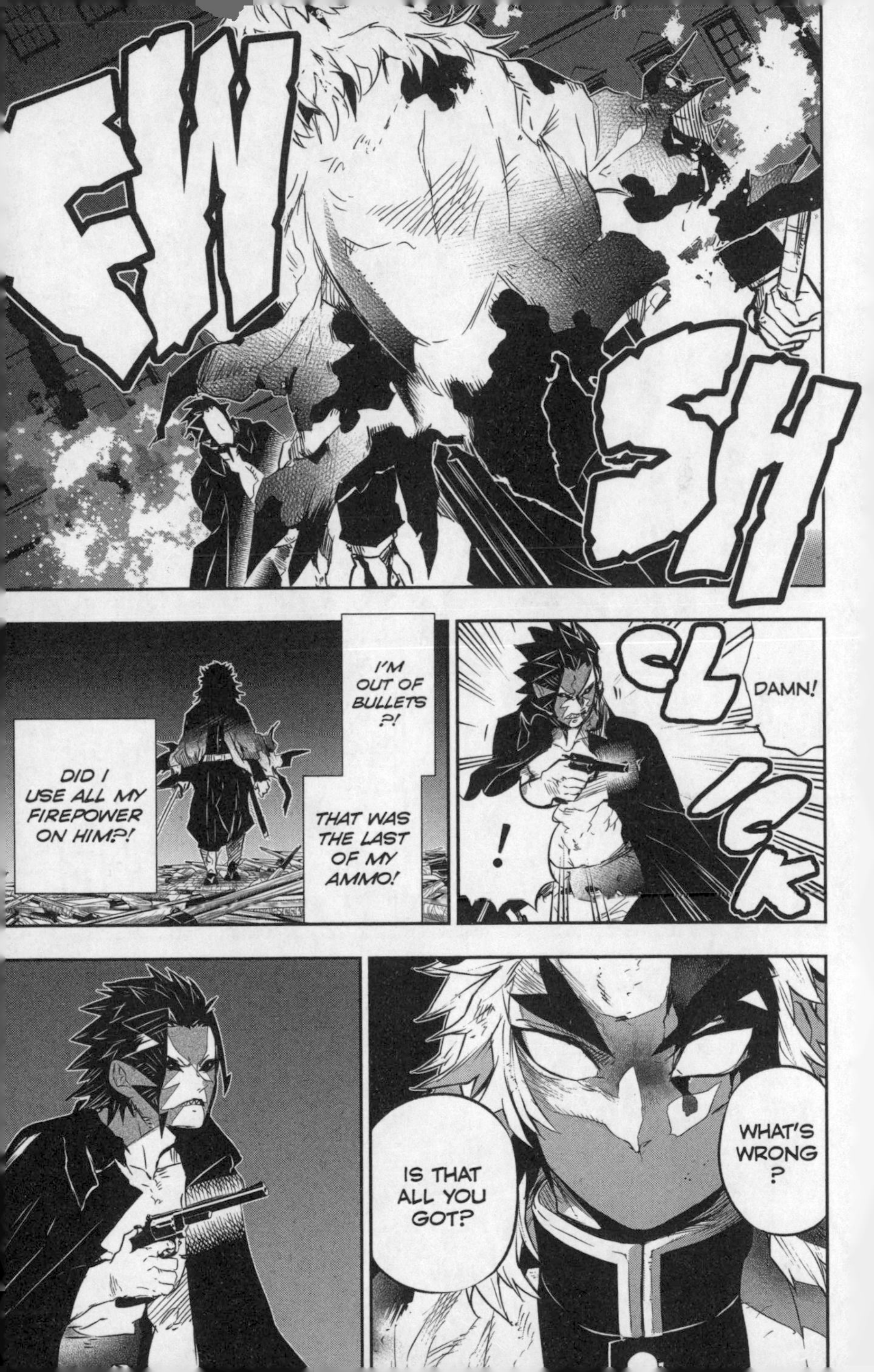
FWSH
CLICK
DAMN!
!
I'M OUT OF BULLETS?!
THAT WAS THE LAST OF MY AMMO!
DID I USE ALL MY FIREPOWER ON HIM?!
WHAT'S WRONG?
IS THAT ALL YOU GOT?

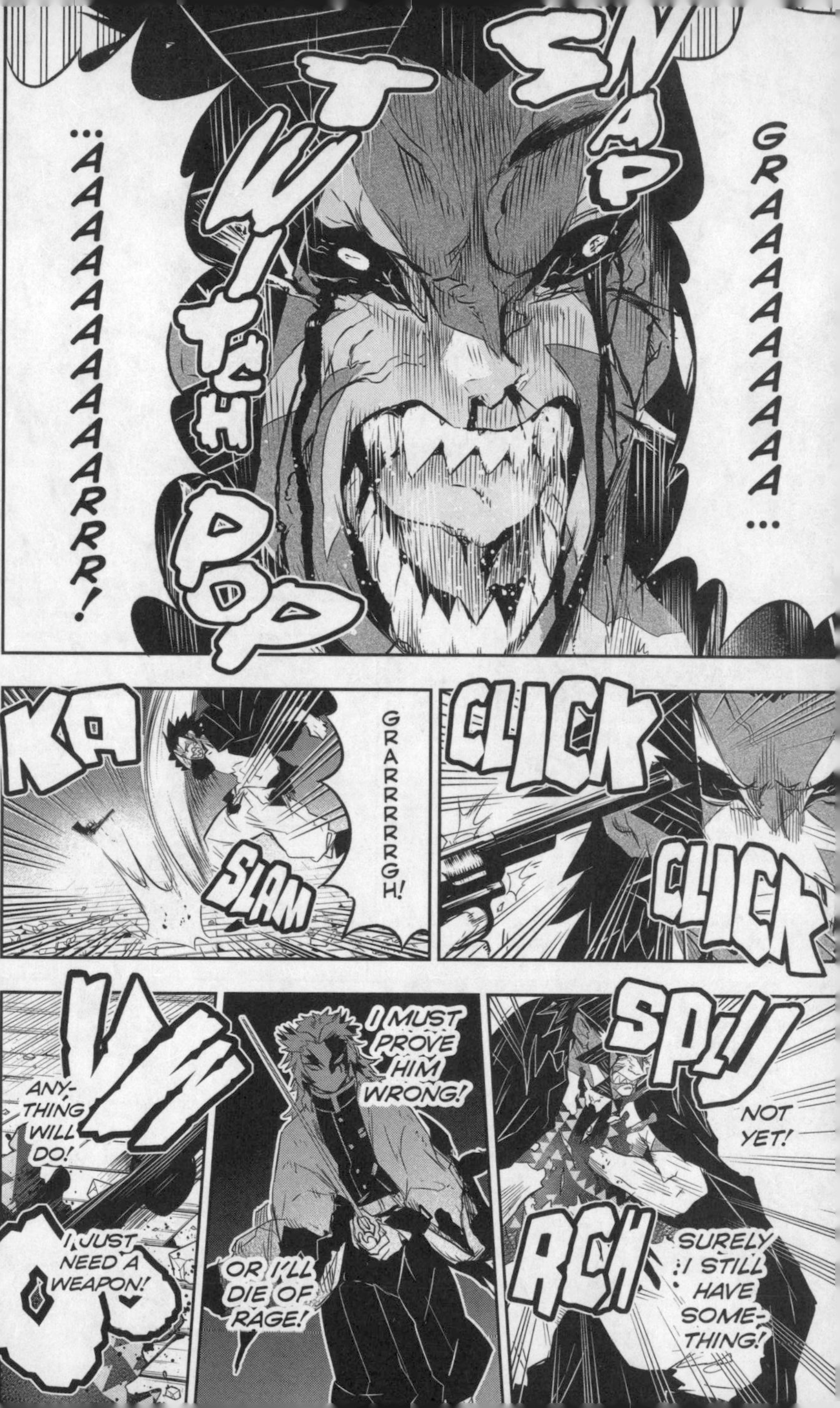
SNAP
GRAAAAAAAAAA...
TWITCH
POP
...AAAAAAAAAAAARRRR!
CLICK
CLICK
KA
GRARRRRRGH!
SLAM
SPLU
RCH
NOT YET!
SURELY I STILL HAVE SOME-THING!
I MUST PROVE HIM WRONG!
OR I'LL DIE OF RAGE!
ANY-THING WILL DO!
I JUST NEED A WEAPON!

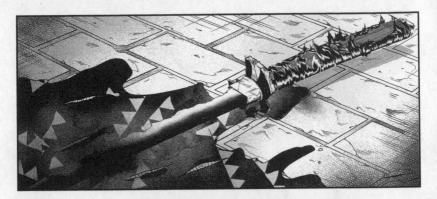

BUSHIDO IS A RELIC OF THE PAST!

HOW PITIFUL!

TRY STOPPING OUR BULLETS WITH BUSHIDO!

HA HA HA HA!

OUR SWORDS NEVER LOSE AGAINST GUNS.

DO NOT WORRY.

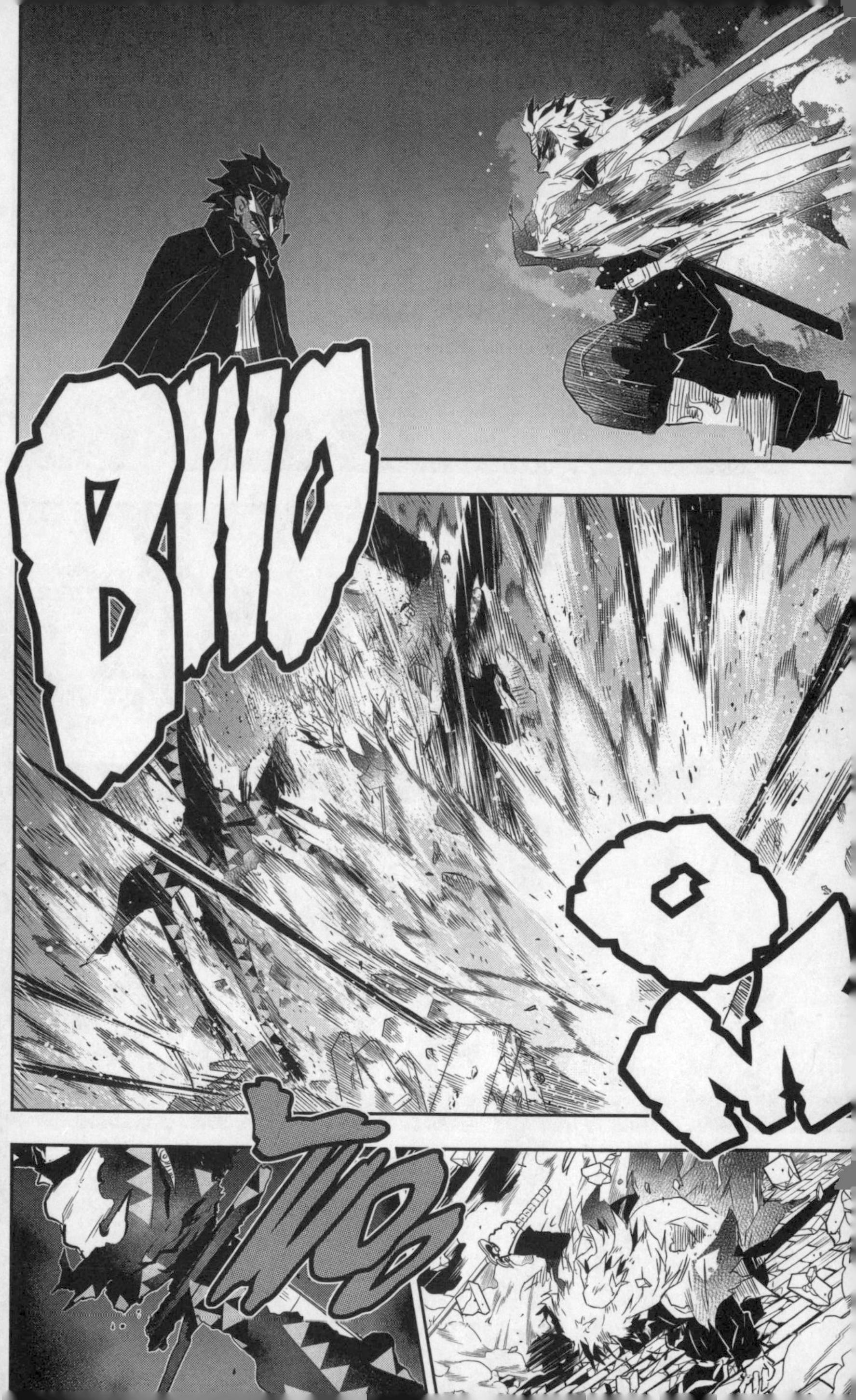

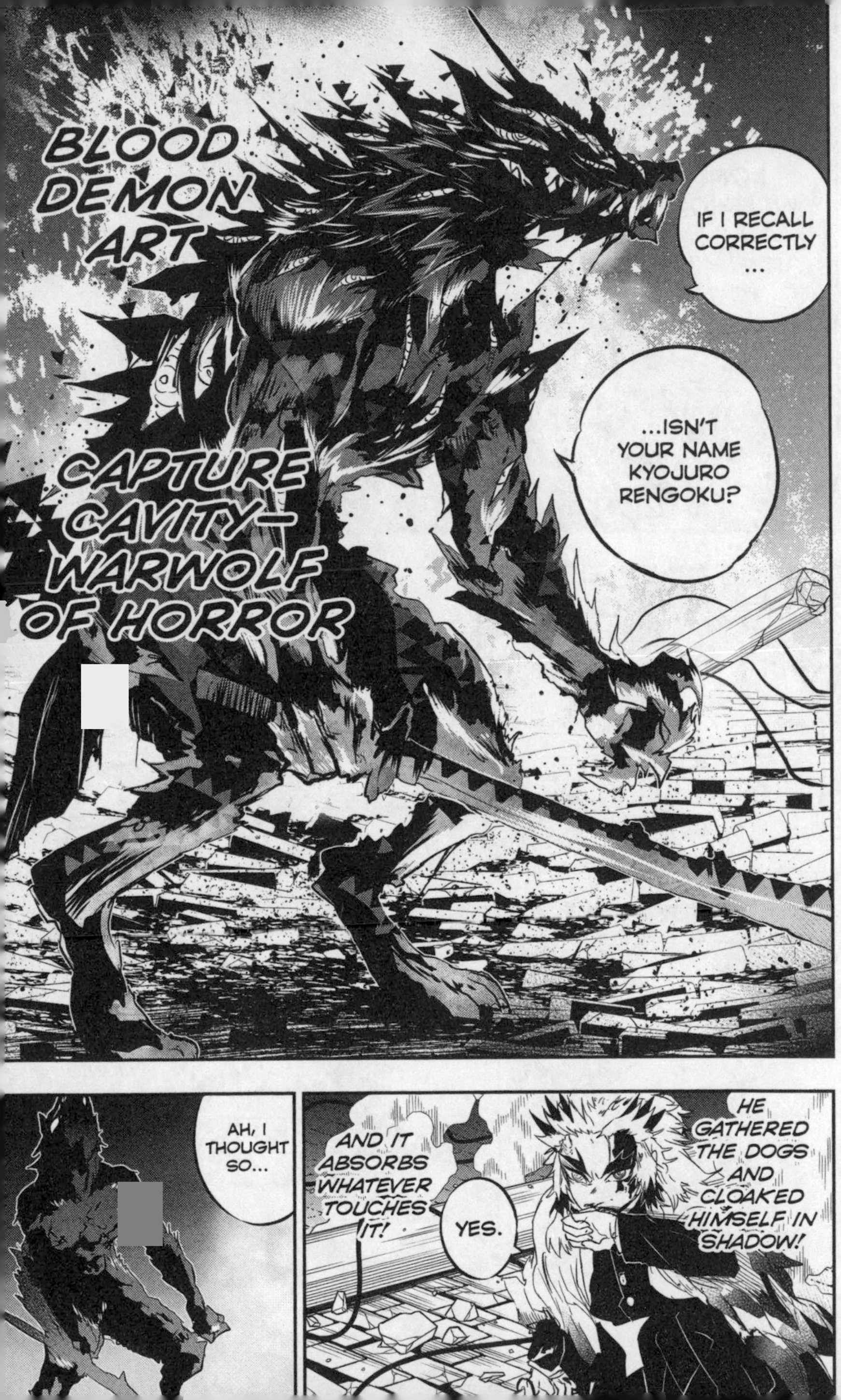
IF I RECALL CORRECTLY ...
...ISN'T YOUR NAME KYOJURO RENGOKU?
BLOOD DEMON ART
CAPTURE CAVITY— WARWOLF OF HORROR
HE GATHERED THE DOGS AND CLOAKED HIMSELF IN SHADOW!
AND IT ABSORBS WHATEVER TOUCHES IT!
YES.
AH, I THOUGHT SO...

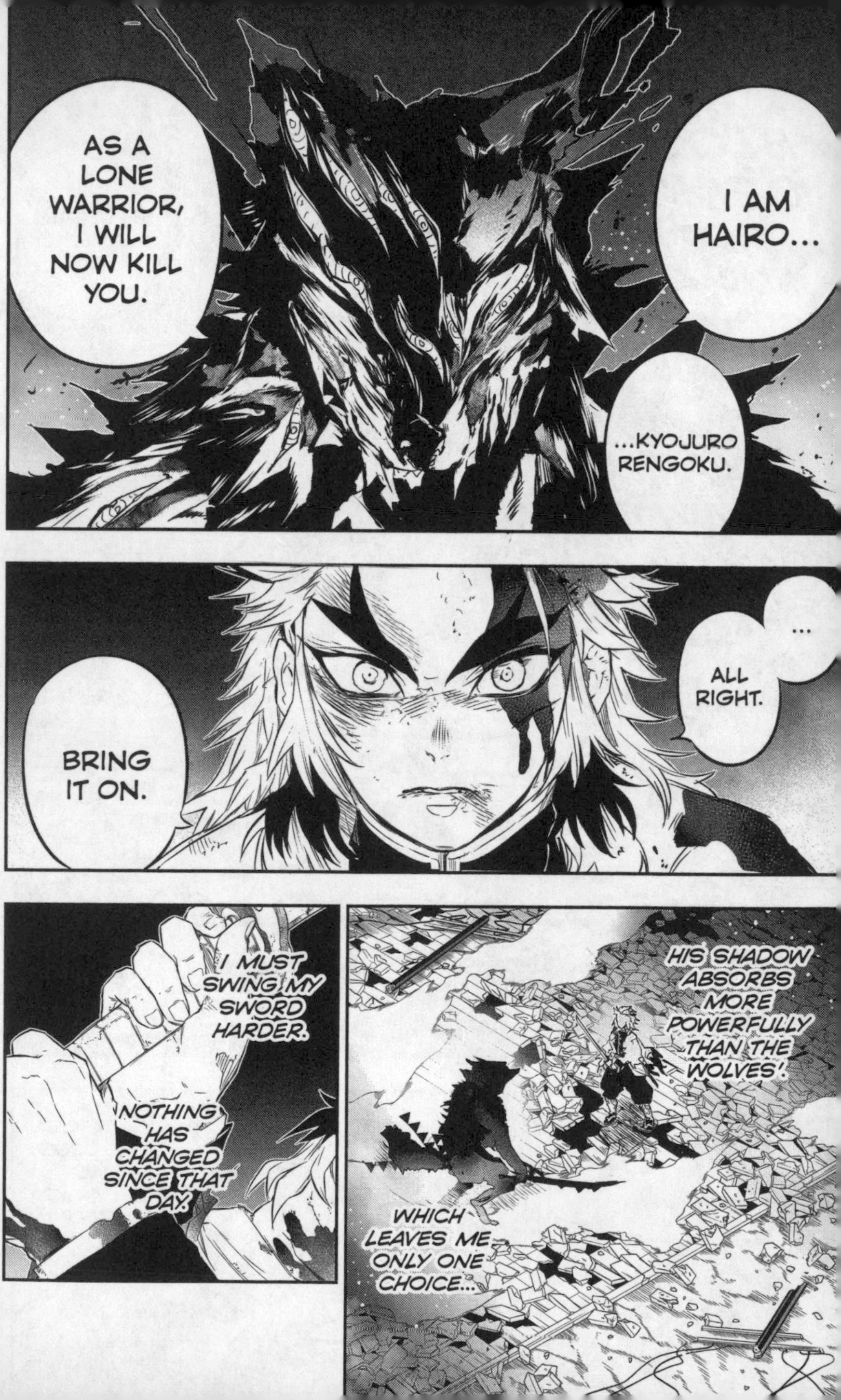
I AM HAIRO...
...KYOJURO RENGOKU.
AS A LONE WARRIOR, I WILL NOW KILL YOU.
... ALL RIGHT.
BRING IT ON.
HIS SHADOW ABSORBS MORE POWERFULLY THAN THE WOLVES!
WHICH LEAVES ME ONLY ONE CHOICE...
I MUST SWING MY SWORD HARDER.
NOTHING HAS CHANGED SINCE THAT DAY.

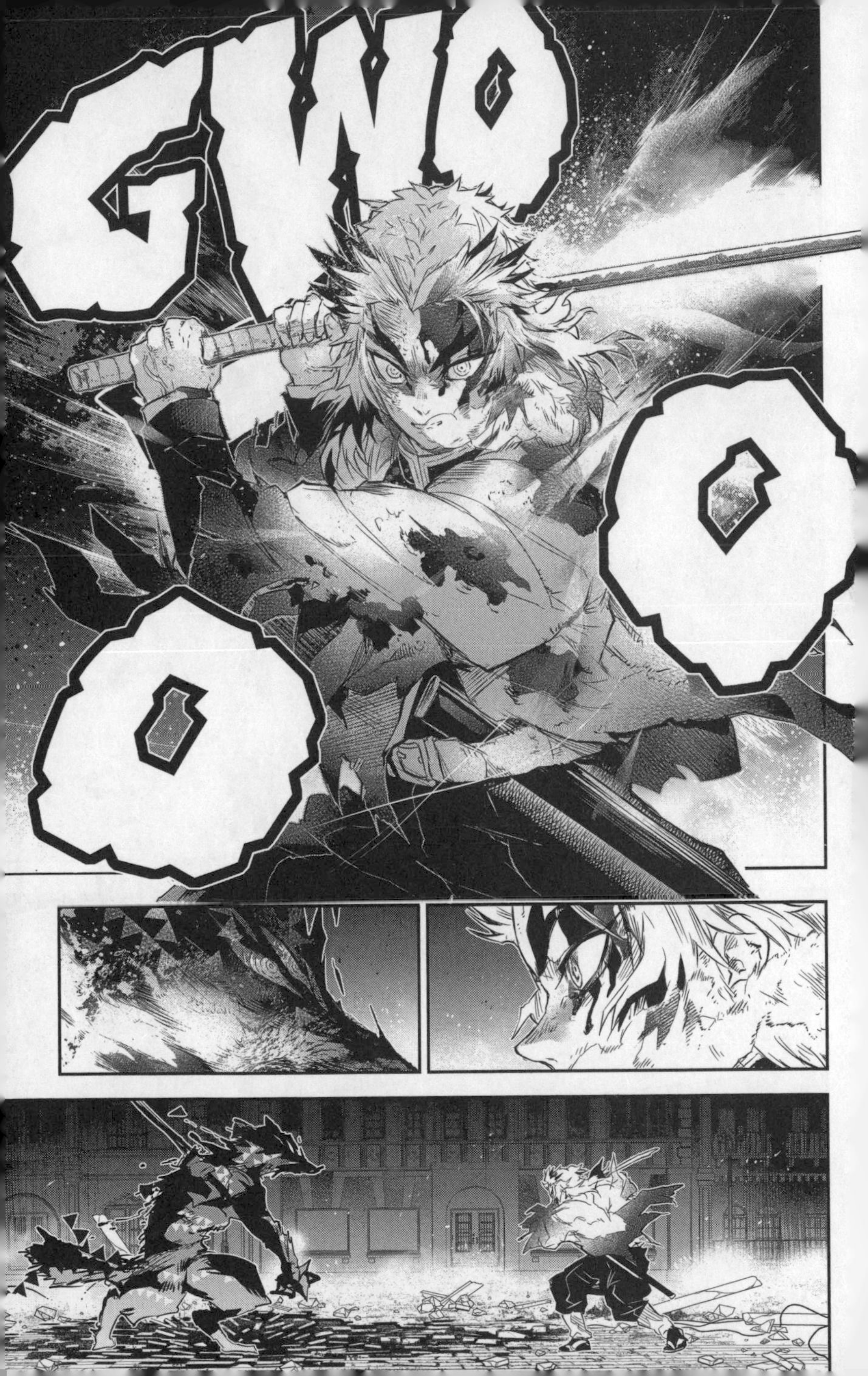
GWOOO

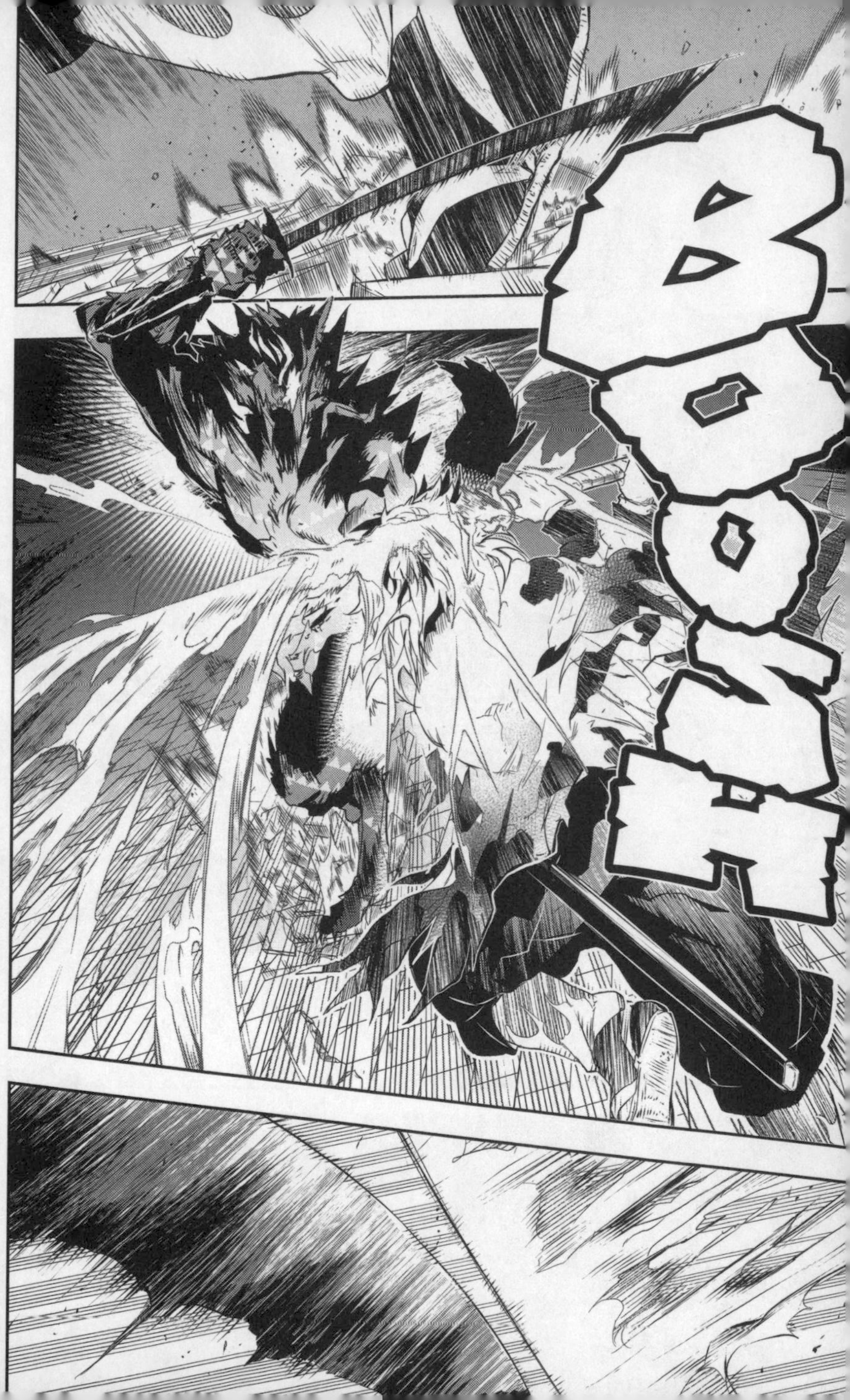
BOOM

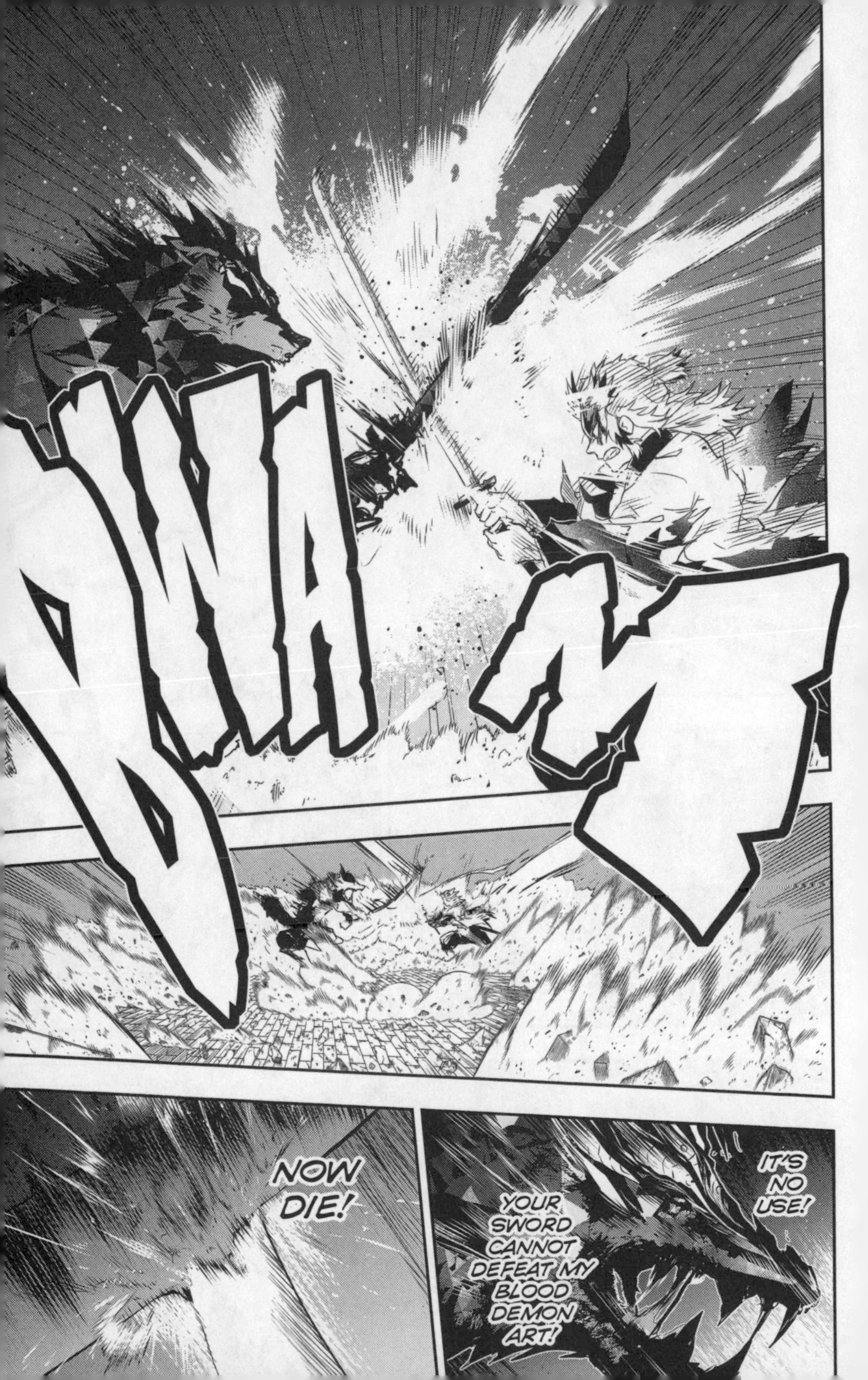
IT'S NO USE!
YOUR SWORD CANNOT DEFEAT MY BLOOD DEMON ART!
NOW DIE!

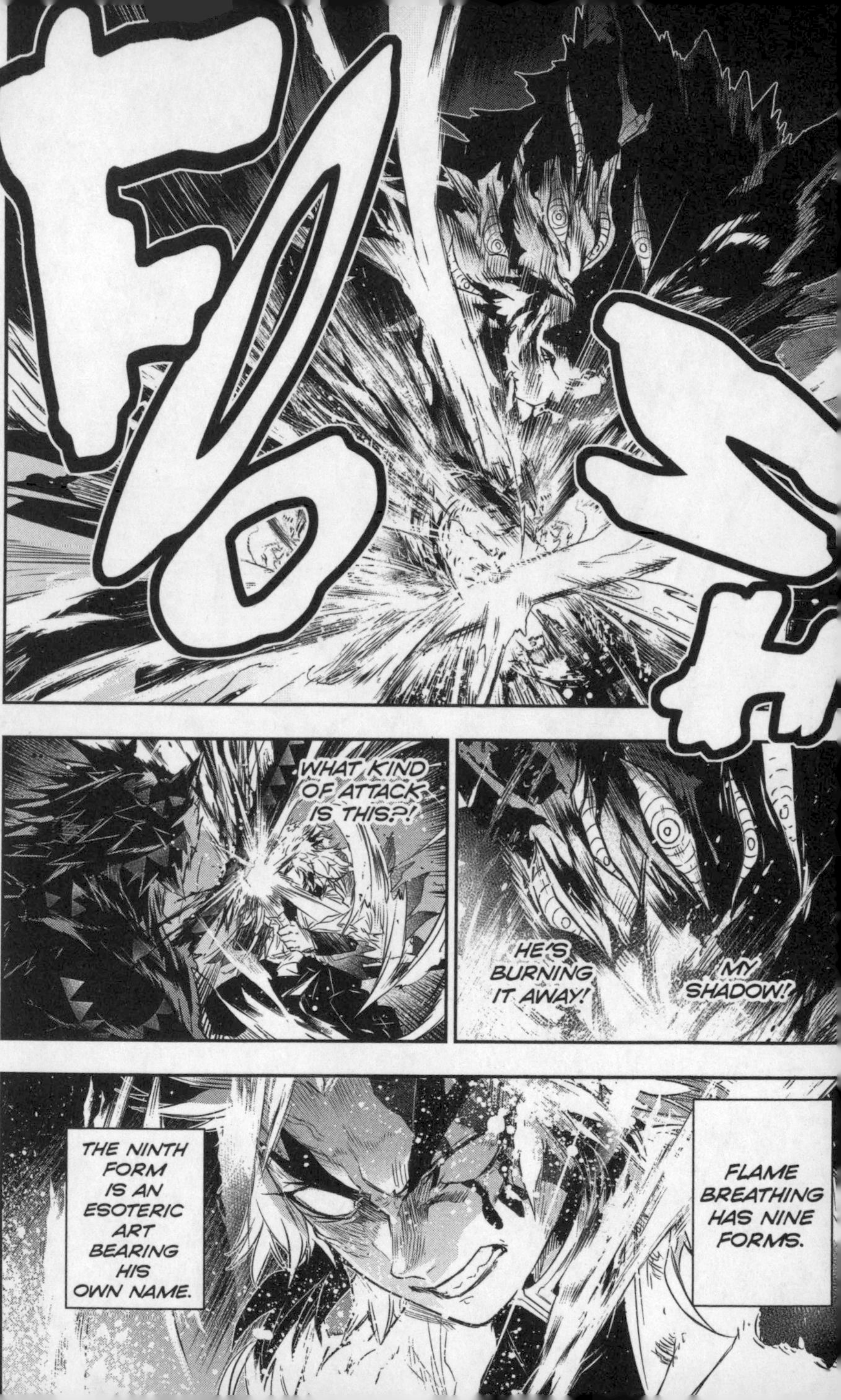

MY SHADOW!
HE'S BURNING IT AWAY!
WHAT KIND OF ATTACK IS THIS?!
FLAME BREATHING HAS NINE FORMS.
THE NINTH FORM IS AN ESOTERIC ART BEARING HIS OWN NAME.

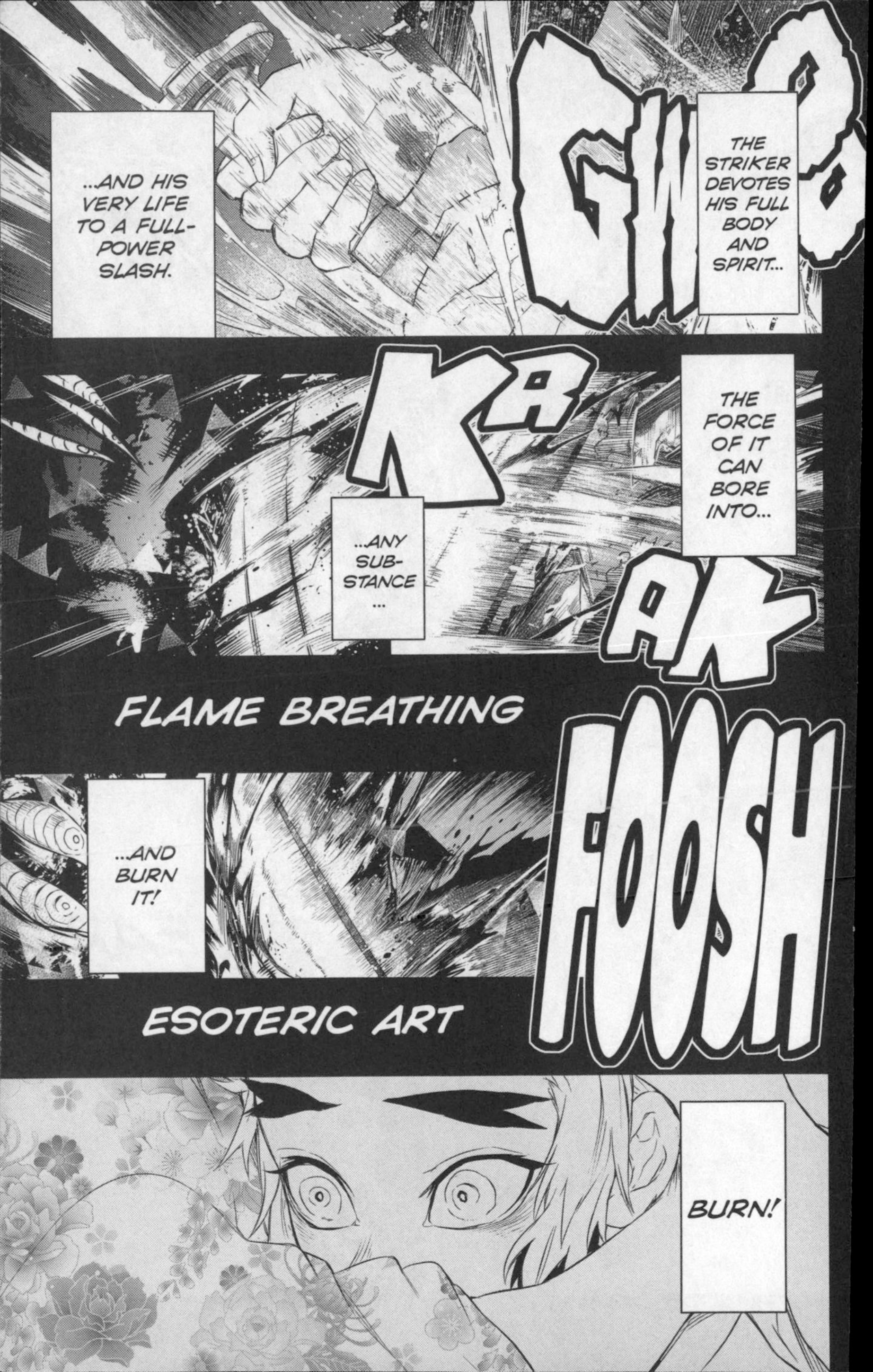
THE STRIKER DEVOTES HIS FULL BODY AND SPIRIT...
...AND HIS VERY LIFE TO A FULL-POWER SLASH.
THE FORCE OF IT CAN BORE INTO...
KRAK
...ANY SUBSTANCE...
FOOSH
FLAME BREATHING
...AND BURN IT!
ESOTERIC ART
BURN!

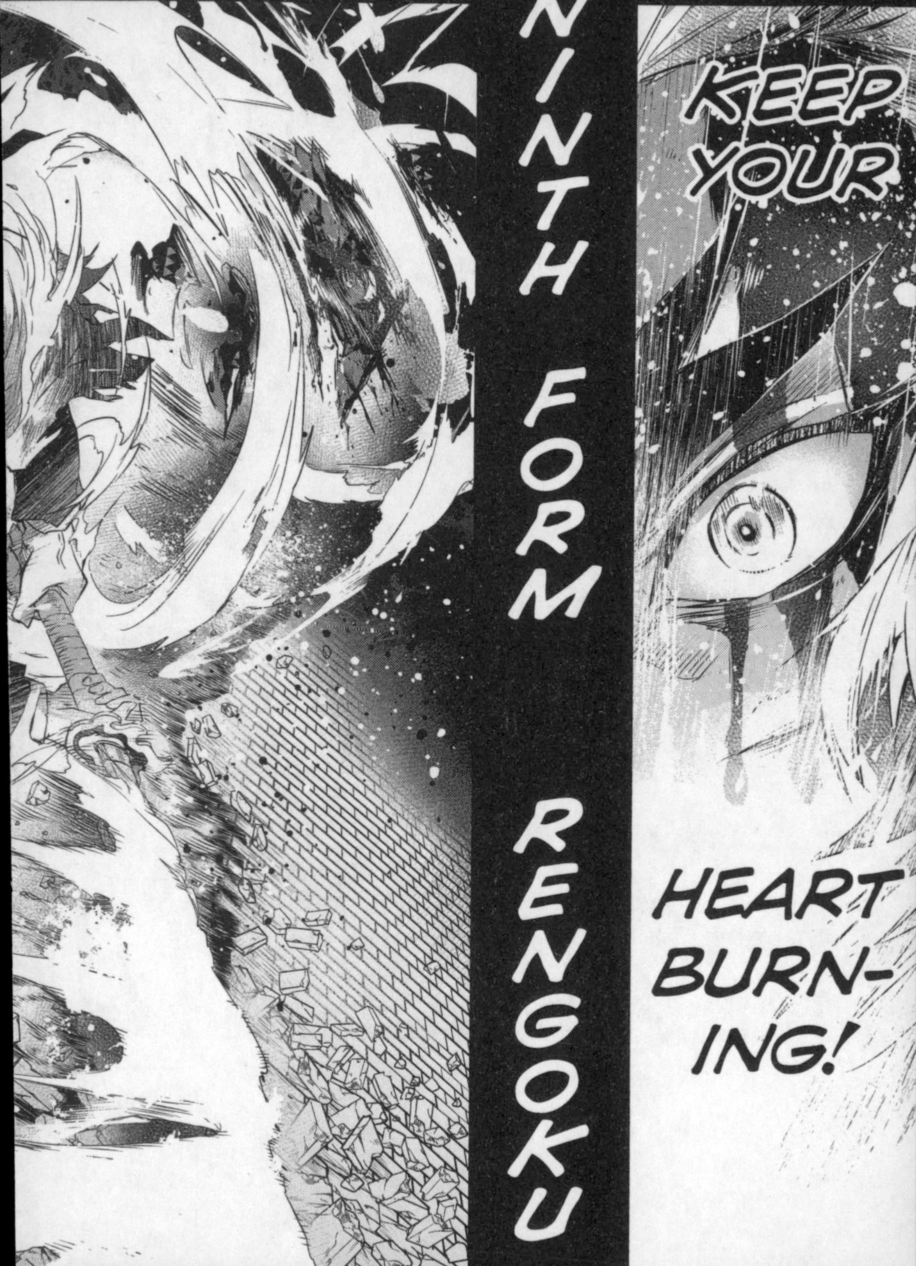
KEEP YOUR HEART BURNING!
NINTH FORM RENGOKU

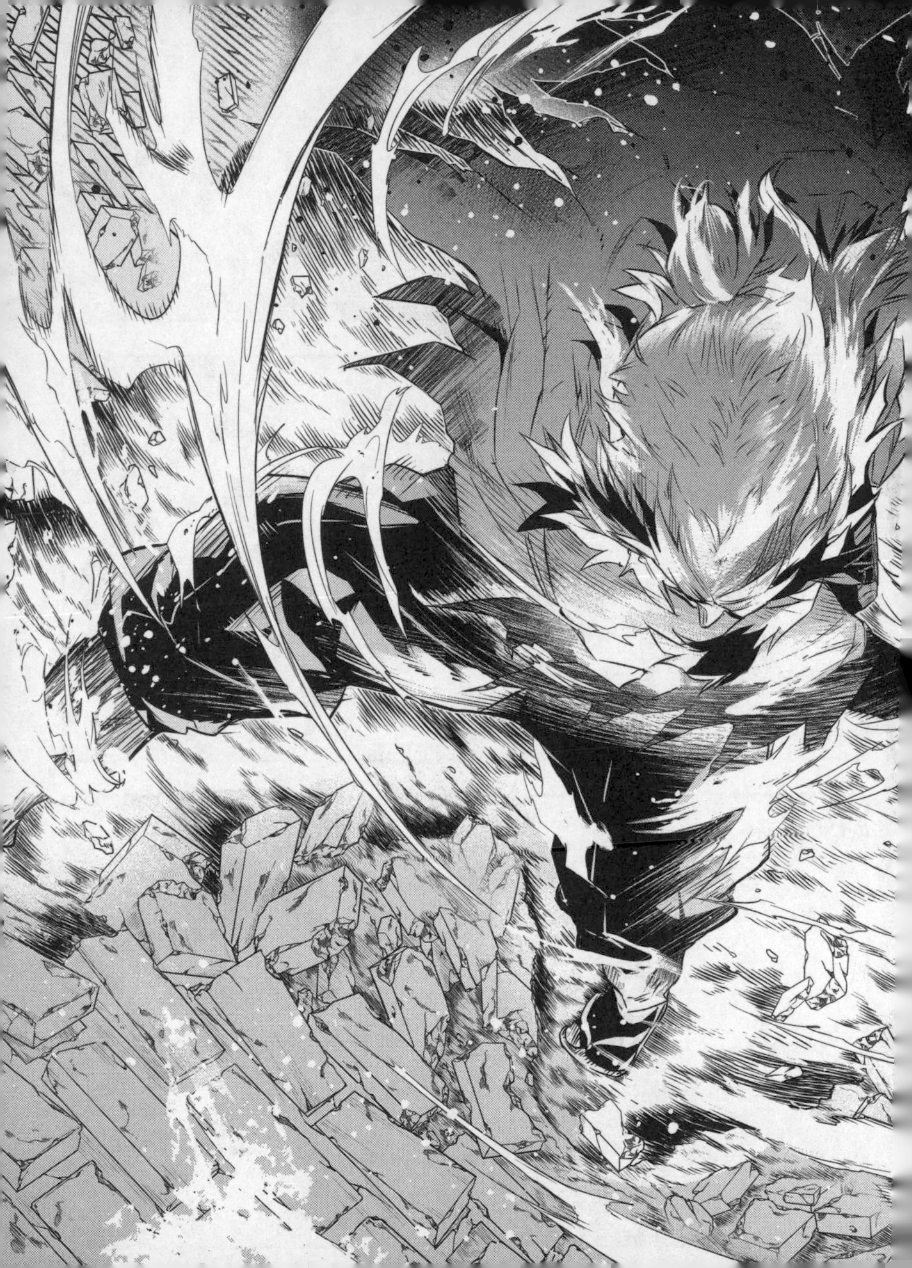

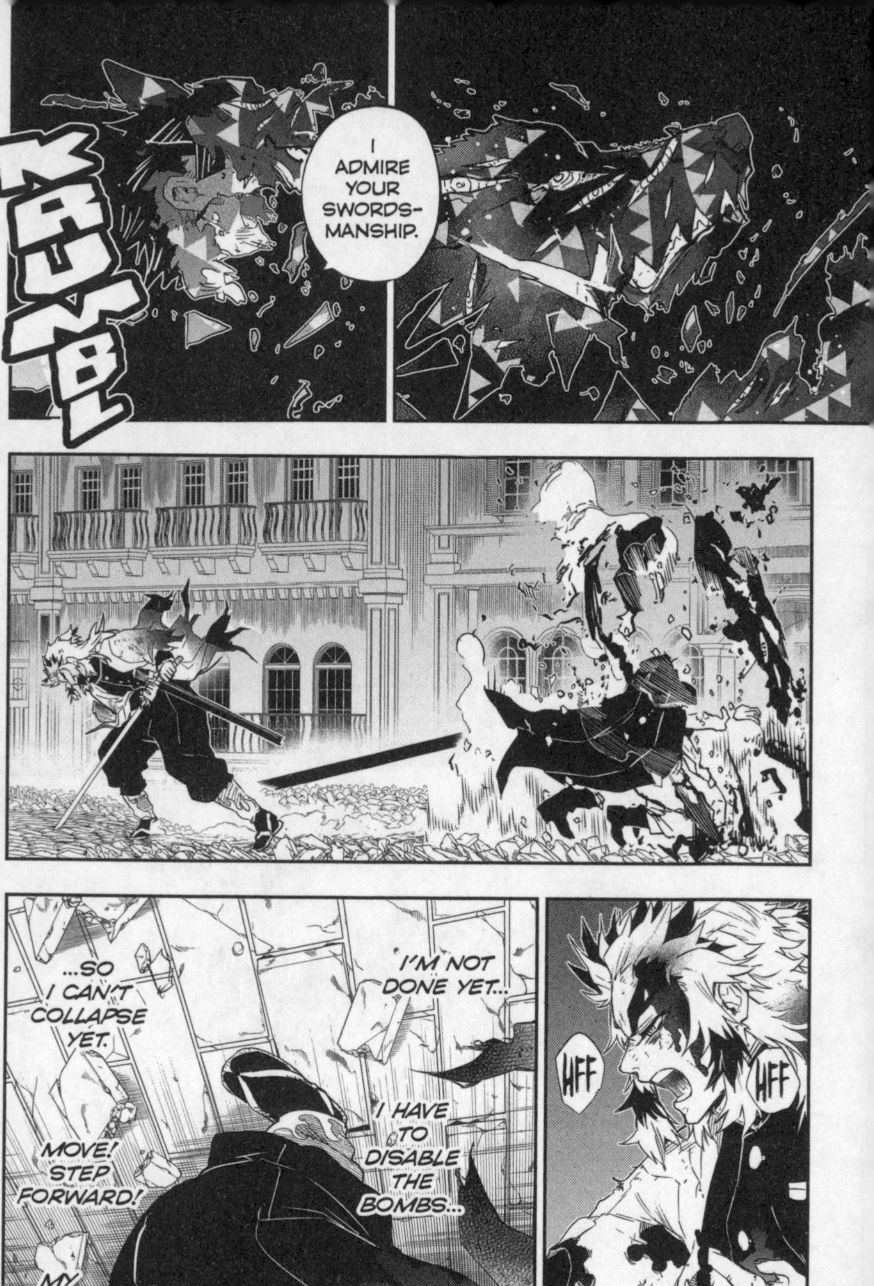
I ADMIRE YOUR SWORDS-MANSHIP.
KRUMBL
HFF
HFF
I'M NOT DONE YET...
I HAVE TO DISABLE THE BOMBS...
...SO I CAN'T COLLAPSE YET.
MOVE! STEP FORWARD!
MY BODY...

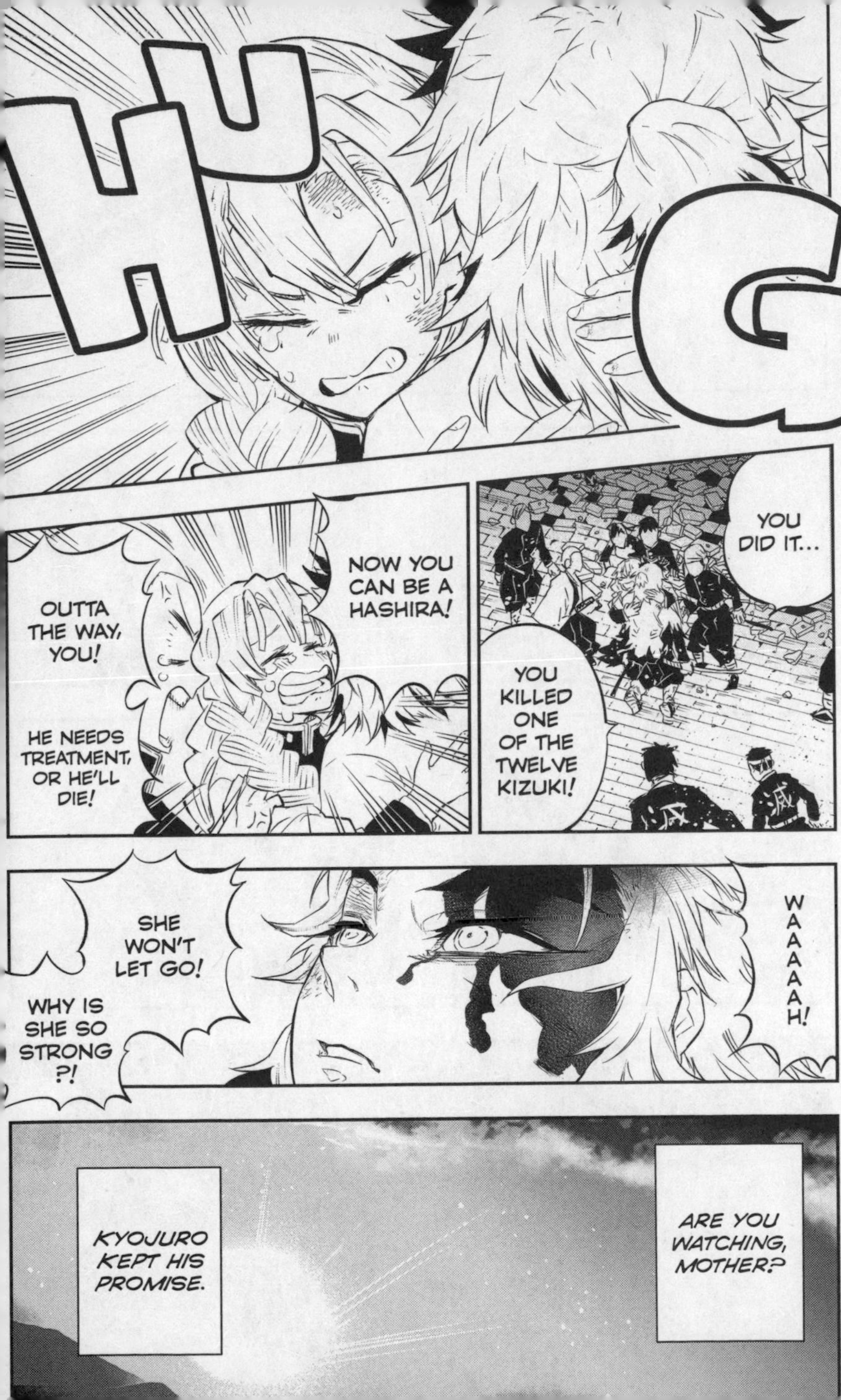
HUG
YOU DID IT...
YOU KILLED ONE OF THE TWELVE KIZUKI!
NOW YOU CAN BE A HASHIRA!
OUTTA THE WAY, YOU!
HE NEEDS TREATMENT, OR HE'LL DIE!
WAAAAAH!
SHE WON'T LET GO!
WHY IS SHE SO STRONG?!
ARE YOU WATCHING, MOTHER?
KYOJURO KEPT HIS PROMISE.

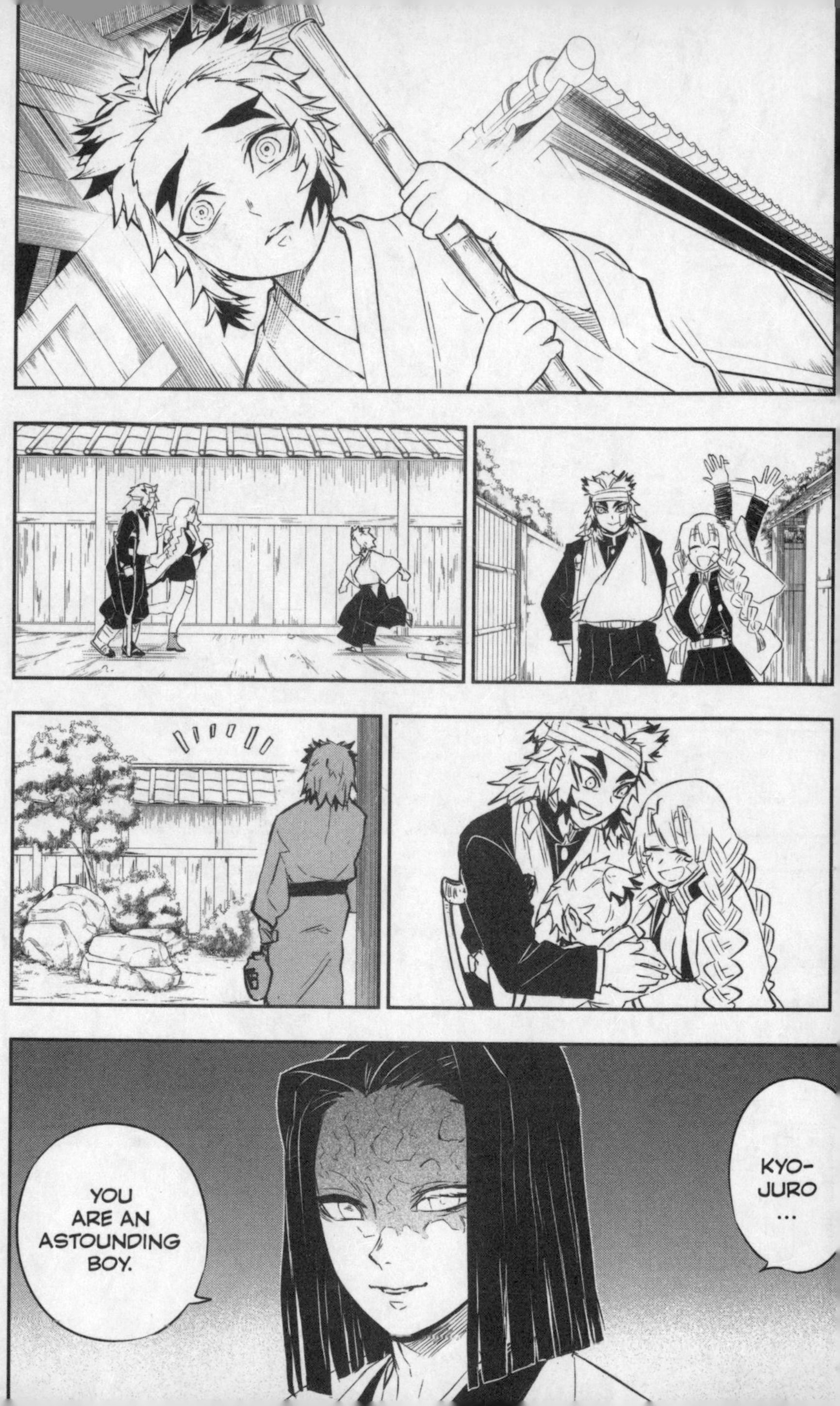
KYO-
JURO
...
YOU
ARE AN
ASTOUNDING
BOY.

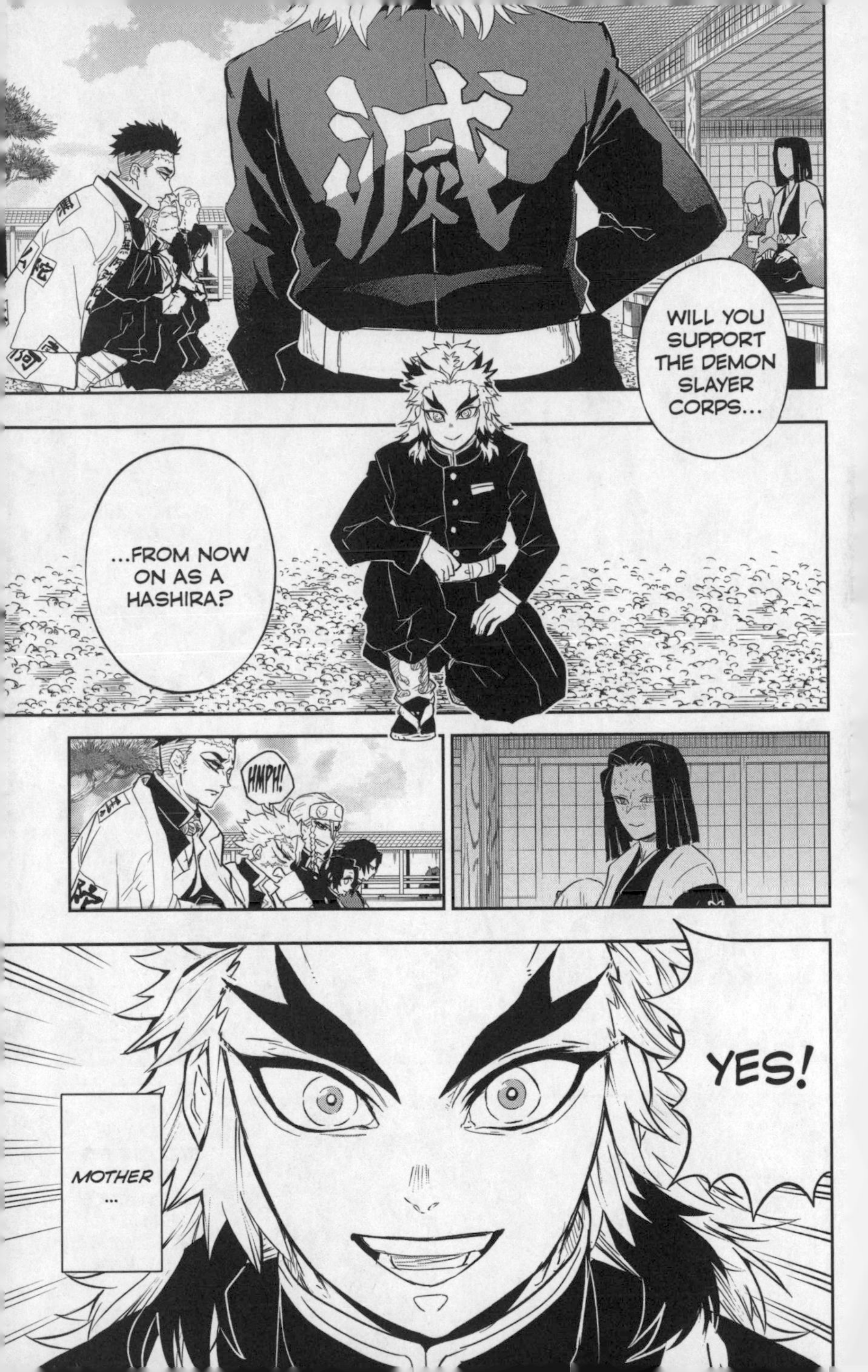
WILL YOU SUPPORT THE DEMON SLAYER CORPS...
...FROM NOW ON AS A HASHIRA?
HMPH!
YES!
MOTHER ...

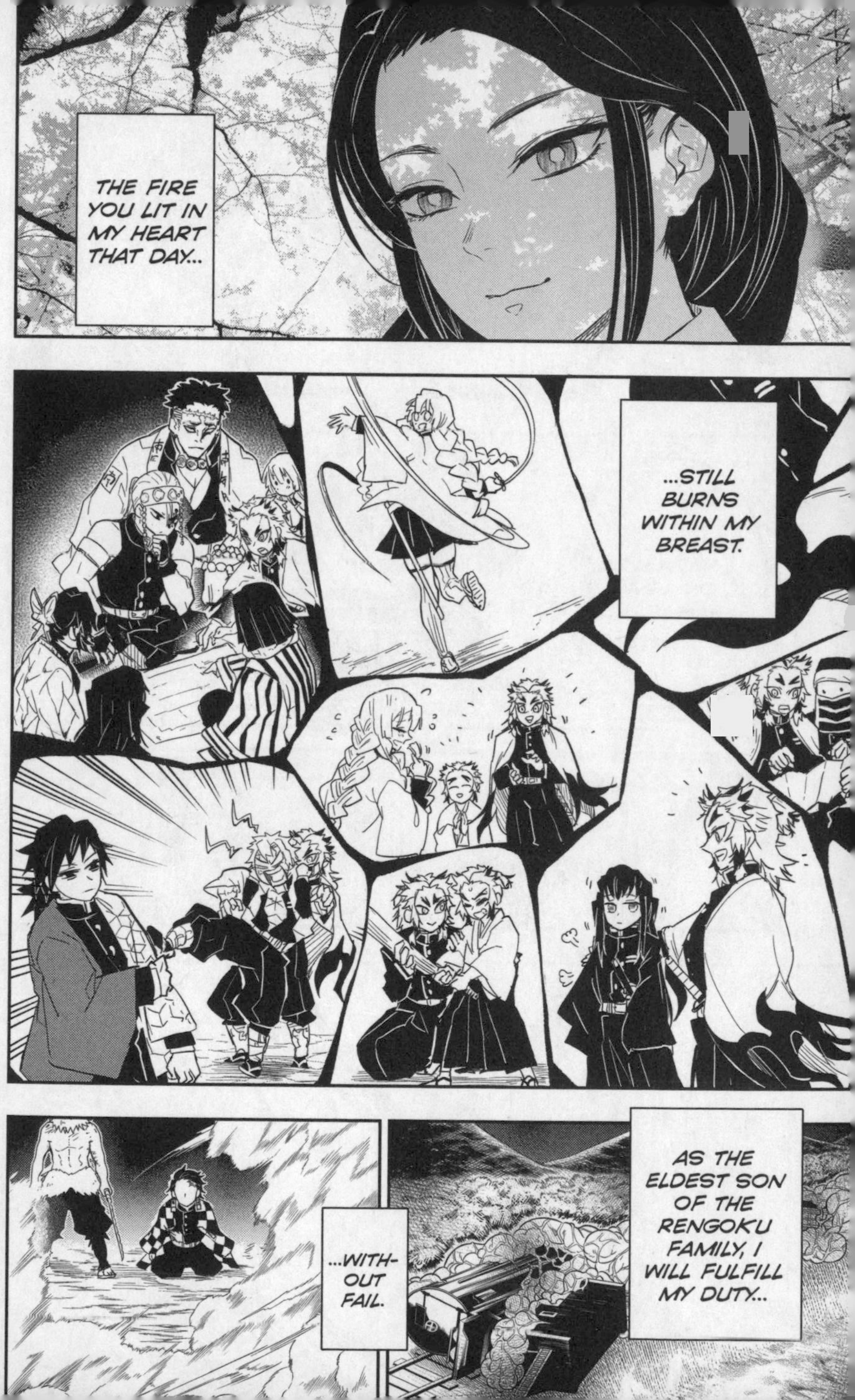
THE FIRE YOU LIT IN MY HEART THAT DAY...
...STILL BURNS WITHIN MY BREAST.
AS THE ELDEST SON OF THE RENGOKU FAMILY, I WILL FULFILL MY DUTY...
...WITH-OUT FAIL.

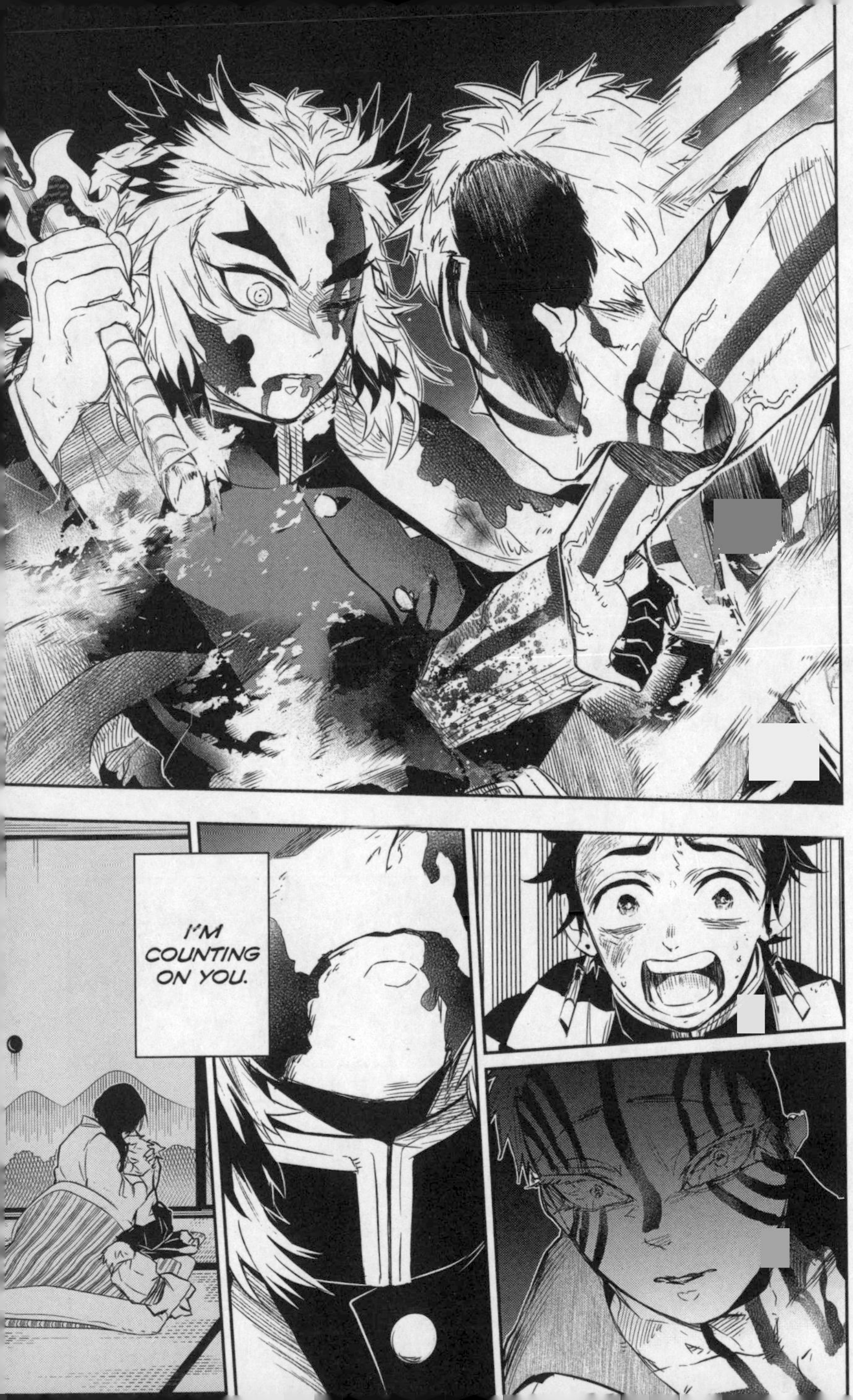
I'M COUNTING ON YOU.

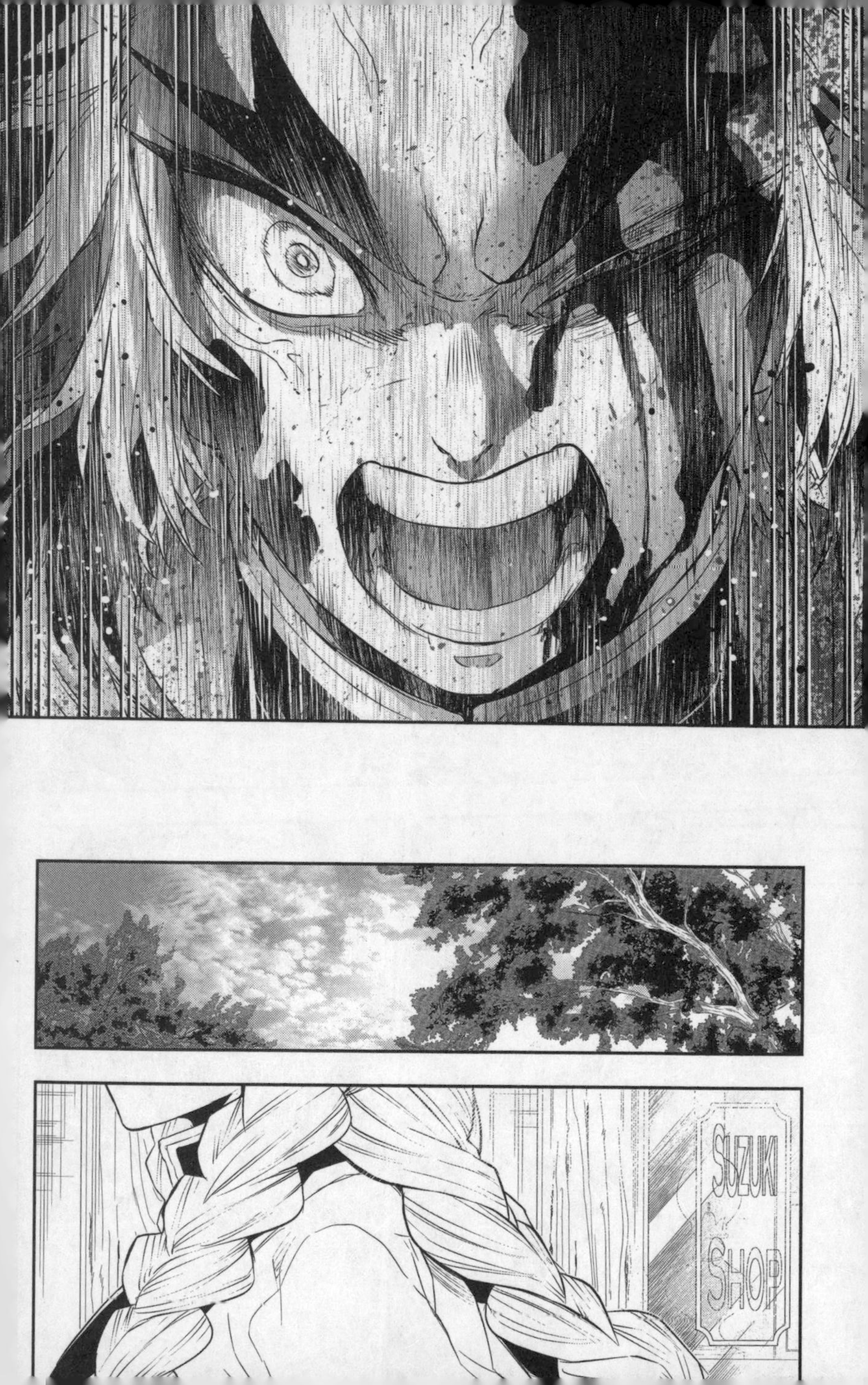
SUZUKI SHOP

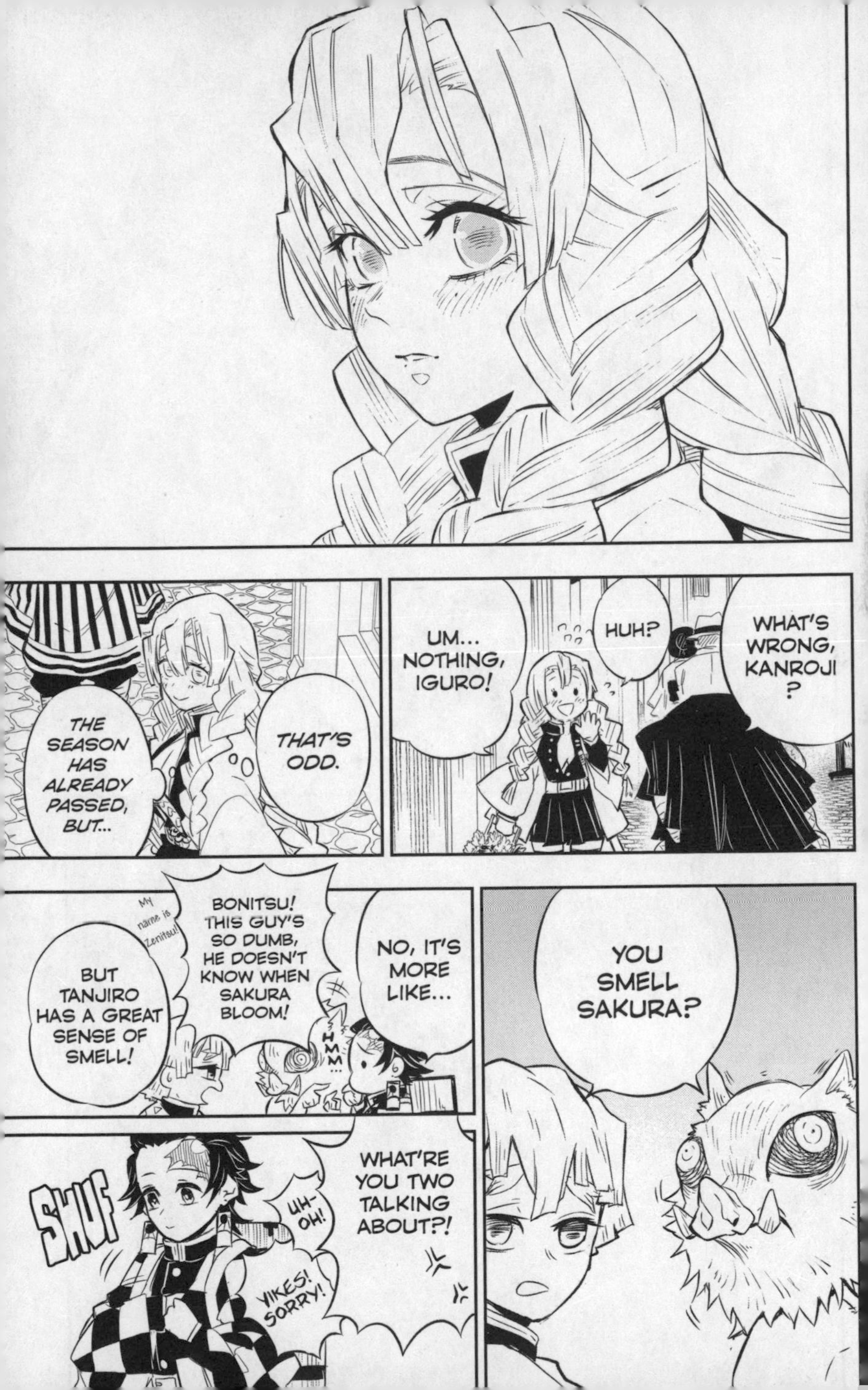
WHAT'S WRONG, KANROJI?
HUH?
UM... NOTHING, IGURO!
THAT'S ODD.
THE SEASON HAS ALREADY PASSED, BUT...
YOU SMELL SAKURA?
NO, IT'S MORE LIKE...
HMM...
BONITSU! THIS GUY'S SO DUMB, HE DOESN'T KNOW WHEN SAKURA BLOOM!
My name is Zenitsu!
BUT TANJIRO HAS A GREAT SENSE OF SMELL!
WHAT'RE YOU TWO TALKING ABOUT?!
UH-OH!
YIKES! SORRY!
SHUF

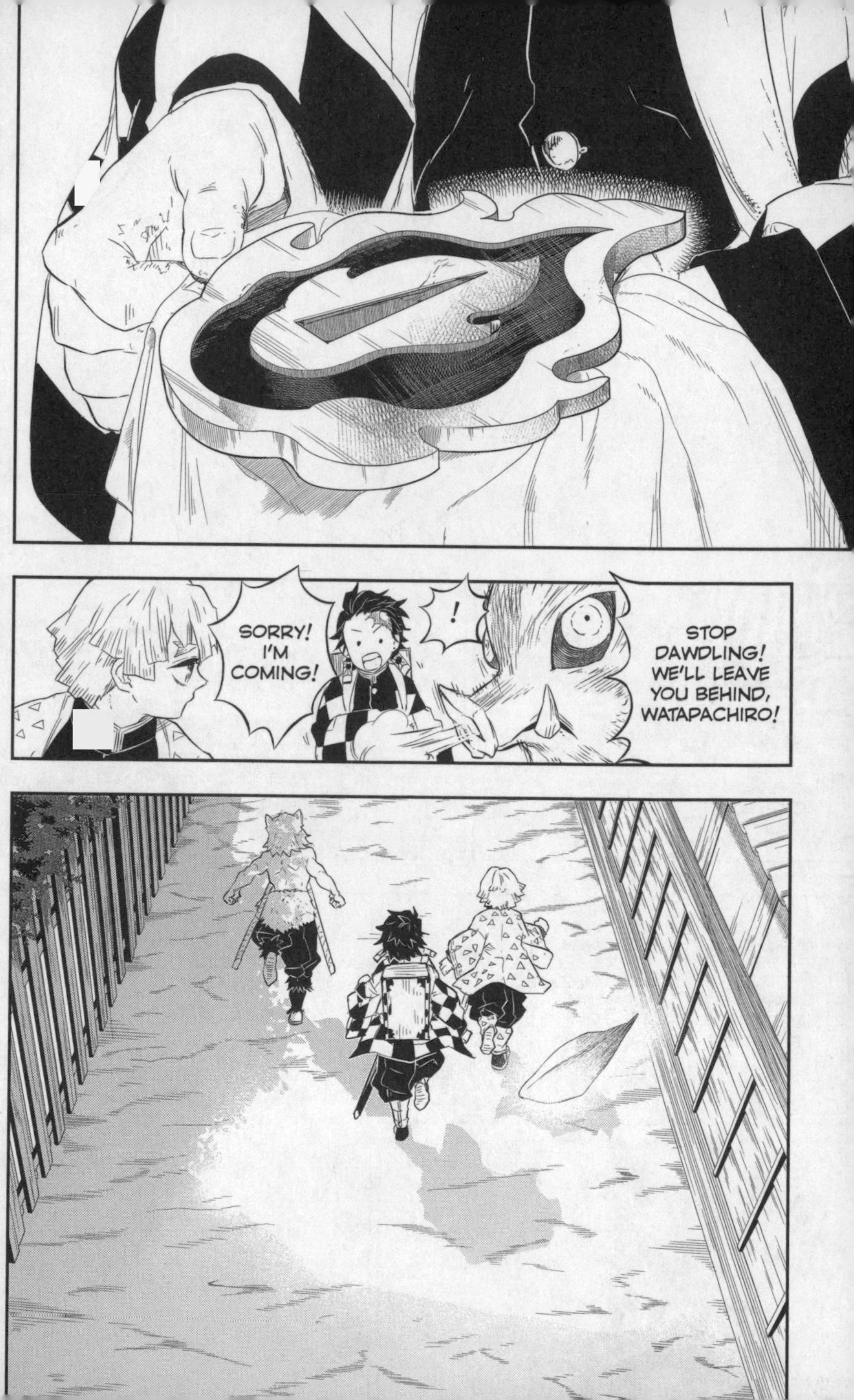
STOP DAWDLING! WE'LL LEAVE YOU BEHIND, WATAPACHIRO!
!
SORRY! I'M COMING!

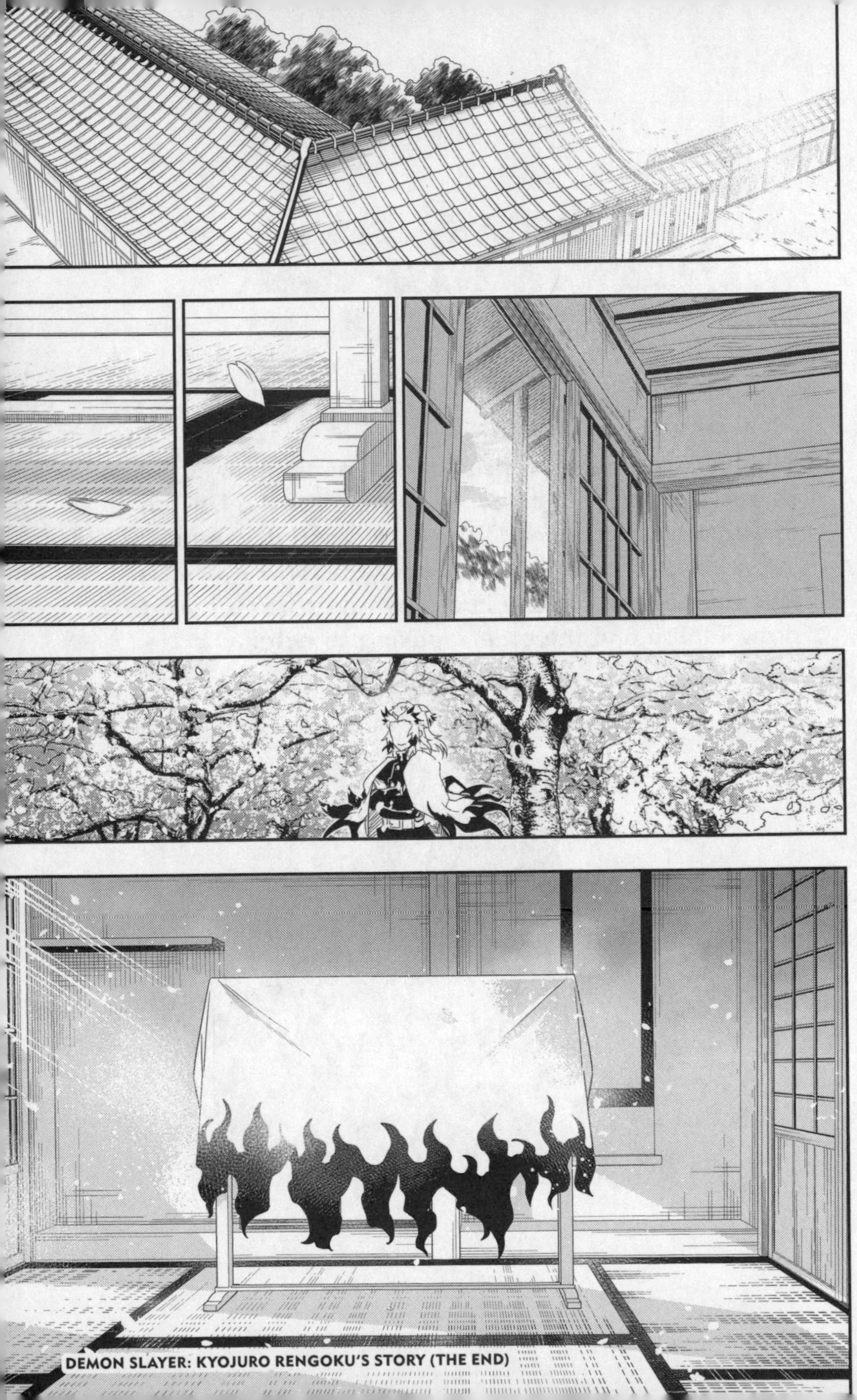
DEMON SLAYER: KYOJURO RENGOKU'S STORY (THE END)

# KIMETSU BETWEEN THE SCENES!

The following pages consist of four-panel manga serialized in *Jump+* as bonus content for the *Demon Slayer* television anime. They were created with the intention of providing further enjoyment for everyone who had watched the anime. Anyway, it was a blast to draw Tanjiro and the others looking so cute!

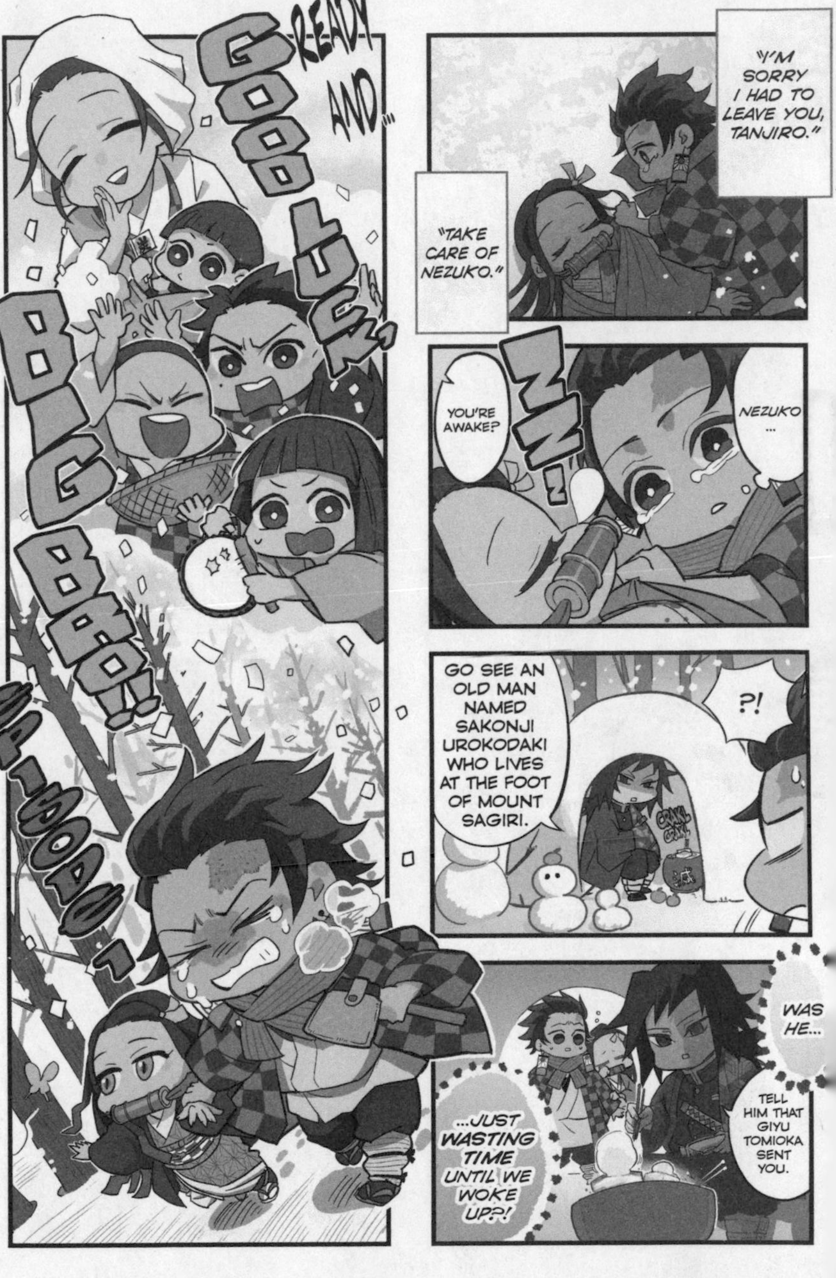
"I'M SORRY I HAD TO LEAVE YOU, TANJIRO."
"TAKE CARE OF NEZUKO."
NEZUKO...
YOU'RE AWAKE?
MN?
?!
GO SEE AN OLD MAN NAMED SAKONJI UROKODAKI WHO LIVES AT THE FOOT OF MOUNT SAGIRI.
WAS HE...
TELL HIM THAT GIYU TOMIOKA SENT YOU.
...JUST WASTING TIME UNTIL WE WOKE UP?!
READY AND...
GOOD LUCK,
BIG BRO!!
EPISODE 7

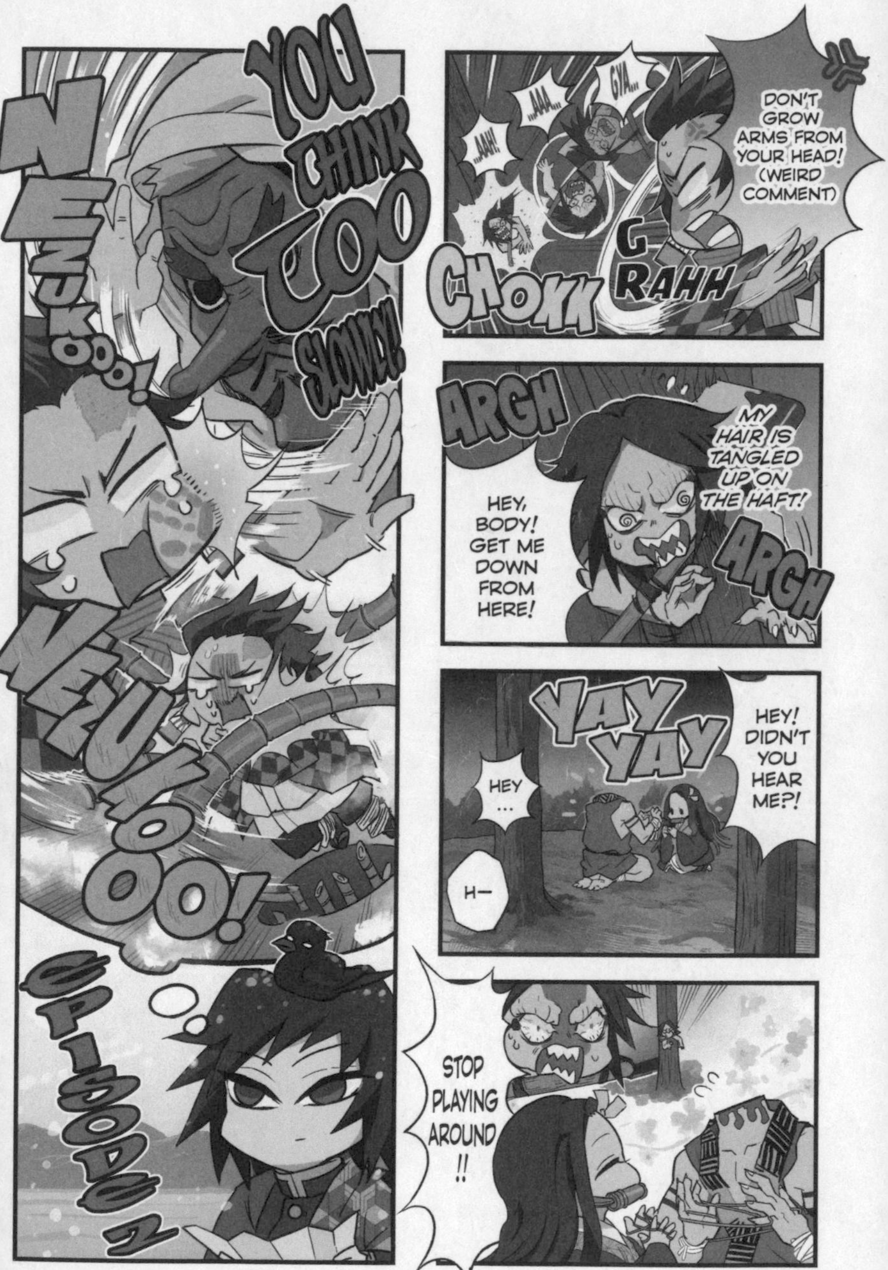
DON'T GROW ARMS FROM YOUR HEAD! (WEIRD COMMENT)
GYA...
...AAA...
...AAH!
G RAHH
CHOKK
MY HAIR IS TANGLED UP ON THE HAFT!
ARGH
HEY, BODY! GET ME DOWN FROM HERE!
ARGH
HEY! DIDN'T YOU HEAR ME?!
YAY YAY
HEY ...
H—
STOP PLAYING AROUND !!
YOU CHINK TOO SLOWLY!
NEZUKOOO!
NEZUKOOO!
EPISODE 2

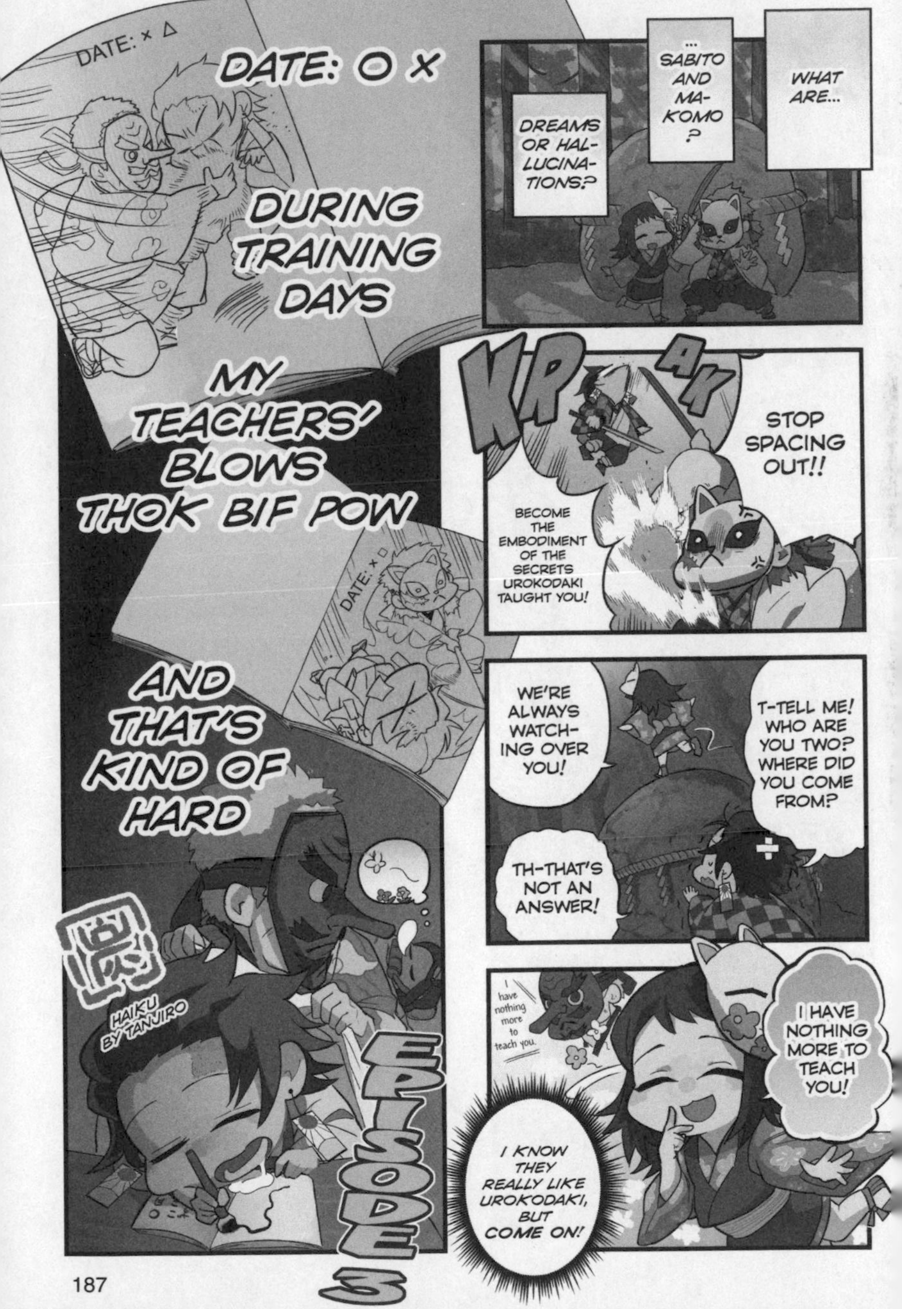

WHAT ARE...
... SABITO AND MA-KOMO?
DREAMS OR HAL-LUCINA-TIONS?
KRAK
STOP SPACING OUT!!
BECOME THE EMBODIMENT OF THE SECRETS UROKODAKI TAUGHT YOU!
T-TELL ME! WHO ARE YOU TWO? WHERE DID YOU COME FROM?
WE'RE ALWAYS WATCH-ING OVER YOU!
TH-THAT'S NOT AN ANSWER!
I HAVE NOTHING MORE TO TEACH YOU!
I have nothing more to teach you.
I KNOW THEY REALLY LIKE UROKODAKI, BUT COME ON!
DATE: × △
DATE: O X
DURING TRAINING DAYS
MY TEACHERS' BLOWS THOK BIF POW
AND THAT'S KIND OF HARD
DATE: × □
HAIKU BY TANJIRO
EPISODE 3

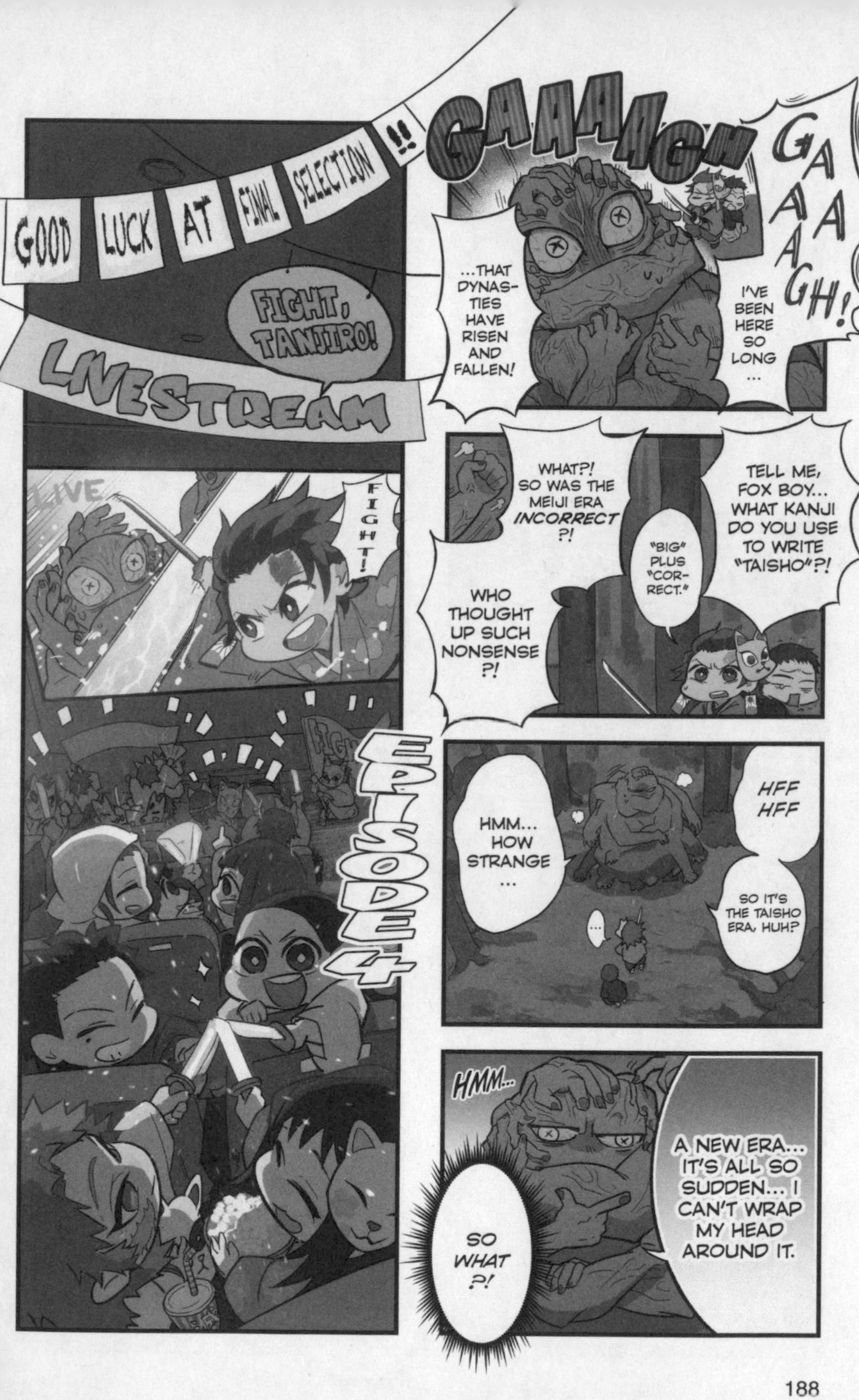

GAAAIGH
GAAAAGH!
I'VE BEEN HERE SO LONG...
...THAT DYNASTIES HAVE RISEN AND FALLEN!
TELL ME, FOX BOY... WHAT KANJI DO YOU USE TO WRITE "TAISHO"?!
"BIG" PLUS "CORRECT."
WHAT?! SO WAS THE MEIJI ERA *INCORRECT*?!
WHO THOUGHT UP SUCH NONSENSE?!
HFF HFF
SO IT'S THE TAISHO ERA, HUH?
HMM... HOW STRANGE...
...
A NEW ERA... IT'S ALL SO SUDDEN... I CAN'T WRAP MY HEAD AROUND IT.
HMM...
SO *WHAT*?!
GOOD LUCK AT FINAL SELECTION!!
FIGHT, TANJIRO!
LIVESTREAM
LIVE
FIGHT!
EPISODE 4

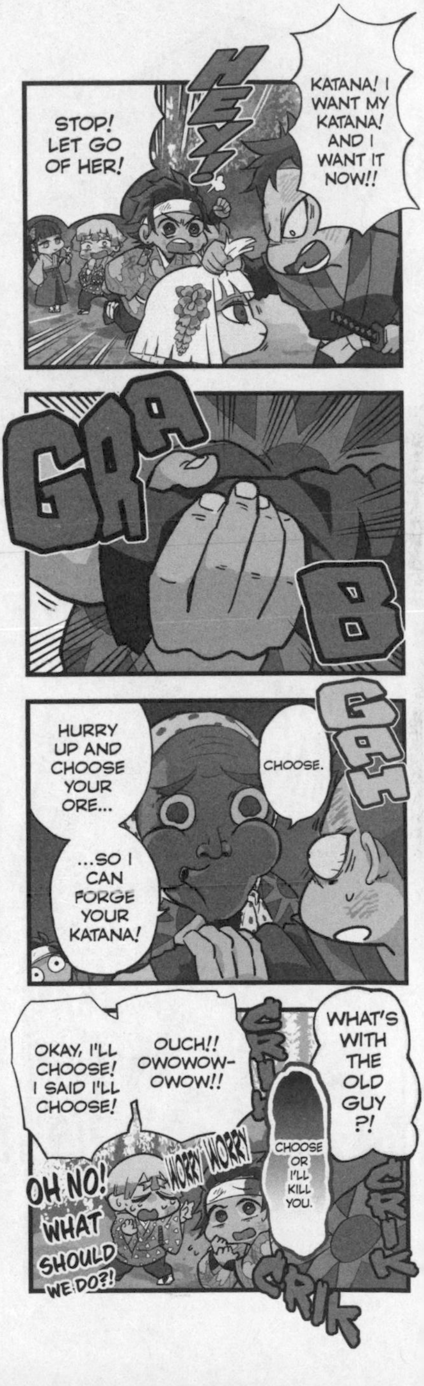
KATANA! I WANT MY KATANA! AND I WANT IT NOW!!
HEY!!
STOP! LET GO OF HER!
GRAB
GASH
CHOOSE.
HURRY UP AND CHOOSE YOUR ORE...
...SO I CAN FORGE YOUR KATANA!
WHAT'S WITH THE OLD GUY?!
CHOOSE OR I'LL KILL YOU.
OUCH!! OWOWOW-OWOW!!
OKAY, I'LL CHOOSE! I SAID I'LL CHOOSE!
CRIK CRIK
WORRY WORRY
OH NO! WHAT SHOULD WE DO?!
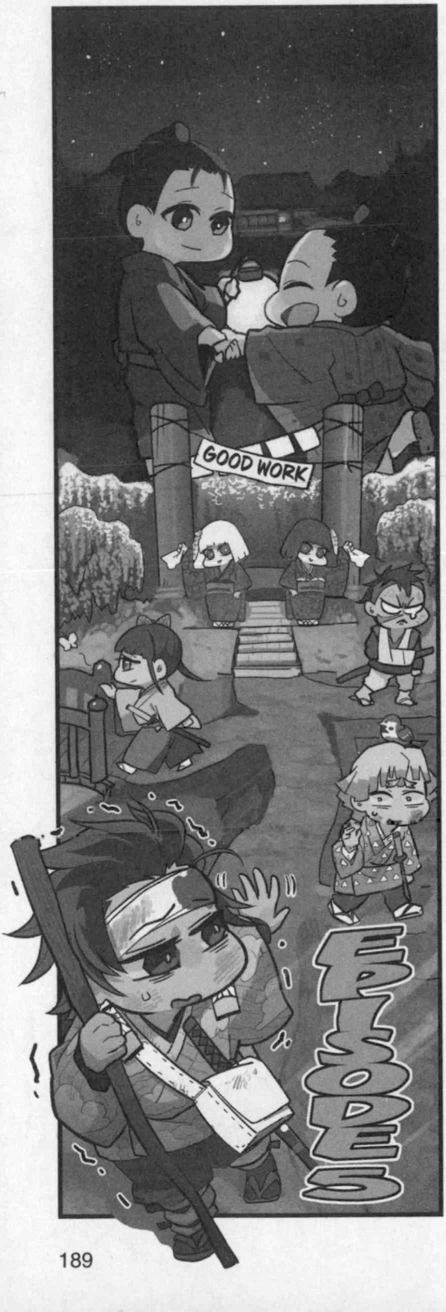
GOOD WORK
EPISODES

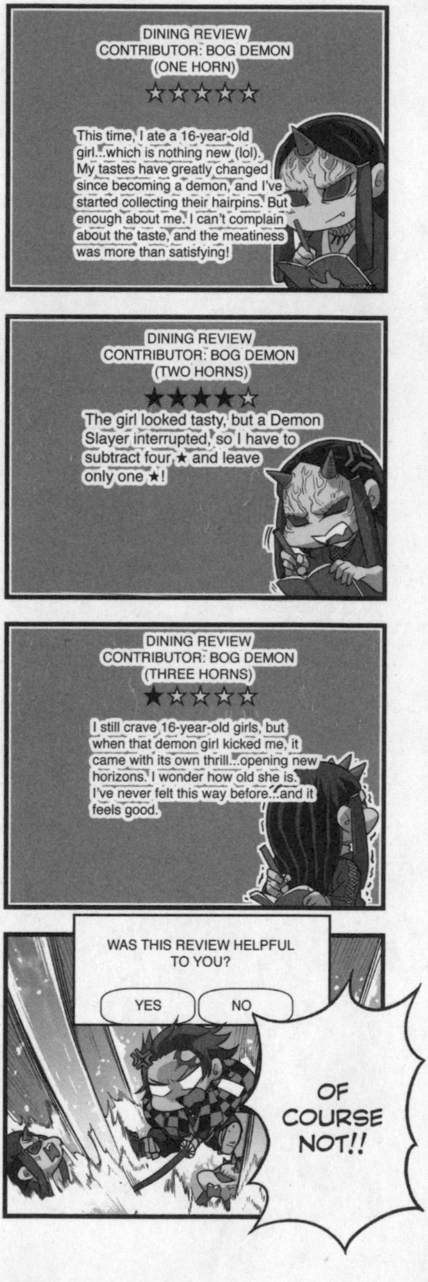
DINING REVIEW
CONTRIBUTOR: BOG DEMON
(ONE HORN)
☆☆☆☆☆
This time, I ate a 16-year-old girl...which is nothing new (lol). My tastes have greatly changed since becoming a demon, and I've started collecting their hairpins. But enough about me. I can't complain about the taste, and the meatiness was more than satisfying!
DINING REVIEW
CONTRIBUTOR: BOG DEMON
(TWO HORNS)
★★★★☆
The girl looked tasty, but a Demon Slayer interrupted, so I have to subtract four ★ and leave only one ★!
DINING REVIEW
CONTRIBUTOR: BOG DEMON
(THREE HORNS)
★☆☆☆☆
I still crave 16-year-old girls, but when that demon girl kicked me, it came with its own thrill...opening new horizons. I wonder how old she is. I've never felt this way before...and it feels good.
WAS THIS REVIEW HELPFUL TO YOU?
YES
NO
OF COURSE NOT!!
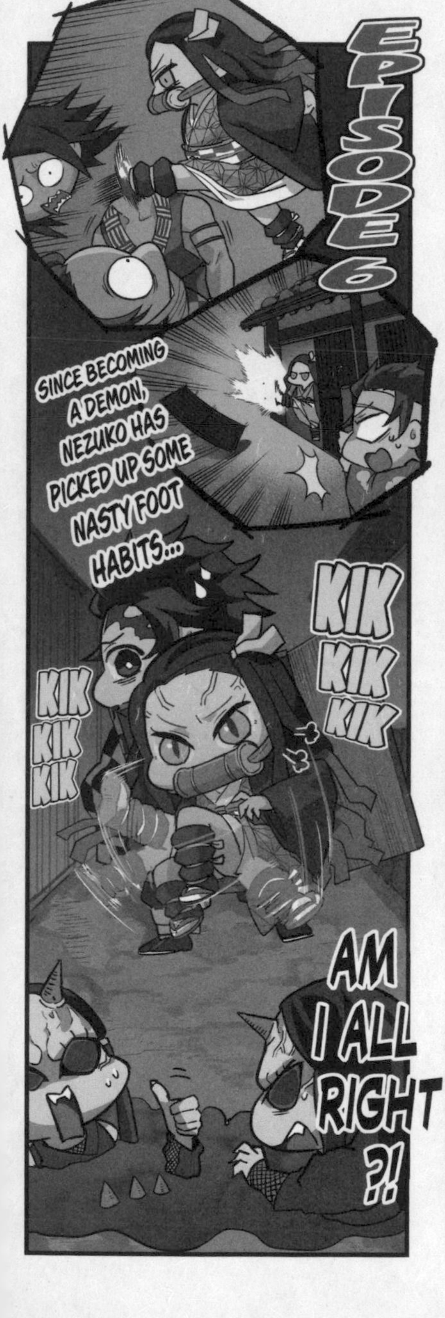
EPISODE 6
SINCE BECOMING A DEMON, NEZUKO HAS PICKED UP SOME NASTY FOOT HABITS...
KIK KIK KIK
KIK KIK KIK
AM I ALL RIGHT ?!

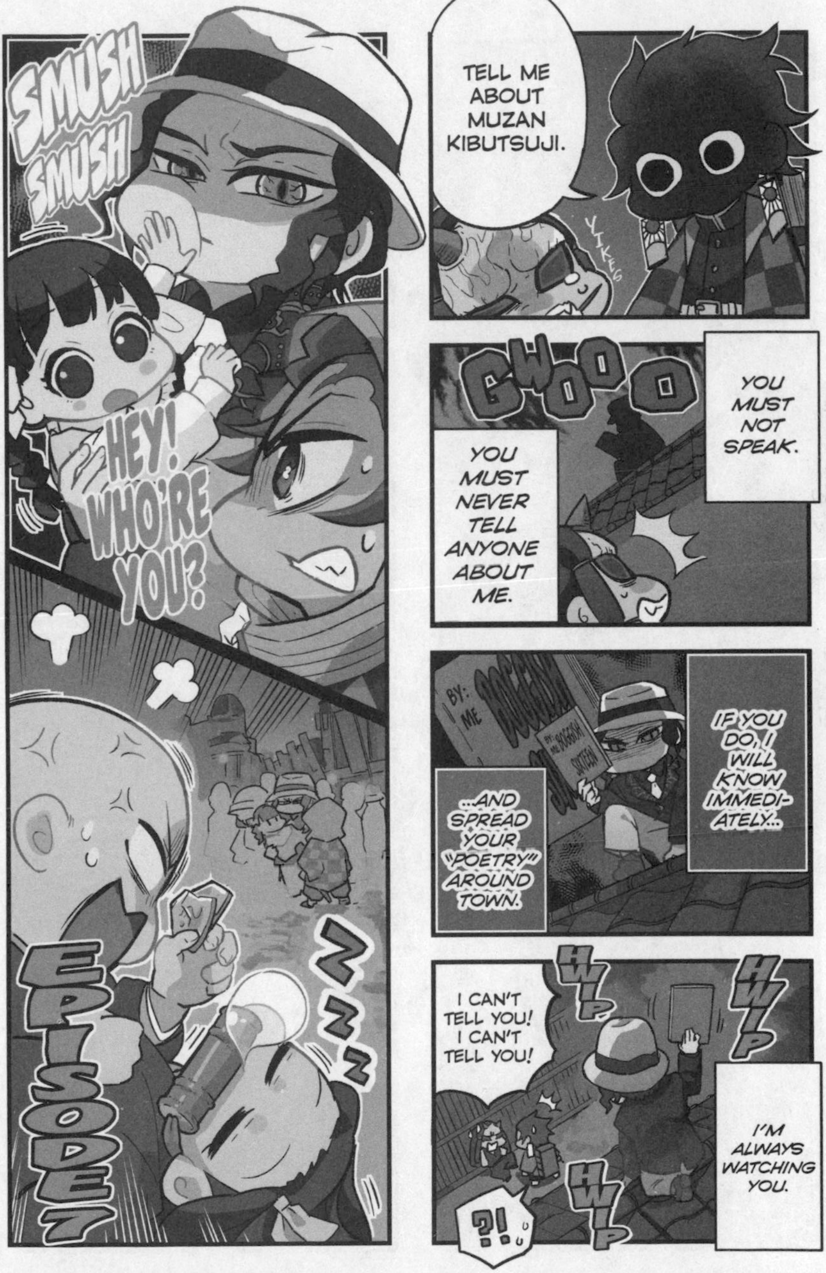
TELL ME ABOUT MUZAN KIBUTSUJI.
YIKES
GWOOO
YOU MUST NOT SPEAK.
YOU MUST NEVER TELL ANYONE ABOUT ME.
IF YOU DO, I WILL KNOW IMMEDI-ATELY...
BY: ME
...AND SPREAD YOUR "POETRY" AROUND TOWN.
HWIP
HWIP
I'M ALWAYS WATCHING YOU.
I CAN'T TELL YOU! I CAN'T TELL YOU!
HWIP
?!
SMUSH SMUSH
HEY! WHO'RE YOU?
Z Z Z
EPISODE 7

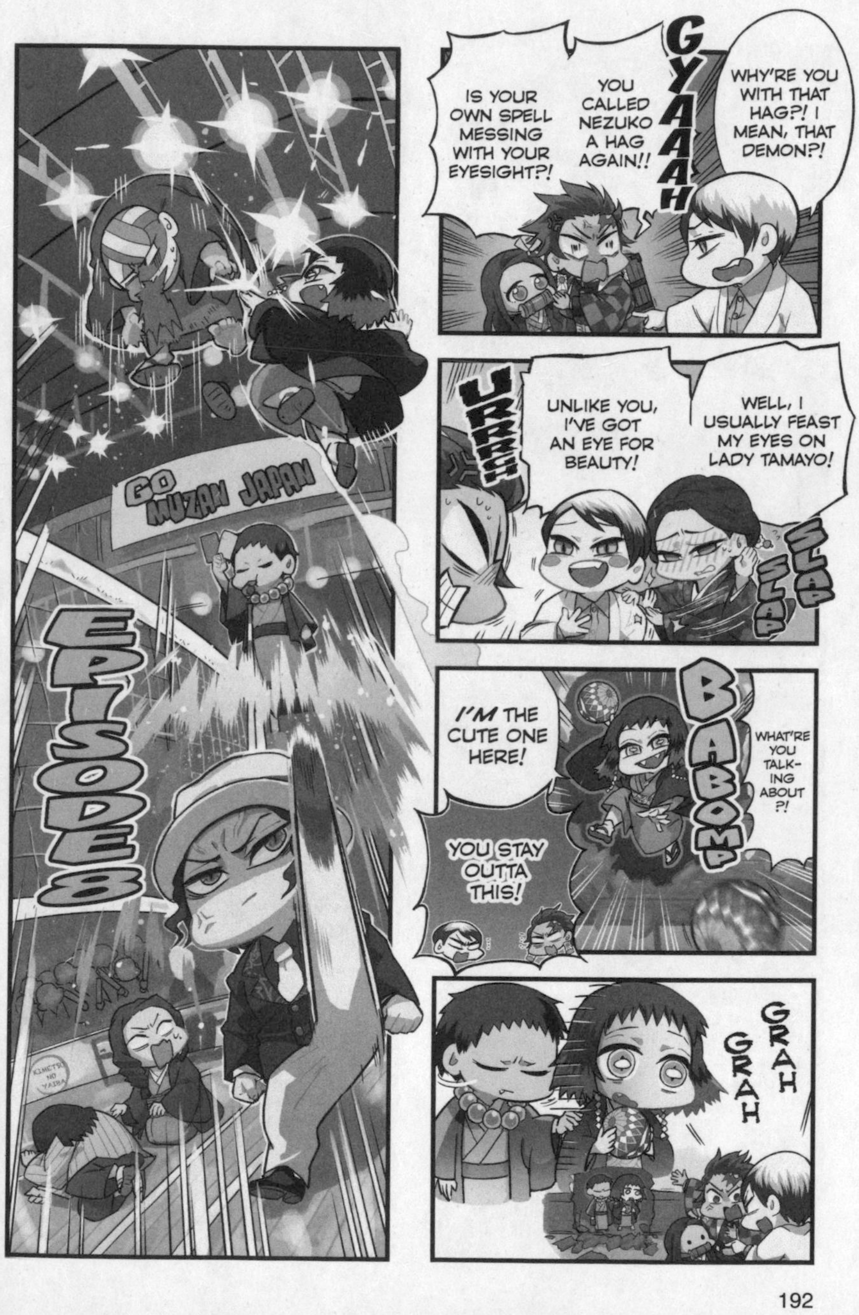
WHY'RE YOU WITH THAT HAG?! I MEAN, THAT DEMON?!
GYAAAAH
YOU CALLED NEZUKO A HAG AGAIN!!
IS YOUR OWN SPELL MESSING WITH YOUR EYESIGHT?!
WELL, I USUALLY FEAST MY EYES ON LADY TAMAYO!
UNLIKE YOU, I'VE GOT AN EYE FOR BEAUTY!
URRRGH
SLAP SLAP
WHAT'RE YOU TALKING ABOUT?!
BABOMP
I'M THE CUTE ONE HERE!
YOU STAY OUTTA THIS!
GRAH GRAH
EPISODE 8
GO MUZAN JAPAN
KIMETSU NO YAIBA

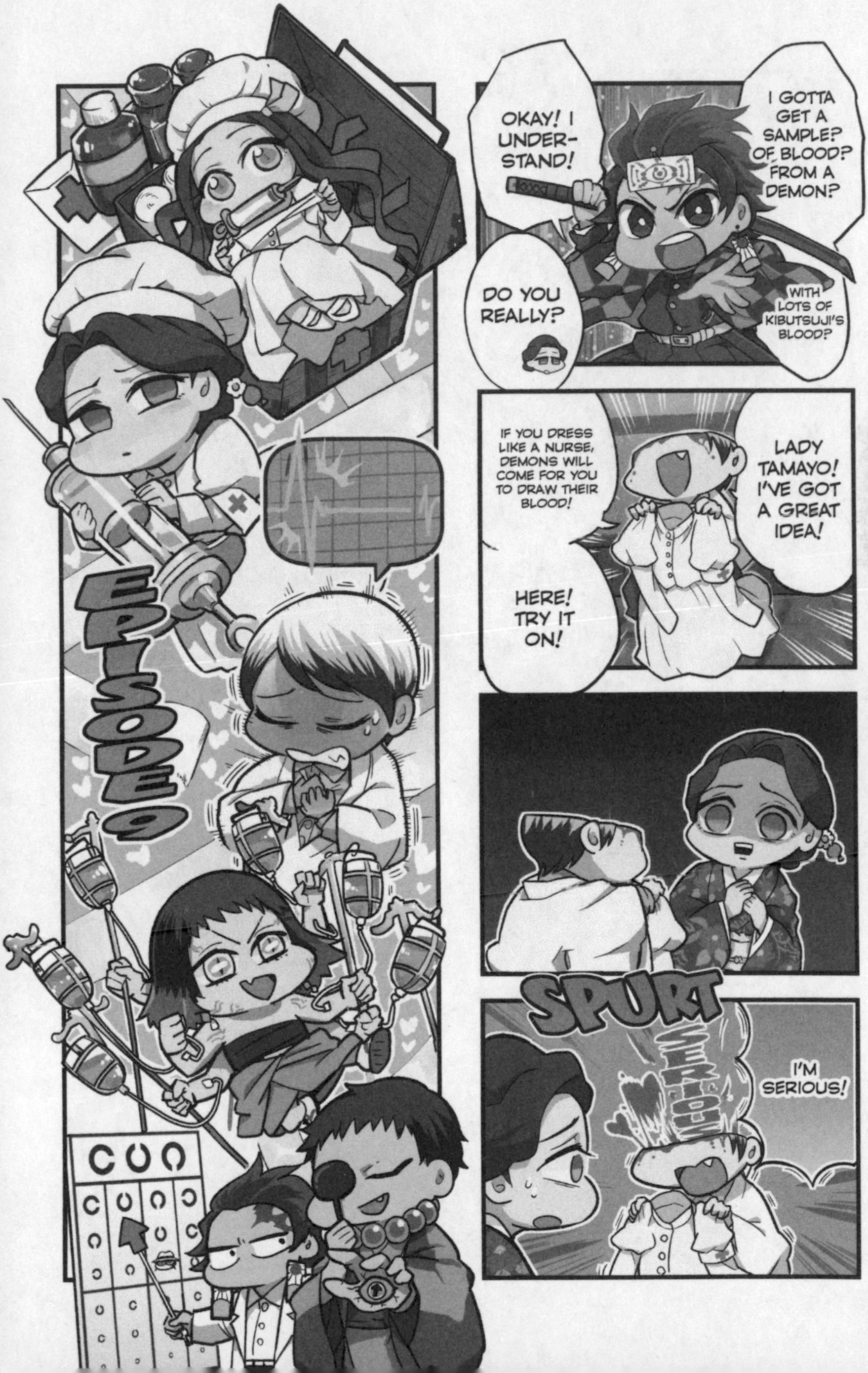
I GOTTA GET A SAMPLE? OF BLOOD? FROM A DEMON?
OKAY! I UNDER-STAND!
WITH LOTS OF KIBUTSUJI'S BLOOD?
DO YOU REALLY?
LADY TAMAYO! I'VE GOT A GREAT IDEA!
IF YOU DRESS LIKE A NURSE, DEMONS WILL COME FOR YOU TO DRAW THEIR BLOOD!
HERE! TRY IT ON!
SPURT
I'M SERIOUS!
SERIOUS
EPISODE 9

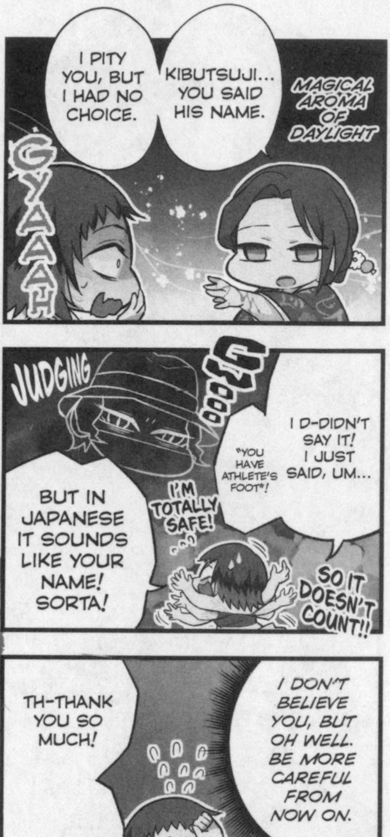
MAGICAL AROMA OF DAYLIGHT
KIBUTSUJI... YOU SAID HIS NAME.
I PITY YOU, BUT I HAD NO CHOICE.
GYAAAAH
I D-DIDN'T SAY IT! I JUST SAID, UM...
"YOU HAVE ATHLETE'S FOOT*!"
G...
JUDGING
I'M TOTALLY SAFE!
BUT IN JAPANESE IT SOUNDS LIKE YOUR NAME! SORTA!
SO IT DOESN'T COUNT!!
I DON'T BELIEVE YOU, BUT OH WELL. BE MORE CAREFUL FROM NOW ON.
TH-THANK YOU SO MUCH!
WHEW
YOU'RE SO FORGIVING, MUZAN!
END

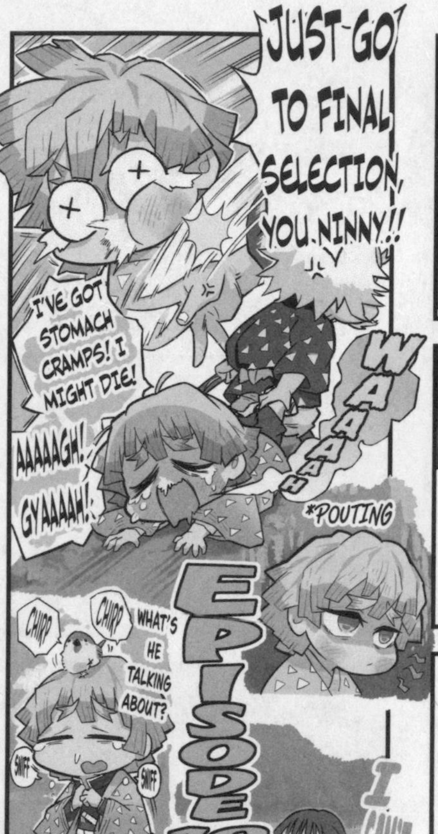
JUST GO TO FINAL SELECTION, YOU NINNY!!
I'VE GOT STOMACH CRAMPS! I MIGHT DIE!
WAAAAAAH
AAAAAGH! GYAAAAH!
*POUTING
EPISODE 10
WHAT'S HE TALKING ABOUT?
CHIRP
CHIRP
SNIFF
SNIFF
I CAN'T DO IT! I'LL DIEEEE!
I DON'T WANNA GOOOOO!

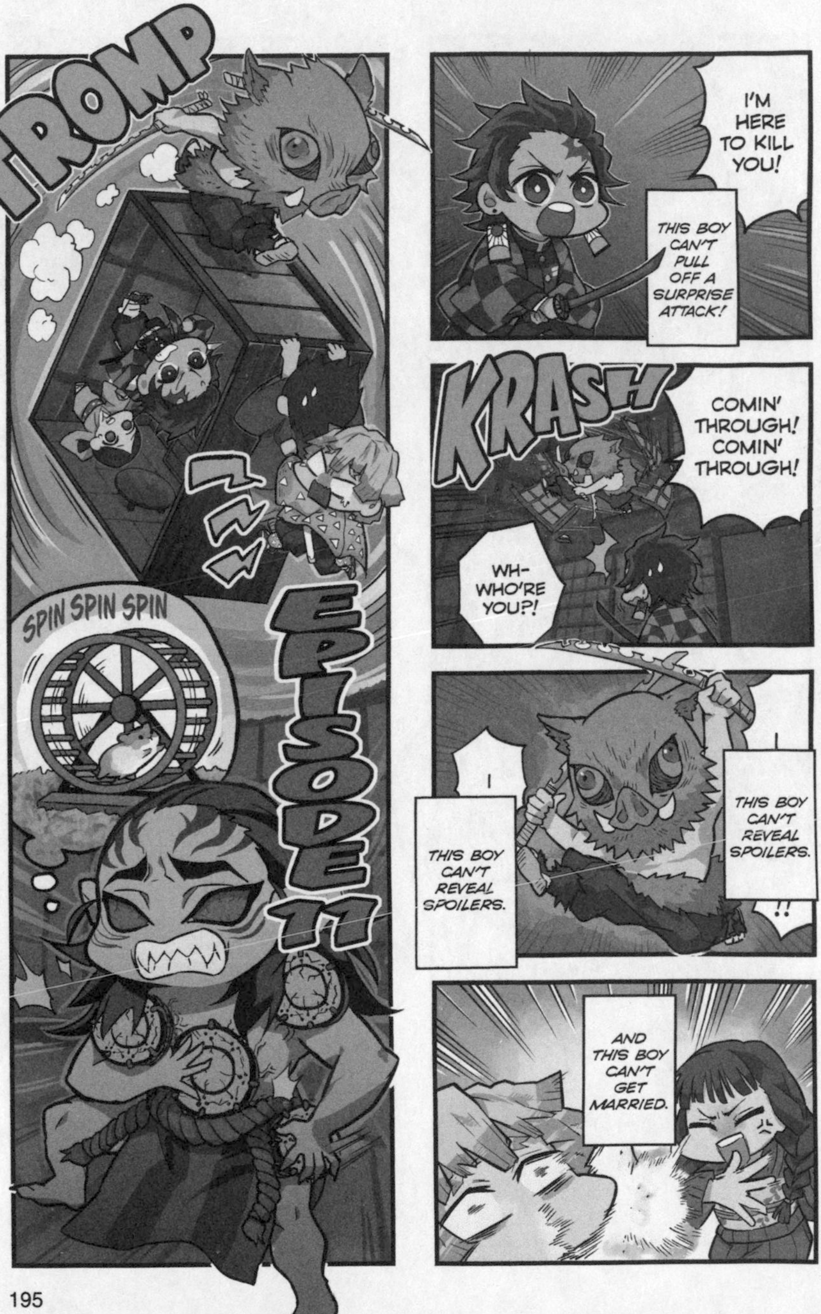
I'M HERE TO KILL YOU!
THIS BOY CAN'T PULL OFF A SURPRISE ATTACK!
KRASH
COMIN' THROUGH! COMIN' THROUGH!
WH- WHO'RE YOU?!
!
THIS BOY CAN'T REVEAL SPOILERS.
!
THIS BOY CAN'T REVEAL SPOILERS.
!!
AND THIS BOY CAN'T GET MARRIED.
TROMP
EPISODE 11
SPIN SPIN SPIN

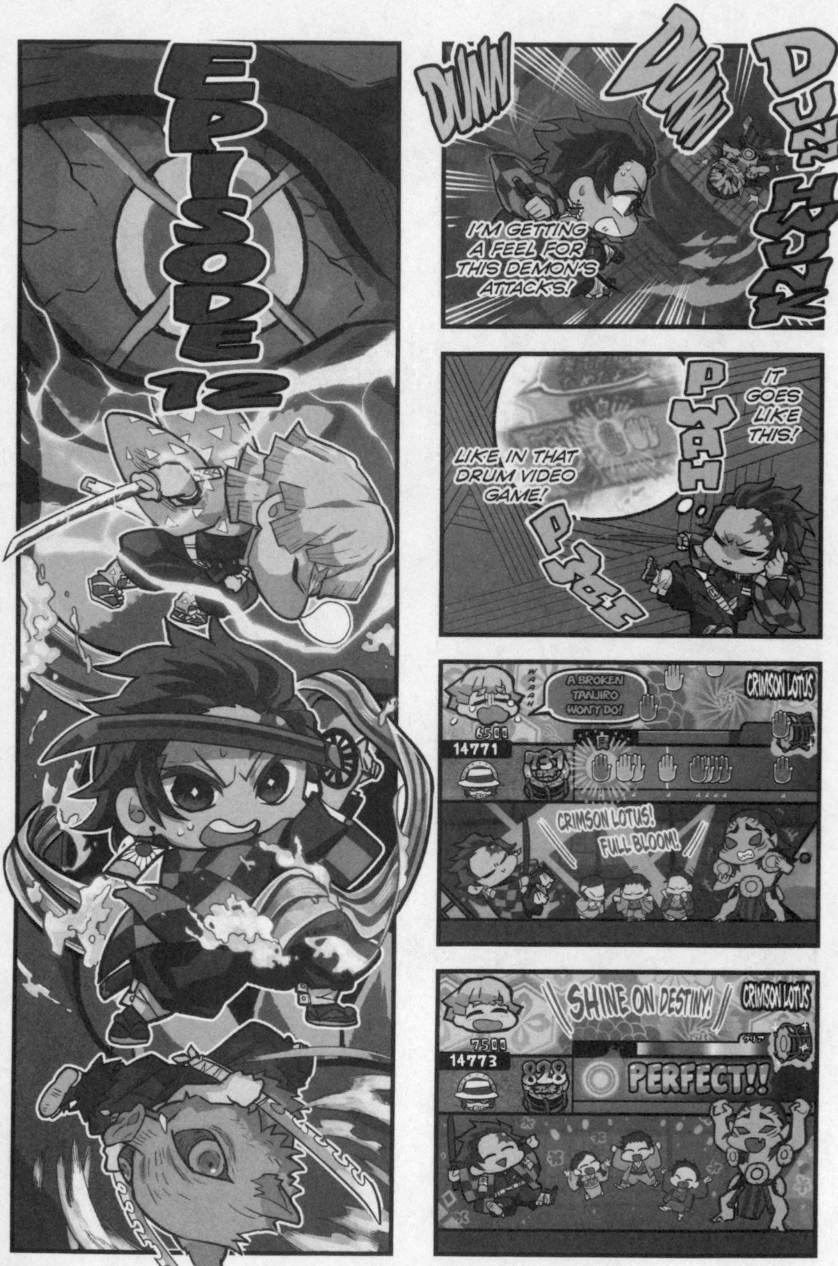
DUNN
DUNN
DUNN
I'M GETTING A FEEL FOR THIS DEMON'S ATTACKS!
IT GOES LIKE THIS!
PWAH
LIKE IN THAT DRUM VIDEO GAME!
CRIMSON LOTUS
A BROKEN TANJIRO WON'T DO!
6500
14771
CRIMSON LOTUS! FULL BLOOM!
CRIMSON LOTUS
SHINE ON DESTINY!
7500
14773
828
PERFECT!!
EPISODE 12

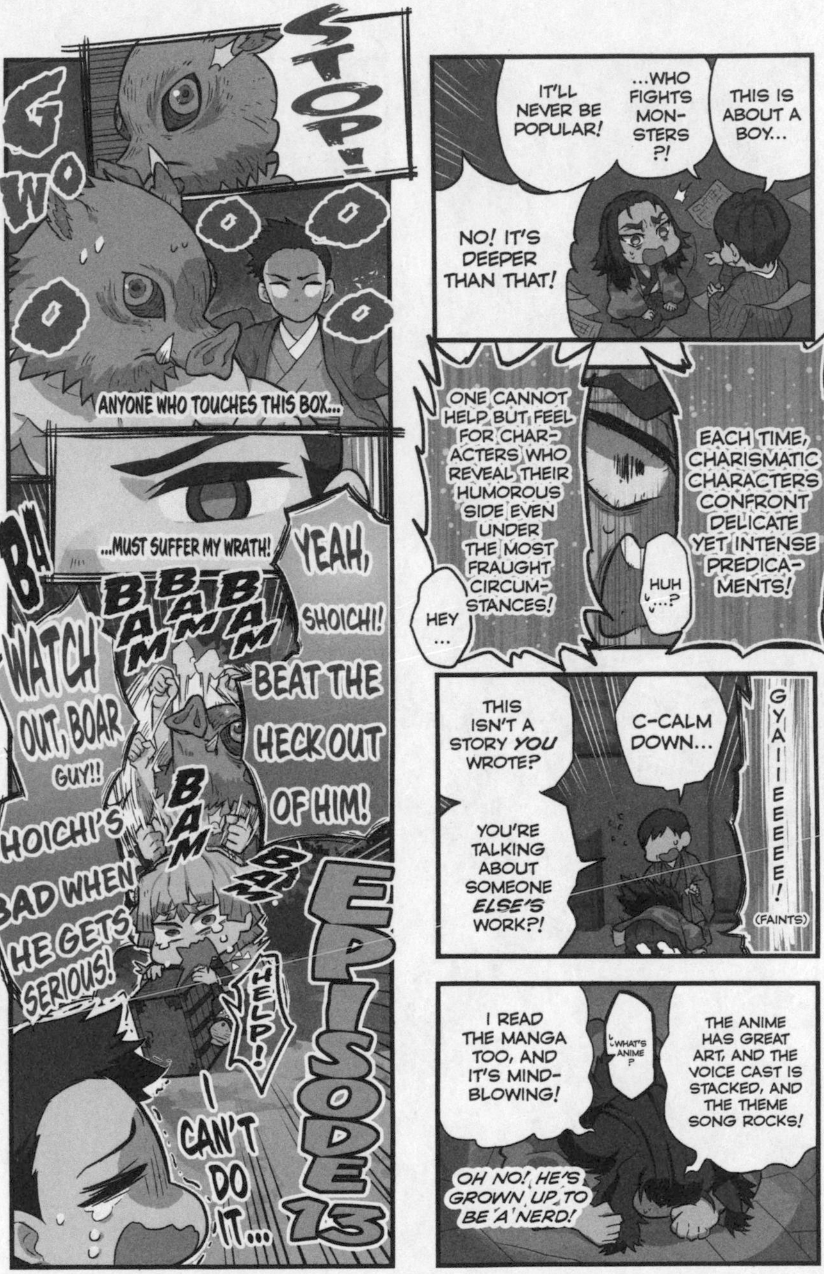
THIS IS ABOUT A BOY...
...WHO FIGHTS MON-STERS?!
IT'LL NEVER BE POPULAR!
NO! IT'S DEEPER THAN THAT!
EACH TIME, CHARISMATIC CHARACTERS CONFRONT DELICATE YET INTENSE PREDICA-MENTS!
HUH...?
ONE CANNOT HELP BUT FEEL FOR CHAR-ACTERS WHO REVEAL THEIR HUMOROUS SIDE EVEN UNDER THE MOST FRAUGHT CIRCUM-STANCES!
HEY...
GYAIIEEEEE!
(FAINTS)
C-CALM DOWN...
THIS ISN'T A STORY *YOU* WROTE?
YOU'RE TALKING ABOUT SOMEONE *ELSE'S* WORK?!
THE ANIME HAS GREAT ART, AND THE VOICE CAST IS STACKED, AND THE THEME SONG ROCKS!
WHAT'S ANIME?
I READ THE MANGA TOO, AND IT'S MIND-BLOWING!
OH NO! HE'S GROWN UP TO BE A NERD!
EPISODE 13
STOP!!
GWOOOOOO
ANYONE WHO TOUCHES THIS BOX...
...MUST SUFFER MY WRATH!
BA
YEAH, SHOICHI!
BAMM BAMM BAMM
BEAT THE HECK OUT OF HIM!
WATCH OUT, BOAR GUY!!
SHOICHI'S BAD WHEN HE GETS SERIOUS!
BAM
BAM
HELP!
I CAN'T DO IT...

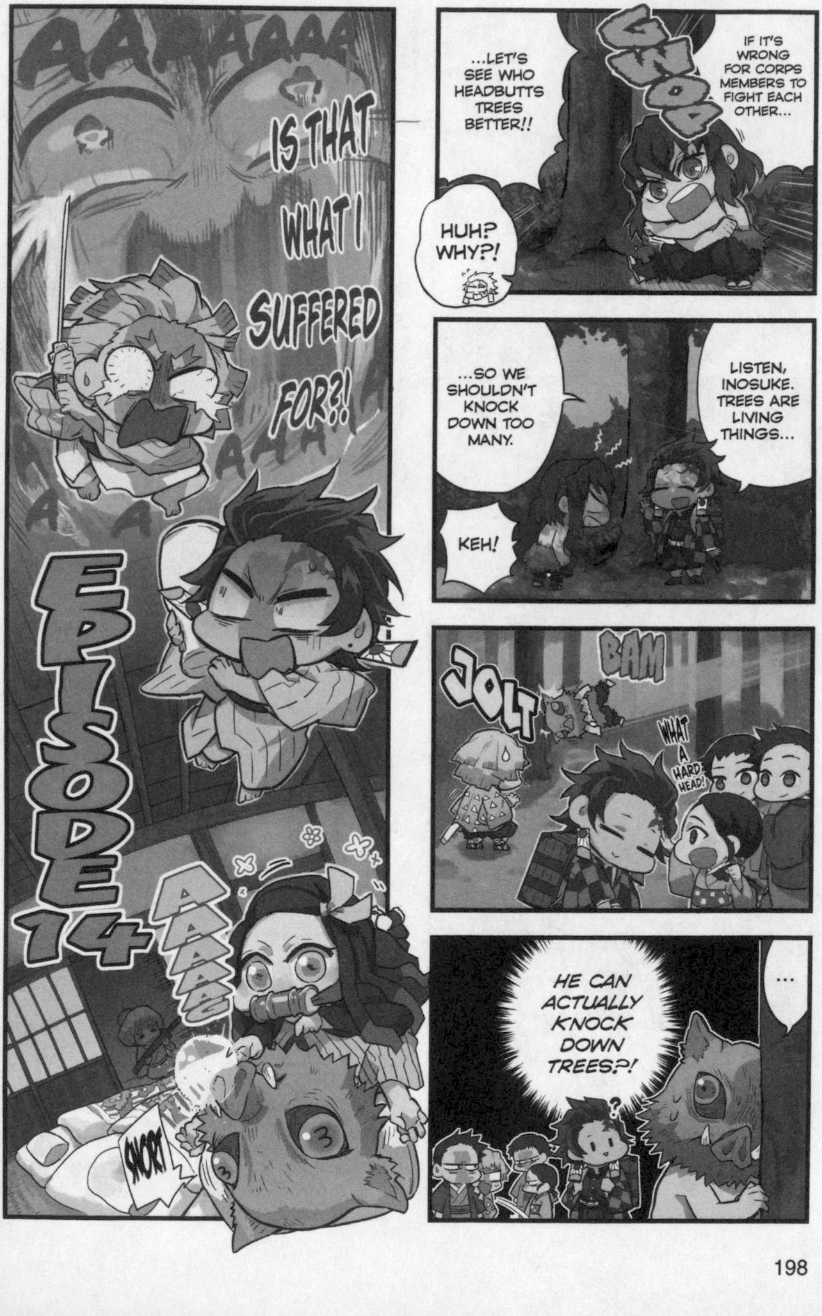
IF IT'S WRONG FOR CORPS MEMBERS TO FIGHT EACH OTHER...
...LET'S SEE WHO HEADBUTTS TREES BETTER!!
HUH? WHY?!
LISTEN, INOSUKE. TREES ARE LIVING THINGS...
...SO WE SHOULDN'T KNOCK DOWN TOO MANY.
KEH!
BAM
JOLT
WHAT A HARD HEAD!
...
HE CAN ACTUALLY KNOCK DOWN TREES?!
?
AAAAAAA
IS THAT WHAT I SUFFERED FOR?!
EPISODE 14
AAAAAG
SNORT

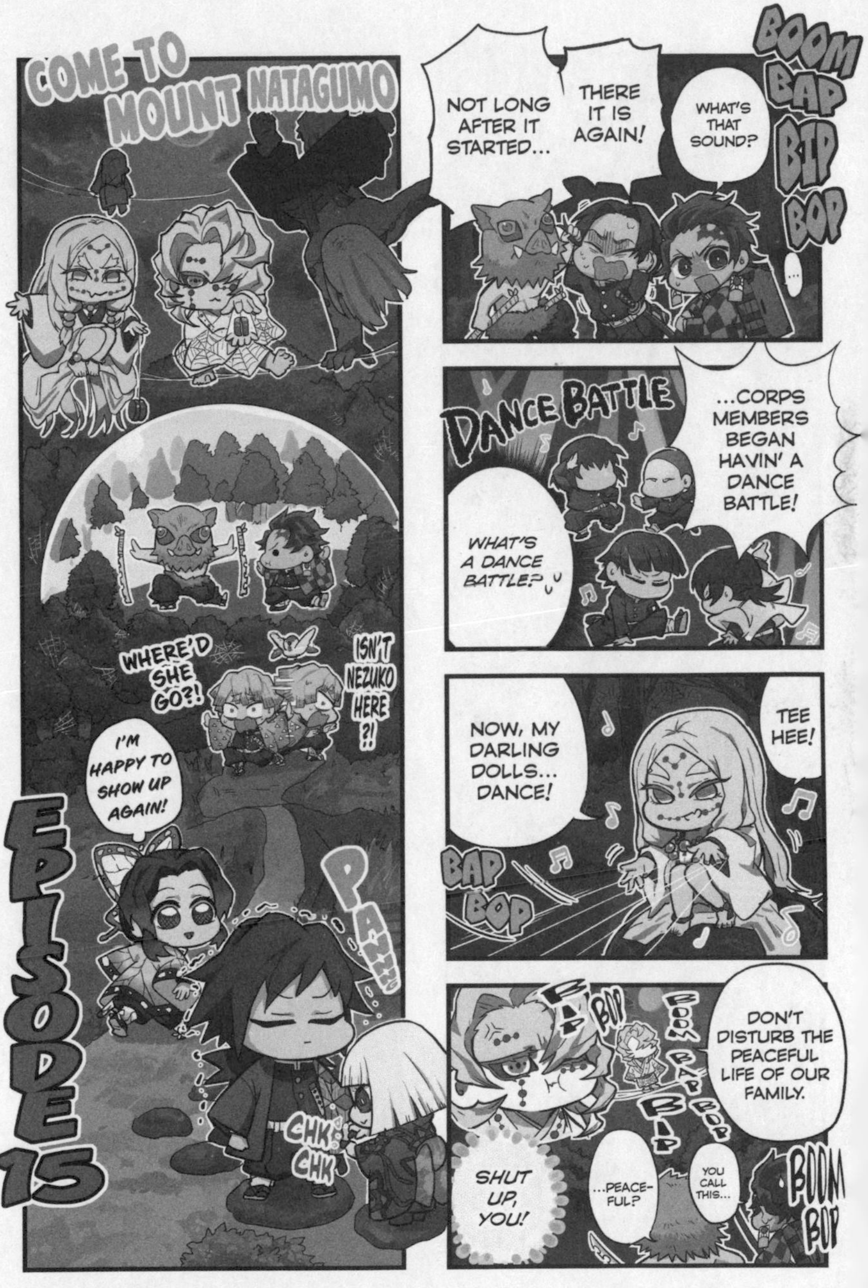
BOOM BAP BIP BOP
WHAT'S THAT SOUND?
THERE IT IS AGAIN!
NOT LONG AFTER IT STARTED...
...
...CORPS MEMBERS BEGAN HAVIN' A DANCE BATTLE!
DANCE BATTLE
WHAT'S A DANCE BATTLE?
TEE HEE!
NOW, MY DARLING DOLLS... DANCE!
BAP BOP
DON'T DISTURB THE PEACEFUL LIFE OF OUR FAMILY.
BOOM BAP BOP
BAP BOP
BIP
BOOM BOP
YOU CALL THIS...
...PEACE-FUL?
SHUT UP, YOU!
COME TO MOUNT NATAGUMO
ISN'T NEZUKO HERE?!
WHERE'D SHE GO?!
I'M HAPPY TO SHOW UP AGAIN!
CHK CHK
EPISODE 15

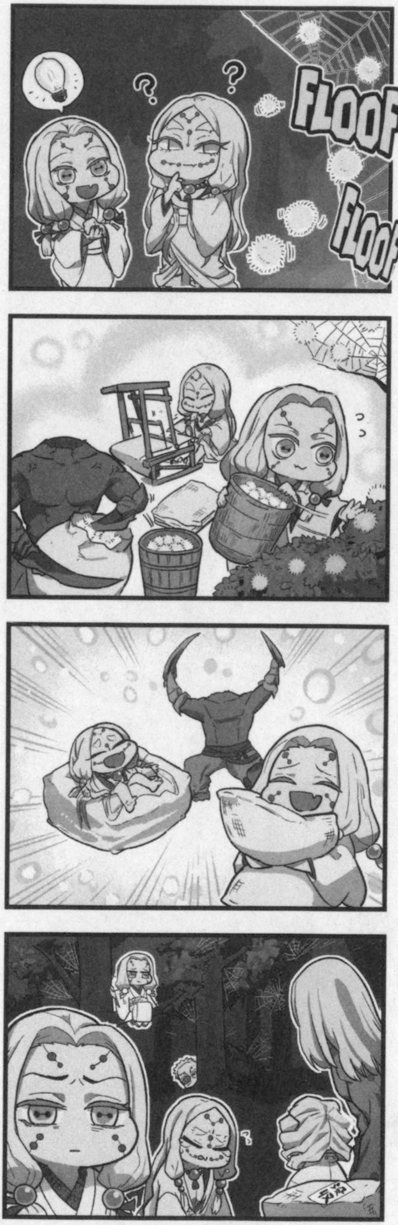

FLOOF
FLOOF


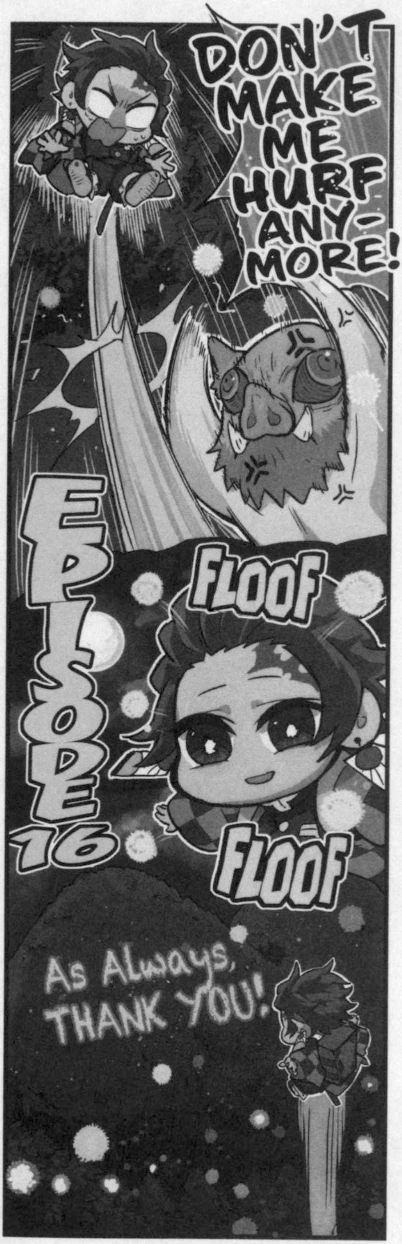

DON'T MAKE ME HURF ANY-MORE!
EPISODE 16
FLOOF
FLOOF
As Always, THANK YOU!

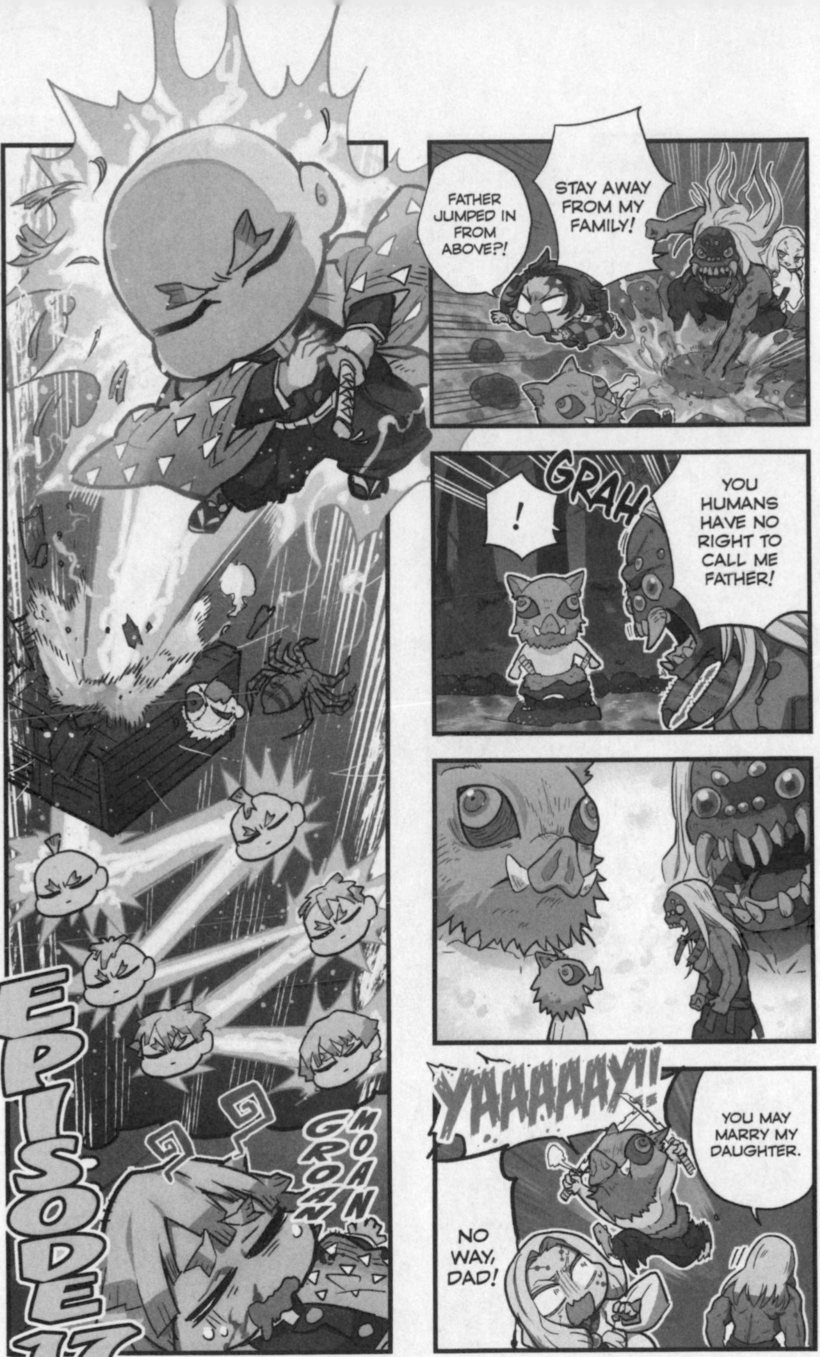
STAY AWAY FROM MY FAMILY!
FATHER JUMPED IN FROM ABOVE?!
YOU HUMANS HAVE NO RIGHT TO CALL ME FATHER!
GRAH
!
YOU MAY MARRY MY DAUGHTER.
YAAAAAY!!
NO WAY, DAD!
MOAN
GROAN
EPISODE 17

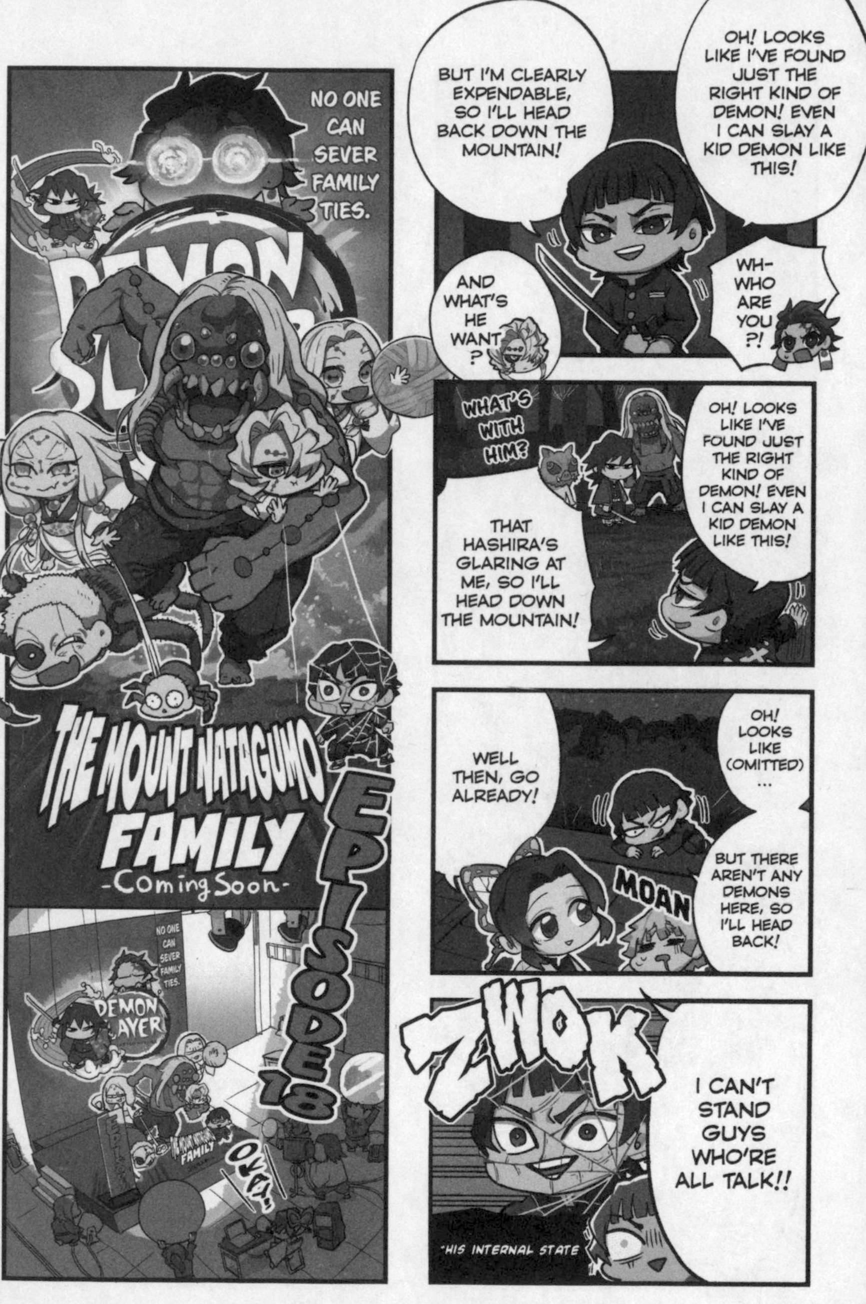
OH! LOOKS LIKE I'VE FOUND JUST THE RIGHT KIND OF DEMON! EVEN I CAN SLAY A KID DEMON LIKE THIS!
BUT I'M CLEARLY EXPENDABLE, SO I'LL HEAD BACK DOWN THE MOUNTAIN!
WH-WHO ARE YOU?!
AND WHAT'S HE WANT?
OH! LOOKS LIKE I'VE FOUND JUST THE RIGHT KIND OF DEMON! EVEN I CAN SLAY A KID DEMON LIKE THIS!
WHAT'S WITH HIM?
THAT HASHIRA'S GLARING AT ME, SO I'LL HEAD DOWN THE MOUNTAIN!
OH! LOOKS LIKE (OMITTED)...
BUT THERE AREN'T ANY DEMONS HERE, SO I'LL HEAD BACK!
MOAN
WELL THEN, GO ALREADY!
ZWOK
I CAN'T STAND GUYS WHO'RE ALL TALK!!
*HIS INTERNAL STATE
NO ONE CAN SEVER FAMILY TIES.
EPISODE 18
THE MOUNT NATAGUMO FAMILY
-Coming Soon-
NO ONE CAN SEVER FAMILY TIES.
THE MOUNT NATAGUMO FAMILY
OKAY!

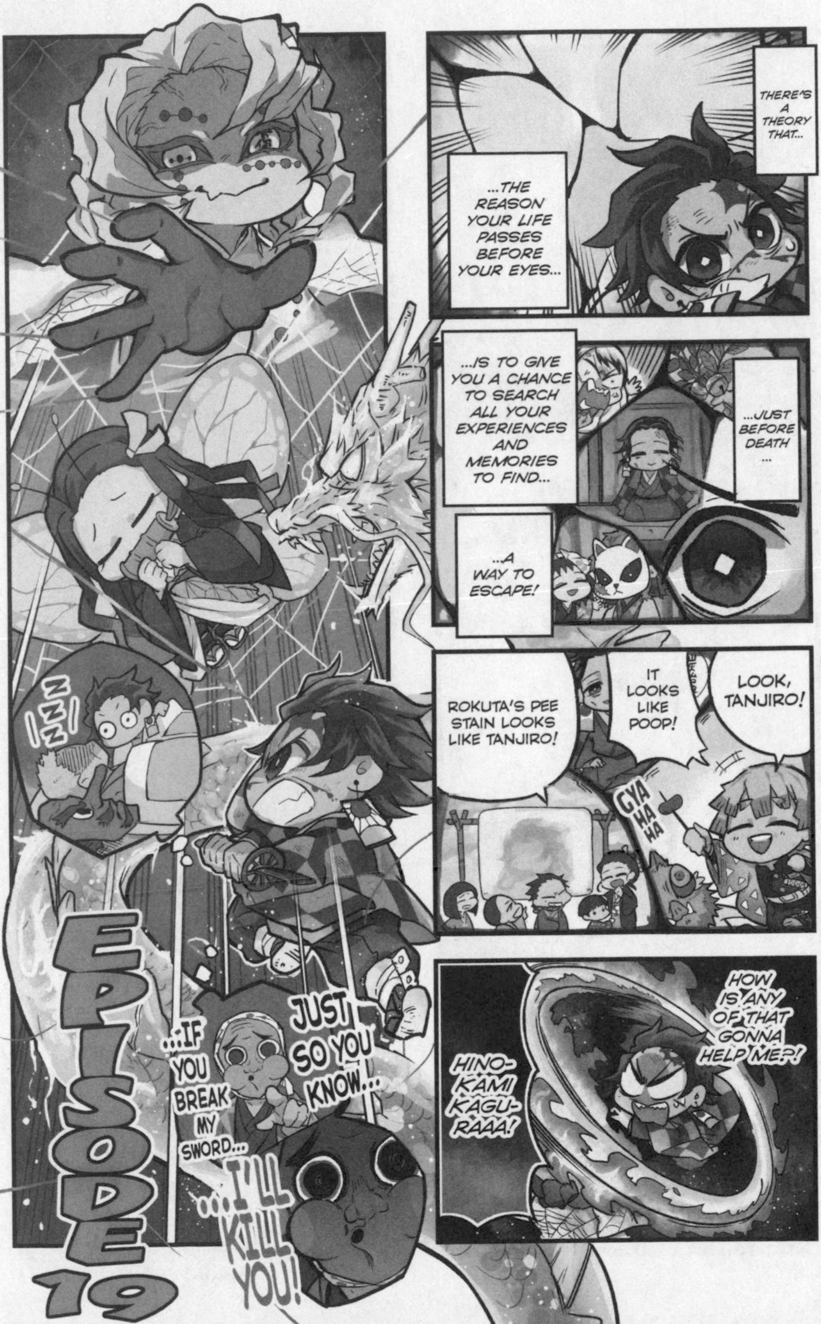
THERE'S A THEORY THAT...
...THE REASON YOUR LIFE PASSES BEFORE YOUR EYES...
...JUST BEFORE DEATH...
...IS TO GIVE YOU A CHANCE TO SEARCH ALL YOUR EXPERIENCES AND MEMORIES TO FIND...
...A WAY TO ESCAPE!
LOOK, TANJIRO!
IT LOOKS LIKE POOP!
ROKUTA'S PEE STAIN LOOKS LIKE TANJIRO!
GYA HA HA
HOW IS ANY OF THAT GONNA HELP ME?!
HINO-KAMI KAGU-RAAA!
ZZZ
JUST SO YOU KNOW...
...IF YOU BREAK MY SWORD...
...I'LL KILL YOU!
EPISODE 19

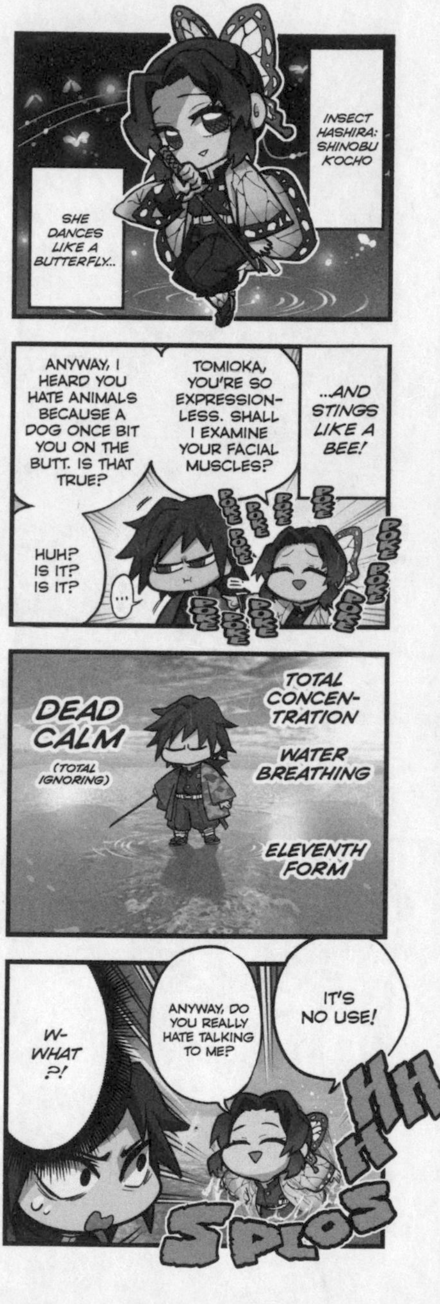
INSECT HASHIRA: SHINOBU KOCHO
SHE DANCES LIKE A BUTTERFLY...
...AND STINGS LIKE A BEE!
TOMIOKA, YOU'RE SO EXPRESSION-LESS. SHALL I EXAMINE YOUR FACIAL MUSCLES?
ANYWAY, I HEARD YOU HATE ANIMALS BECAUSE A DOG ONCE BIT YOU ON THE BUTT. IS THAT TRUE?
POKE POKE POKE POKE POKE POKE POKE POKE POKE POKE POKE POKE
HUH? IS IT? IS IT?
...
TOTAL CONCEN-TRATION
WATER BREATHING
ELEVENTH FORM
DEAD CALM
(TOTAL IGNORING)
IT'S NO USE!
ANYWAY, DO YOU REALLY HATE TALKING TO ME?
W-WHAT?!
SPLOSHHH

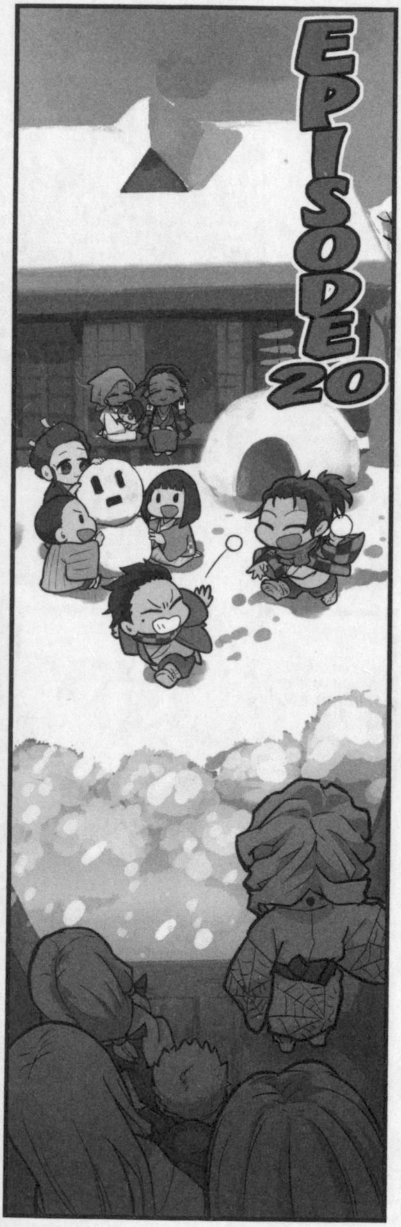
EPISODE 20

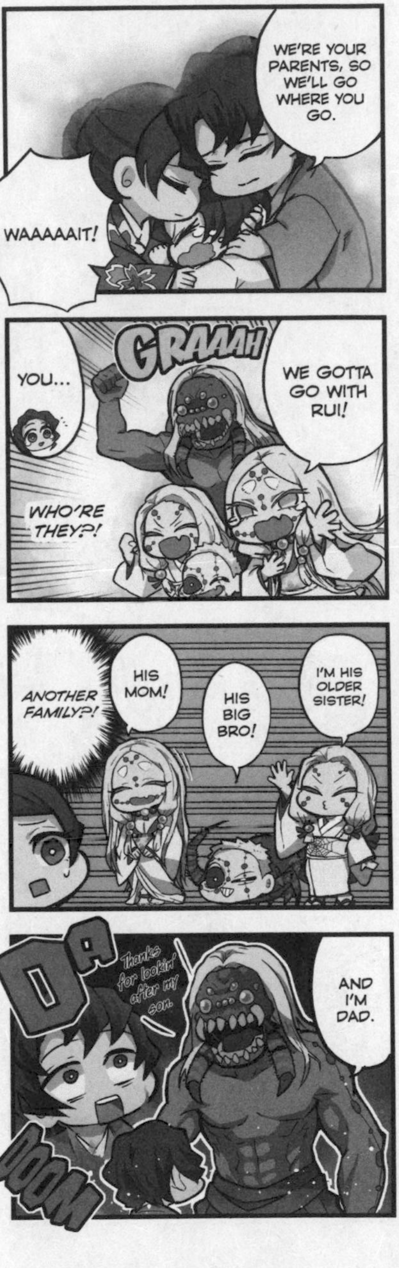
WE'RE YOUR PARENTS, SO WE'LL GO WHERE YOU GO.
WAAAAAIT!
GRAAAH
WE GOTTA GO WITH RUI!
YOU...
WHO'RE THEY?!
I'M HIS OLDER SISTER!
HIS BIG BRO!
HIS MOM!
ANOTHER FAMILY?!
AND I'M DAD.
Thanks for lookin' after my son.
DA
DOOM

*BANDAGE TAG: TREATMENT COMPLETE

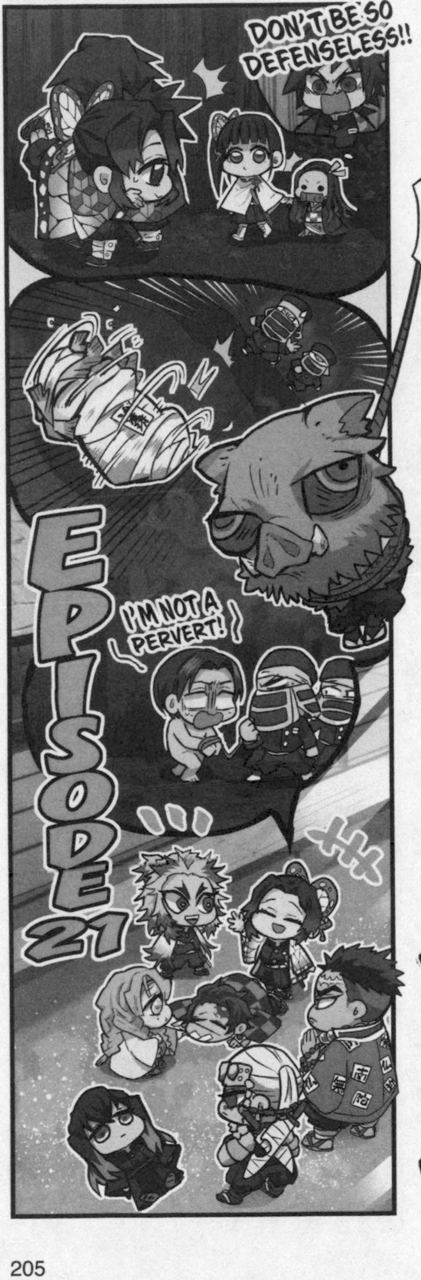
DON'T BE SO DEFENSELESS!!
I'M NOT A PERVERT!
EPISODE 21
...

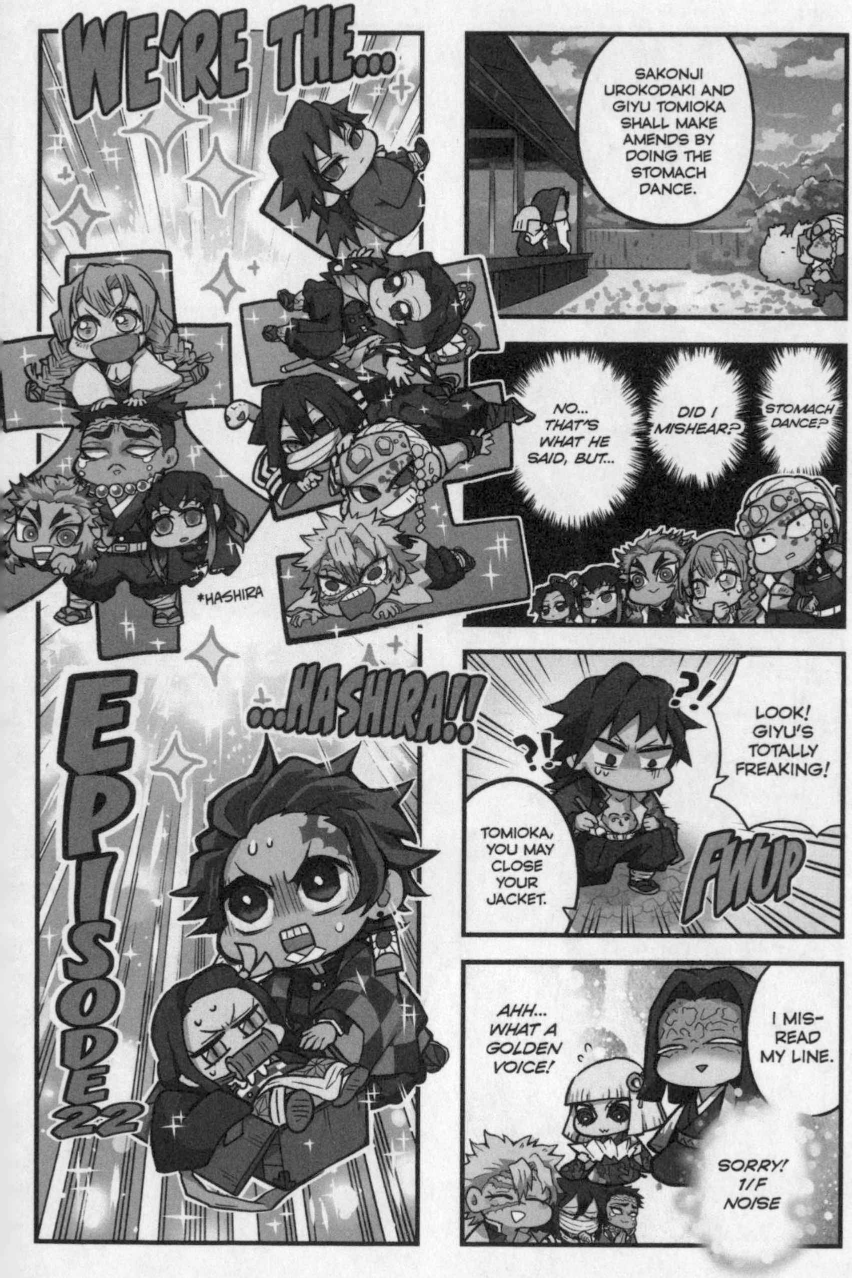
SAKONJI UROKODAKI AND GIYU TOMIOKA SHALL MAKE AMENDS BY DOING THE STOMACH DANCE.
STOMACH DANCE?
DID I MISHEAR?
NO... THAT'S WHAT HE SAID, BUT...
?!
LOOK! GIYU'S TOTALLY FREAKING!
?!
FWUP
TOMIOKA, YOU MAY CLOSE YOUR JACKET.
I MIS-READ MY LINE.
AHH... WHAT A GOLDEN VOICE!
SORRY! 1/F NOISE
WE'RE THE...
*HASHIRA
...HASHIRA!!
EPISODE 22

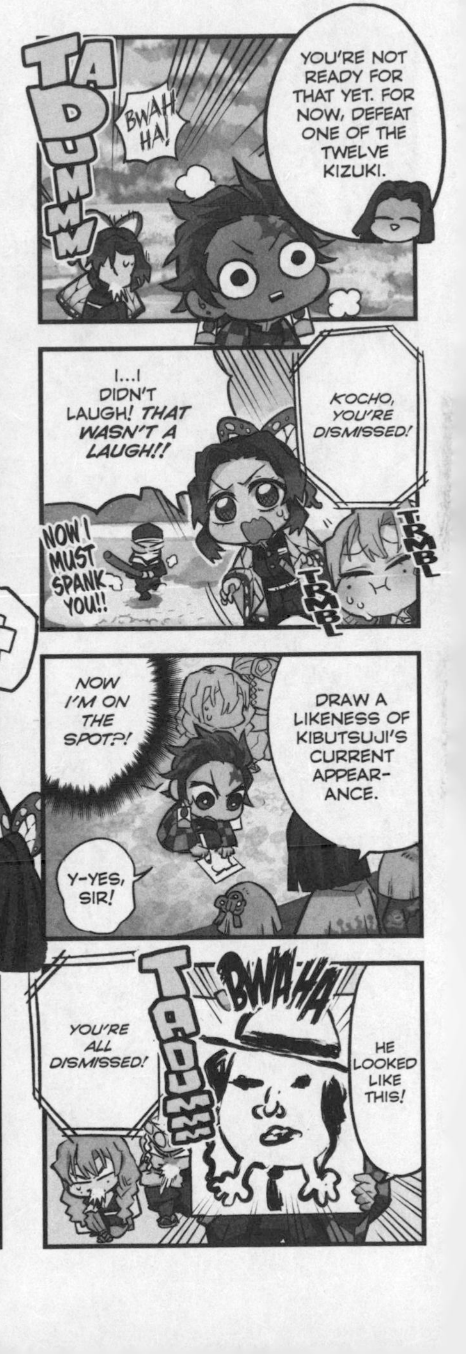
YOU'RE NOT READY FOR THAT YET. FOR NOW, DEFEAT ONE OF THE TWELVE KIZUKI.
BWAH HA!
TA DUMMM
KOCHO, YOU'RE DISMISSED!
TRMBL
TRMBL
I...I DIDN'T LAUGH! THAT WASN'T A LAUGH!!
NOW I MUST SPANK YOU!!
DRAW A LIKENESS OF KIBUTSUJI'S CURRENT APPEAR-ANCE.
NOW I'M ON THE SPOT?!
Y-YES, SIR!
HE LOOKED LIKE THIS!
BWAHAHA
TA DUMMM
YOU'RE ALL DISMISSED!

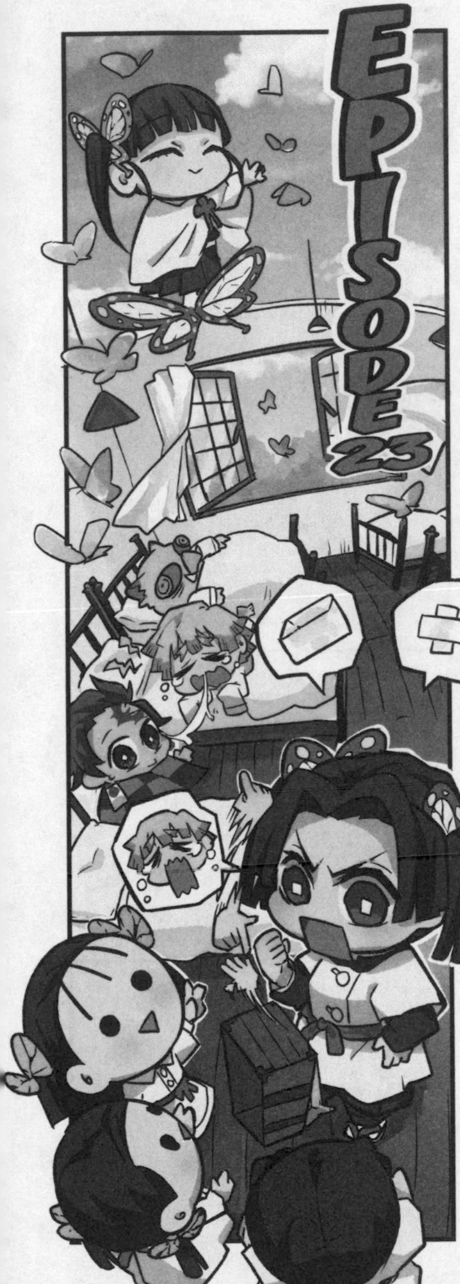
EPISODE 23

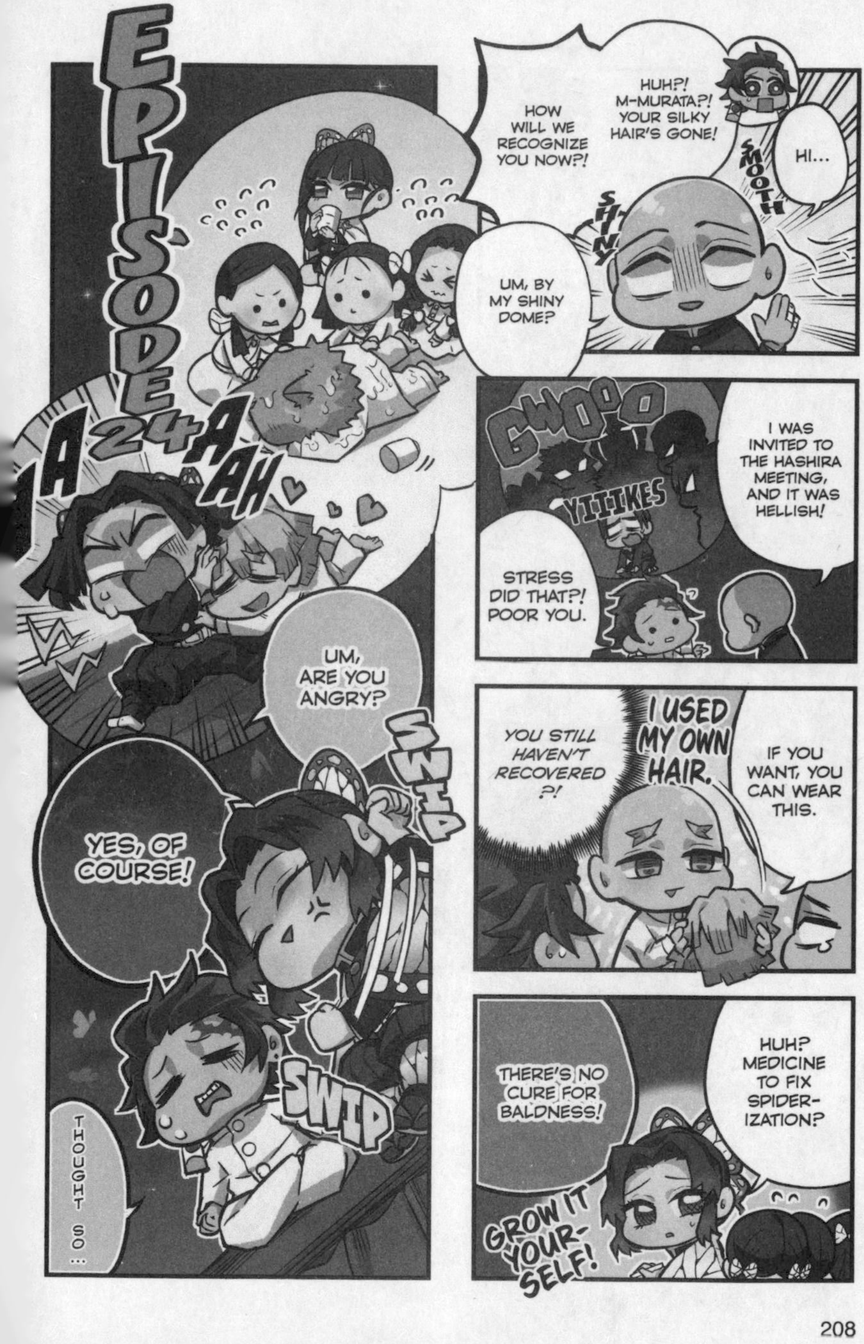
HI...
SMOOTH
SHINY
HUH?! M-MURATA?! YOUR SILKY HAIR'S GONE!
HOW WILL WE RECOGNIZE YOU NOW?!
UM, BY MY SHINY DOME?
I WAS INVITED TO THE HASHIRA MEETING, AND IT WAS HELLISH!
GWOOOO
YIIIKES
STRESS DID THAT?! POOR YOU.
IF YOU WANT, YOU CAN WEAR THIS.
I USED MY OWN HAIR.
YOU STILL HAVEN'T RECOVERED ?!
HUH? MEDICINE TO FIX SPIDER-IZATION?
THERE'S NO CURE FOR BALDNESS!
GROW IT YOUR-SELF!
EPISODE 24
AAAAH
UM, ARE YOU ANGRY?
SWIP
YES, OF COURSE!
SWIP
THOUGHT SO...

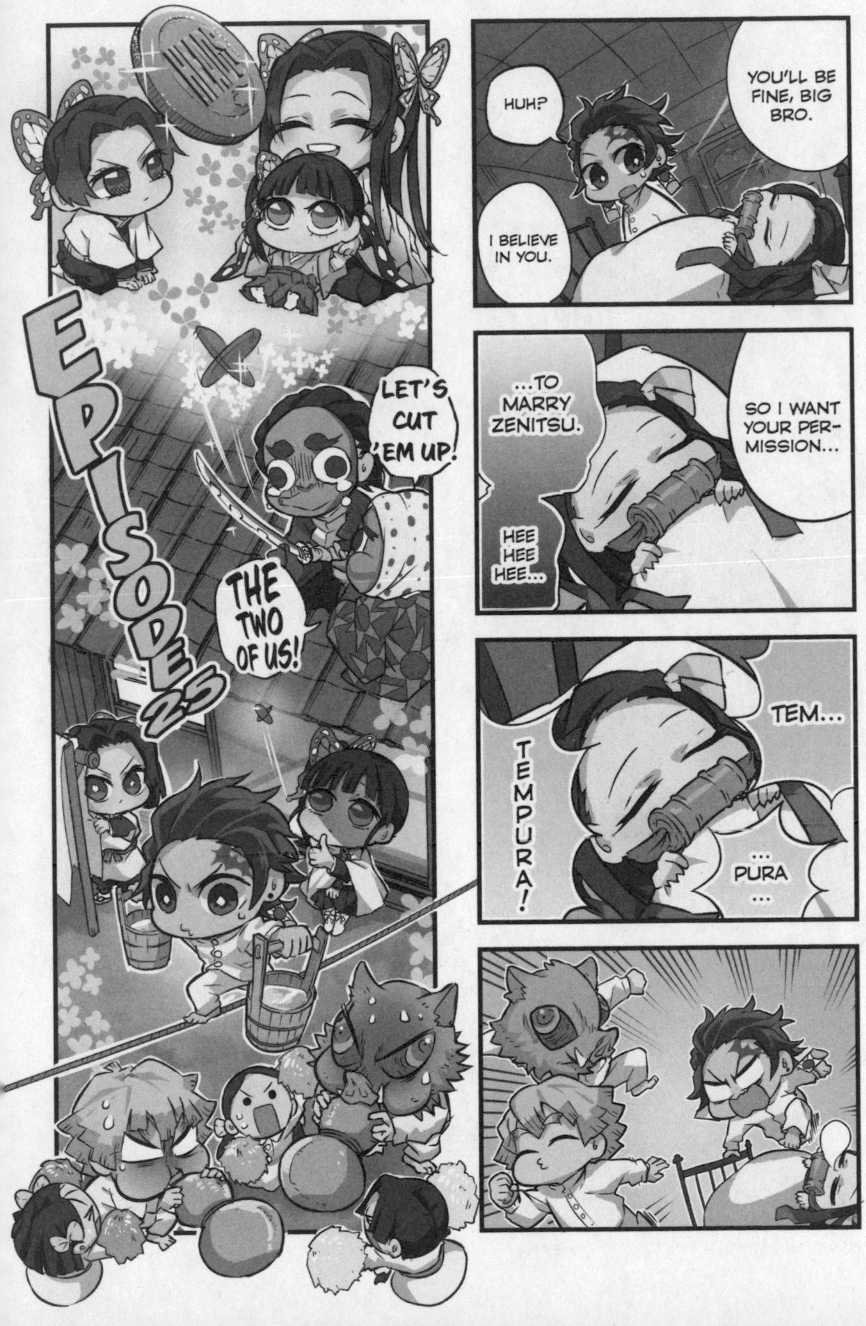
YOU'LL BE FINE, BIG BRO.
HUH?
I BELIEVE IN YOU.
SO I WANT YOUR PER-MISSION...
...TO MARRY ZENITSU.
HEE HEE HEE...
TEM...
TEMPURA!
... PURA ...
EPISODE 25
LET'S CUT 'EM UP!
THE TWO OF US!

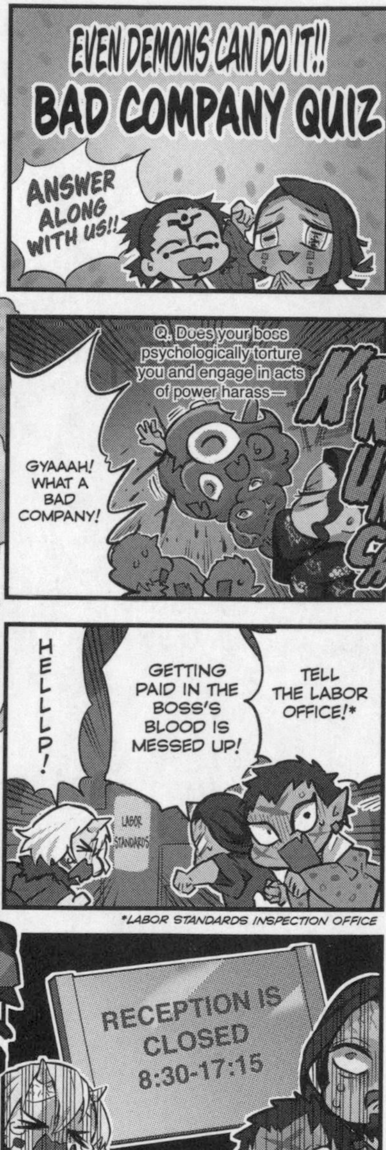
EVEN DEMONS CAN DO IT!!
BAD COMPANY QUIZ
ANSWER ALONG WITH US!!
Q. Does your boss psychologically torture you and engage in acts of power harass—
KRUNCH
GYAAAH! WHAT A BAD COMPANY!
TELL THE LABOR OFFICE!*
GETTING PAID IN THE BOSS'S BLOOD IS MESSED UP!
HELLLP!
LABOR STANDARDS
*LABOR STANDARDS INSPECTION OFFICE
RECEPTION IS CLOSED 8:30-17:15

*TRAIN: INFINITY

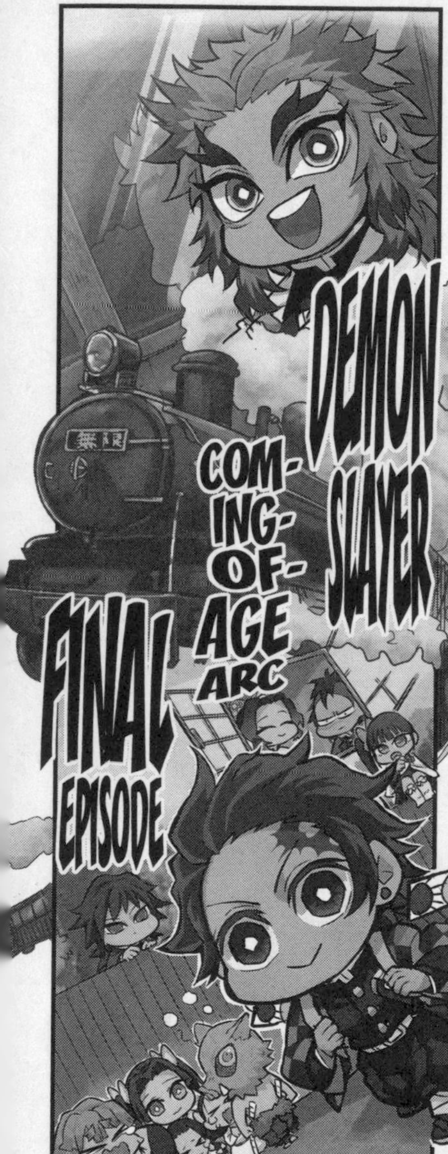
無限
DEMON SLAYER
COMING-OF-AGE ARC
FINAL EPISODE

KIMETSU BETWEEN THE SCENES! (THE END)

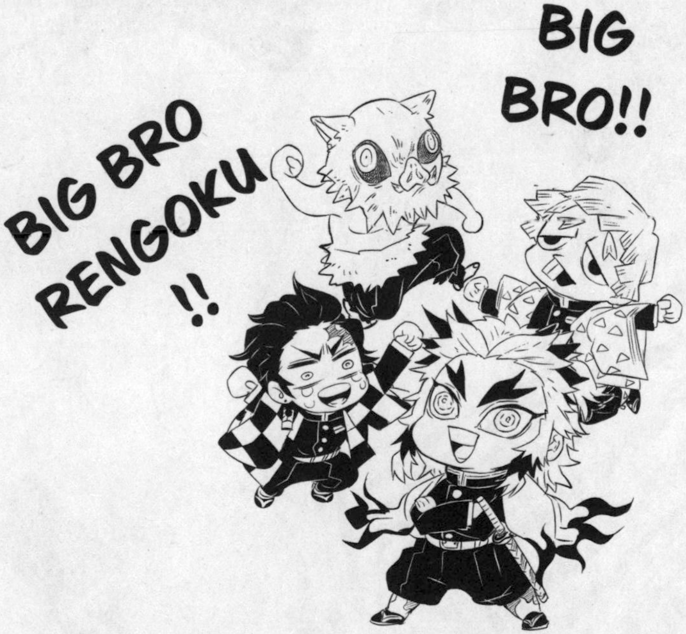
BIG BRO!!
BIG BRO RENGOKU!!

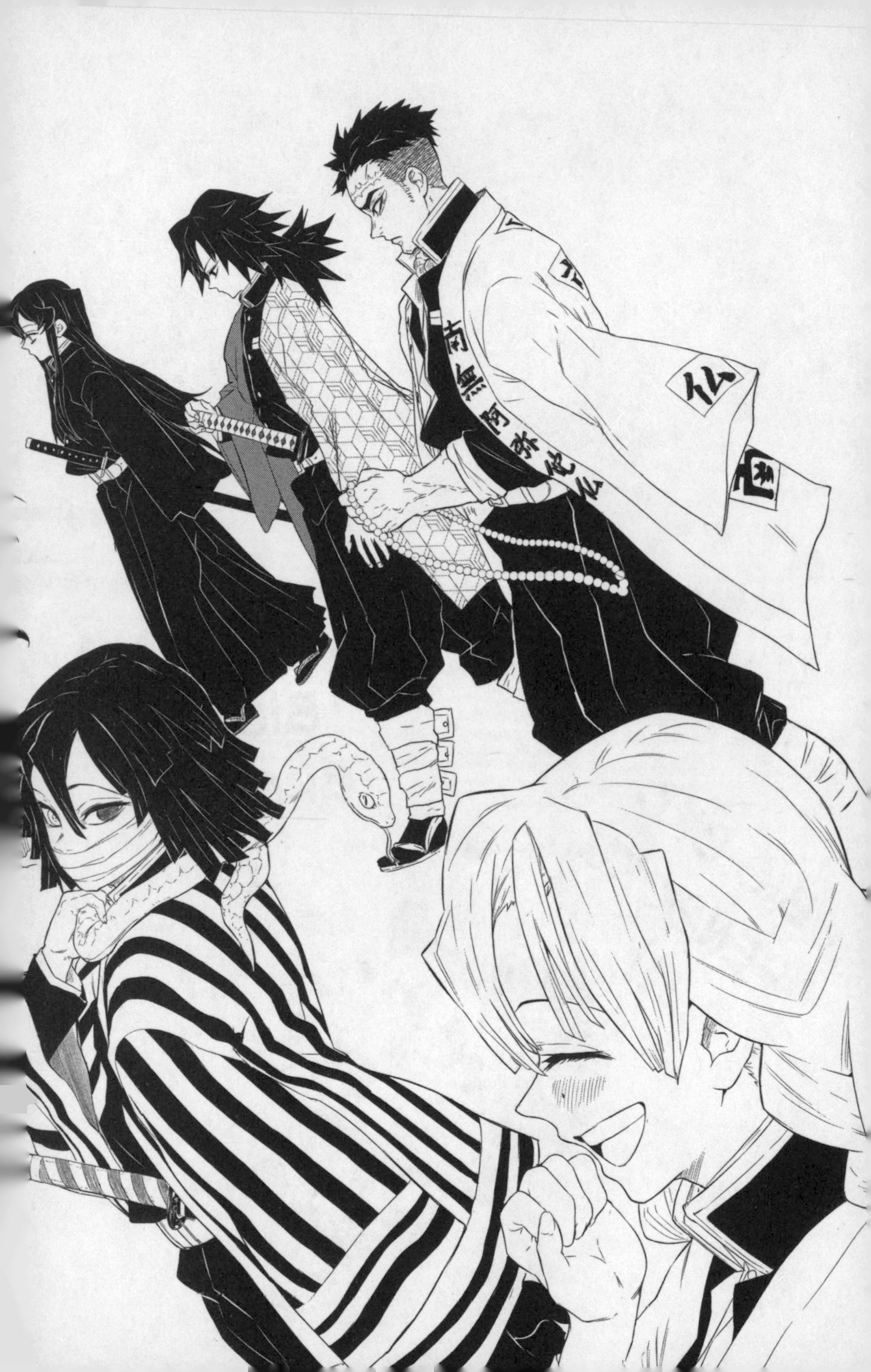
南無阿弥陀仏
仏

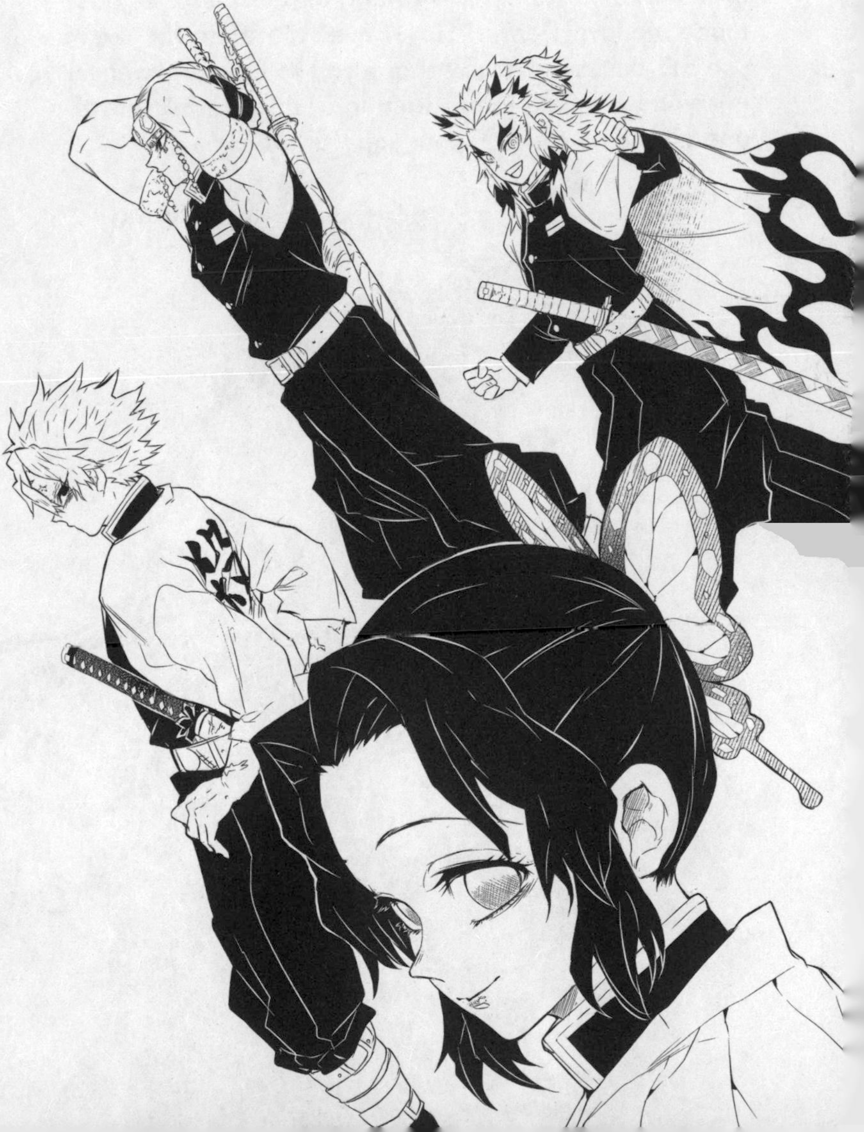

## AFTERWORD

I am deeply grateful to Gotouge Sensei for taking time out of a busy schedule to check my rough layouts and even make corrections. Working on these stories has made me love *Demon Slayer* even more! So I'd like to use this occasion to say thank you to Gotouge Sensei, everyone involved in production of this graphic novel, and all the readers. Thank you very much!

Ryoji Hirano

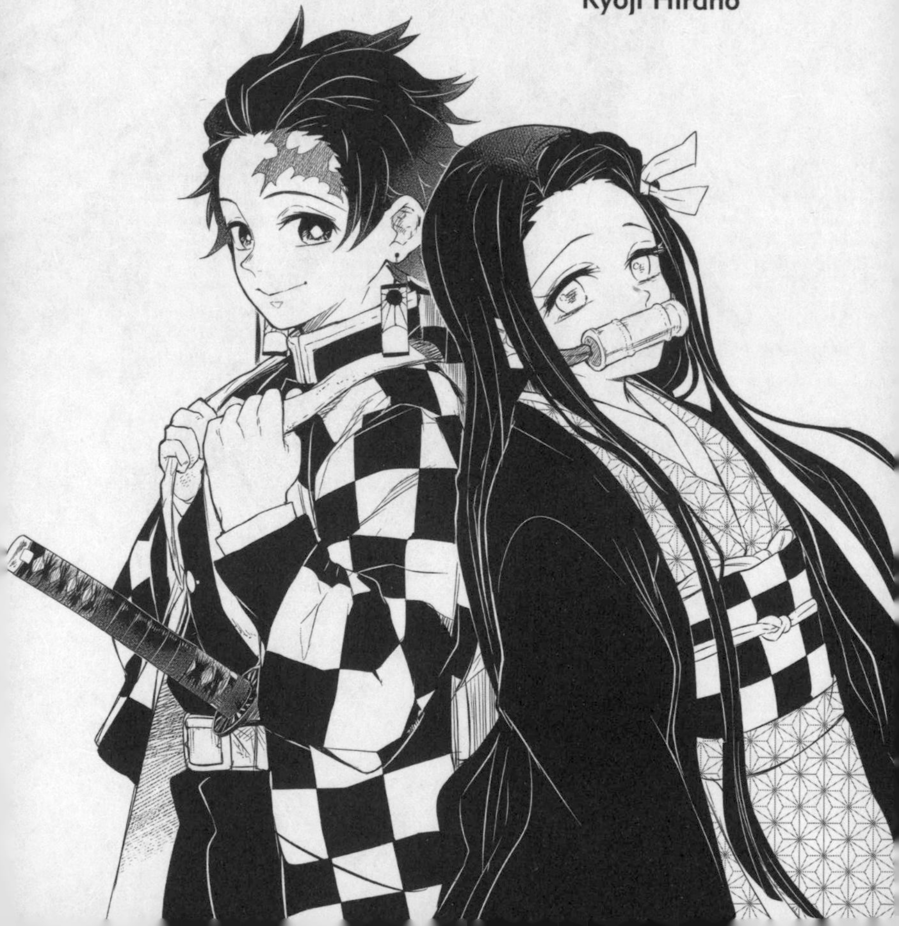

## GOOD WORK! THIS IS GOTOUGE!

I was very happy to have Hirano Sensei create these stories. When I had the chance to meet him at a New Year's party, I had no idea fate would bring us together like this. Many things showed me how closely he read *Demon Slayer*, so I was hap-hap-happy! I wish Hirano Sensei, everyone in his family, and the entire staff the best of health!

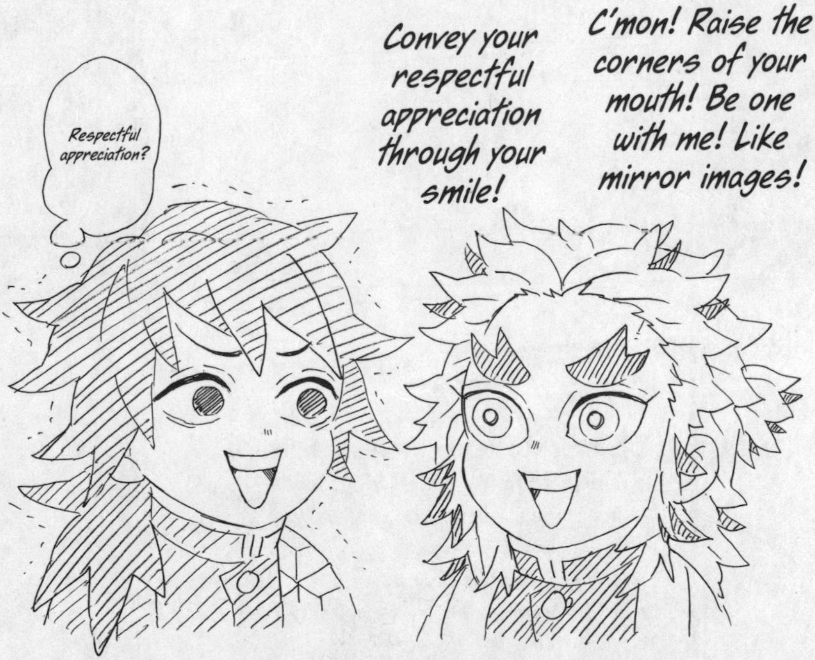
C'mon! Raise the corners of your mouth! Be one with me! Like mirror images!
Convey your respectful appreciation through your smile!
Respectful appreciation?

# YOU'RE READING THE
# WRONG WAY!

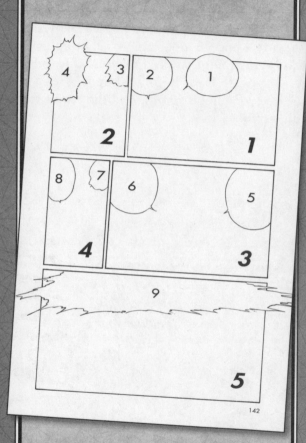

**DEMON SLAYER: KIMETSU NO YAIBA—
STORIES OF WATER AND FLAME** reads
from right to left, starting in the upper-
right corner. Japanese is read from right to
left, meaning that action, sound effects, and
word-balloon order are completely reversed
from English order.